AF413207

Catalogue Raisonné

(Clichés)

CATALOGUE RAISONNÉ

(CLICHÉS)

I—XI A—B

PLATES

(CLICHÉ OF A FLOWER BOUQUET) I

(CLICHÉ OF A FLOWER BOUQUET) I

(CLICHÉ OF A FLOWER BOUQUET) I

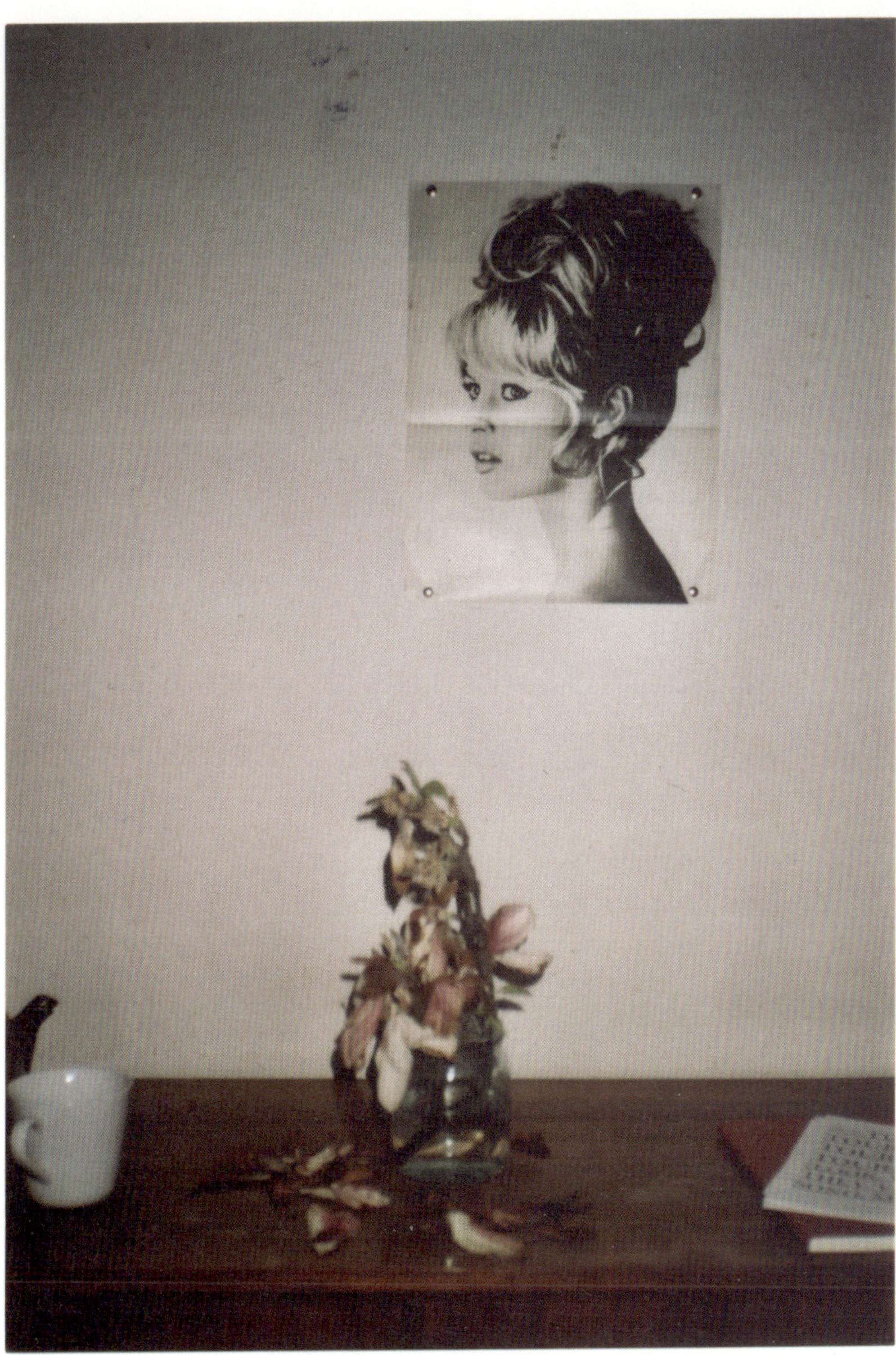

(CLICHÉ OF A FLOWER BOUQUET) XXII

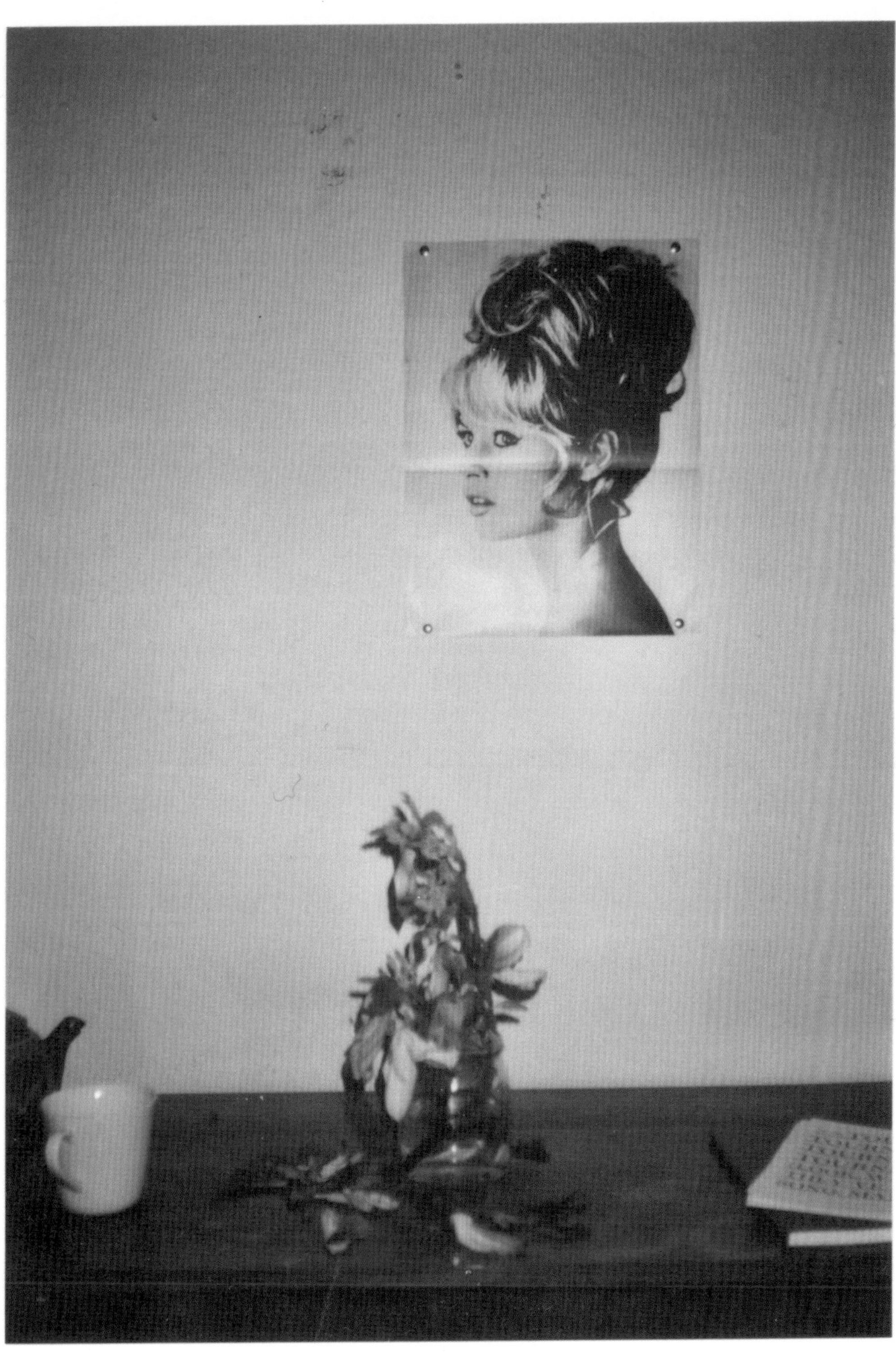

(CLICHÉ OF A FLOWER BOUQUET) XXII

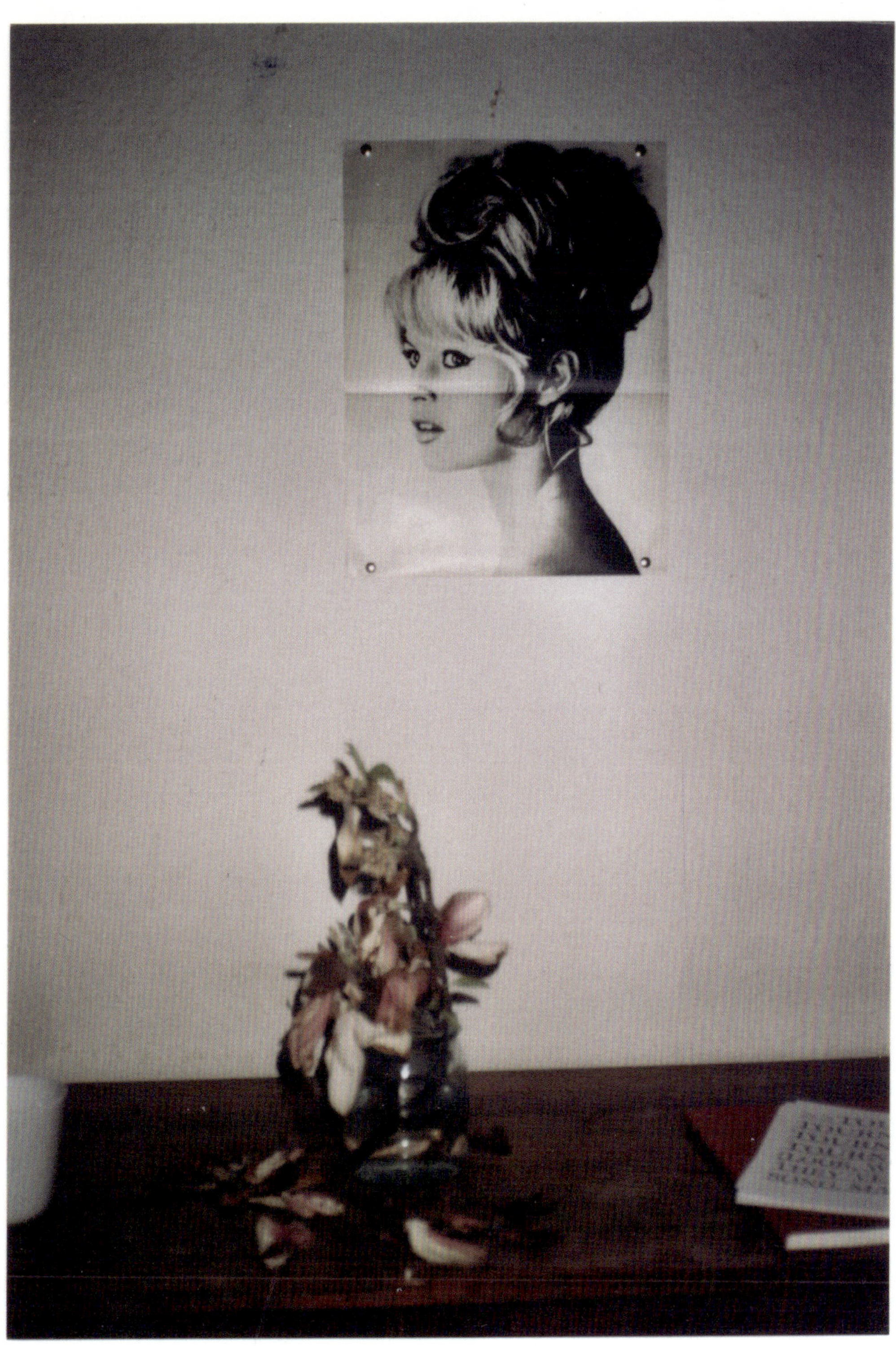

(CLICHÉ OF A FLOWER BOUQUET) XXII

(CLICHÉ OF A MAN, NUDE TORSO) III

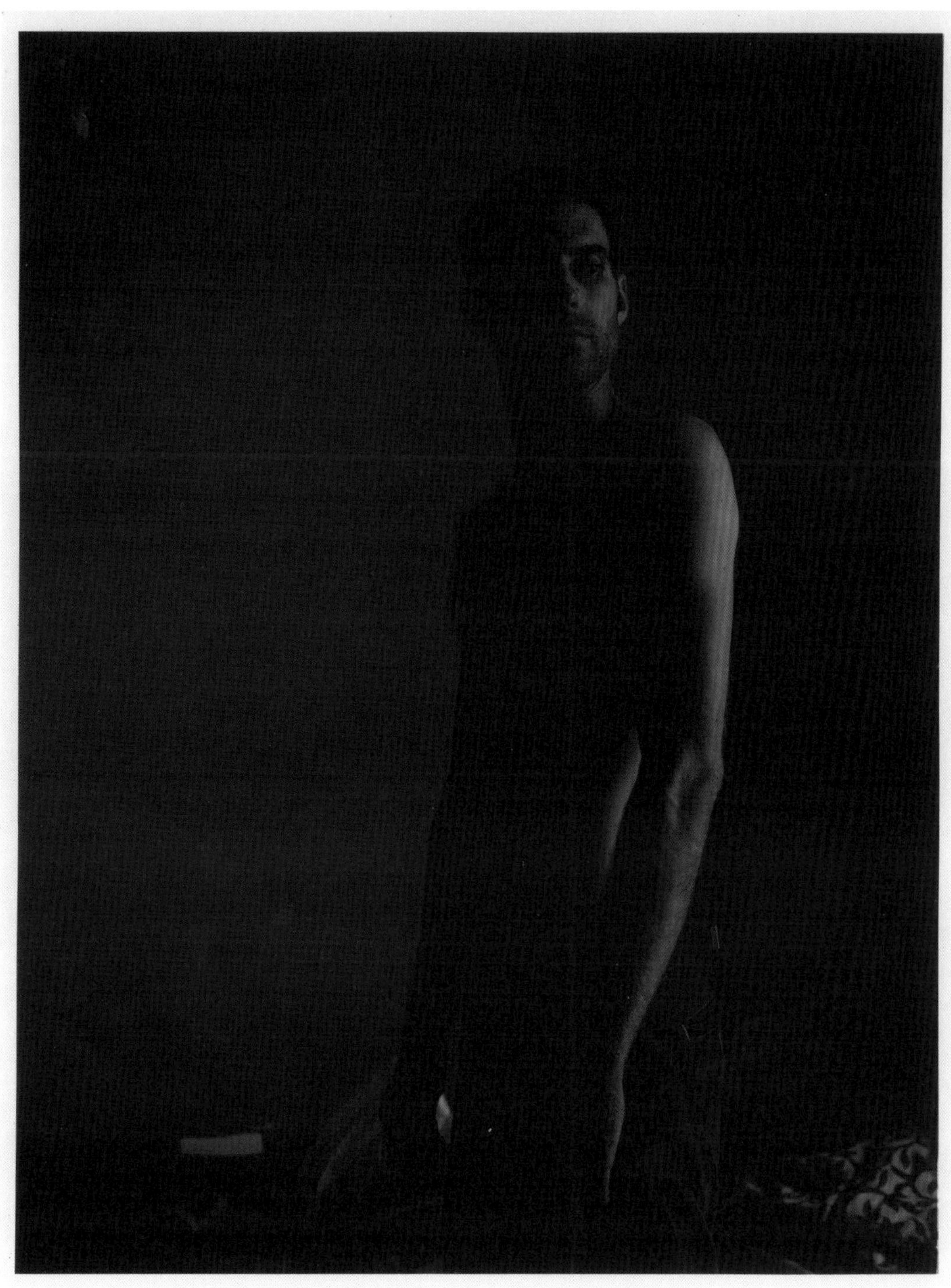

(CLICHÉ OF A MAN, NUDE TORSO) III

(CLICHÉ OF A MAN, NUDE TORSO) III

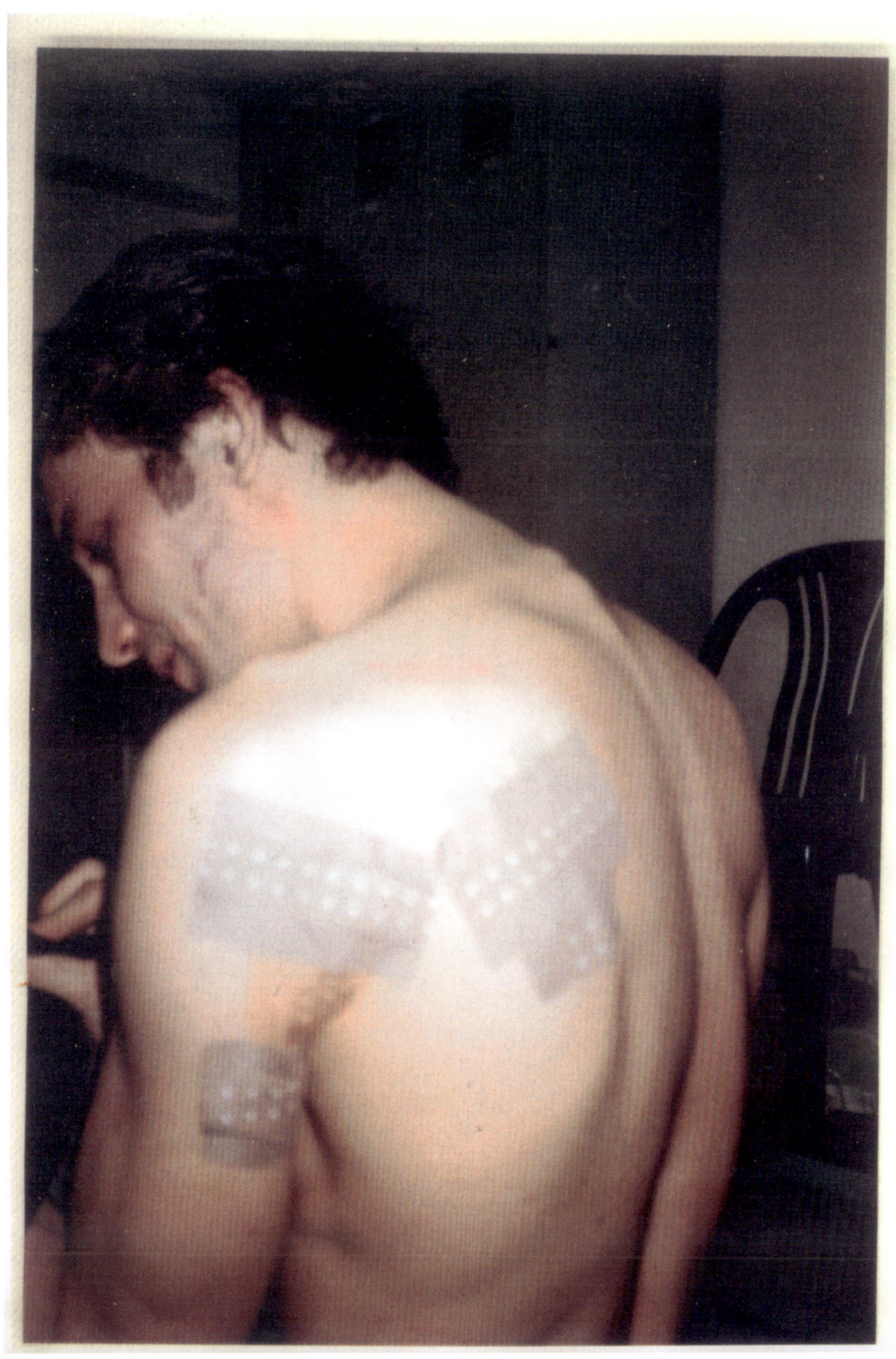

(CLICHÉ OF A MAN, NUDE TORSO) IV

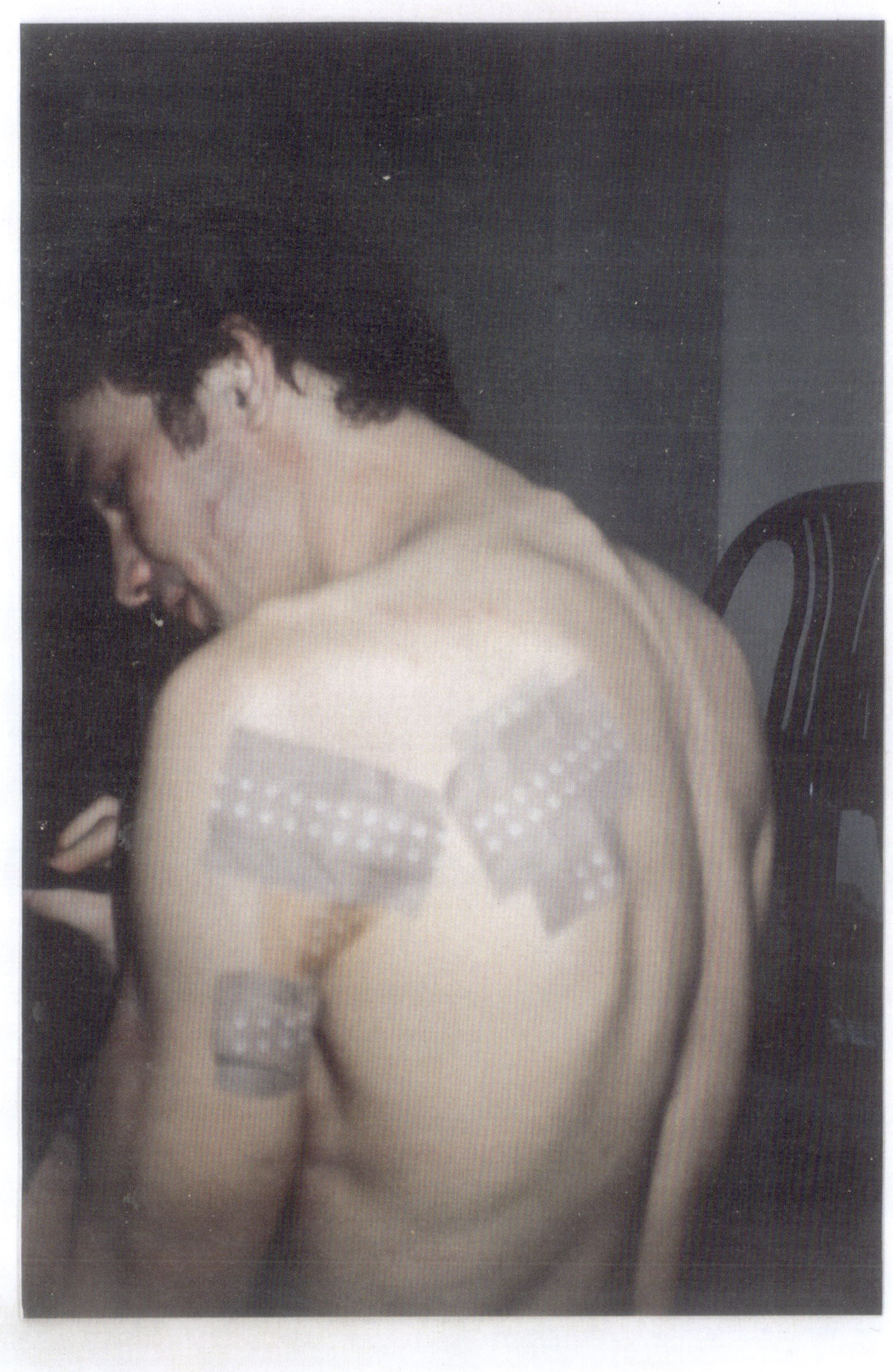

(CLICHÉ OF A MAN, NUDE TORSO) IV

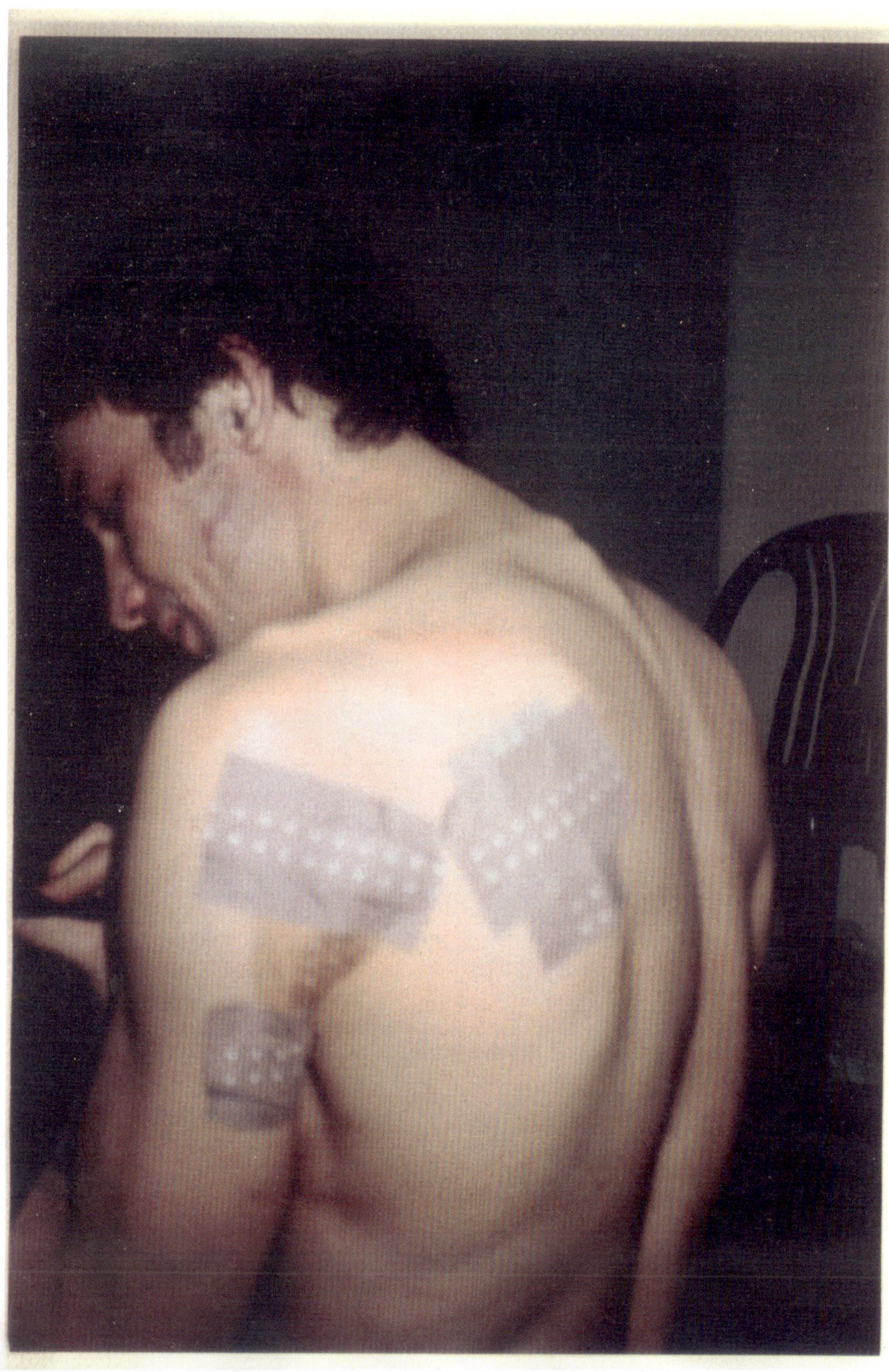

(CLICHÉ OF A MAN, NUDE TORSO) IV

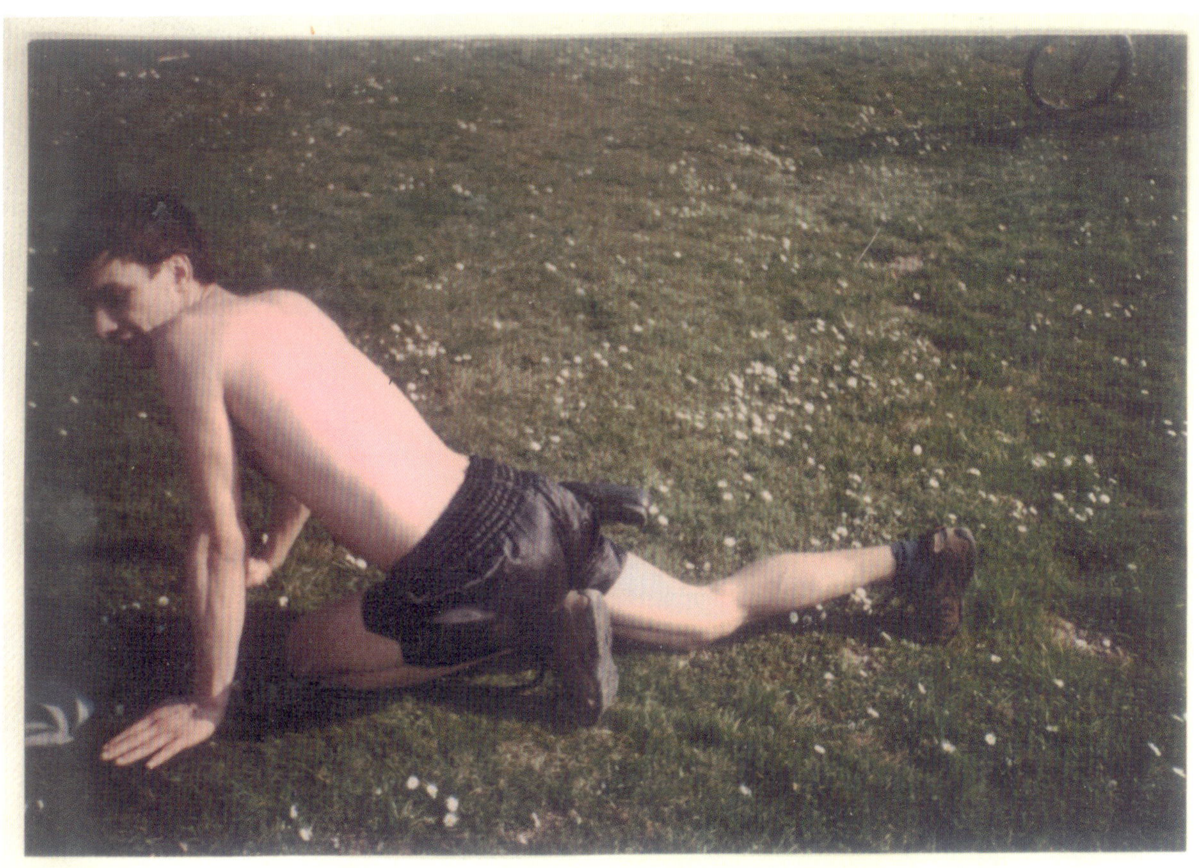

(CLICHÉ OF A MAN, LYING FIGURE, IN GREEN GRASS) II

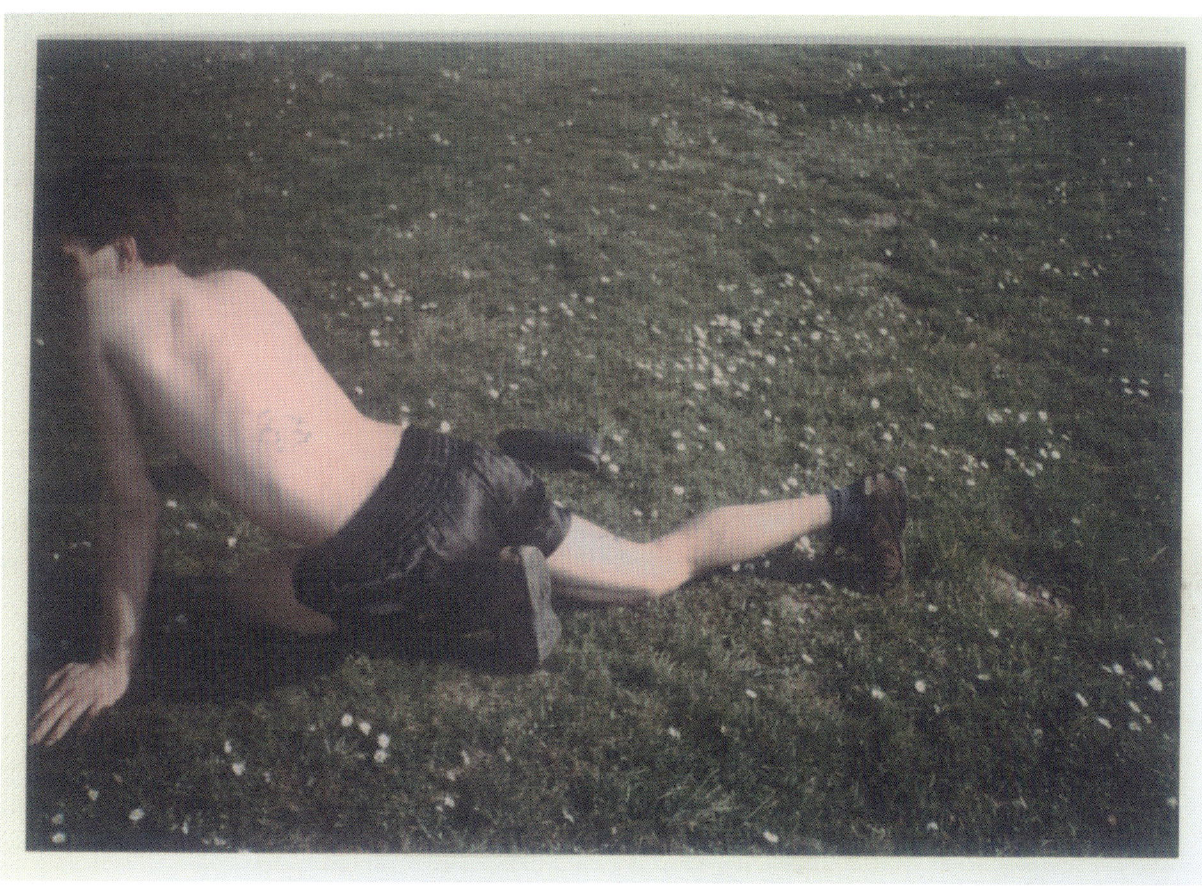

(CLICHÉ OF A MAN, LYING FIGURE, IN GREEN GRASS) II

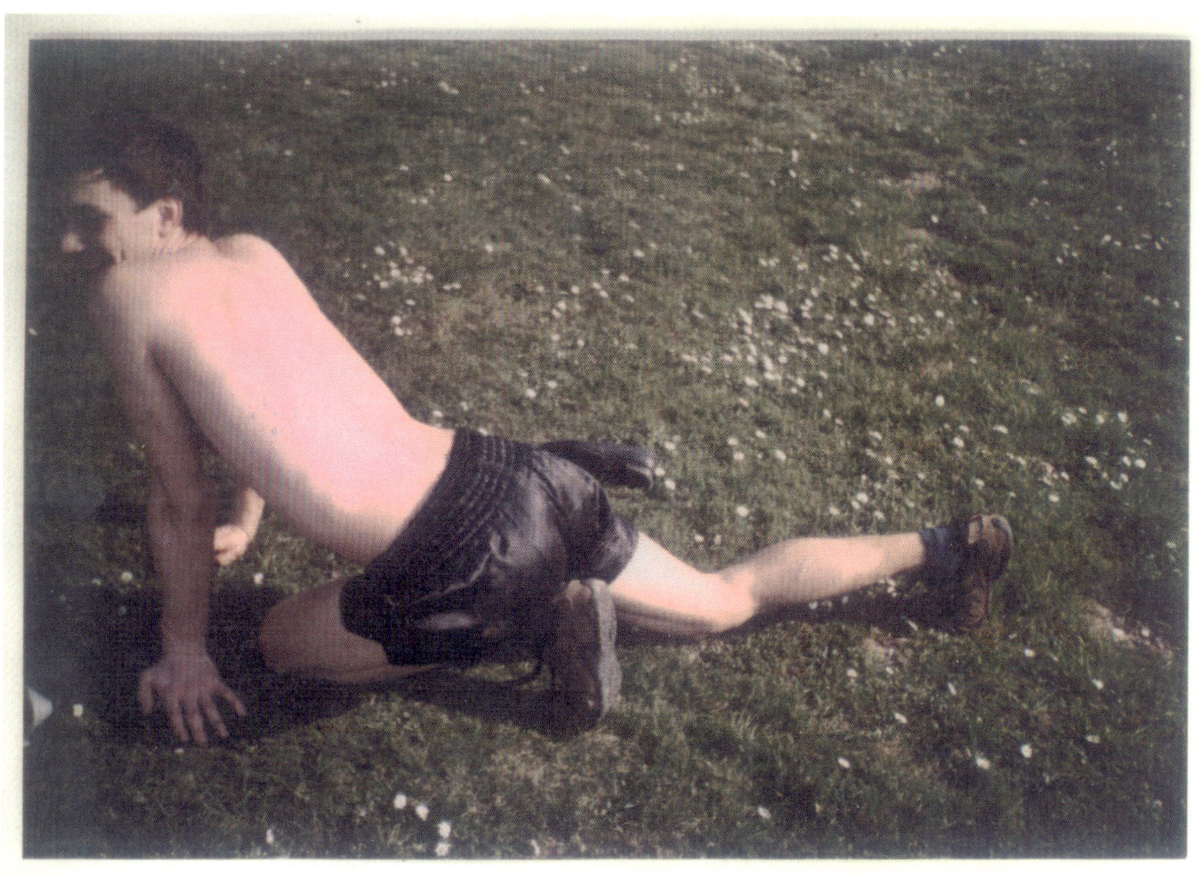

(CLICHÉ OF A MAN, LYING FIGURE, IN GREEN GRASS) II

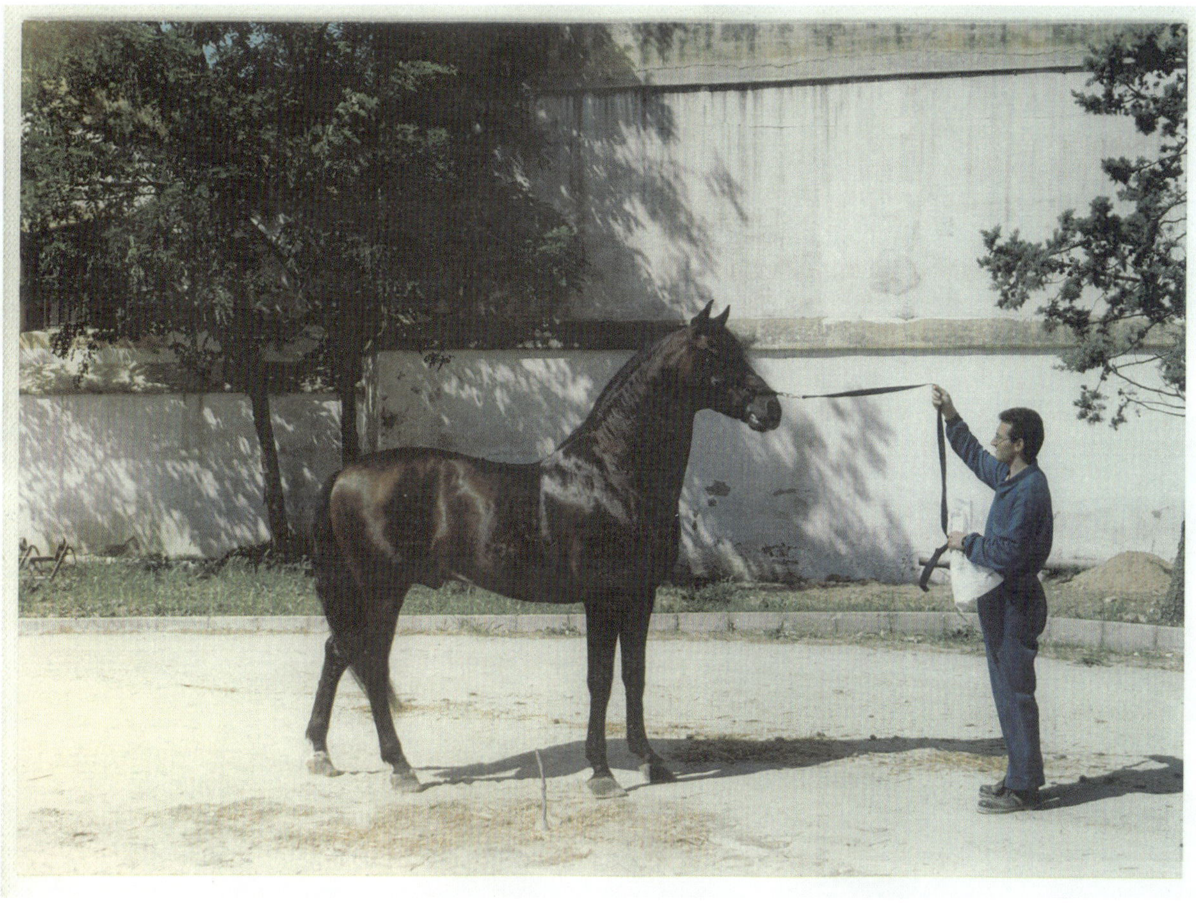

(CLICHÉ OF AN ANIMAL, HORSE, STALLION)

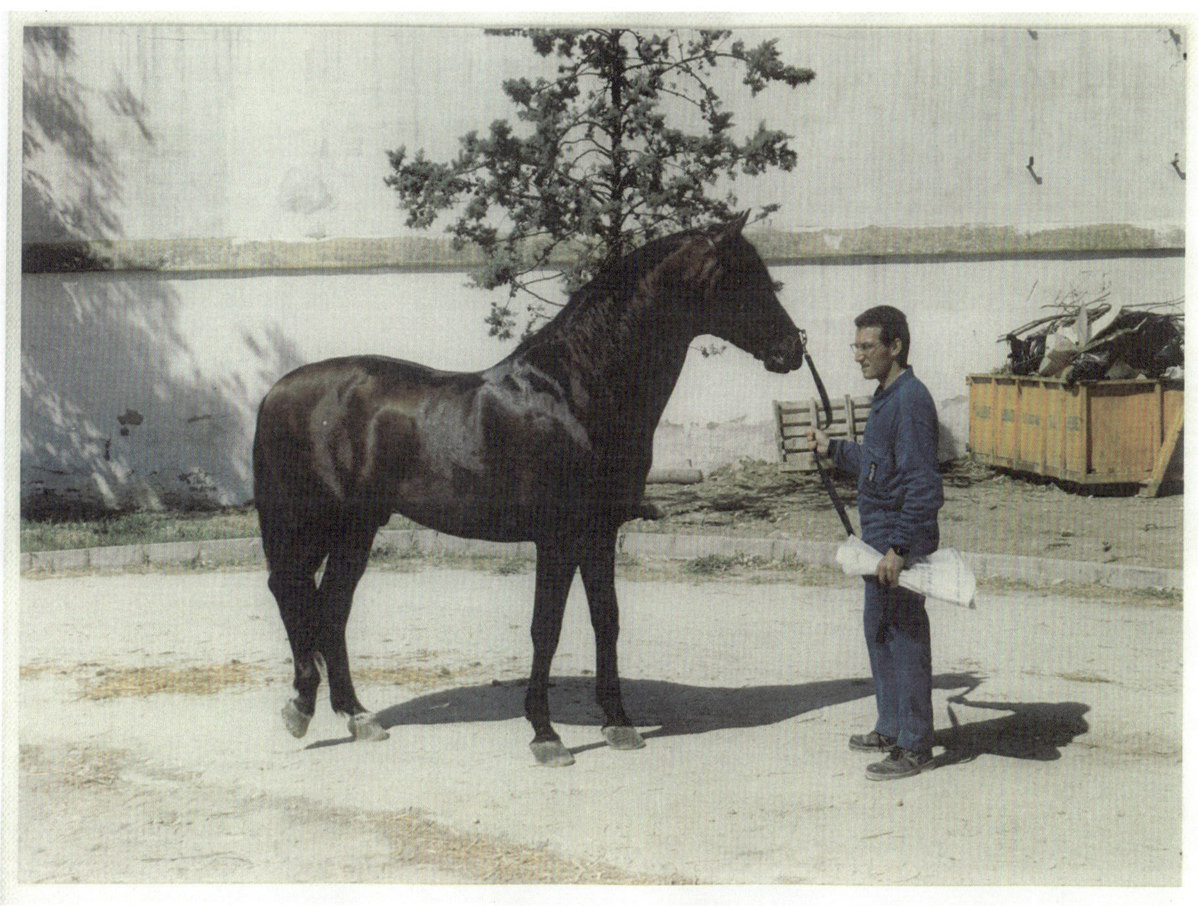

(CLICHÉ OF AN ANIMAL, HORSE, STALLION)

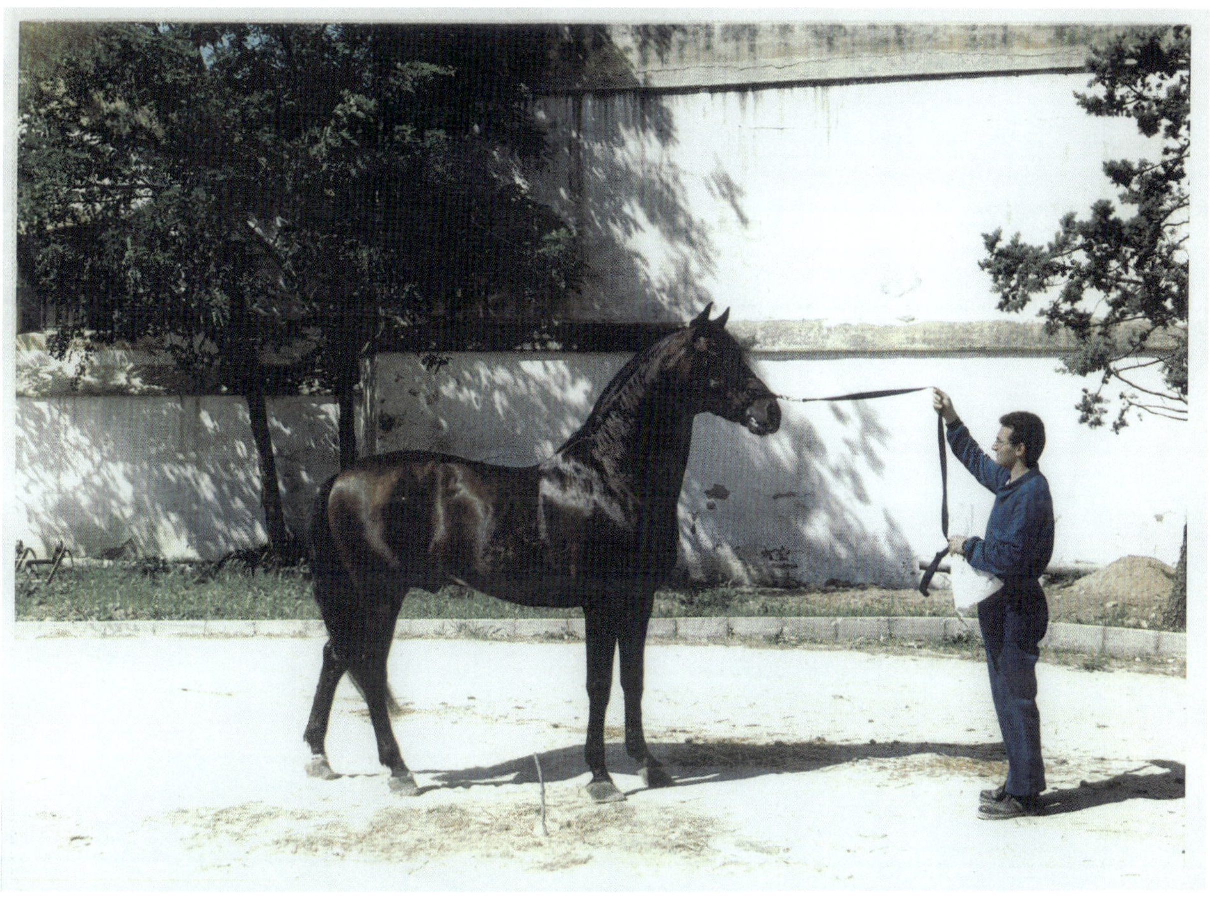

(CLICHÉ OF AN ANIMAL, HORSE, STALLION)

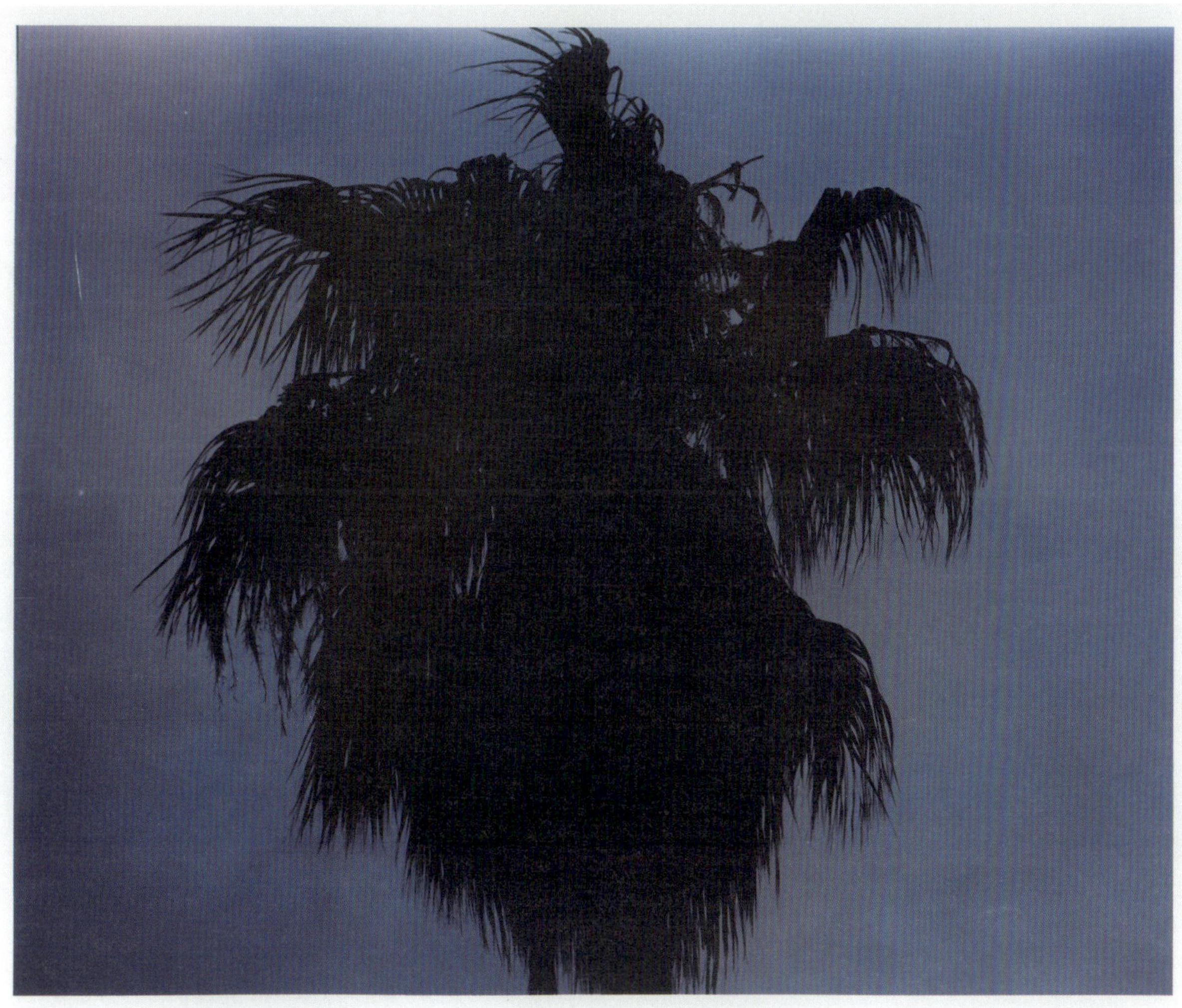

(CLICHÉ OF A PALM TREE) I

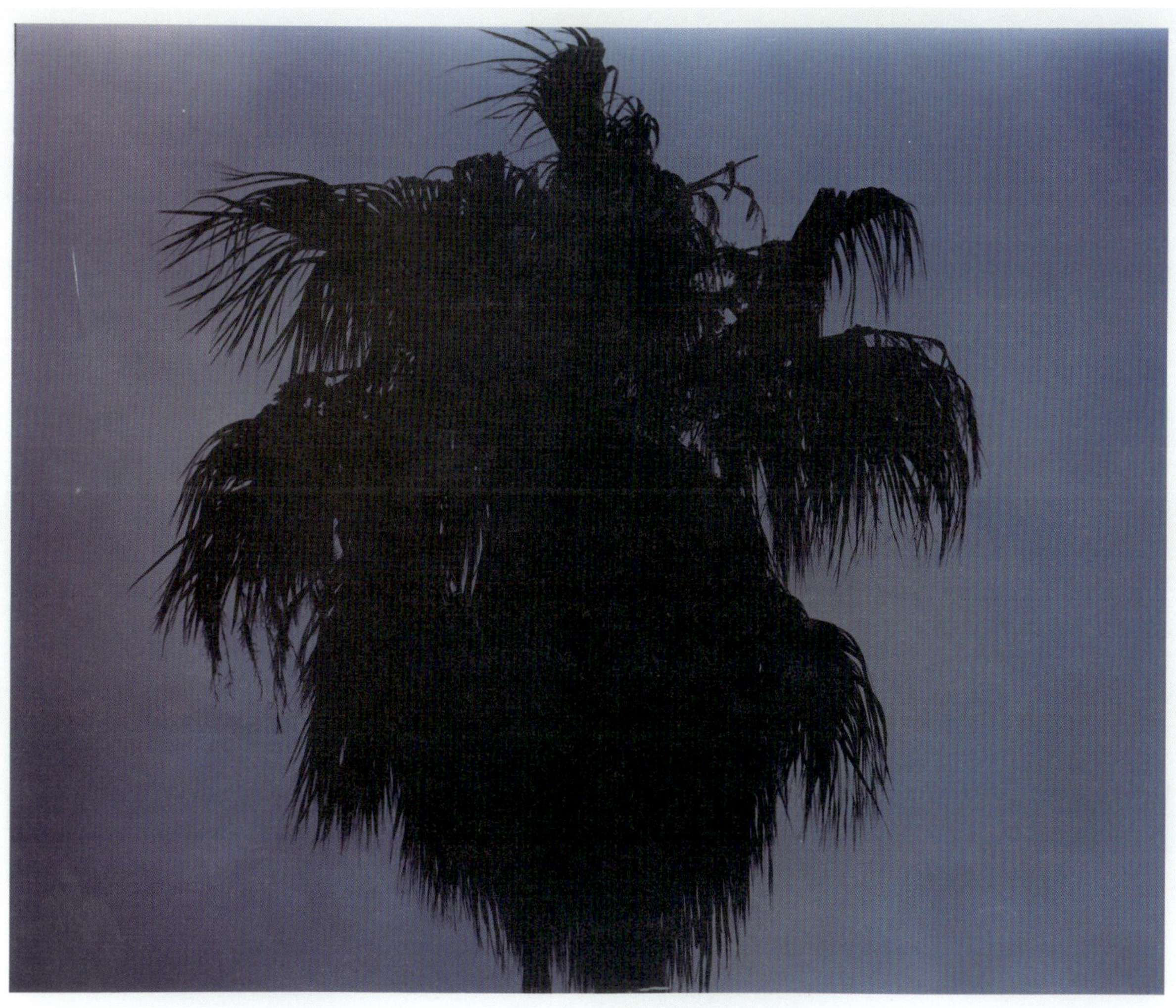

(CLICHÉ OF A PALM TREE) I

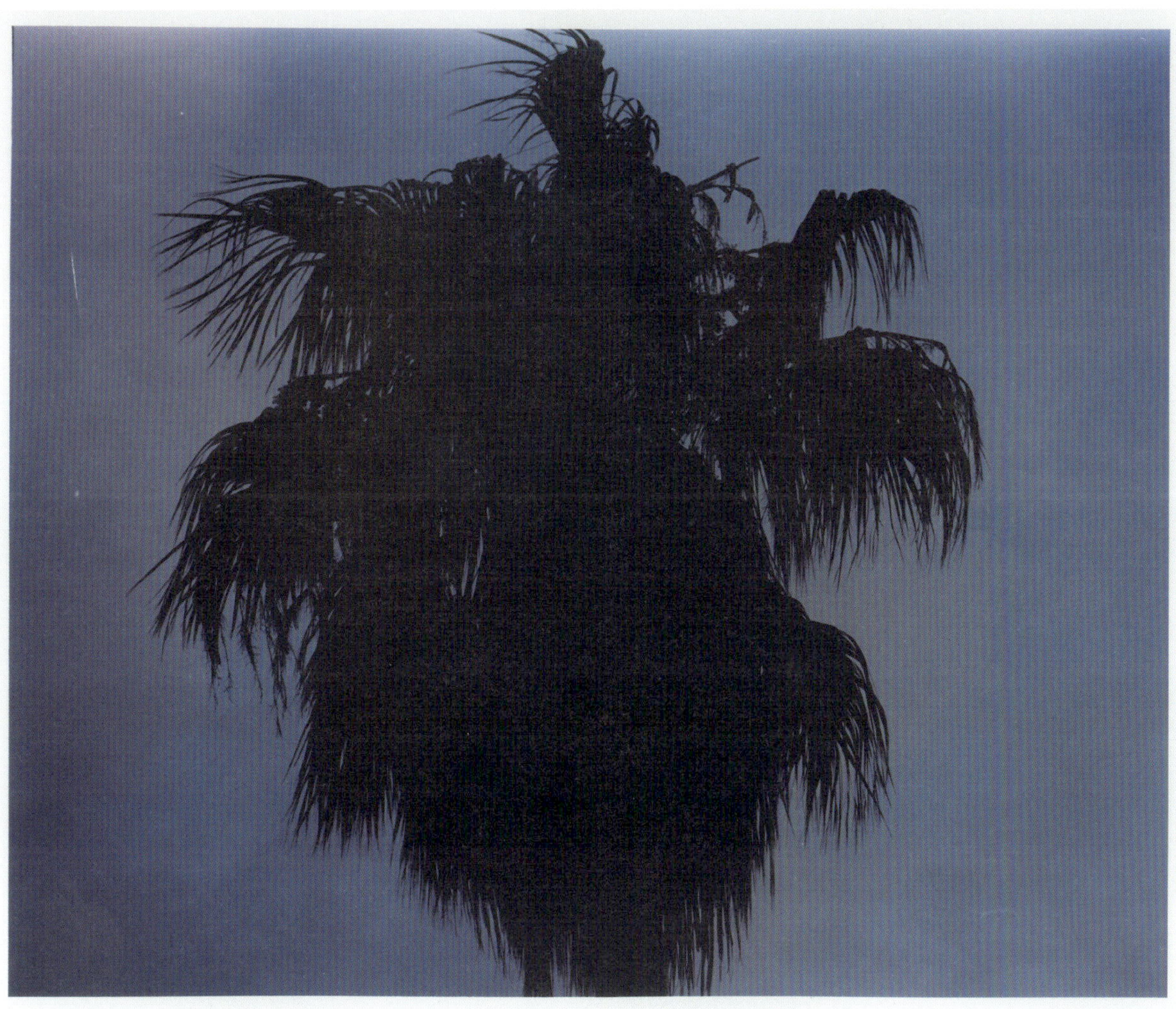

(CLICHÉ OF A PALM TREE) I

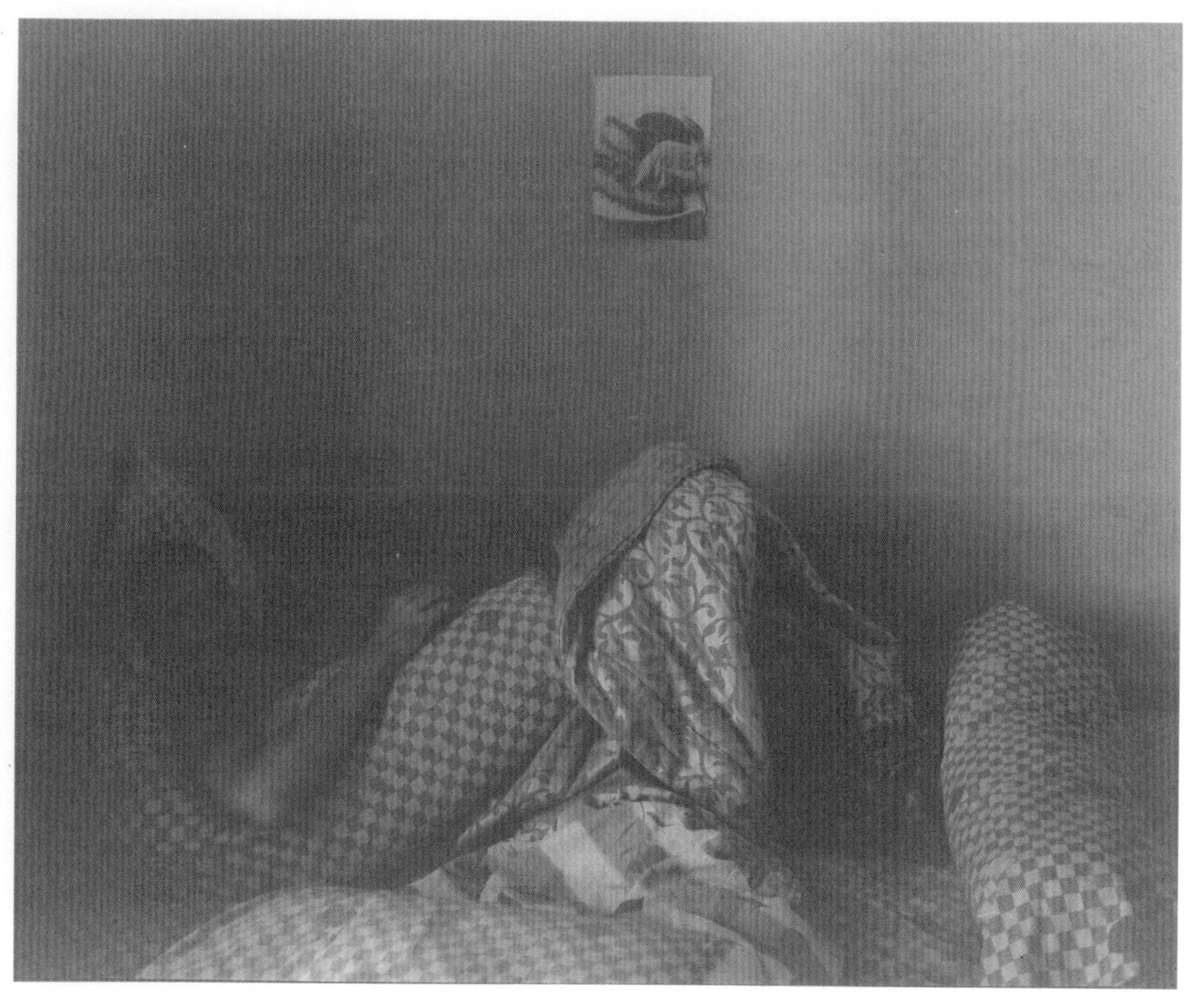

(CLICHÉ OF A MAN, LYING FIGURE) III

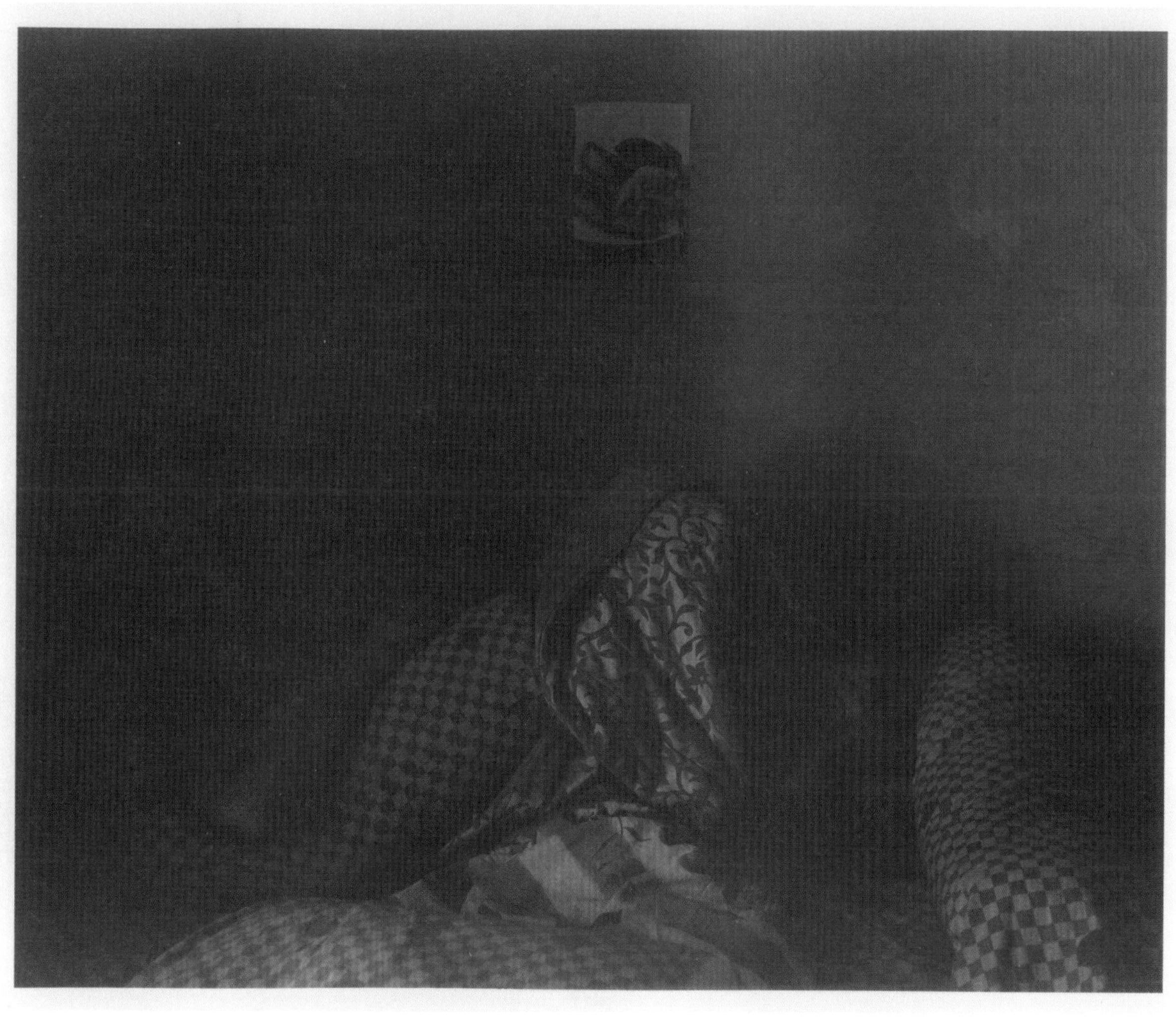

(CLICHÉ OF A MAN, LYING FIGURE) III

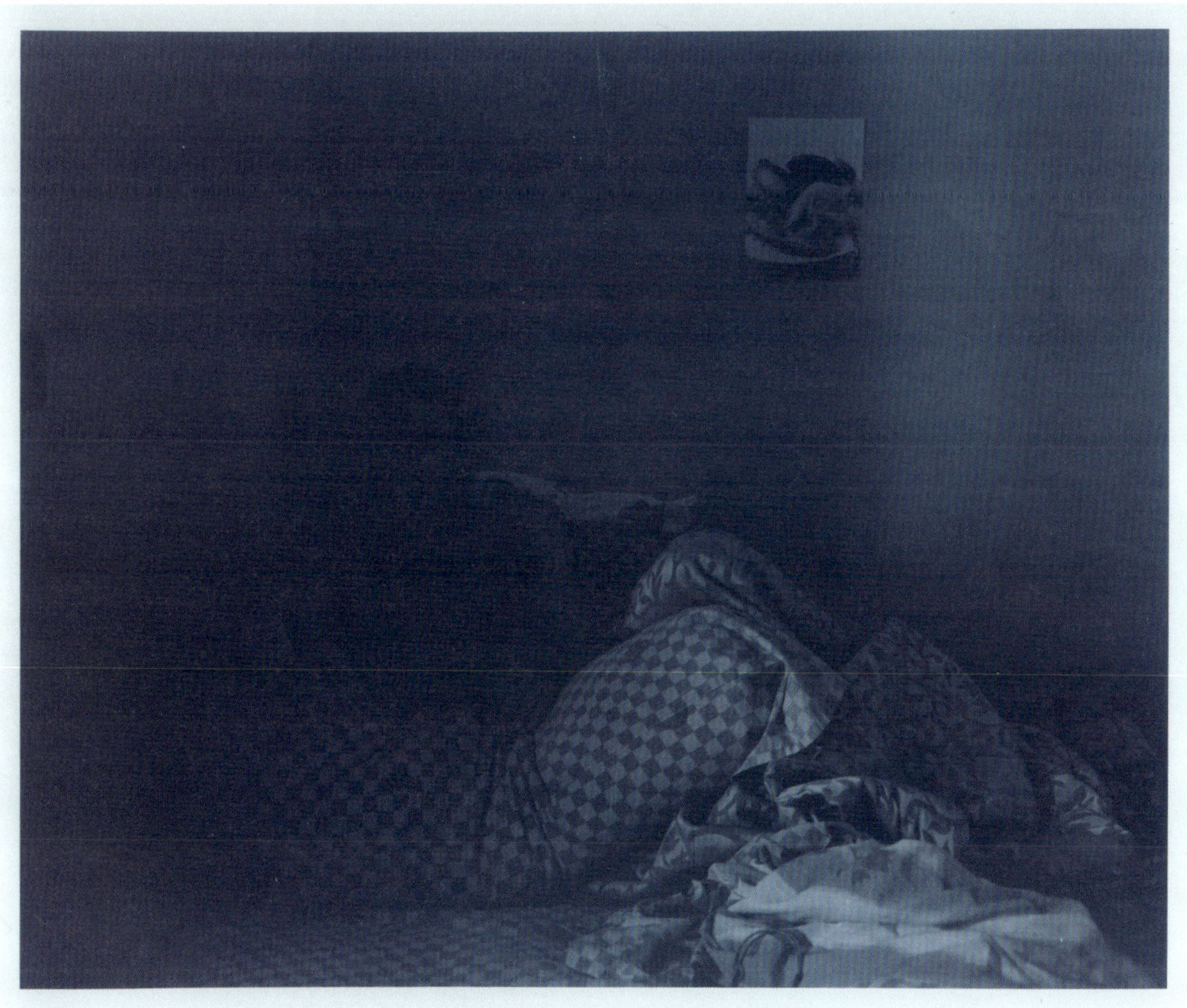

(CLICHÉ OF A MAN, LYING FIGURE) III

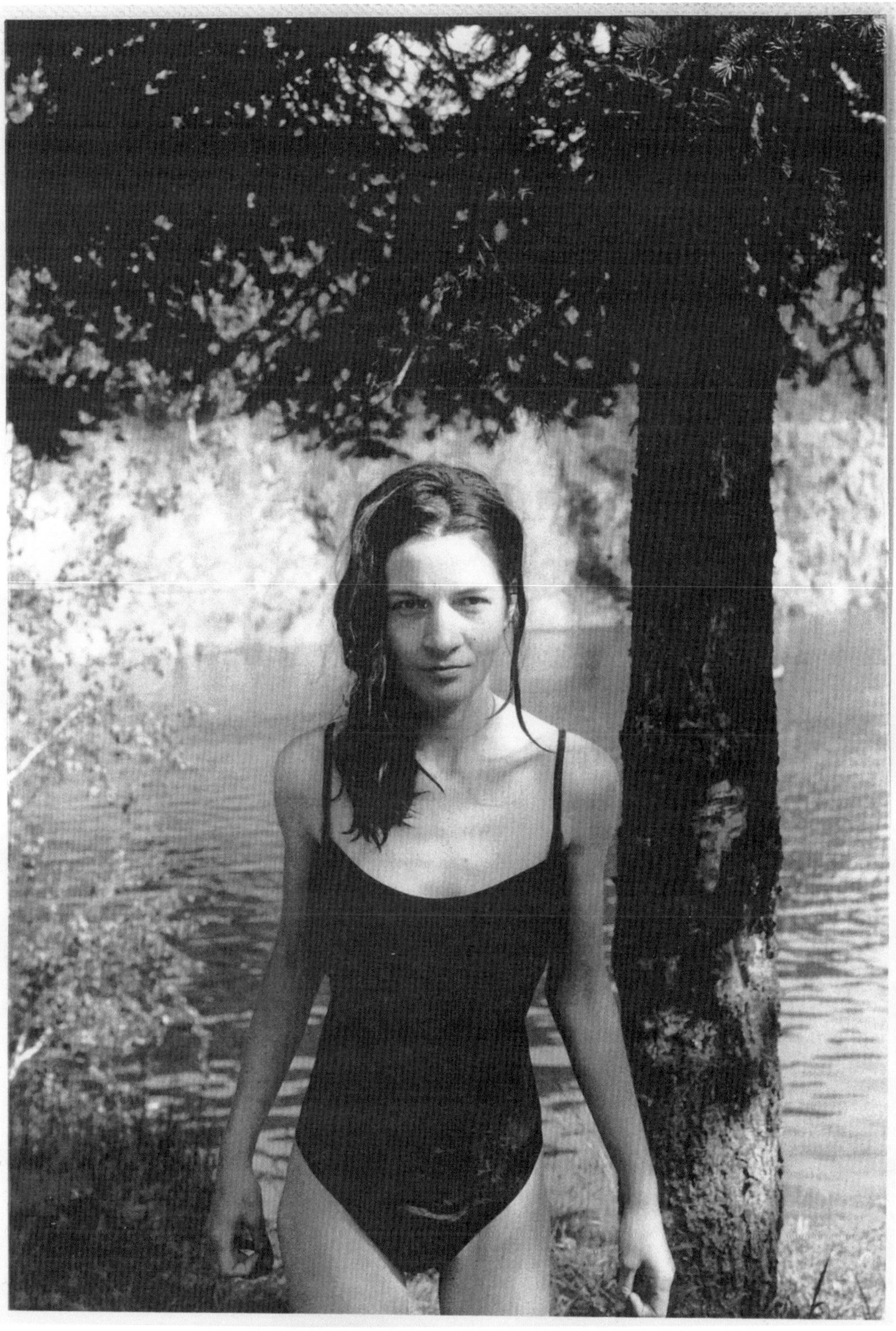

(CLICHÉ OF A WOMAN, STANDING FIGURE, AT THE LAKE)

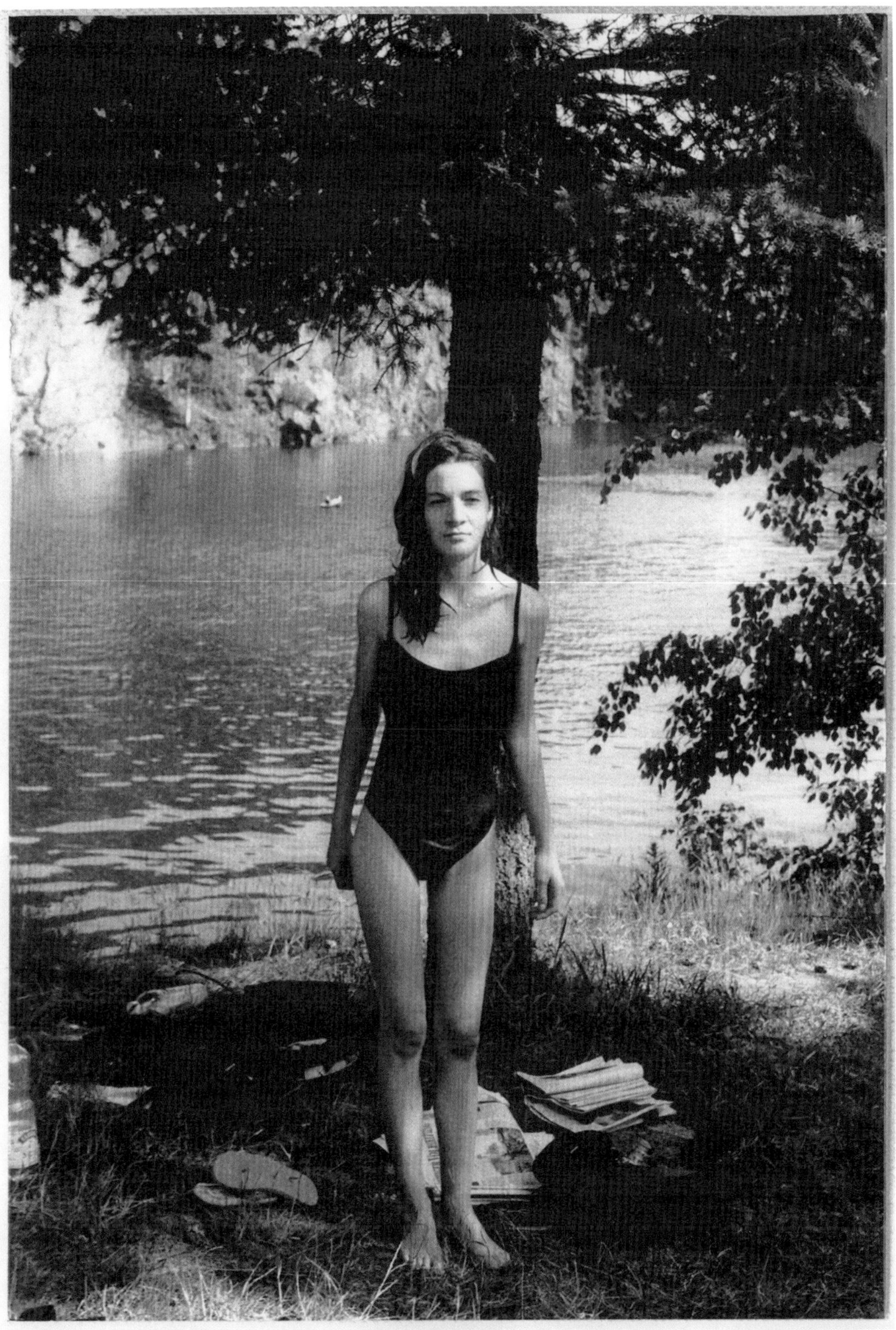

(CLICHÉ OF A WOMAN, STANDING FIGURE, AT THE LAKE)

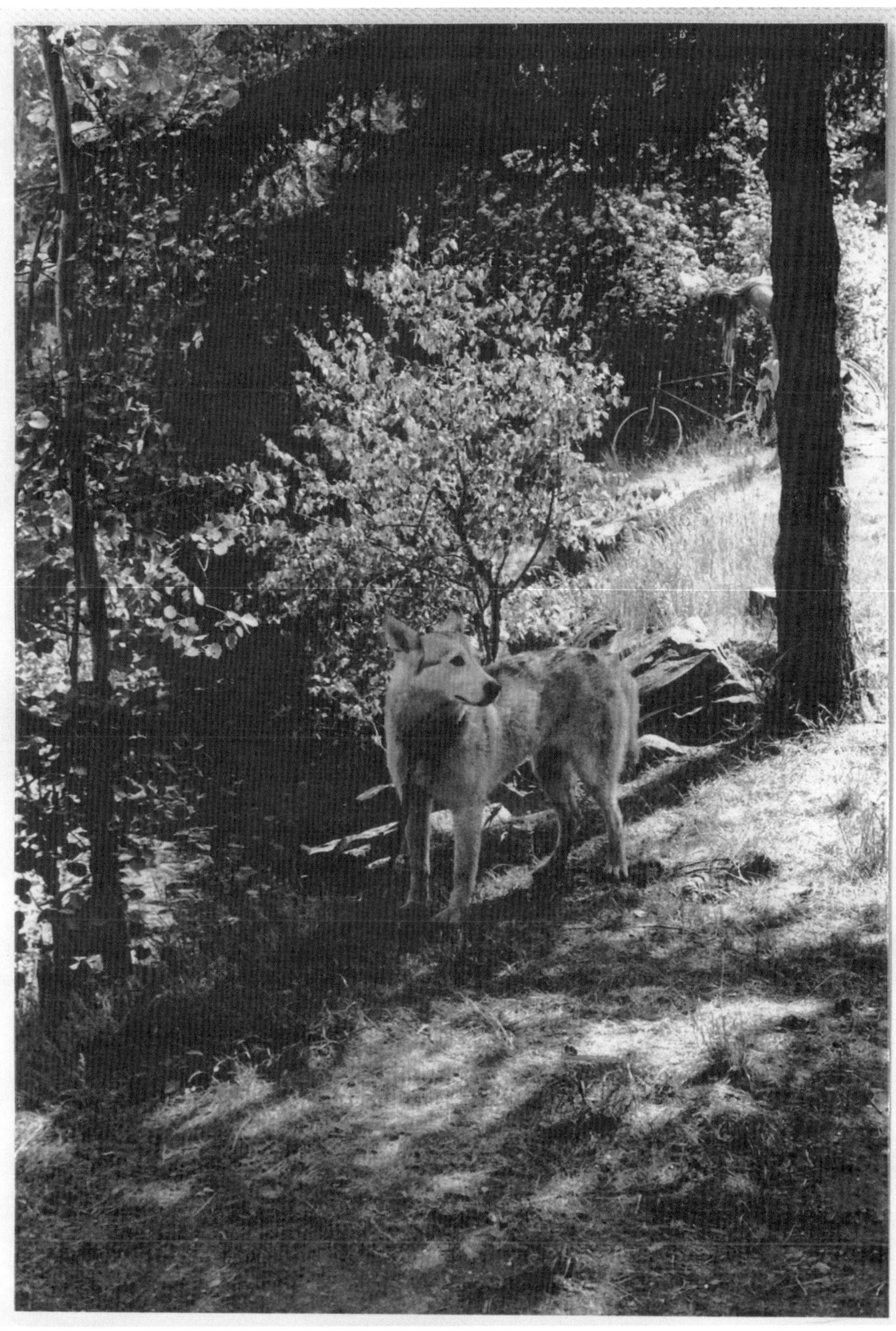

(CLICHÉ OF A WOMAN, STANDING FIGURE, AT THE LAKE)

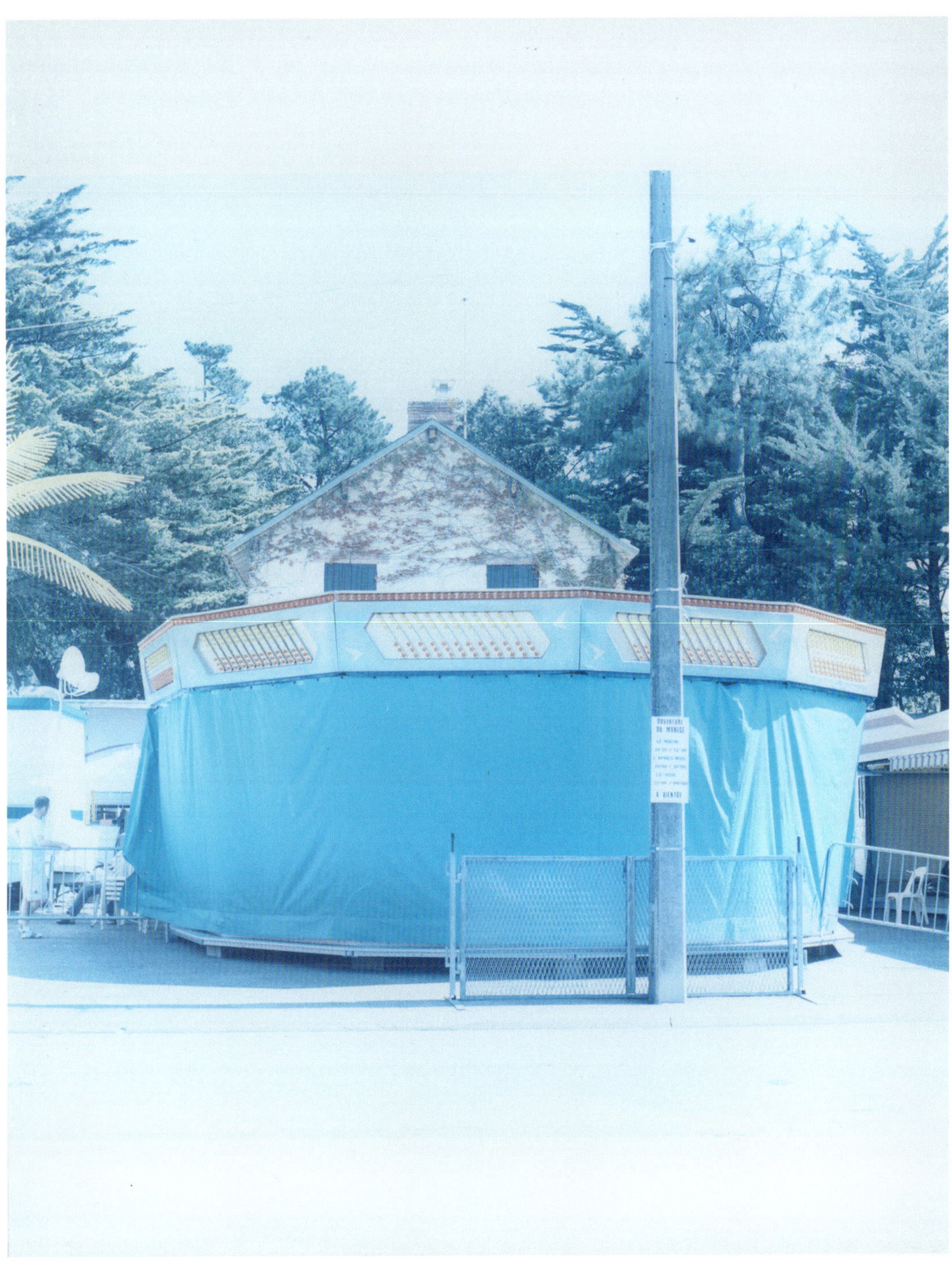

(CLICHÉ OF A CAROUSSEL) I

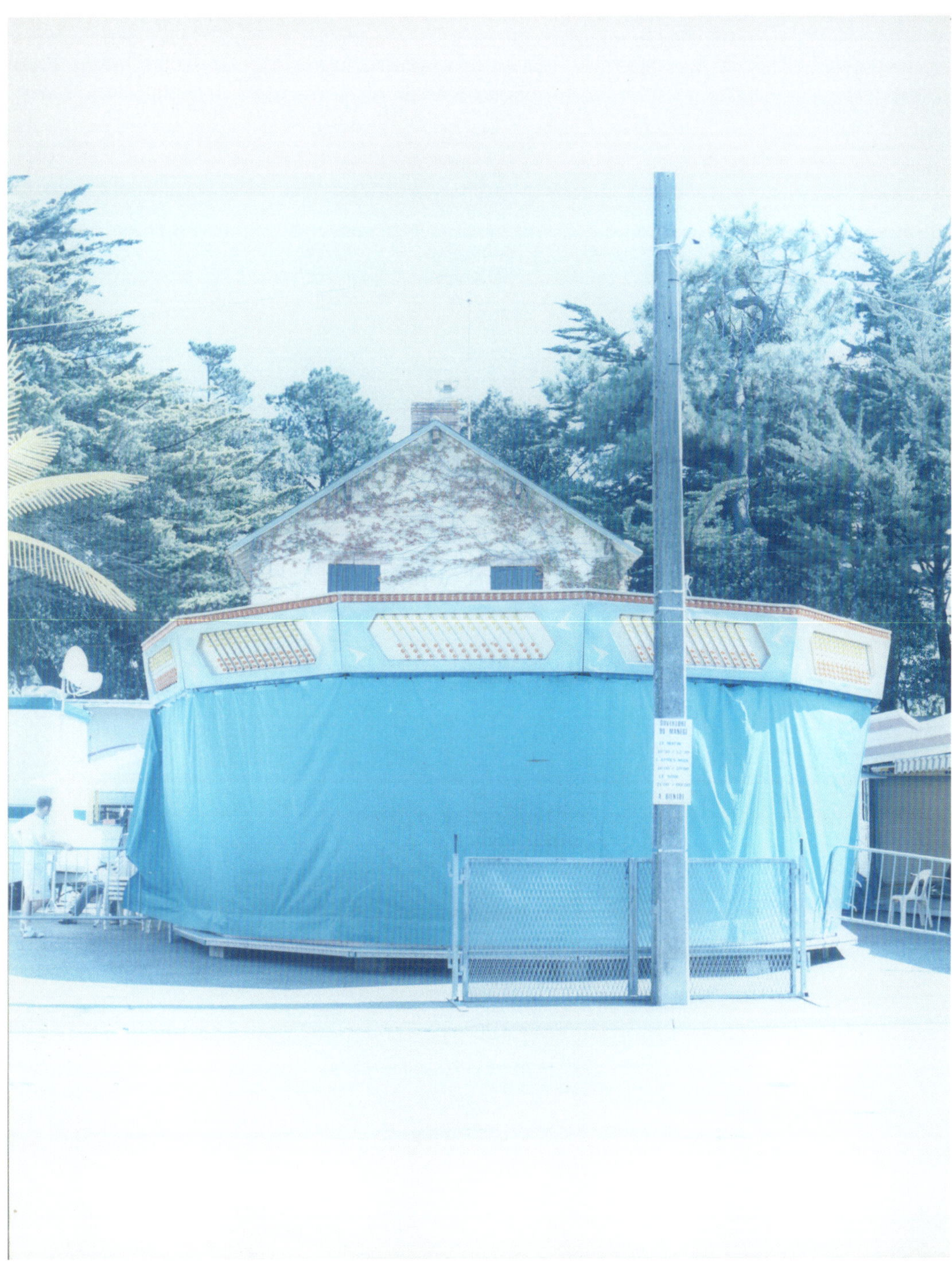

(CLICHÉ OF A CAROUSSEL) I

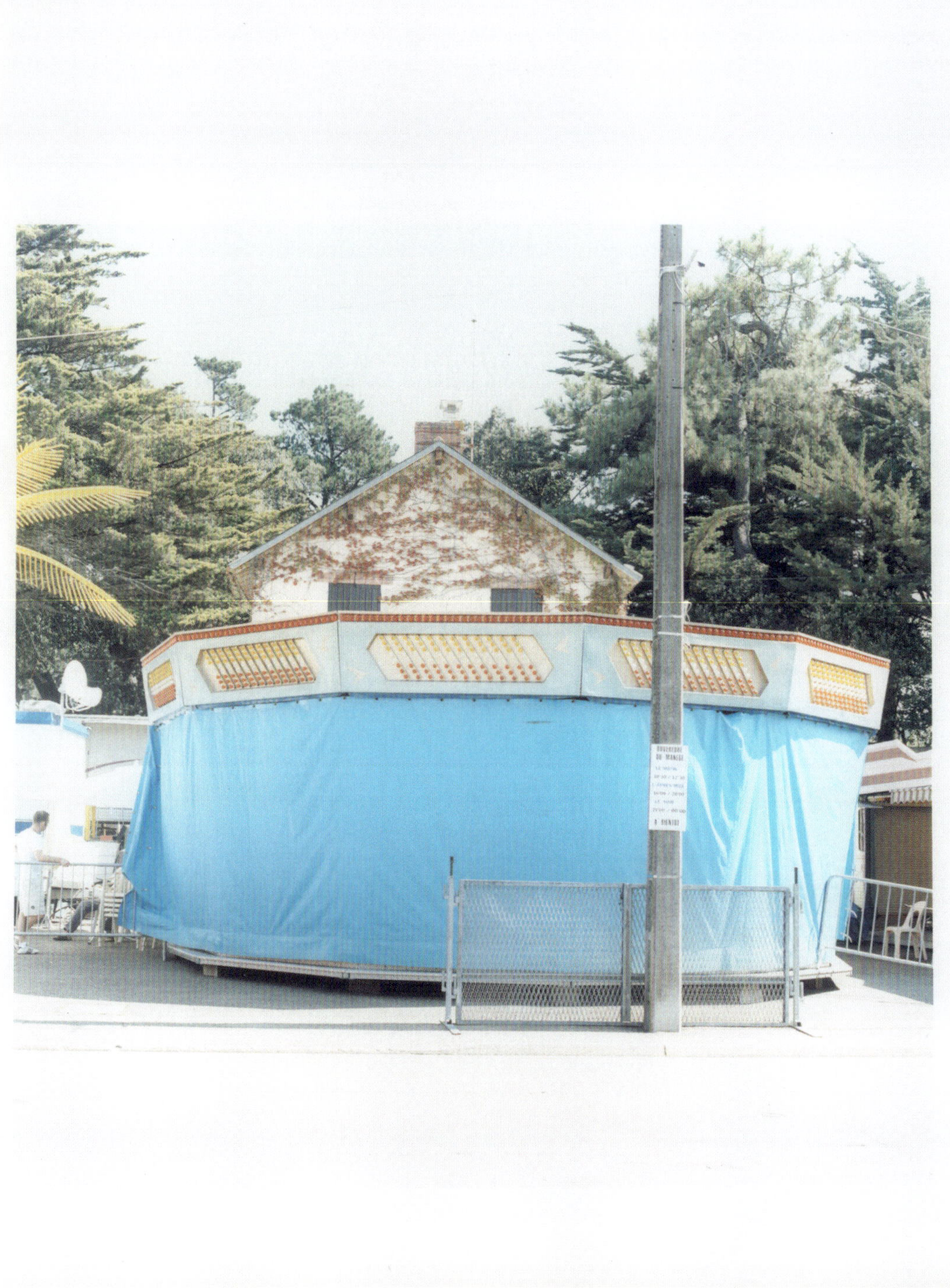

(CLICHÉ OF A CAROUSSEL) I

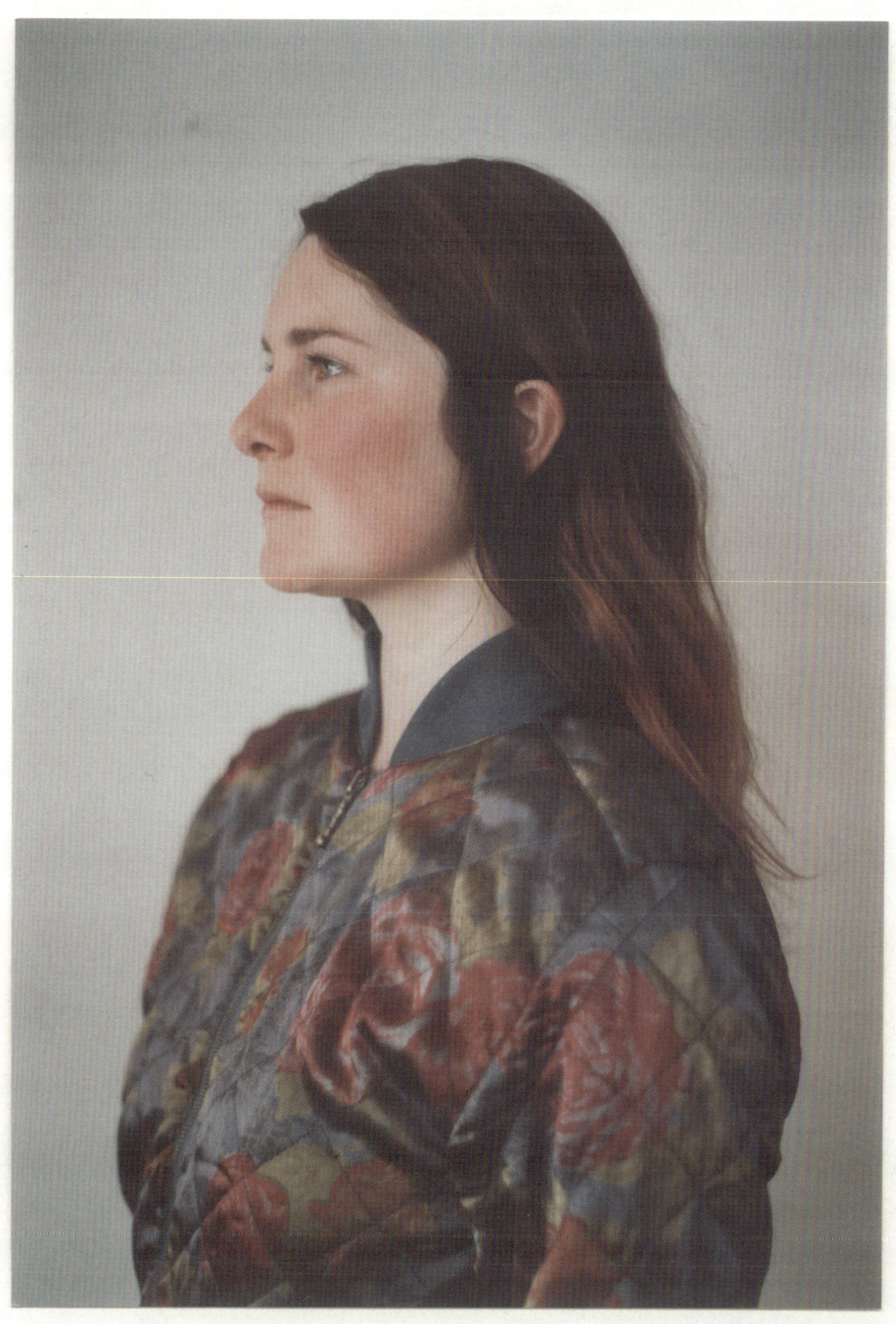

KRISTINA SCHULDT (P. OF A P.) I

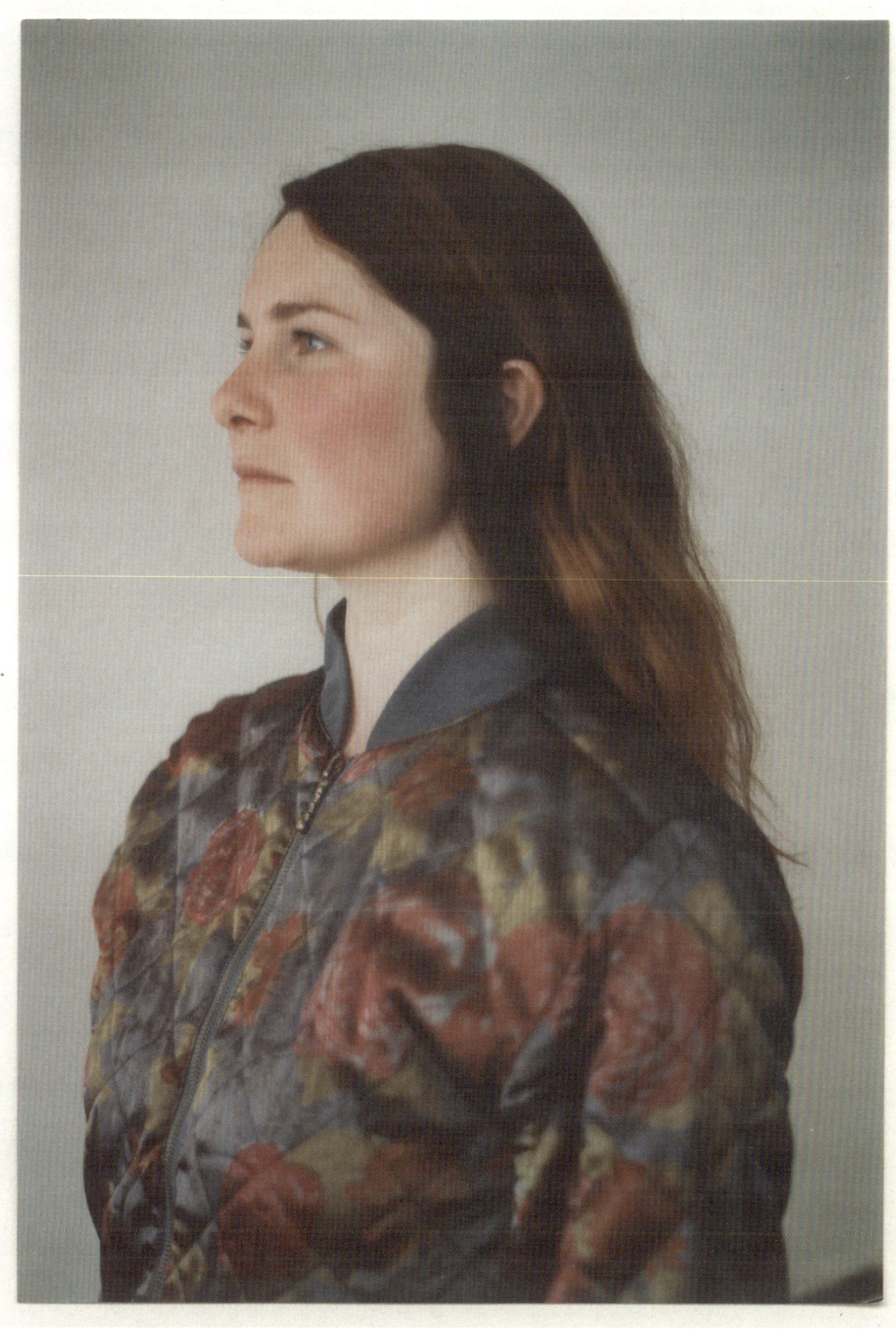

KRISTINA SCHULDT (P. OF A P.) I

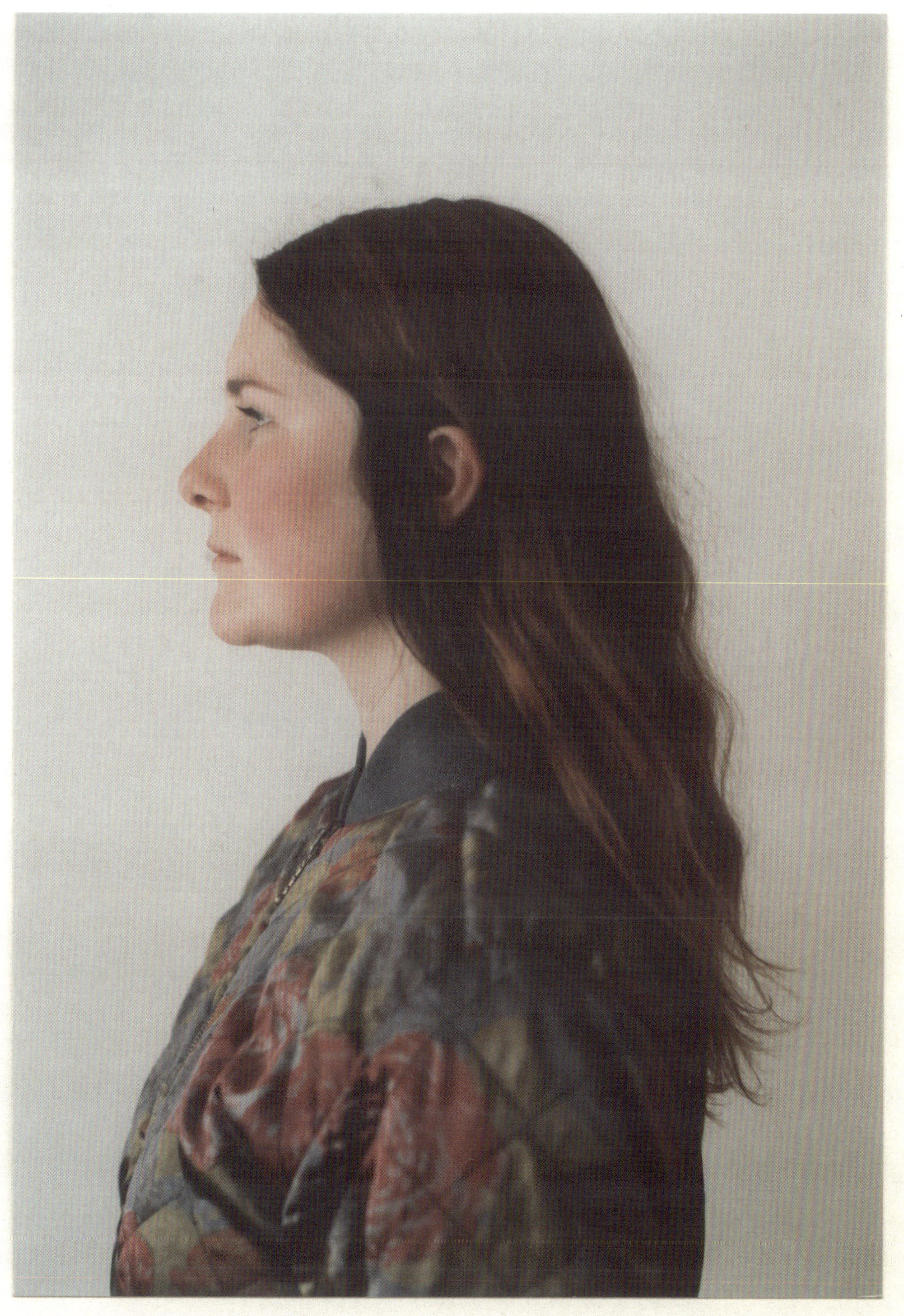

KRISTINA SCHULDT (P. OF A P.) I

CATALOGUE

I—XI

FLOWERS
LANDSCAPES
POW WOW
PLANTS
MEN
WOMEN
CITY
CIRCUS
GROUPS / PAIRS
CHILDREN
ANIMALS

A—B

PICTURE OF A PAINTER (P. OF A P.) I
DOUBLES (P. OF A P.) II

I

FLOWERS

Plate 1
(Cliché of a Flower Bouquet) I

Plate 2
(Cliché of a Flower Bouquet) I

Plate 3
(Cliché of a Flower Bouquet) I

Plate 6
(Cliché of a Flower Bouquet) II

Plate 7
(Cliché of a Flower Bouquet) II

Plate 8
(Cliché of a Flower Bouquet) II

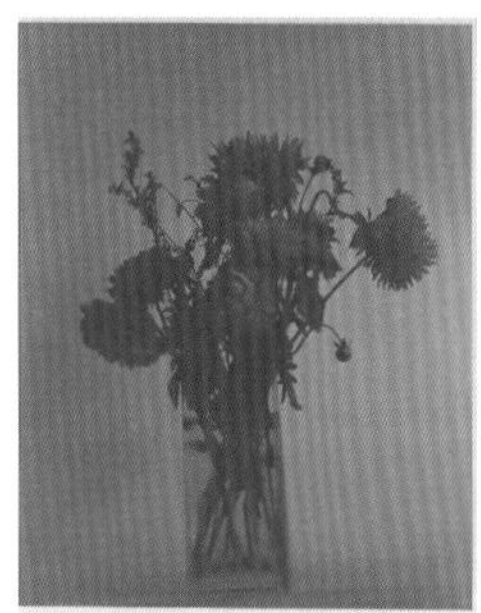

Plate 9
(Cliché of a Flower Bouquet) III

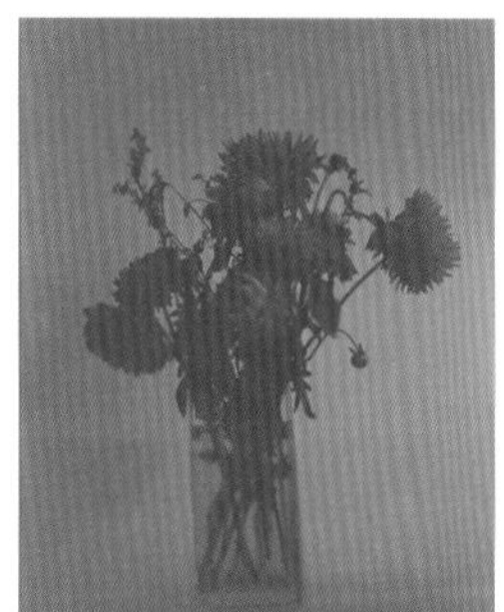

Plate 10
(Cliché of a Flower Bouquet) III

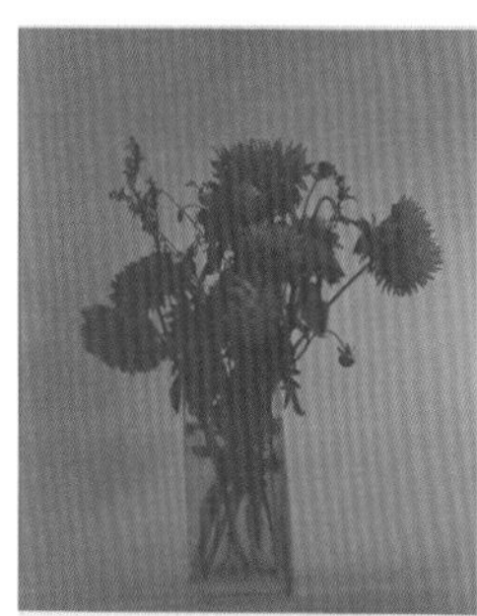

Plate 11
(Cliché of a Flower Bouquet) III

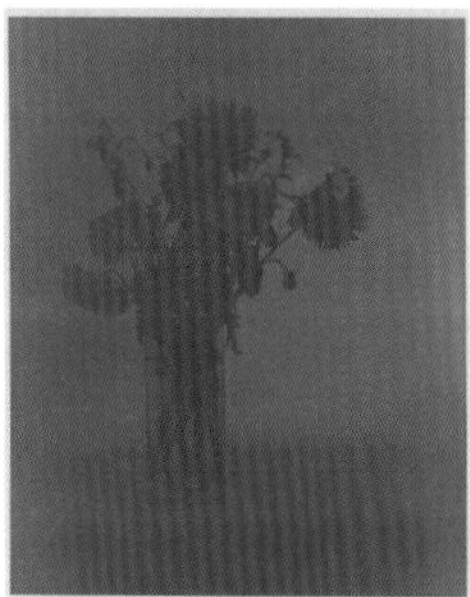

Plate 12
(Cliché of a Flower Bouquet) IV

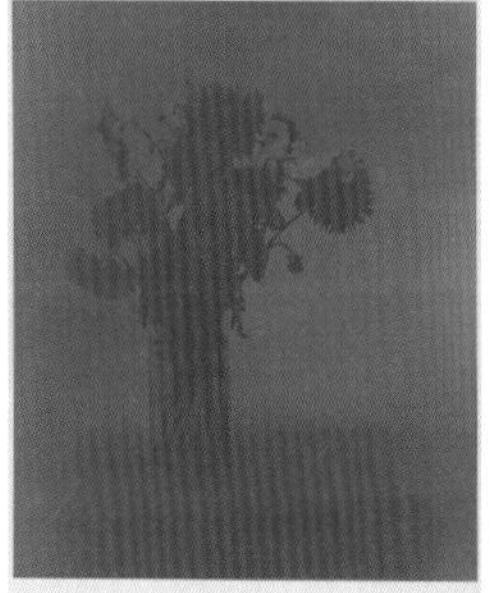

Plate 13
(Cliché of a Flower Bouquet) IV

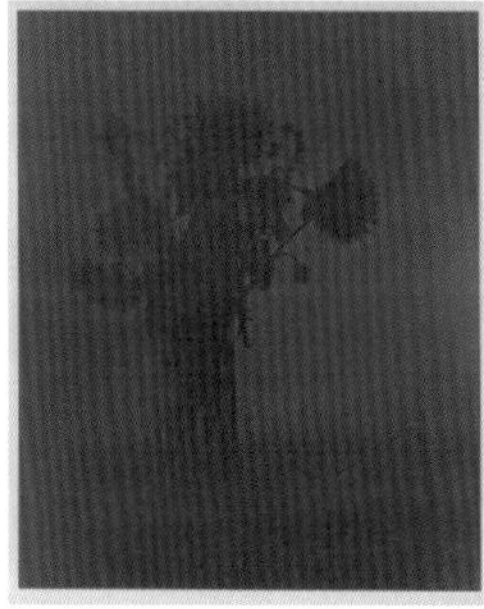

Plate 14
(Cliché of a Flower Bouquet) IV

Plate 4
(Cliché of a Flower Bouquet) I

Plate 5
(Cliché of a Flower Bouquet) I

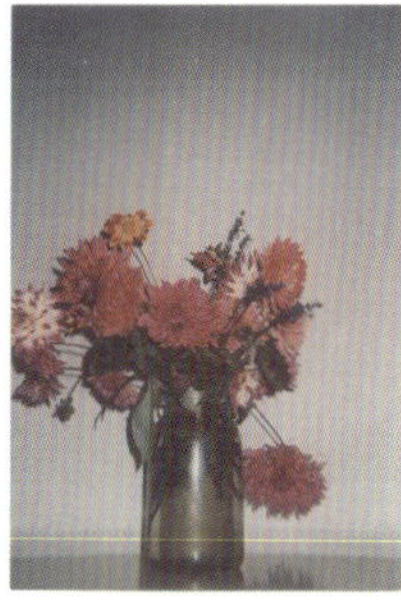

Plate 15
(Cliché of a Flower Bouquet) V

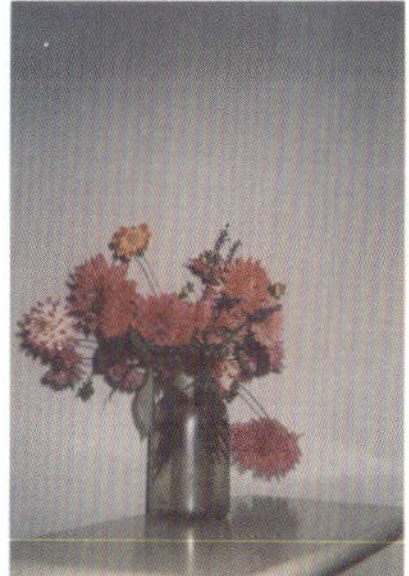

Plate 16
(Cliché of a Flower Bouquet) V

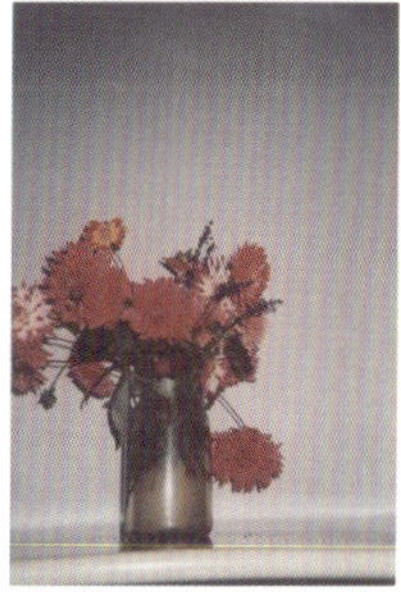

Plate 17
(Cliché of a Flower Bouquet) V

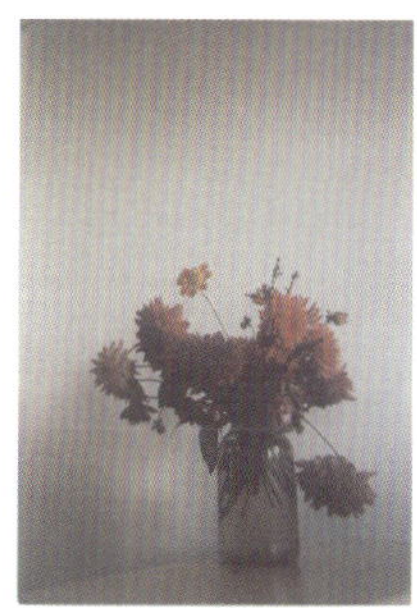

Plate 18
(Cliché of a Flower Bouquet) VI

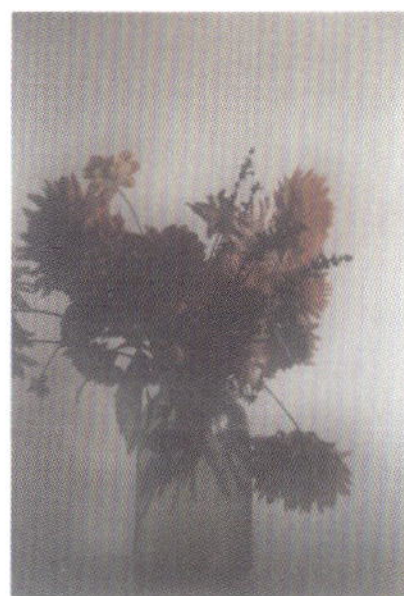

Plate 19
(Cliché of a Flower Bouquet) VI

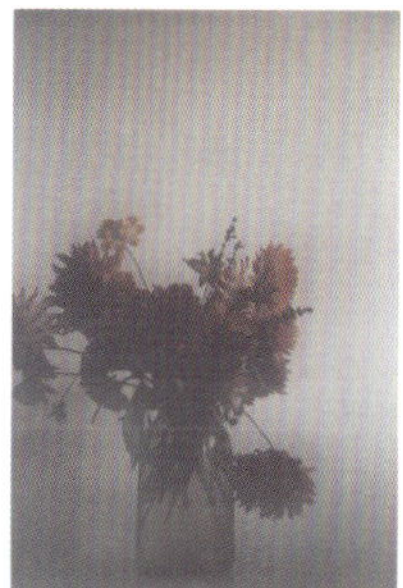

Plate 20
(Cliché of a Flower Bouquet) VI

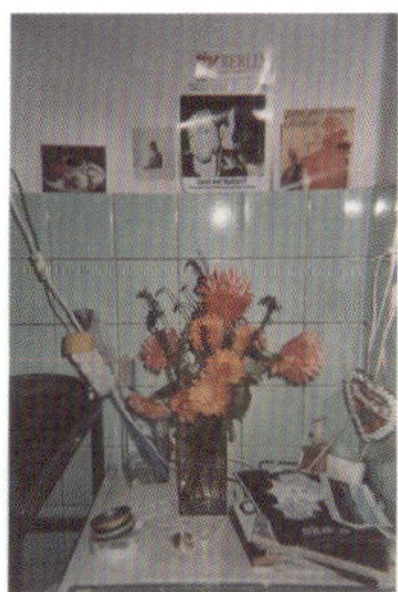

Plate 21
(Cliché of a Flower Bouquet) VII

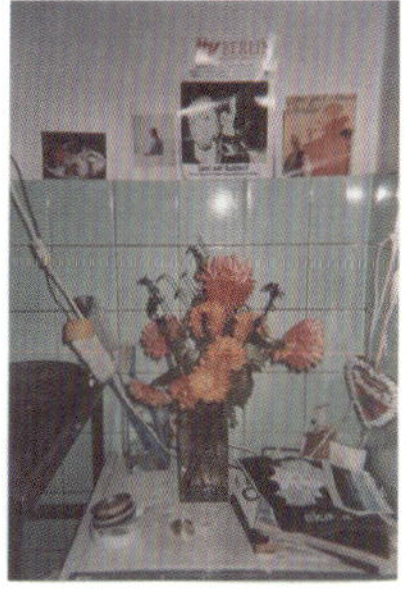

Plate 22
(Cliché of a Flower Bouquet) VII

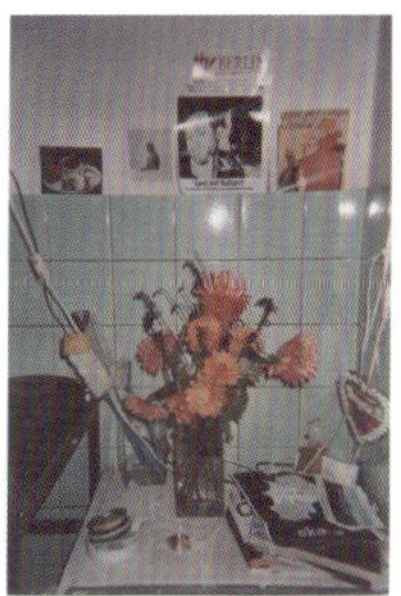

Plate 23
(Cliché of a Flower Bouquet) VII

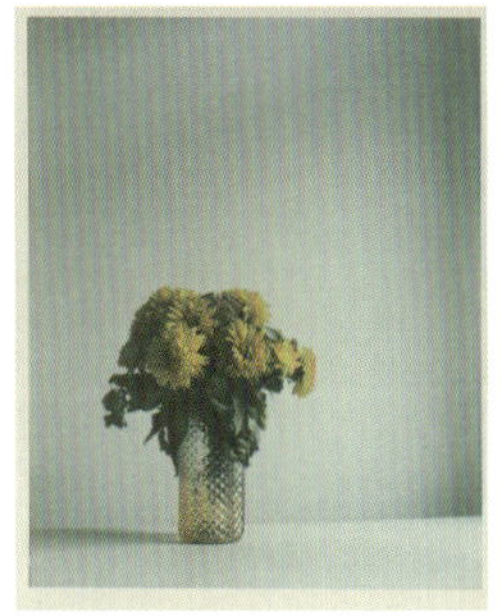

Plate 24
(Cliché of a Flower Bouquet) VIII

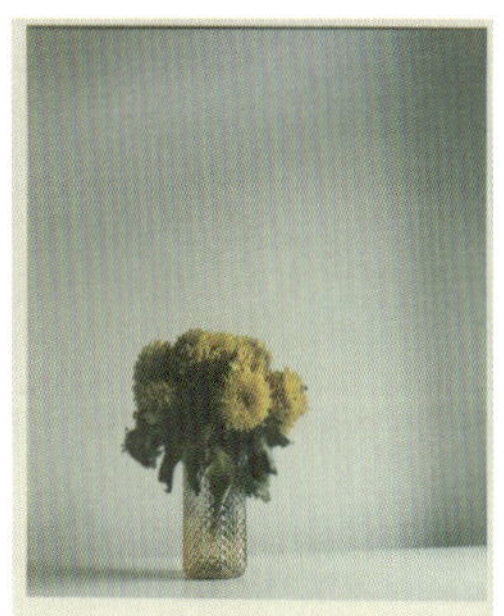

Plate 25
(Cliché of a Flower Bouquet) VIII

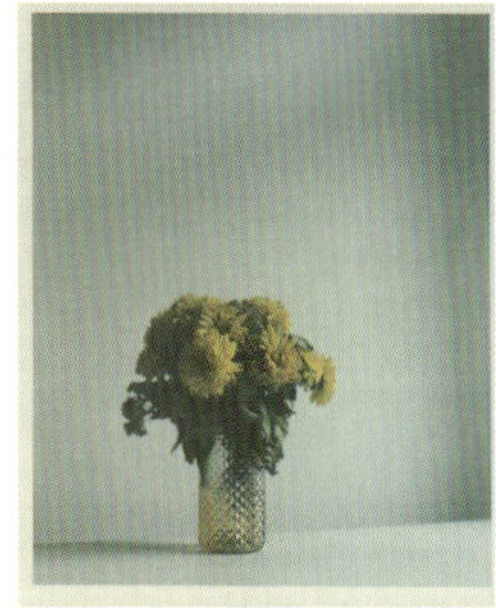

Plate 26
(Cliché of a Flower Bouquet) VIII

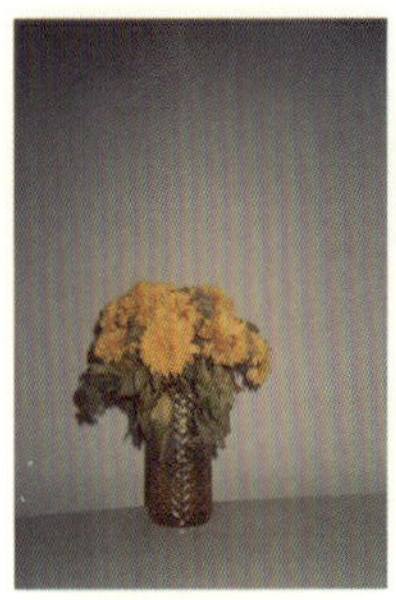

Plate 29
(Cliché of a Flower Bouquet) IX

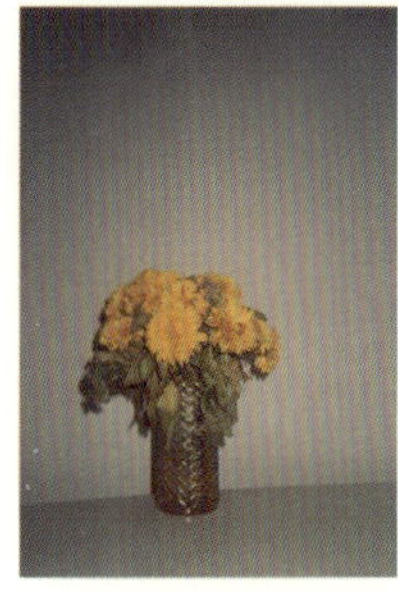

Plate 30
(Cliché of a Flower Bouquet) IX

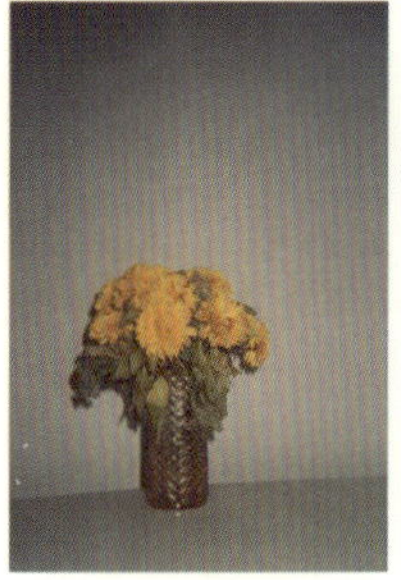

Plate 31
(Cliché of a Flower Bouquet) IX

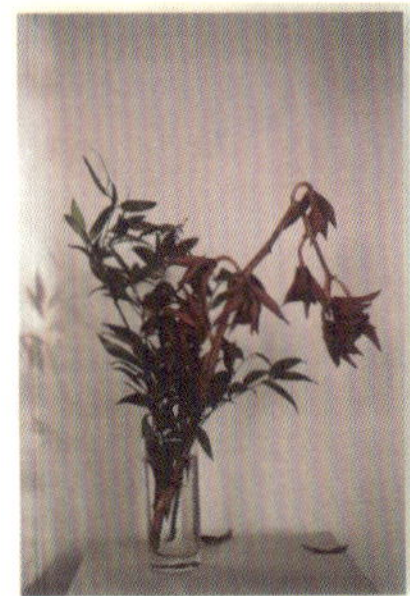

Plate 34
(Cliché of a Flower Bouquet) X

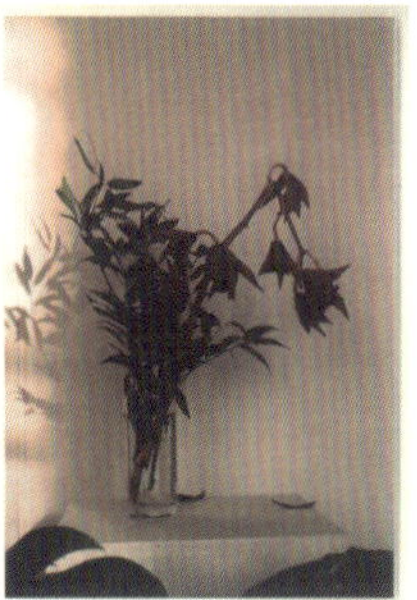

Plate 35
(Cliché of a Flower Bouquet) X

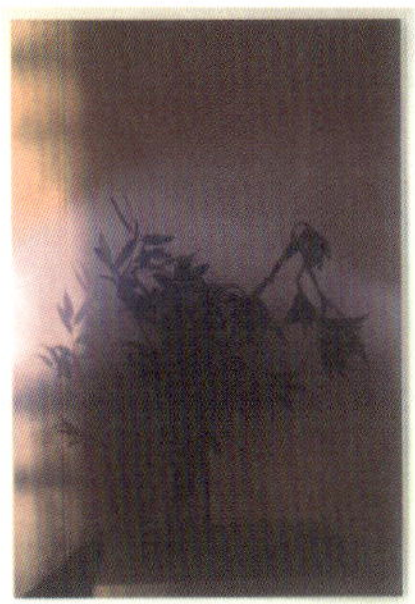

Plate 36
(Cliché of a Flower Bouquet) X

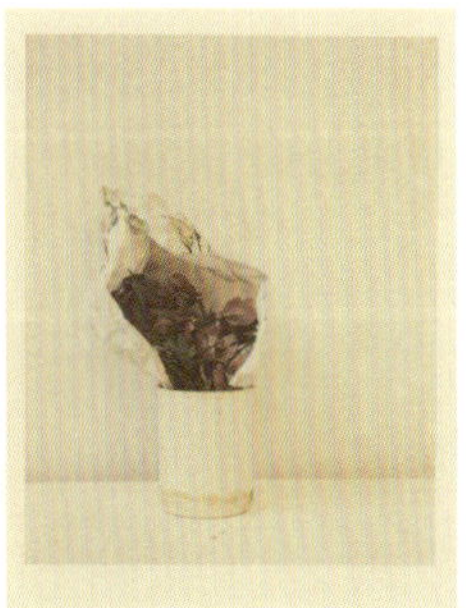

Plate 37
(Cliché of a Flower Bouquet) XI

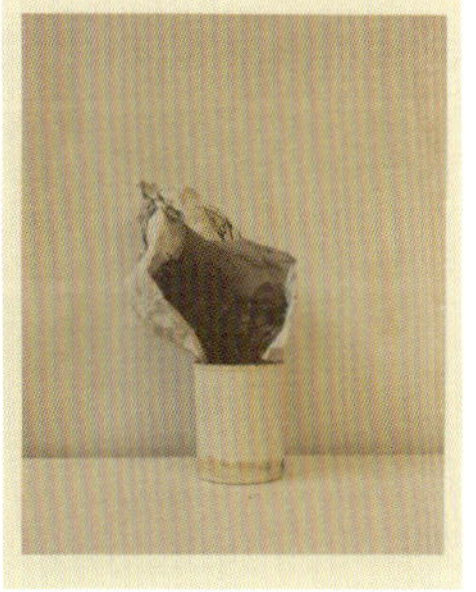

Plate 38
(Cliché of a Flower Bouquet) XI

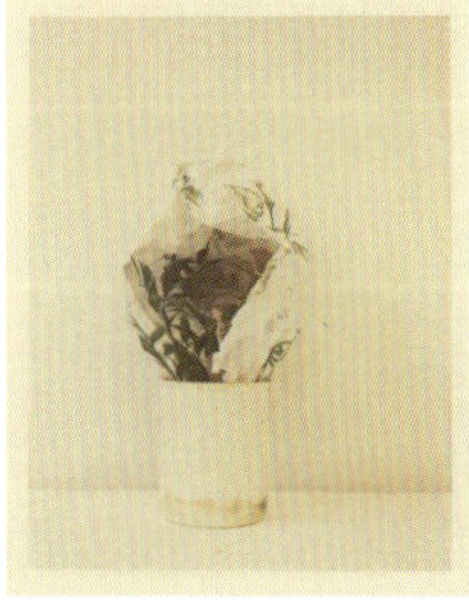

Plate 39
(Cliché of a Flower Bouquet) XI

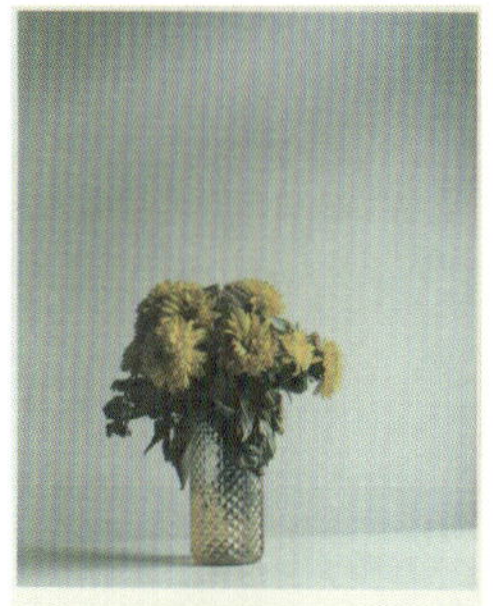

Plate 27
(Cliché of a Flower Bouquet) VIII

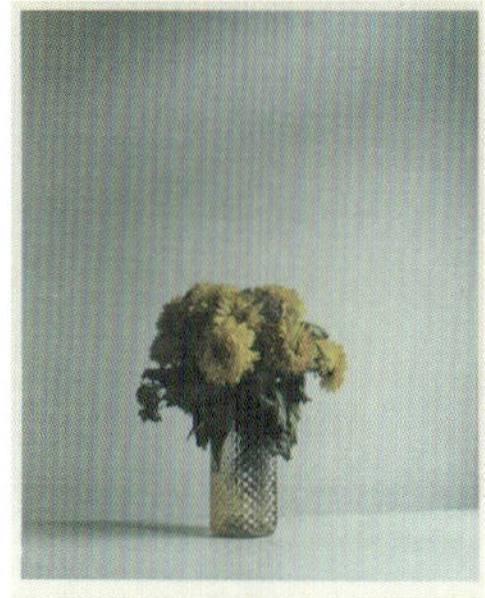

Plate 28
(Cliché of a Flower Bouquet) VIII

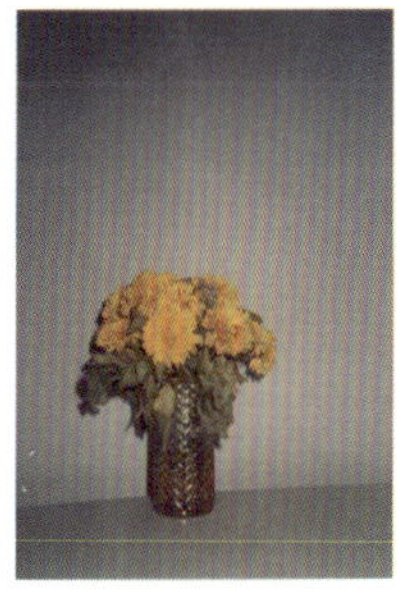

Plate 32
(Cliché of a Flower Bouquet) IX

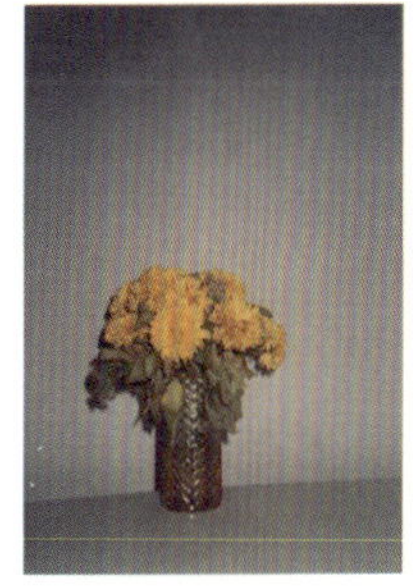

Plate 33
(Cliché of a Flower Bouquet) IX

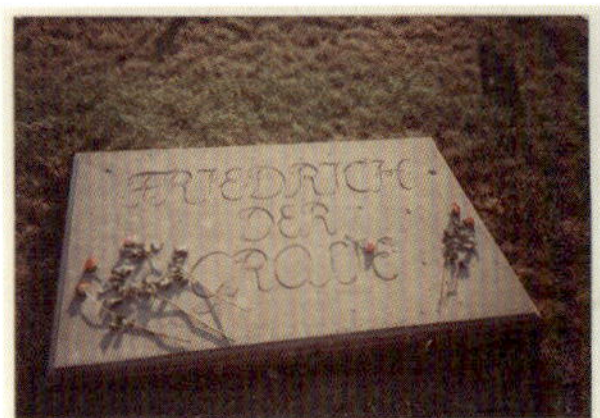

Plate 40
(Cliché of a Flower Bouquet) XII

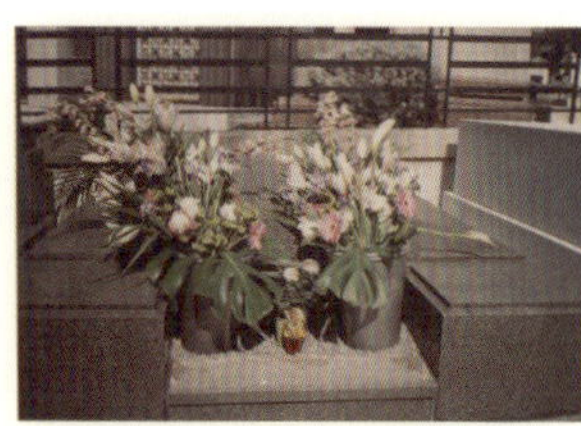

Plate 43
(Cliché of a Flower Bouquet) XIII

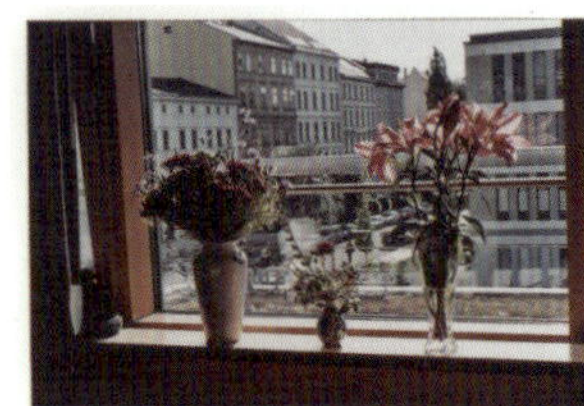

Plate 46
(Cliché of a Flower Bouquet) XIV

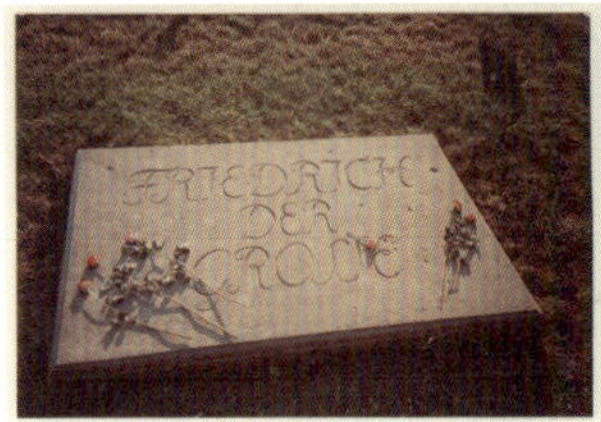

Plate 41
(Cliché of a Flower Bouquet) XII

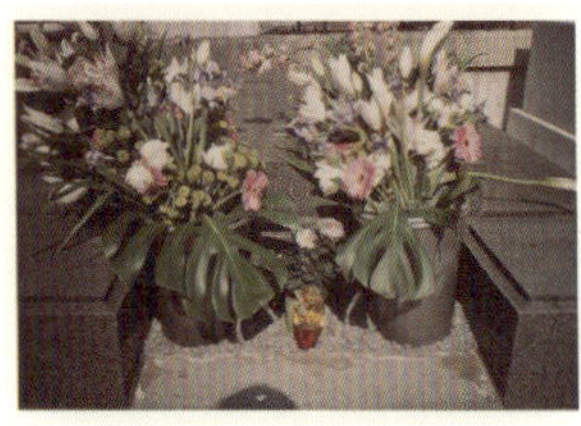

Plate 44
(Cliché of a Flower Bouquet) XIII

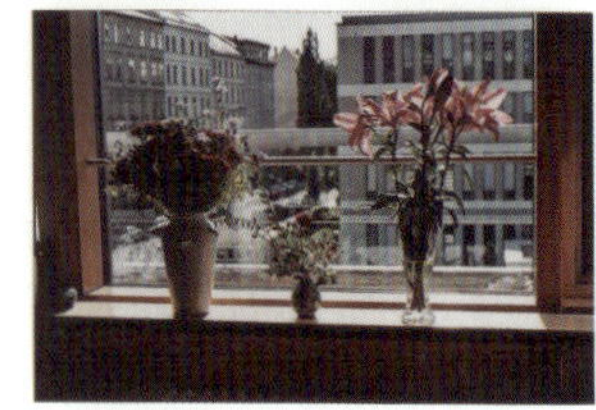

Plate 47
(Cliché of a Flower Bouquet) XIV

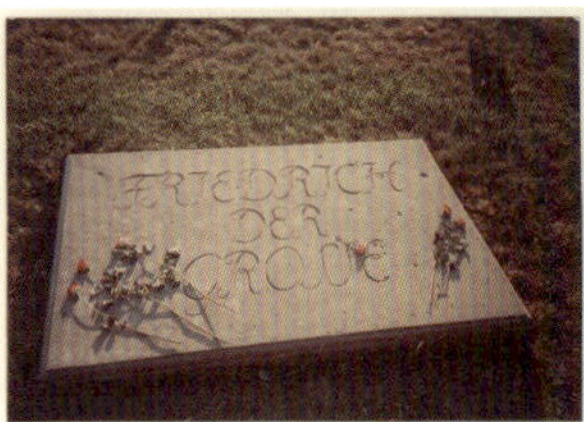

Plate 42
(Cliché of a Flower Bouquet) XII

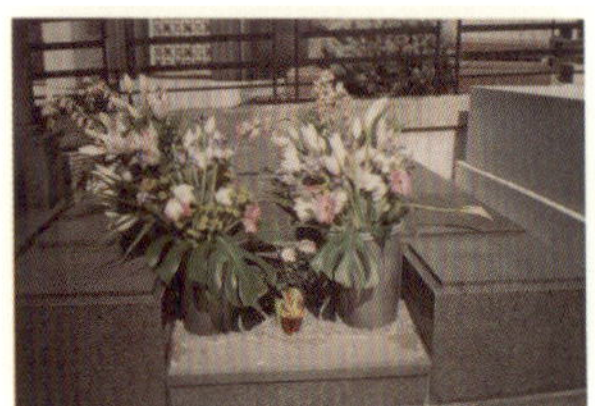

Plate 45
(Cliché of a Flower Bouquet) XIII

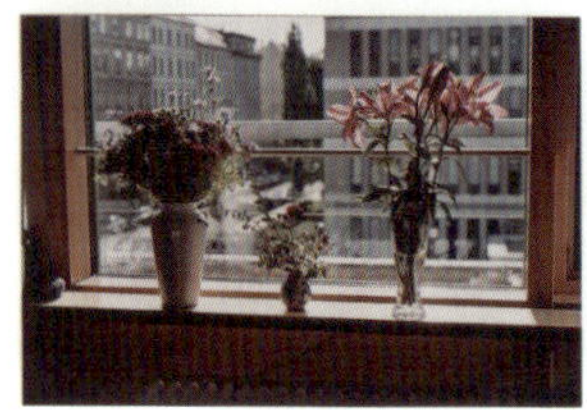

Plate 48
(Cliché of a Flower Bouquet) XIV

Plate 49
(Cliché of a Flower Bouquet) XV

Plate 50
(Cliché of a Flower Bouquet) XV

Plate 51
(Cliché of a Flower Bouquet) XV

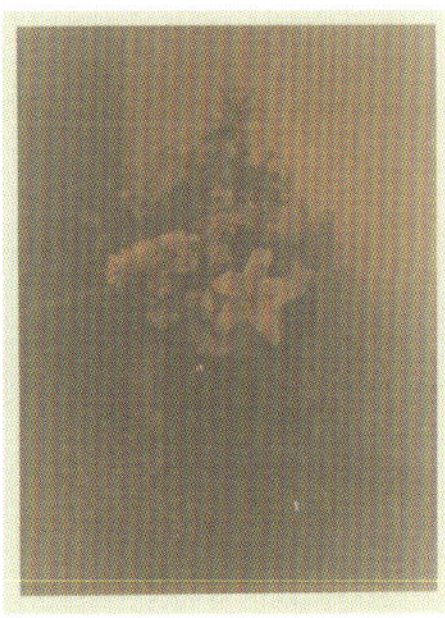

Plate 52
(Cliché of a Flower Bouquet) XVI

Plate 53
(Cliché of a Flower Bouquet) XVI

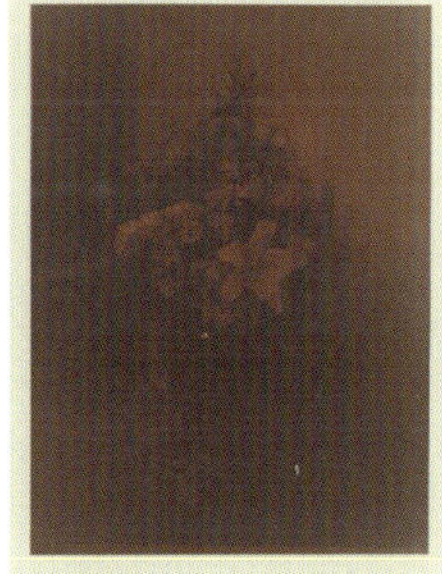

Plate 54
(Cliché of a Flower Bouquet) XVI

Plate 55
(Cliché of a Flower Bouquet) XVII

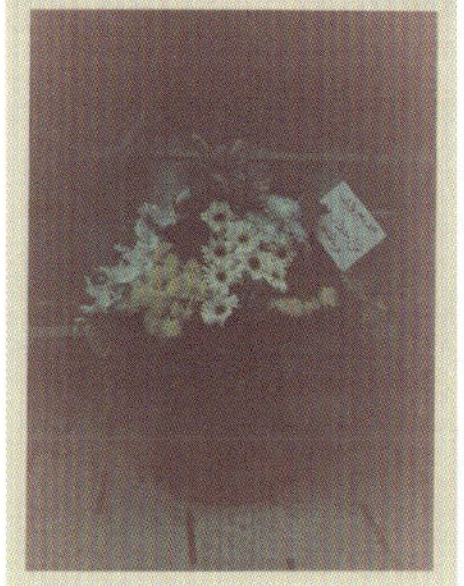

Plate 56
(Cliché of a Flower Bouquet) XVII

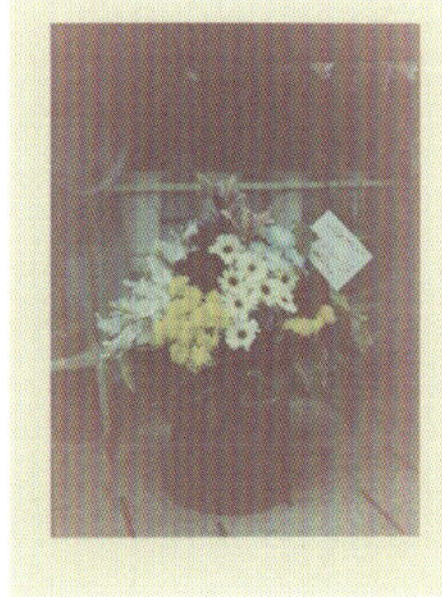

Plate 57
(Cliché of a Flower Bouquet) XVII

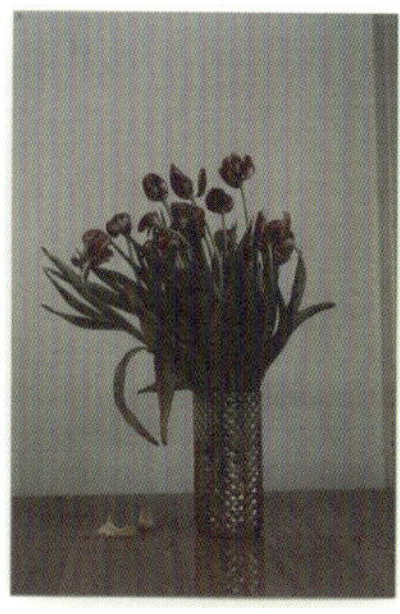

Plate 58
(Cliché of a Flower Bouquet) XVIII

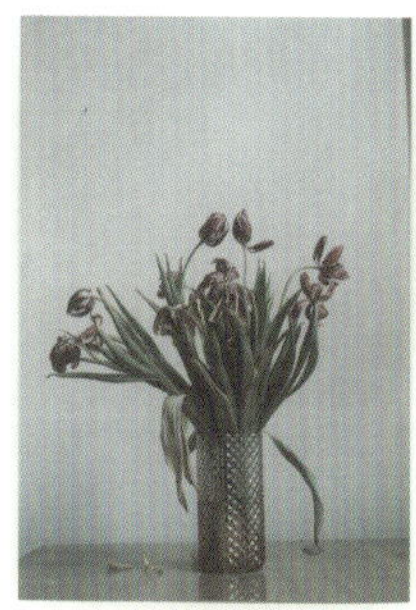

Plate 59
(Cliché of a Flower Bouquet) XVIII

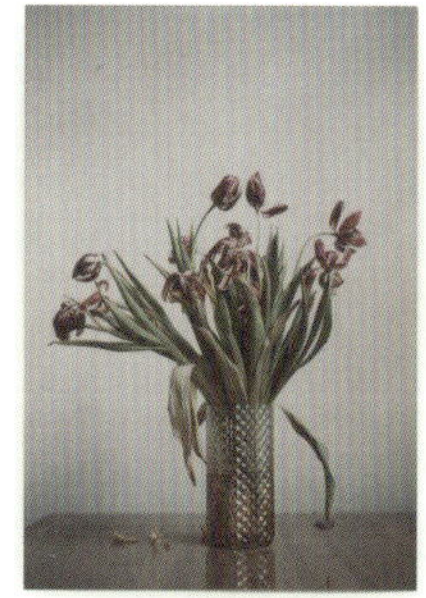

Plate 60
(Cliché of a Flower Bouquet) XVIII

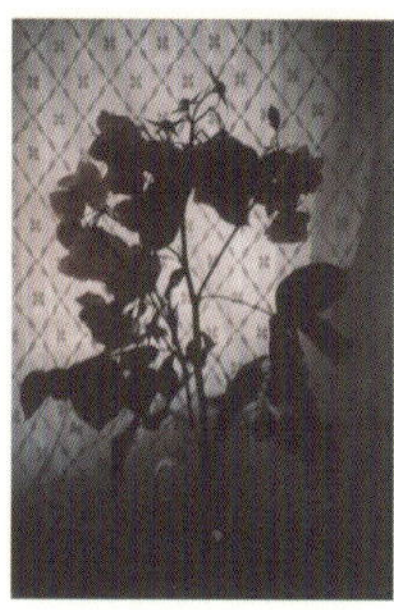

Plate 63
(Cliché of a Flower Bouquet) XIX

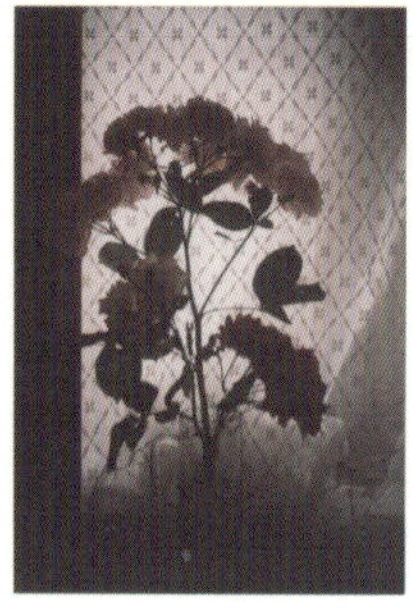

Plate 64
(Cliché of a Flower Bouquet) XIX

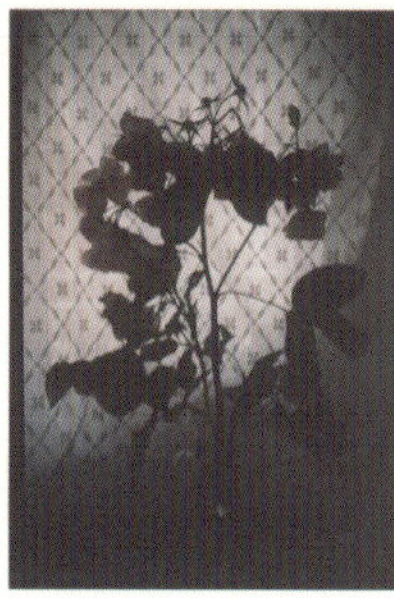

Plate 65
(Cliché of a Flower Bouquet) XIX

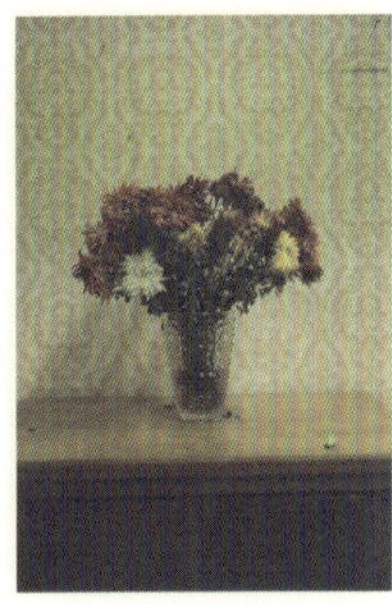

Plate 66
(Cliché of a Flower Bouquet) XX

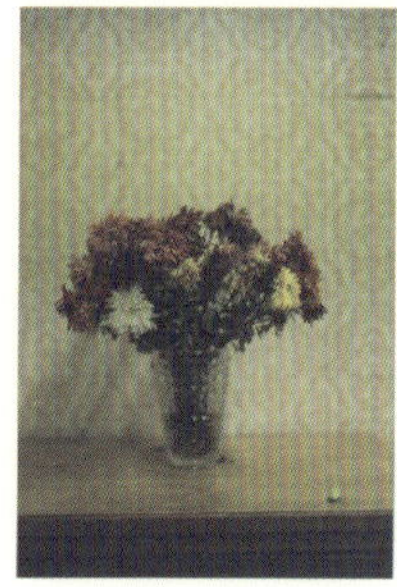

Plate 67
(Cliché of a Flower Bouquet) XX

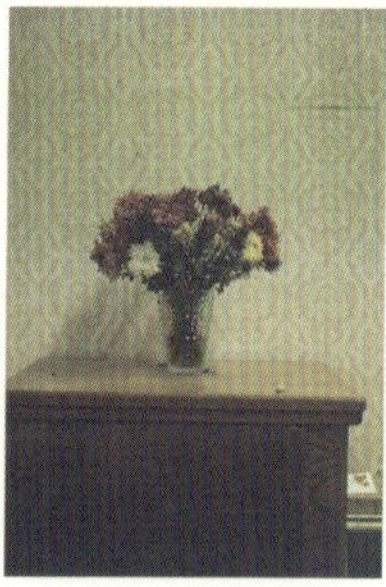

Plate 68
(Cliché of a Flower Bouquet) XX

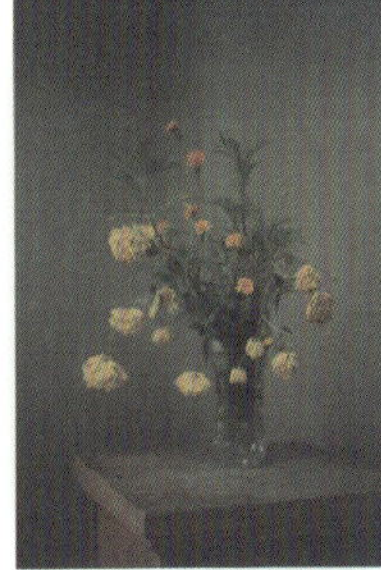

Plate 69
(Cliché of a Flower Bouquet) XXI

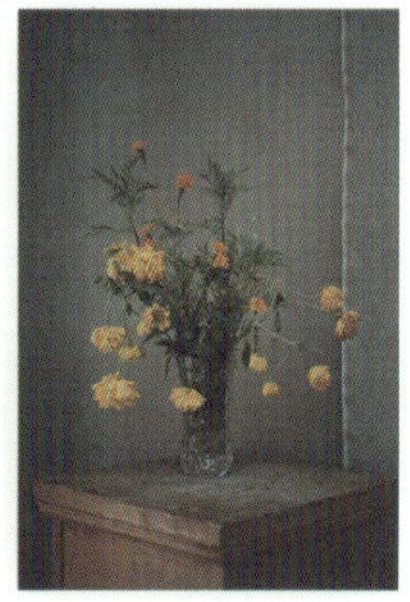

Plate 70
(Cliché of a Flower Bouquet) XXI

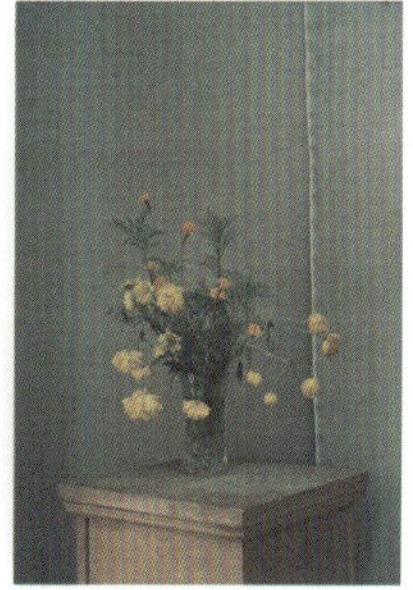

Plate 71
(Cliché of a Flower Bouquet) XXI

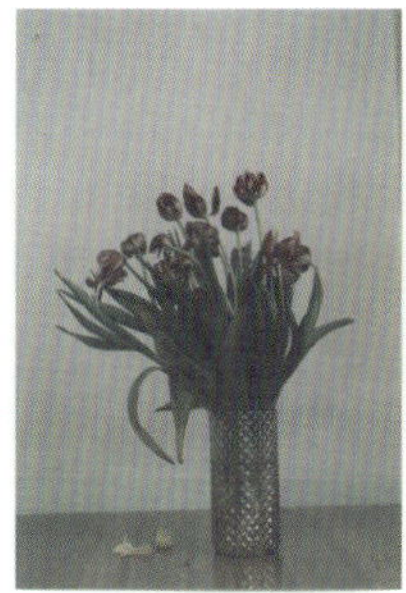

Plate 61
(Cliché of a Flower Bouquet) XVIII

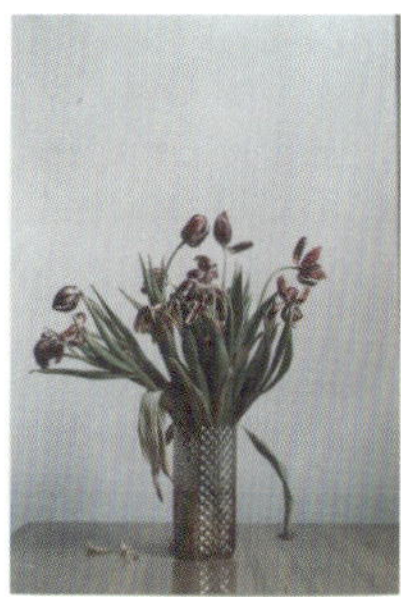

Plate 62
(Cliché of a Flower Bouquet) XVIII

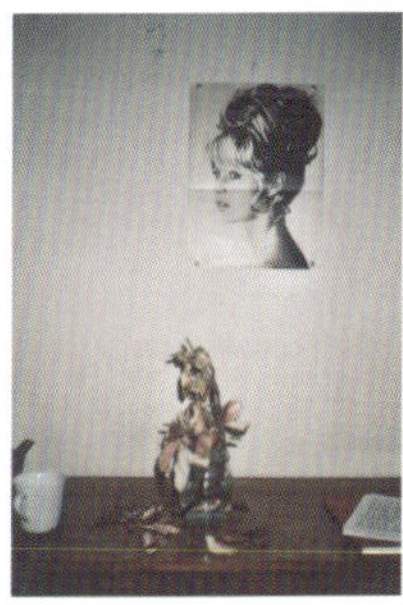

Plate 72
(Cliché of a Flower Bouquet) XXII

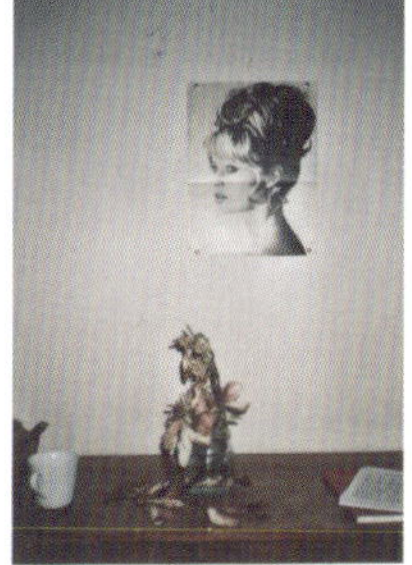

Plate 73
(Cliché of a Flower Bouquet) XXII

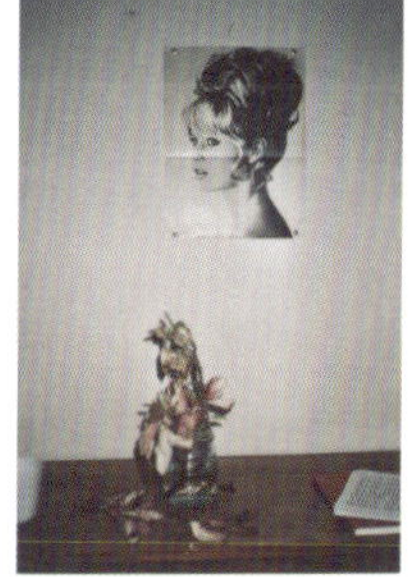

Plate 74
(Cliché of a Flower Bouquet) XXII

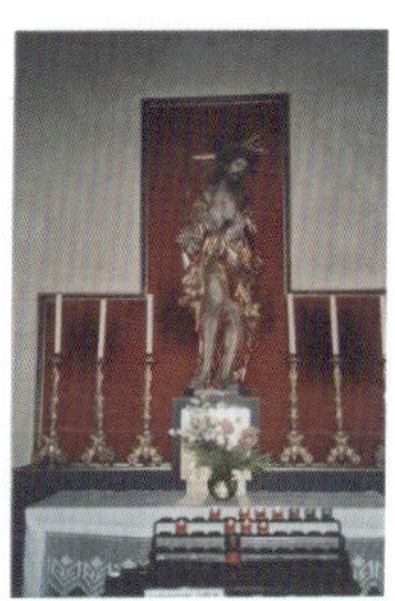

Plate 75
(Cliché of a Flower Bouquet) XXIII

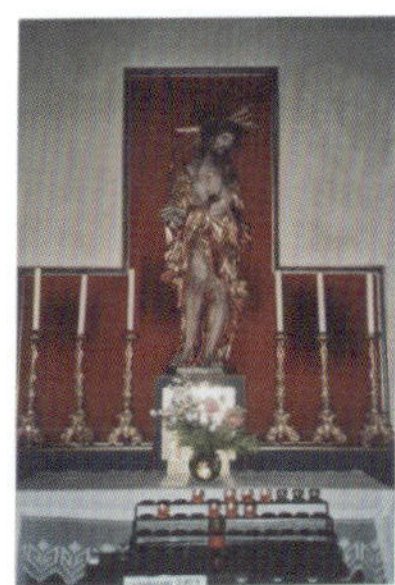

Plate 76
(Cliché of a Flower Bouquet) XXIII

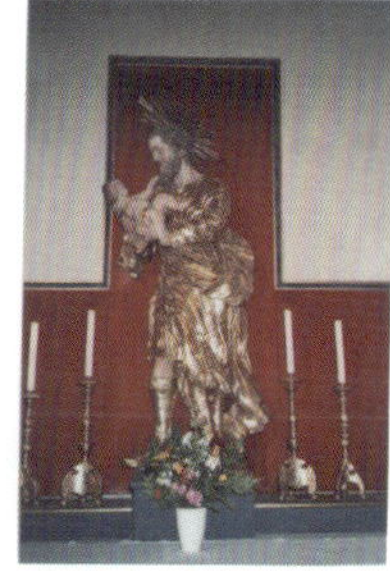

Plate 77
(Cliché of a Flower Bouquet) XXIII

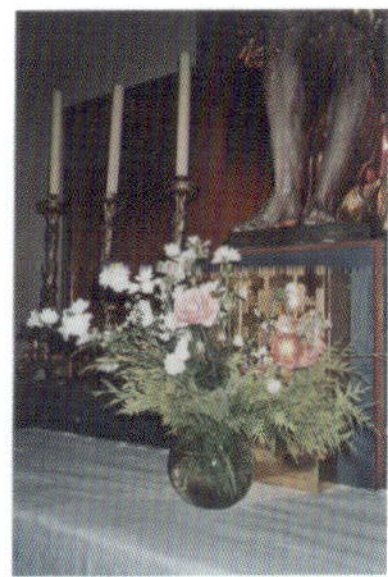

Plate 78
(Cliché of a Flower Bouquet) XXIV

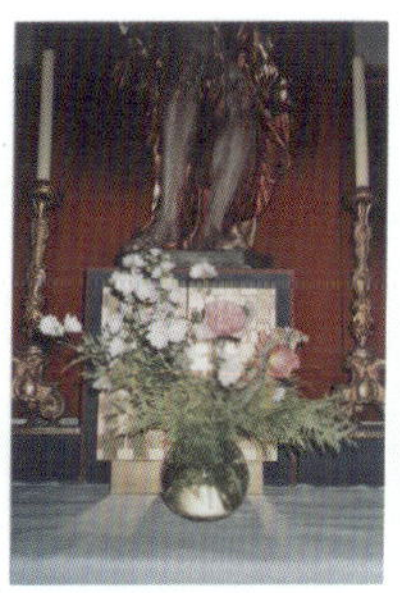

Plate 79
(Cliché of a Flower Bouquet) XXIV

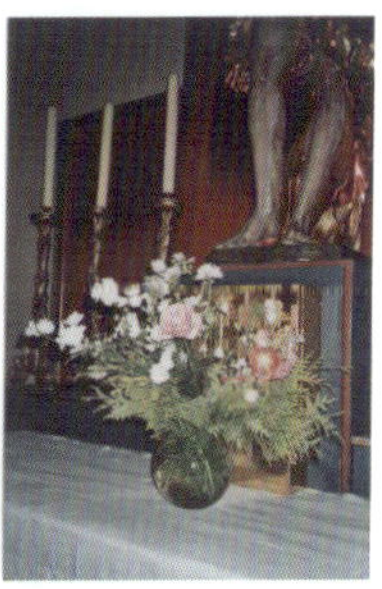

Plate 80
(Cliché of a Flower Bouquet) XXIV

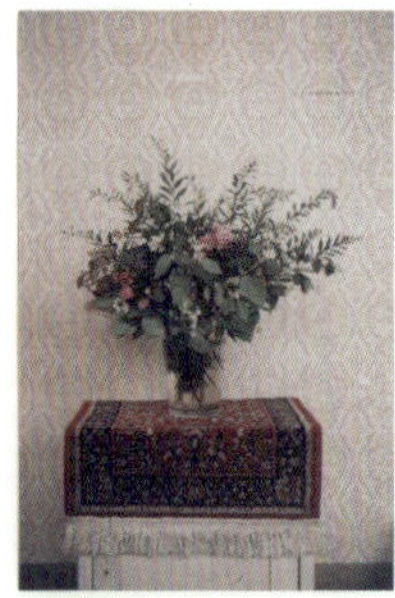

Plate 81
(Cliché of a Flower Bouquet) XXV

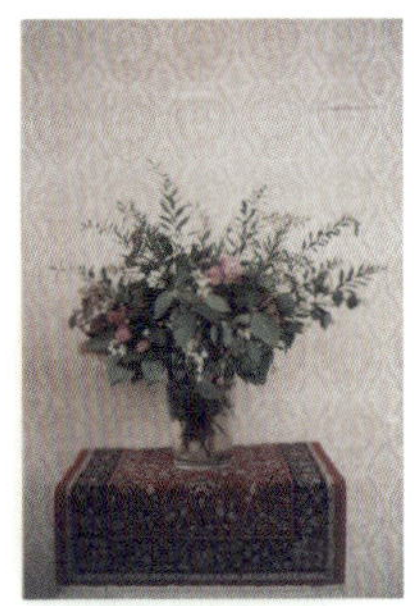

Plate 82
(Cliché of a Flower Bouquet) XXV

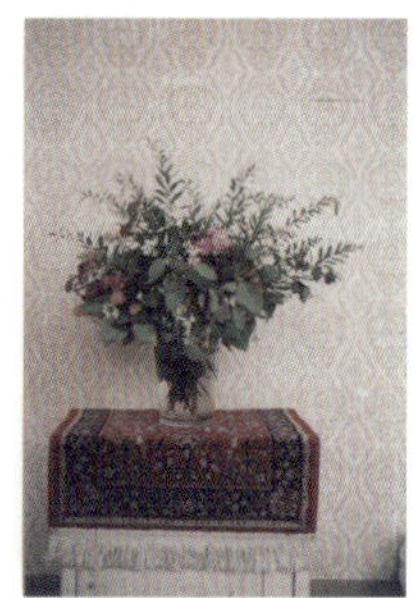

Plate 83
(Cliché of a Flower Bouquet) XXV

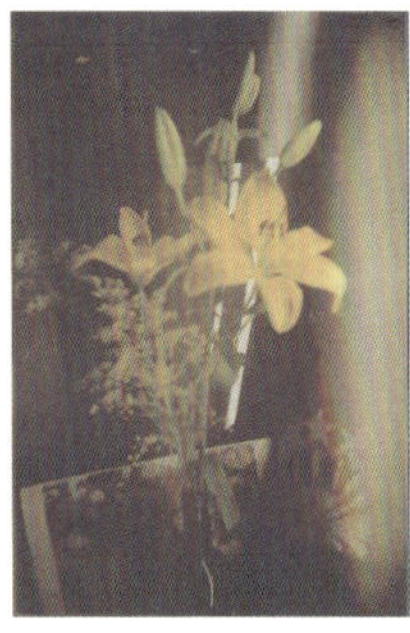

Plate 84
(Cliché of a Flower Bouquet) XXVI

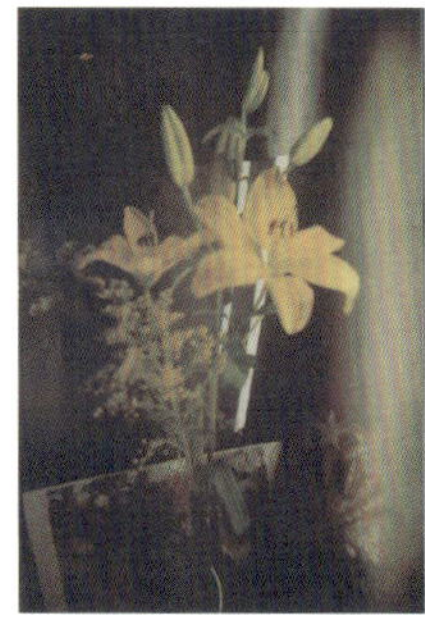

Plate 85
(Cliché of a Flower Bouquet) XXVI

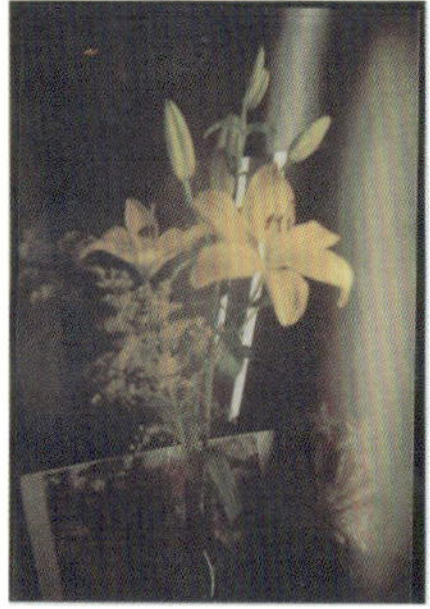

Plate 86
(Cliché of a Flower Bouquet) XXVI

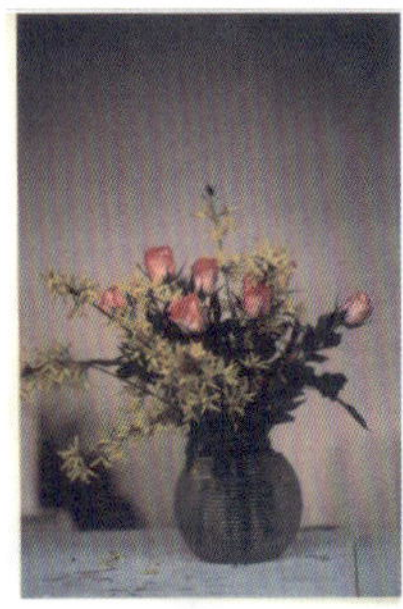

Plate 87
(Cliché of a Flower Bouquet) XXVII

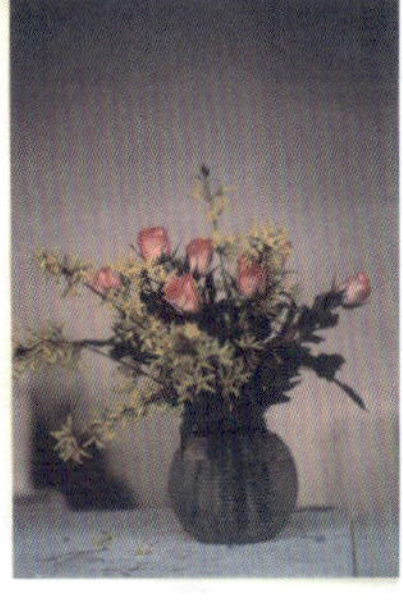

Plate 88
(Cliché of a Flower Bouquet) XXVII

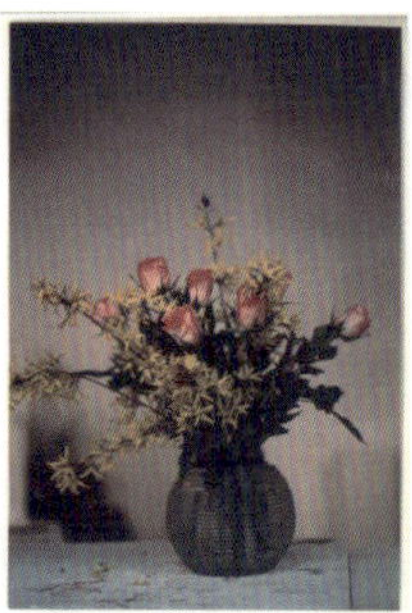

Plate 89
(Cliché of a Flower Bouquet) XXVII

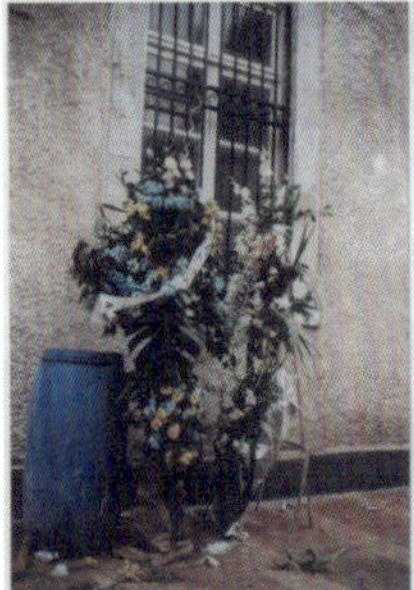

Plate 90
(Cliché of a Flower Bouquet) XXVIII

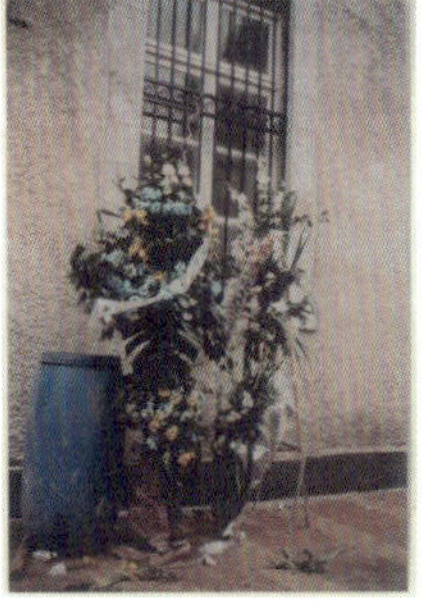

Plate 91
(Cliché of a Flower Bouquet) XXVIII

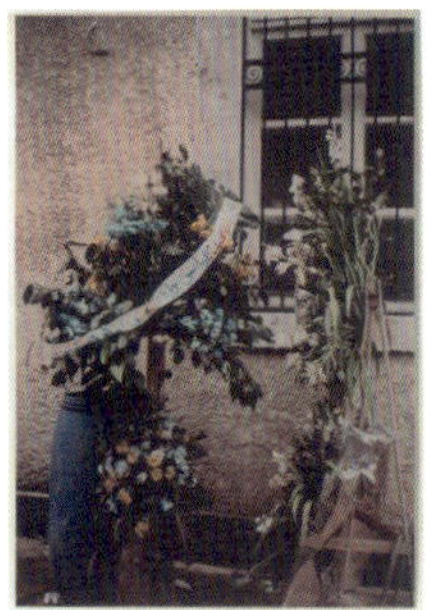

Plate 92
(Cliché of a Flower Bouquet) XXVIII

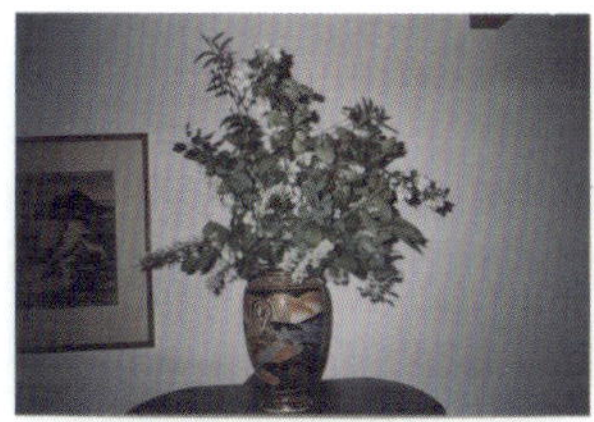

Plate 93
(Cliché of a Flower Bouquet) XXIX

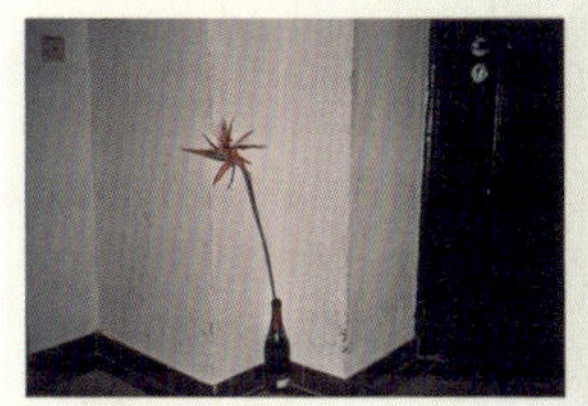

Plate 96
(Cliché of a Flower Bouquet) XXX

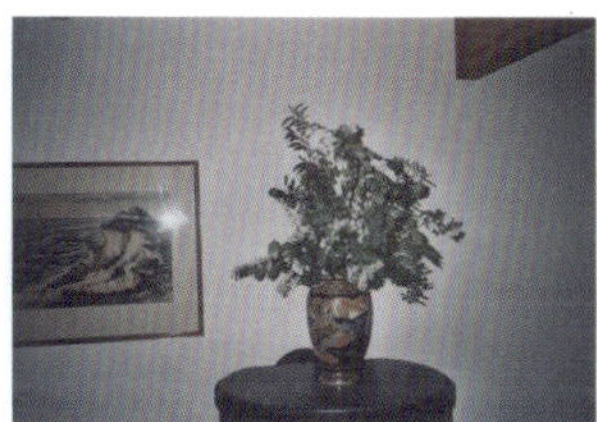

Plate 94
(Cliché of a Flower Bouquet) XXIX

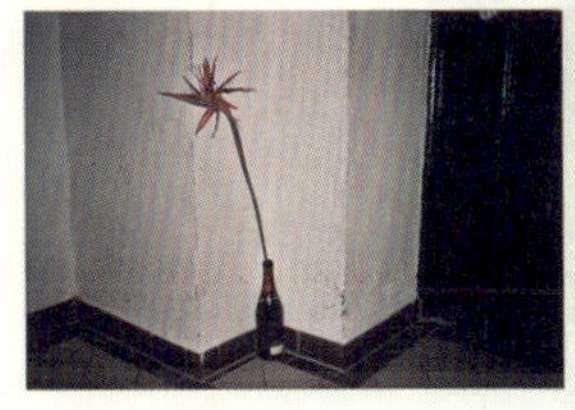

Plate 97
(Cliché of a Flower Bouquet) XXX

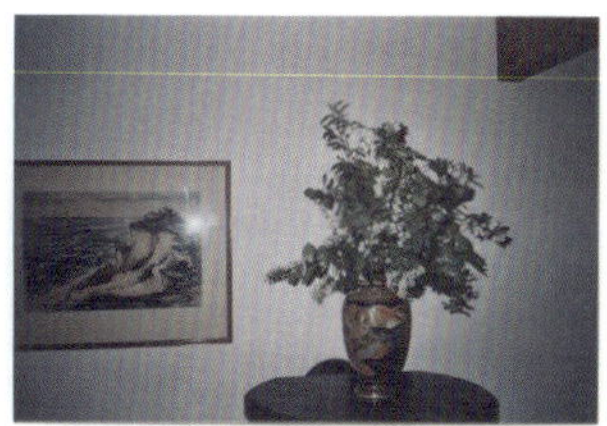

Plate 95
(Cliché of a Flower Bouquet) XXIX

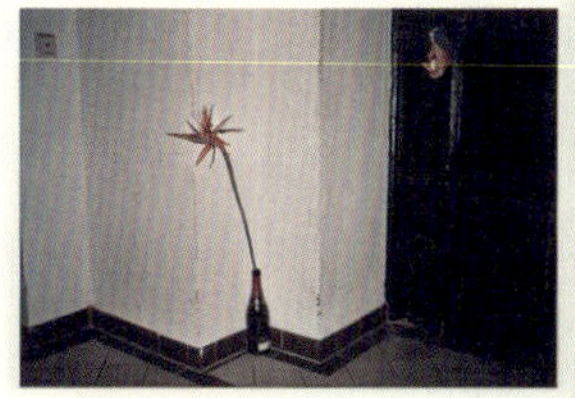

Plate 98
(Cliché of a Flower Bouquet) XXX

II

LANDSCAPES

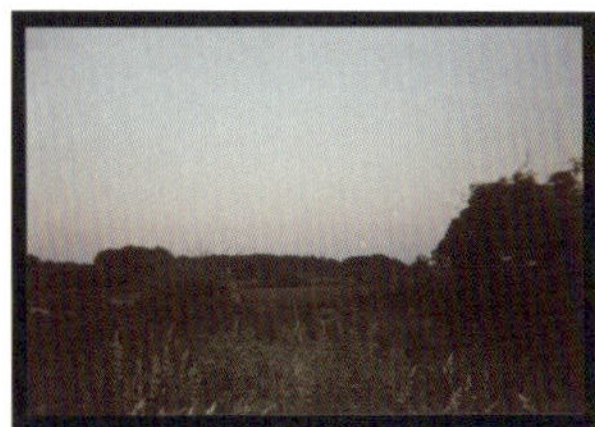
Plate 99
(Cliché of a Landcsape, Moonrise)

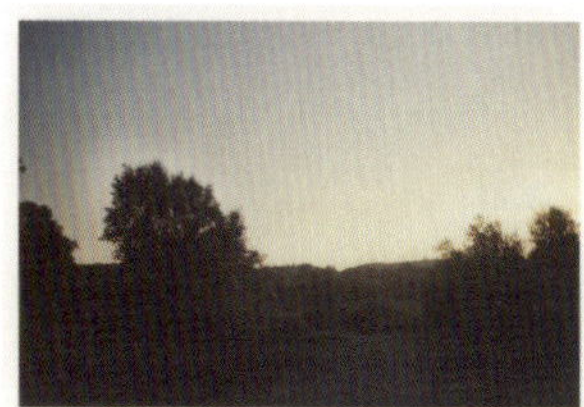
Plate 102
(Cliché of a Landcsape, Sunset) I

Plate 105
(Cliché of a Landcsape, Sunset) II

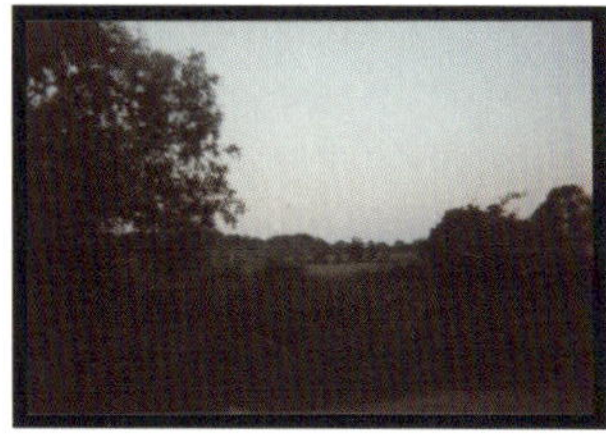
Plate 100
(Cliché of a Landcsape, Moonrise)

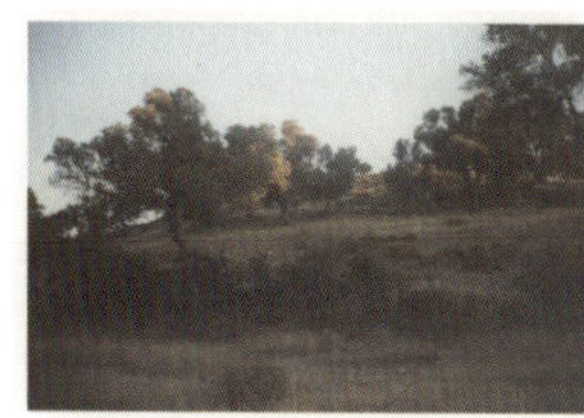
Plate 103
(Cliché of a Landcsape, Sunset) I

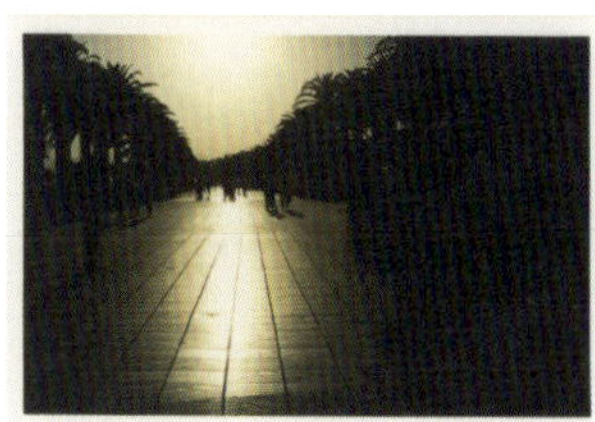
Plate 106
(Cliché of a Landcsape, Sunset) II

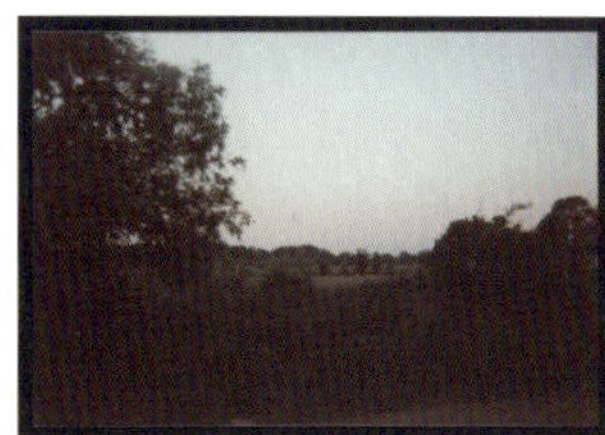
Plate 101
(Cliché of a Landcsape, Moonrise)

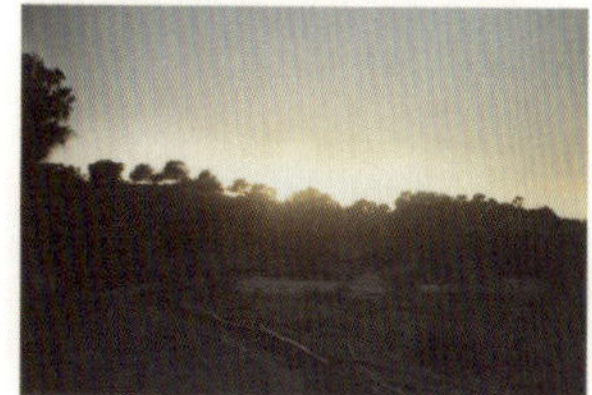
Plate 104
(Cliché of a Landcsape, Sunset) I

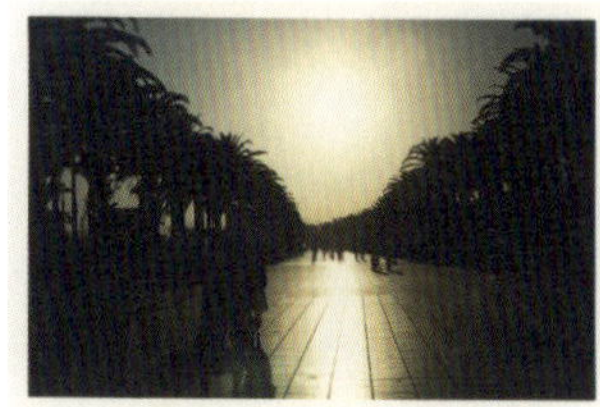
Plate 107
(Cliché of a Landcsape, Sunset) II

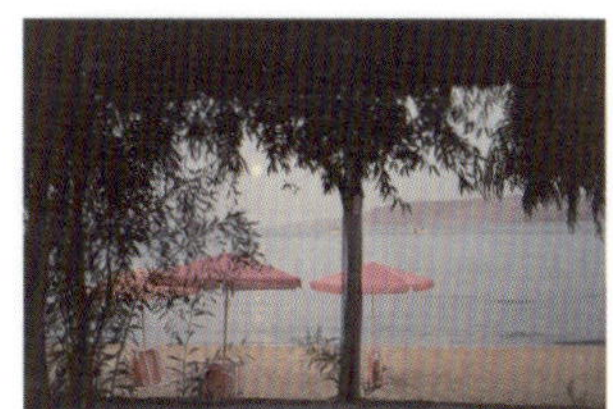

Plate 108
(Cliché of a Landcsape, Sunset, Moonrise)

Plate 111
(Cliché of a Landcsape, Sunset) III

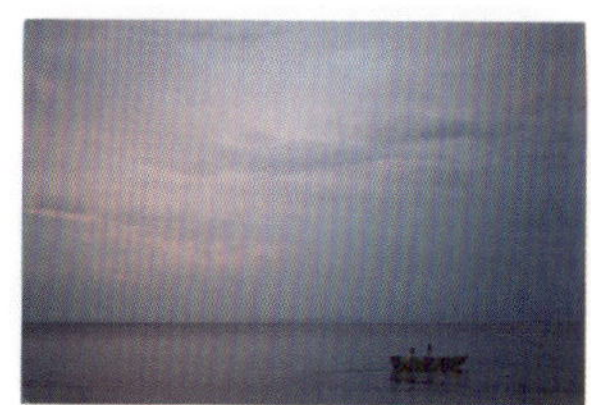

Plate 114
(Cliché of a Landcsape, Sunset) IV

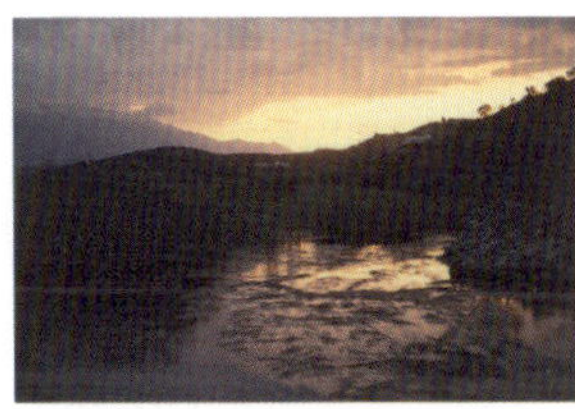

Plate 109
(Cliché of a Landcsape, Sunset, Moonrise)

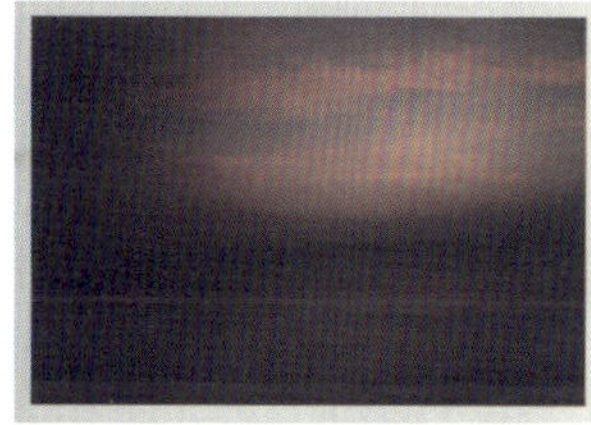

Plate 112
(Cliché of a Landcsape, Sunset) III

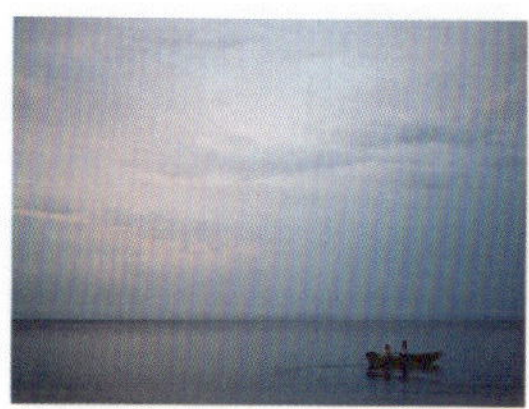

Plate 115
(Cliché of a Landcsape, Sunset) IV

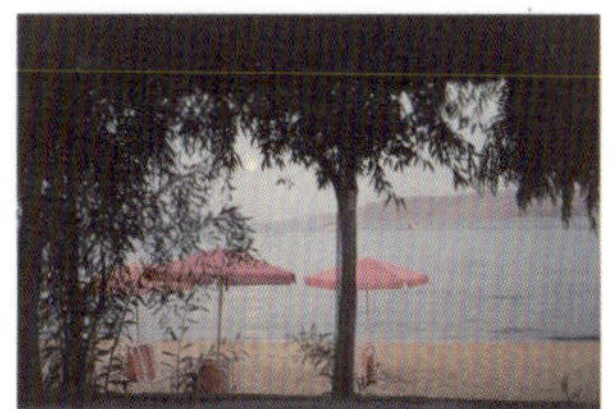

Plate 110
(Cliché of a Landcsape, Sunset, Moonrise)

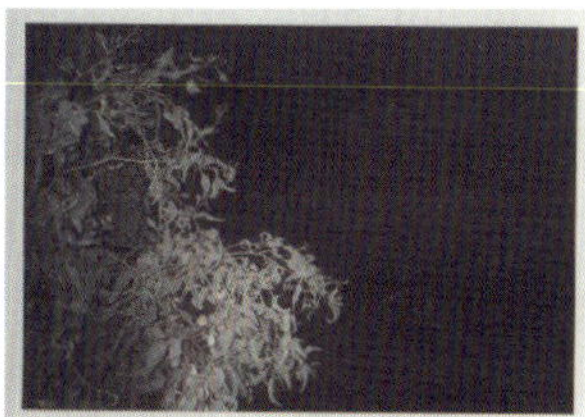

Plate 113
(Cliché of a Landcsape, Sunset) III

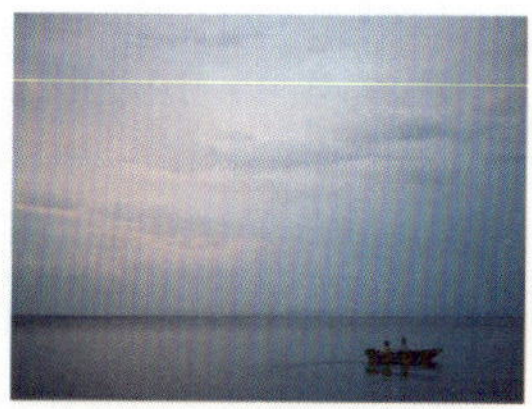

Plate 116
(Cliché of a Landcsape, Sunset) IV

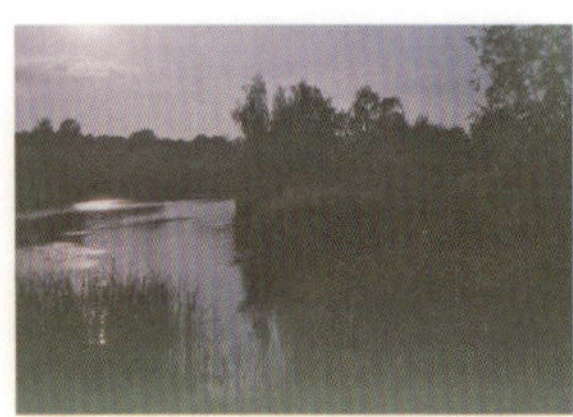

Plate 117
(Cliché of a Landcsape, Sunset) V

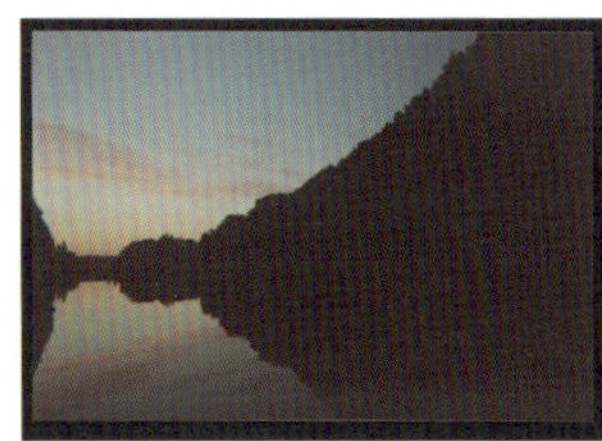

Plate 120
(Cliché of a Landcsape, Sunset,
on a River)

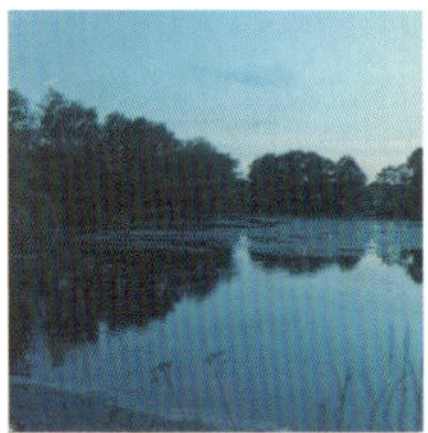

Plate 123
(Cliché of a Landcsape, Sunset,
on a Lake)

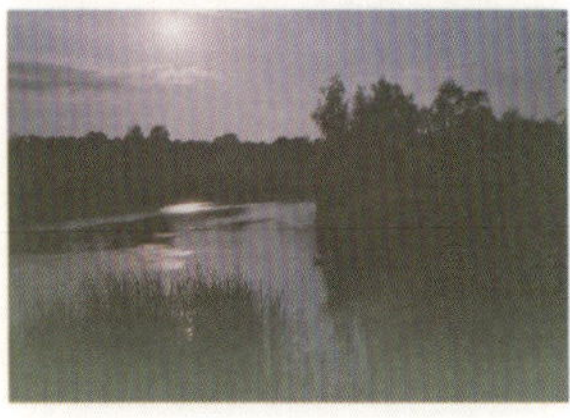

Plate 118
(Cliché of a Landcsape, Sunset) V

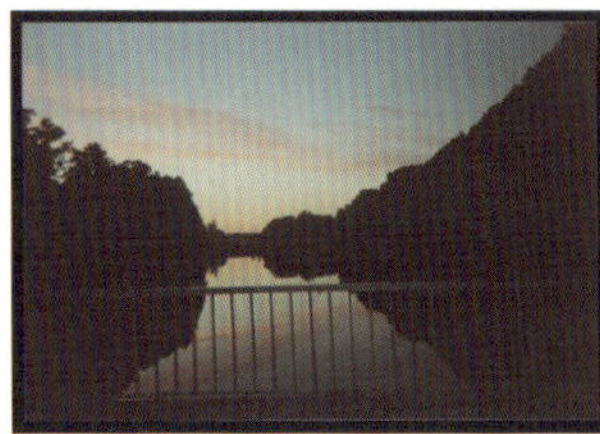

Plate 121
(Cliché of a Landcsape, Sunset,
on a River)

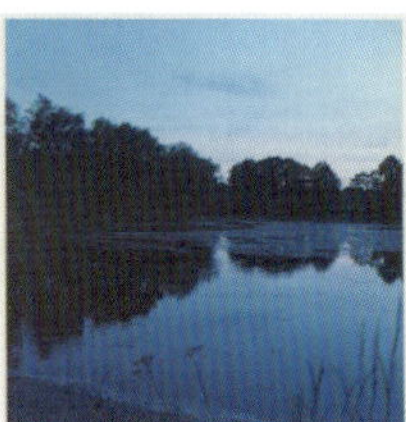

Plate 124
(Cliché of a Landcsape, Sunset,
on a Lake)

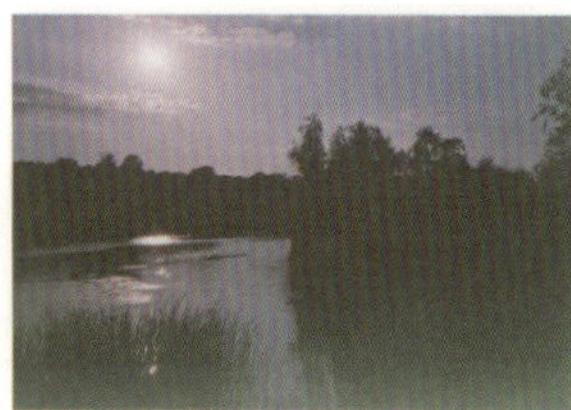

Plate 119
(Cliché of a Landcsape, Sunset) V

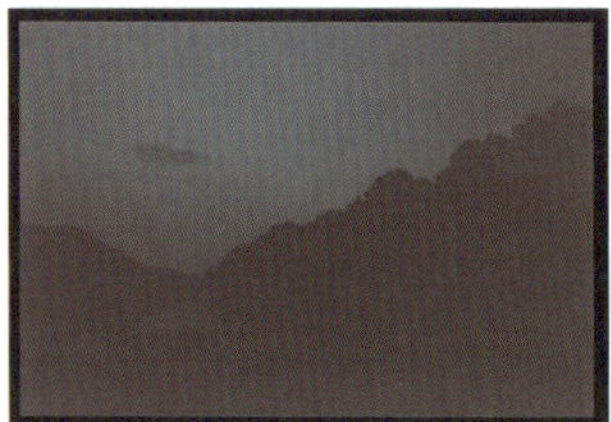

Plate 122
(Cliché of a Landcsape, Sunset,
on a River)

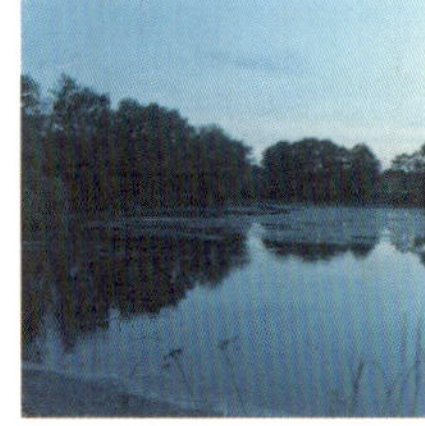

Plate 125
(Cliché of a Landcsape, Sunset,
on a Lake)

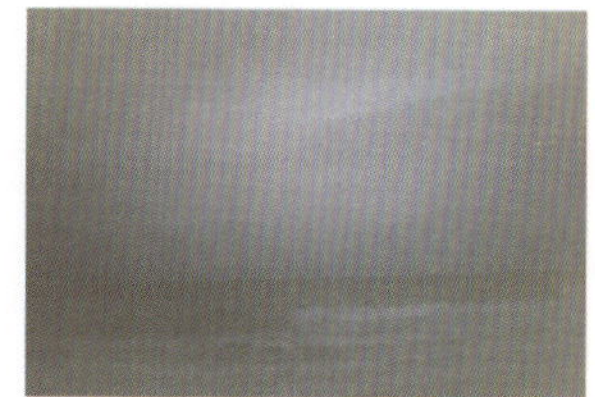

Plate 126
(Cliché of a Landcsape, Sea) I

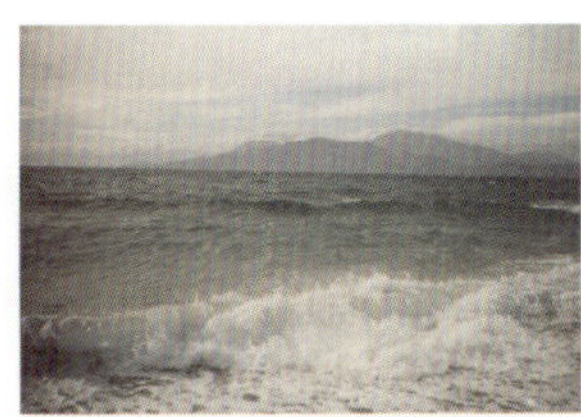

Plate 129
(Cliché of a Landcsape, Sea) II

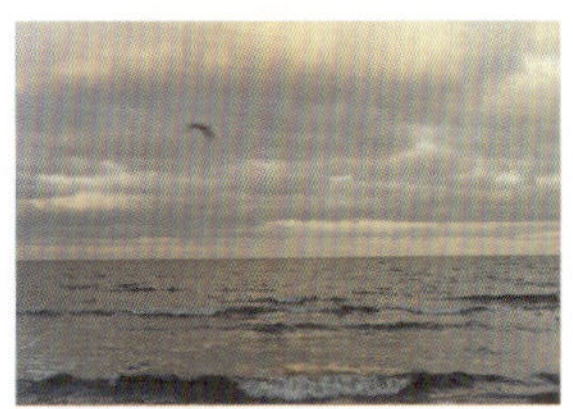

Plate 132
(Cliché of a Landcsape, Sea) III

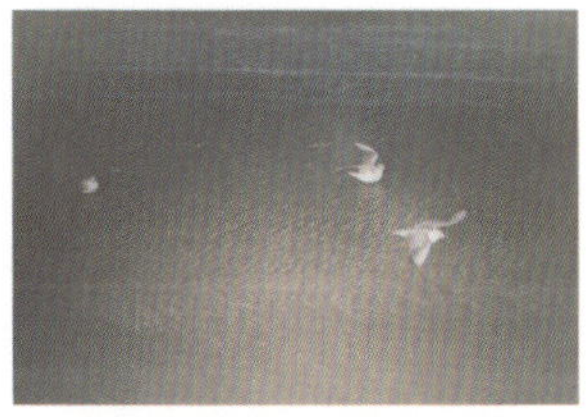

Plate 127
(Cliché of a Landcsape, Sea) I

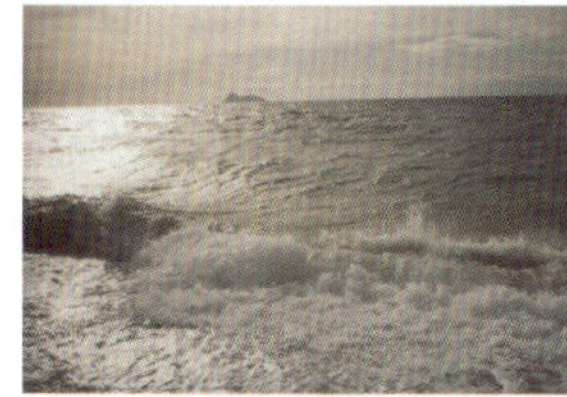

Plate 130
(Cliché of a Landcsape, Sea) II

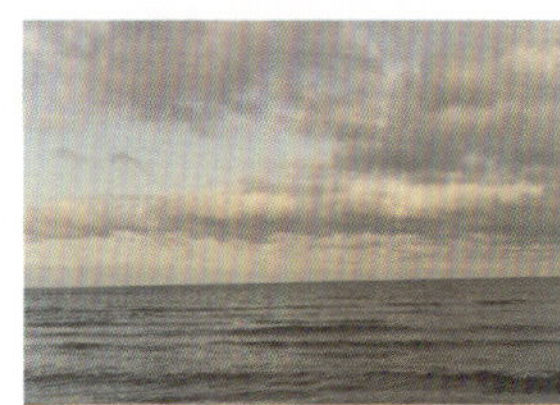

Plate 133
(Cliché of a Landcsape, Sea) III

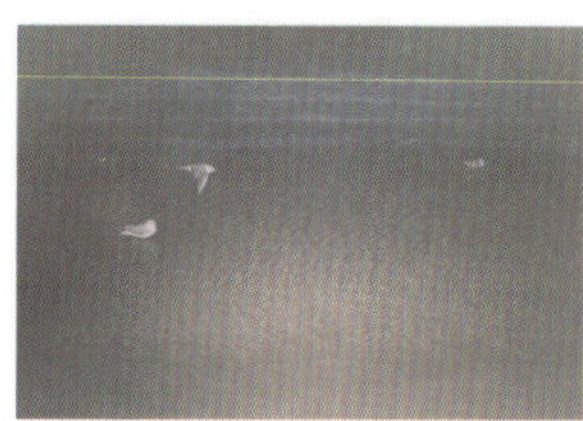

Plate 128
(Cliché of a Landcsape, Sea) I

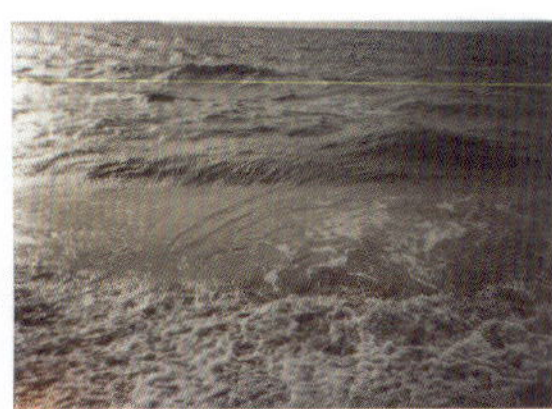

Plate 131
(Cliché of a Landcsape, Sea) II

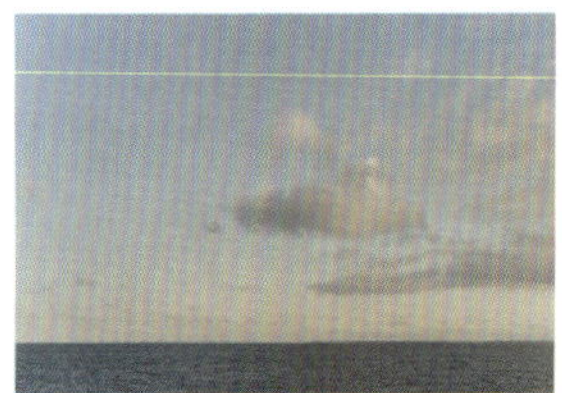

Plate 134
(Cliché of a Landcsape, Sea) III

Plate 135
(Cliché of a Landcsape, Watergate)

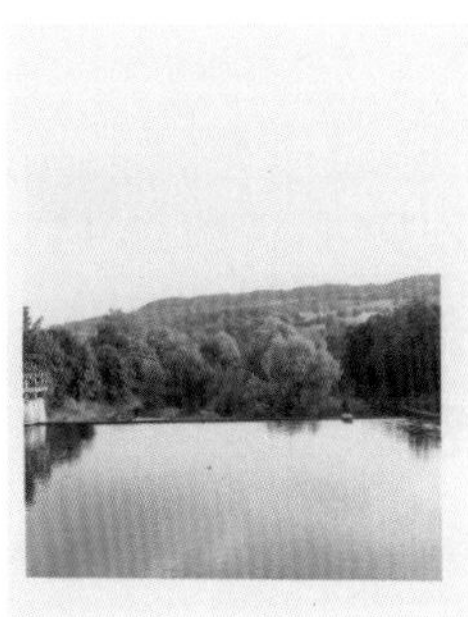

Plate 136
(Cliché of a Landcsape, Watergate)

Plate 137
(Cliché of a Landcsape, Watergate)

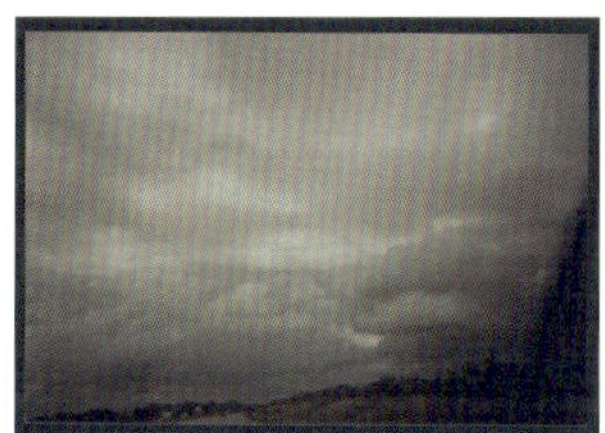

Plate 138
(Cliché of a Landcsape, Sky) I

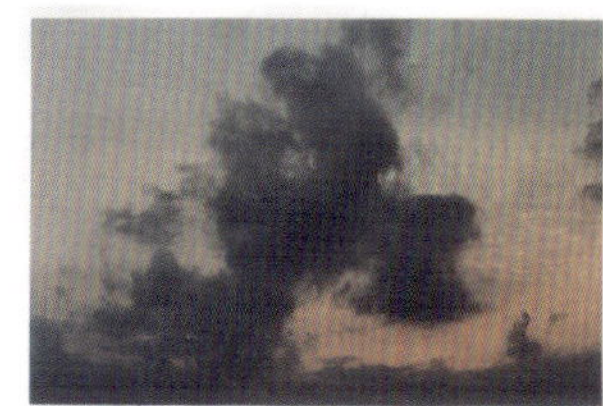

Plate 141
(Cliché of a Landcsape, Sky) II

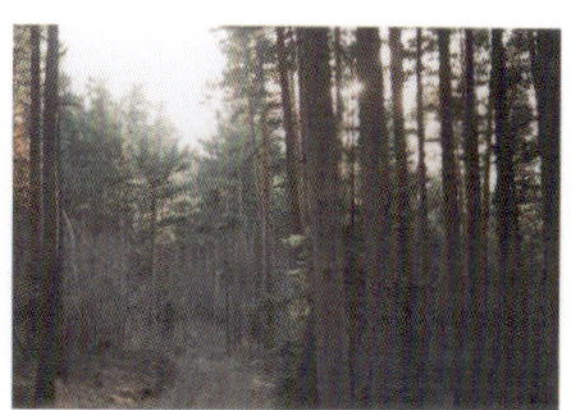

Plate 144
(Cliché of a Landcsape, Wood) I

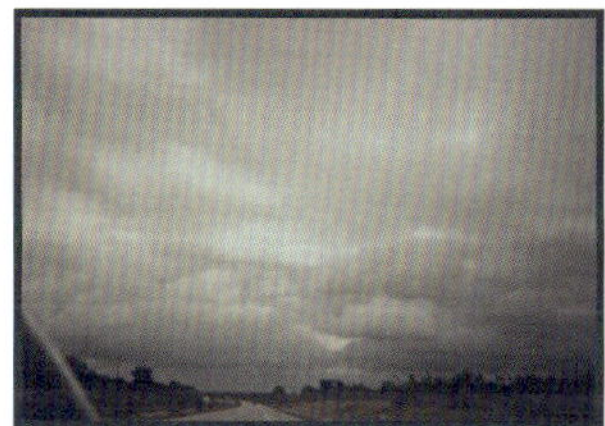

Plate 139
(Cliché of a Landcsape, Sky) I

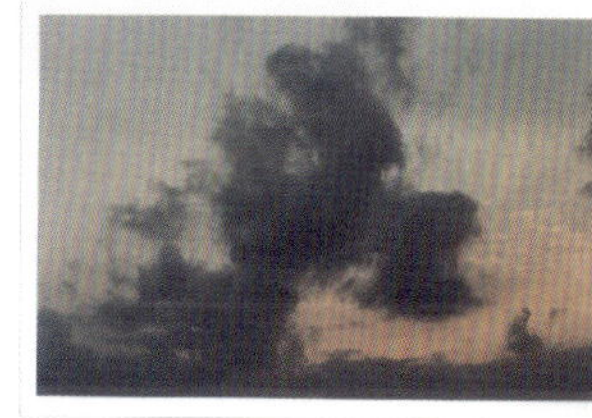

Plate 142
(Cliché of a Landcsape, Sky) II

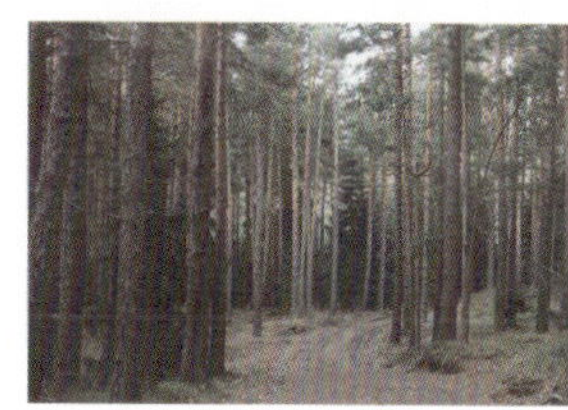

Plate 145
(Cliché of a Landcsape, Wood) I

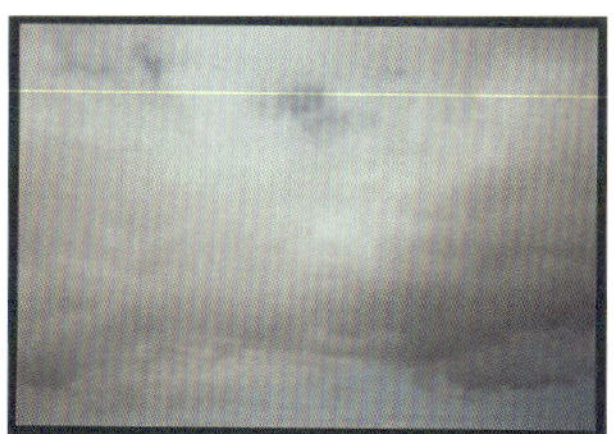

Plate 140
(Cliché of a Landcsape, Sky) I

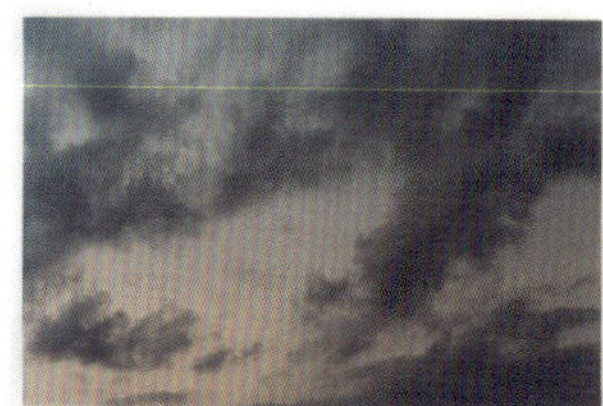

Plate 143
(Cliché of a Landcsape, Sky) II

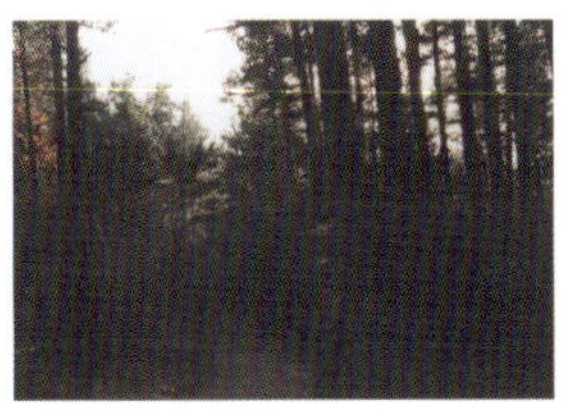

Plate 146
(Cliché of a Landcsape, Wood) I

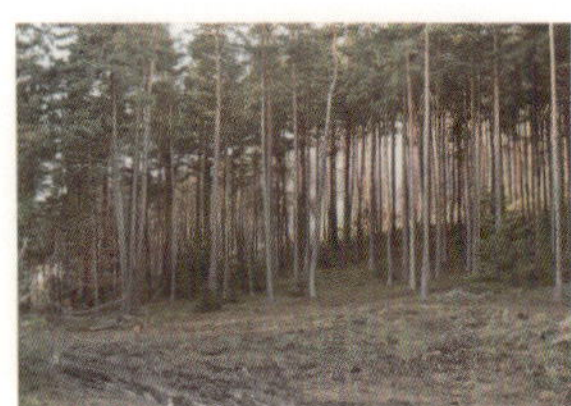

Plate 147
(Cliché of a Landcsape, Wood) II

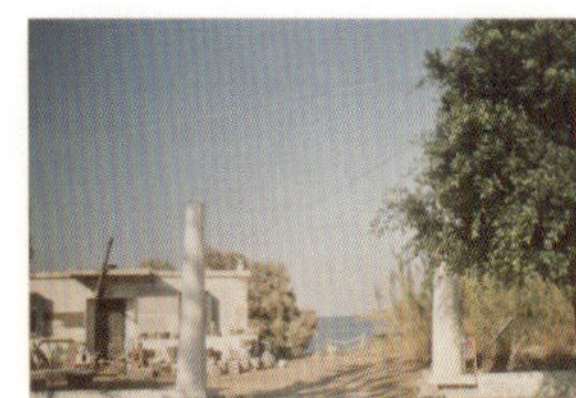

Plate 150
(Cliché of a Landscape, House near
the Beach)

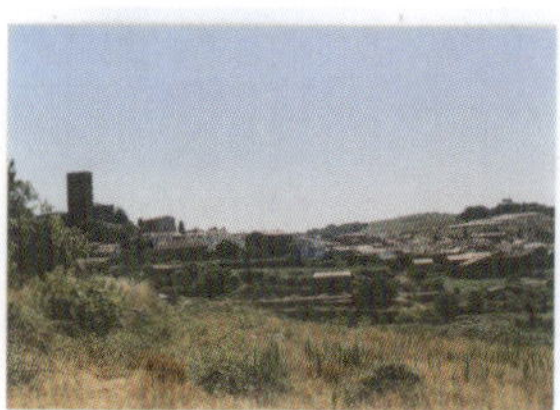

Plate 153
(Cliché of a Landscape)

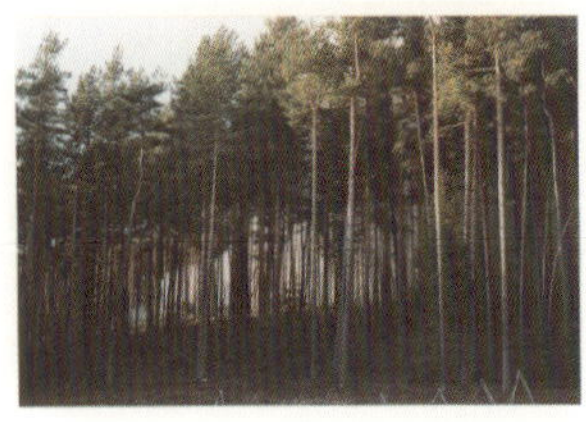

Plate 148
(Cliché of a Landcsape, Wood) II

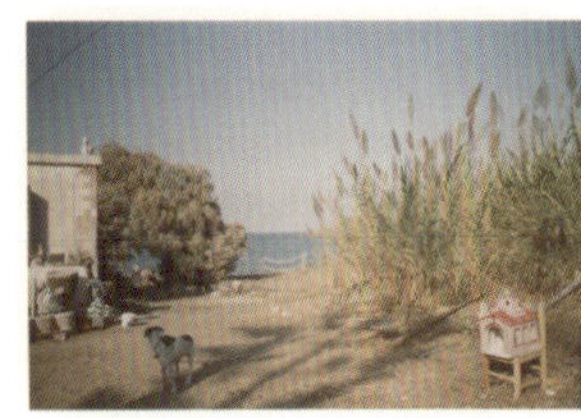

Plate 151
(Cliché of a Landscape, House near
the Beach)

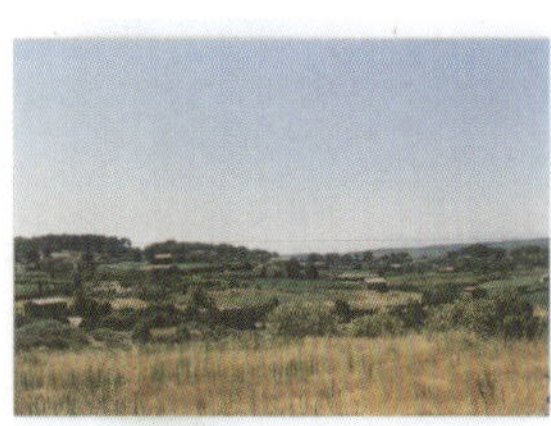

Plate 154
(Cliché of a Landscape)

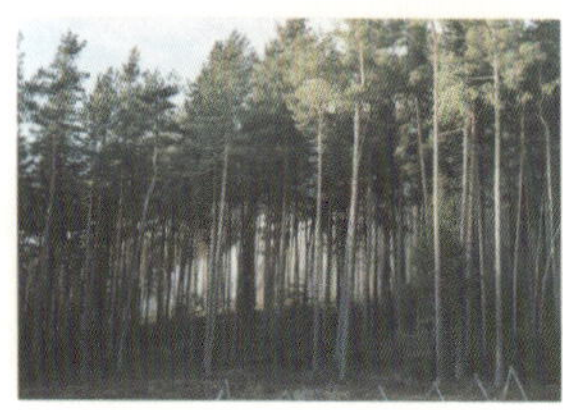

Plate 149
(Cliché of a Landcsape, Wood) II

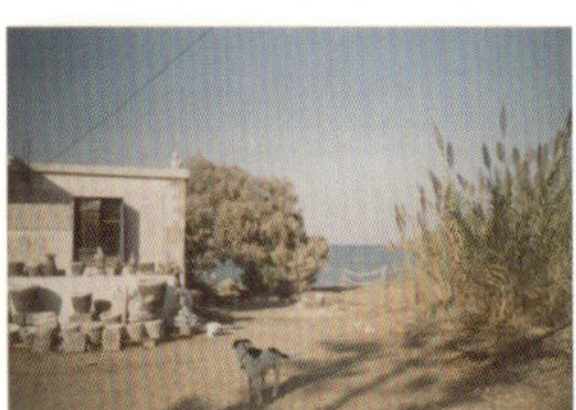

Plate 152
(Cliché of a Landscape, House near
the Beach)

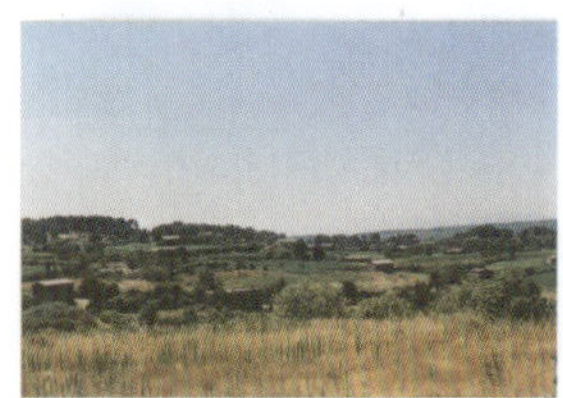

Plate 155
(Cliché of a Landscape)

III

POW WOW

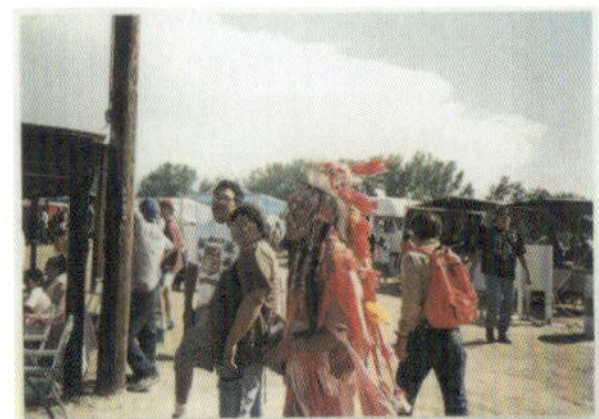

Plate 156
(Cliché of a Pow Wow) I

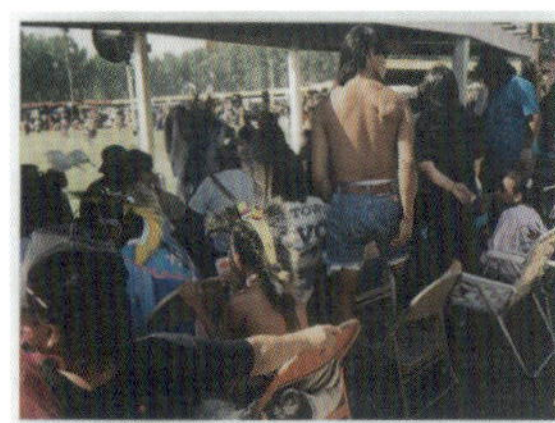

Plate 159
(Cliché of a Pow Wow) II

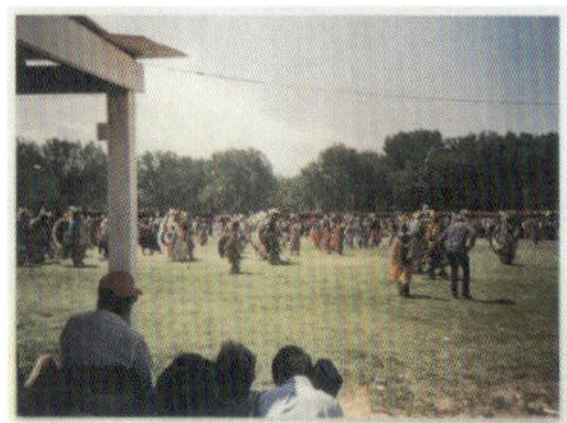

Plate 162
(Cliché of a Pow Wow) III

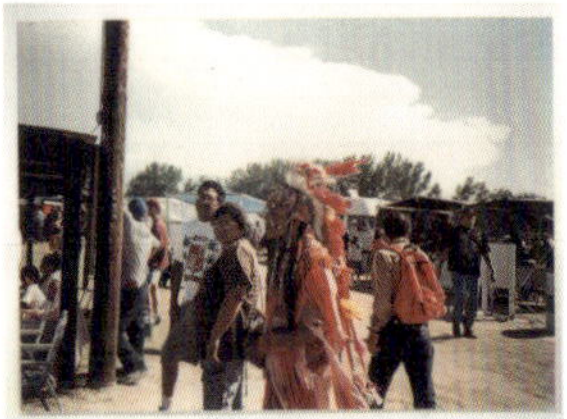

Plate 157
(Cliché of a Pow Wow) I

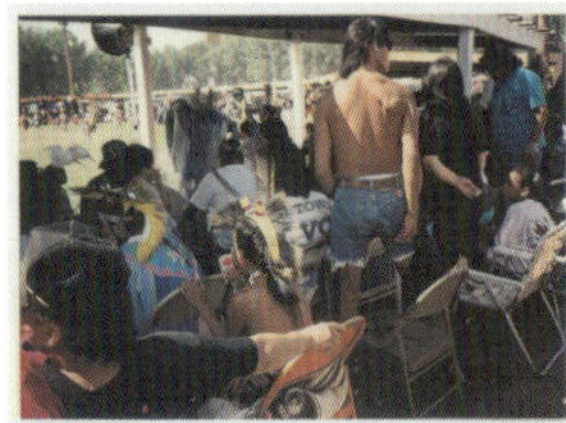

Plate 160
(Cliché of a Pow Wow) II

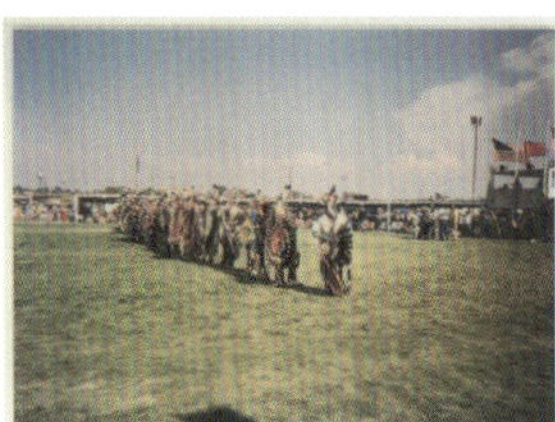

Plate 163
(Cliché of a Pow Wow) III

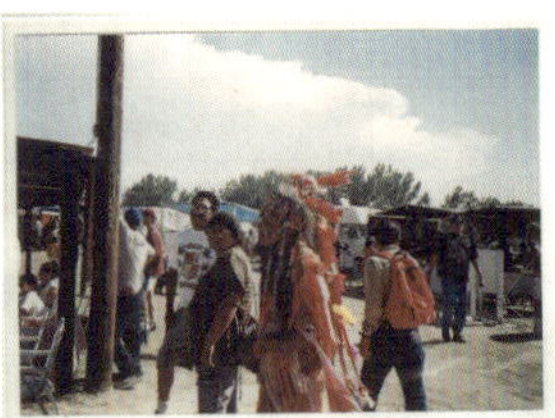

Plate 158
(Cliché of a Pow Wow) I

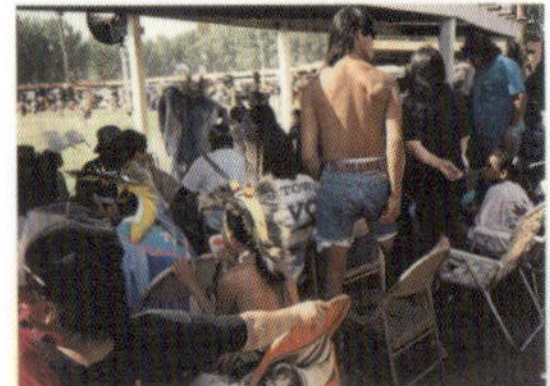

Plate 161
(Cliché of a Pow Wow) II

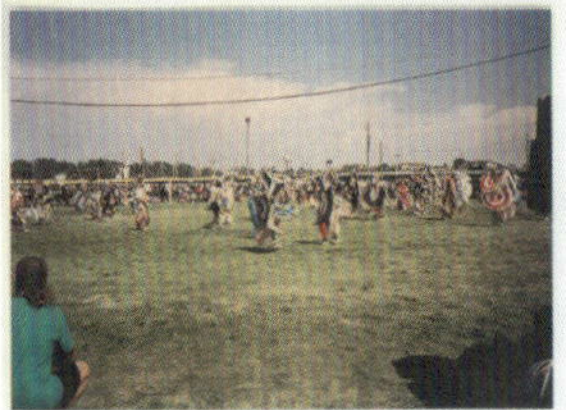

Plate 164
(Cliché of a Pow Wow) III

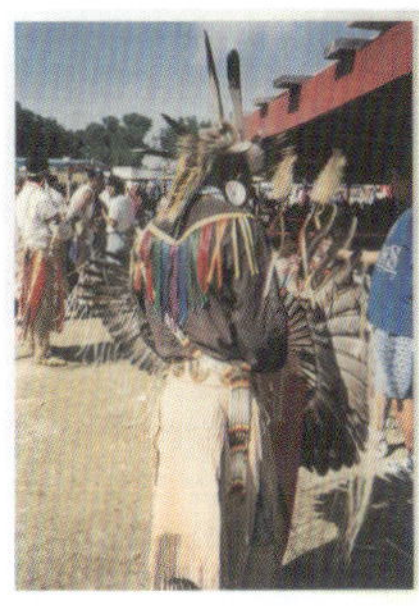

Plate 165
(Cliché of a Pow Wow) IV

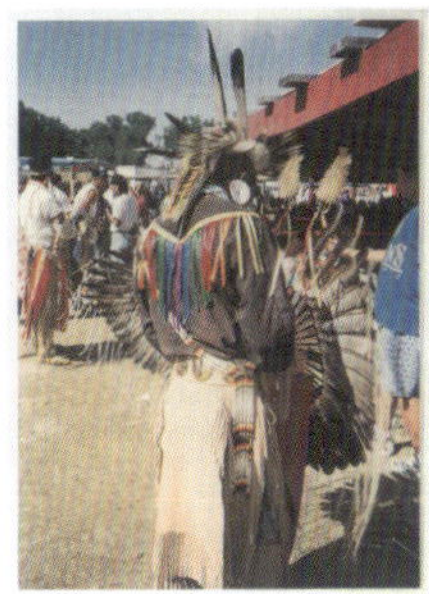

Plate 166
(Cliché of a Pow Wow) IV

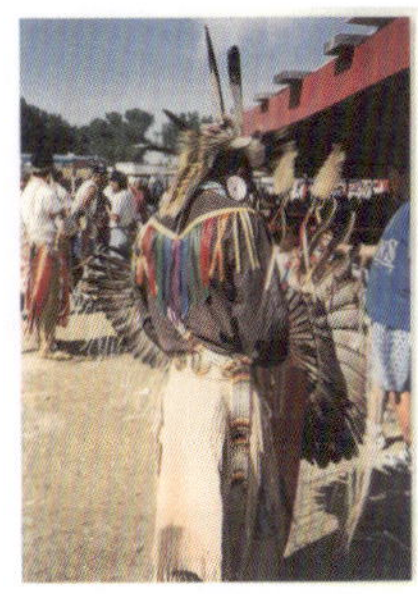

Plate 167
(Cliché of a Pow Wow) IV

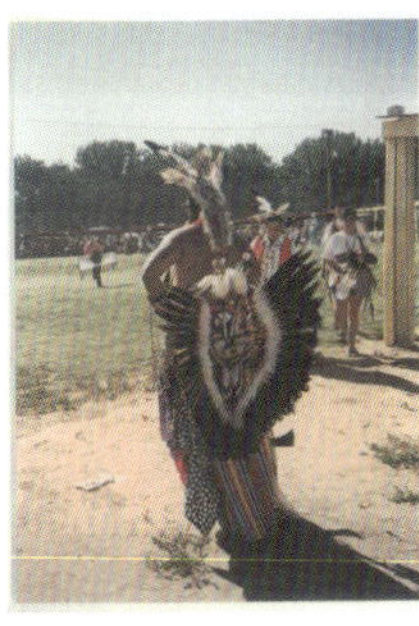

Plate 168
(Cliché of a Pow Wow) V

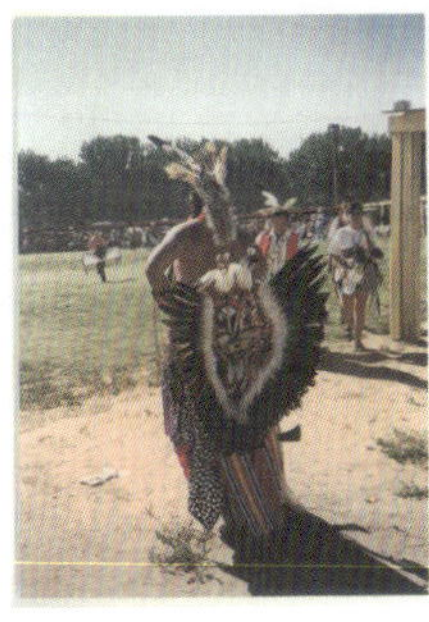

Plate 169
(Cliché of a Pow Wow) V

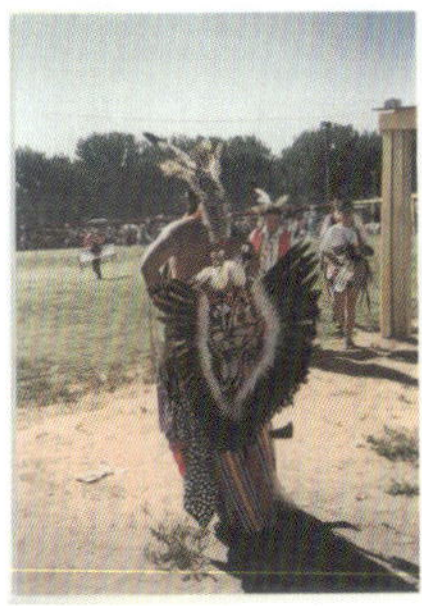

Plate 170
(Cliché of a Pow Wow) V

IV

PLANTS

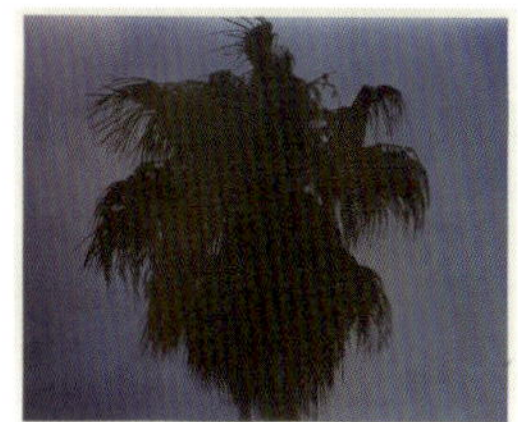

Plate 171
(Cliché of a Palm Tree) I

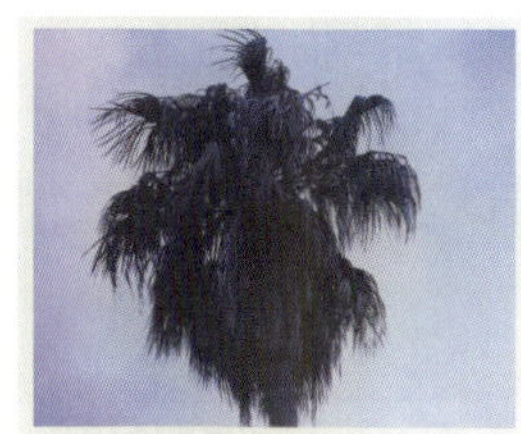

Plate 174
(Cliché of a Palm Tree) II

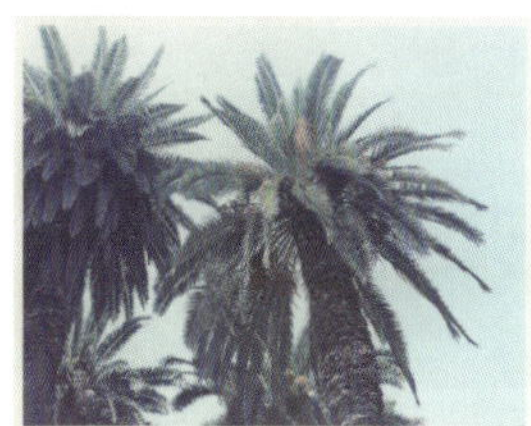

Plate 177
(Cliché of Palm Trees) I

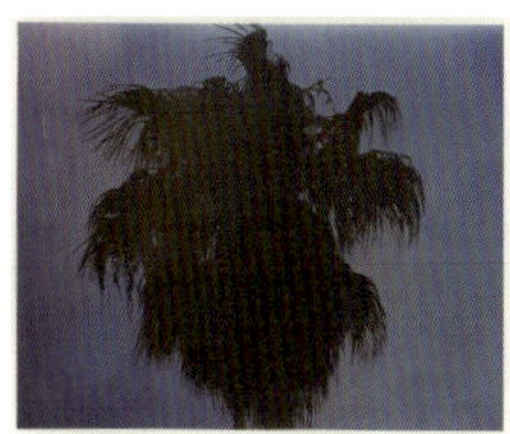

Plate 172
(Cliché of a Palm Tree) I

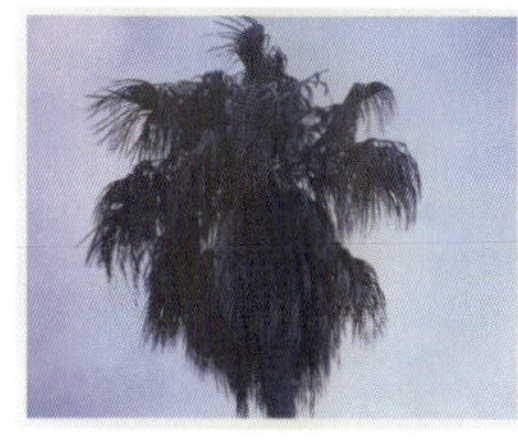

Plate 175
(Cliché of a Palm Tree) II

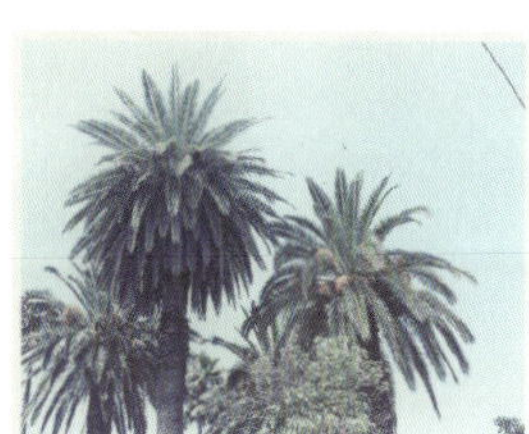

Plate 178
(Cliché of Palm Trees) I

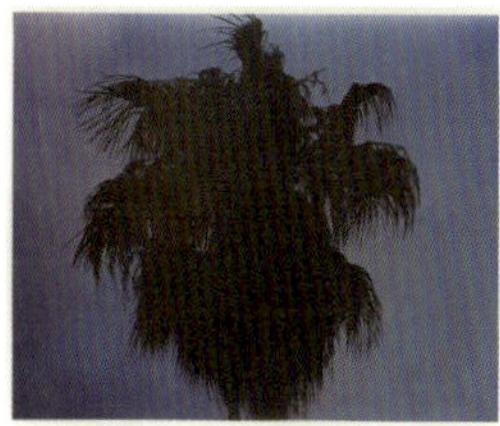

Plate 173
(Cliché of a Palm Tree) I

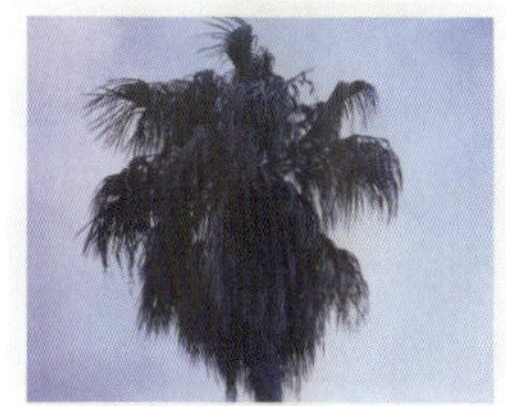

Plate 176
(Cliché of a Palm Tree) II

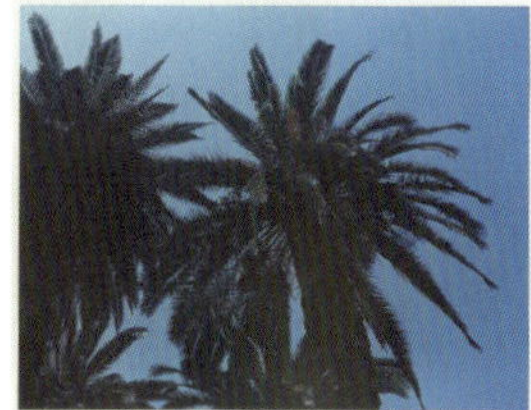

Plate 179
(Cliché of Palm Trees) I

IV

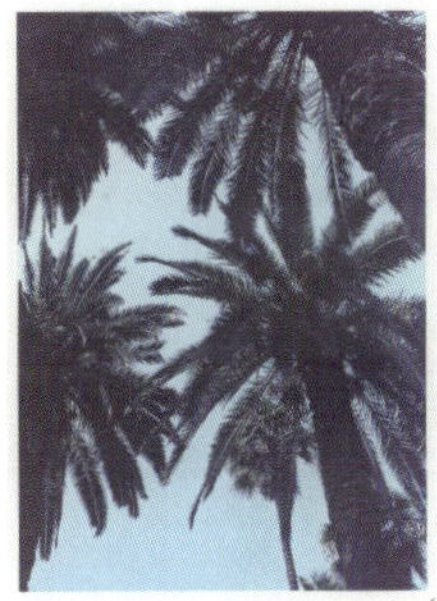

Plate 180
(Cliché of Palm Trees) II

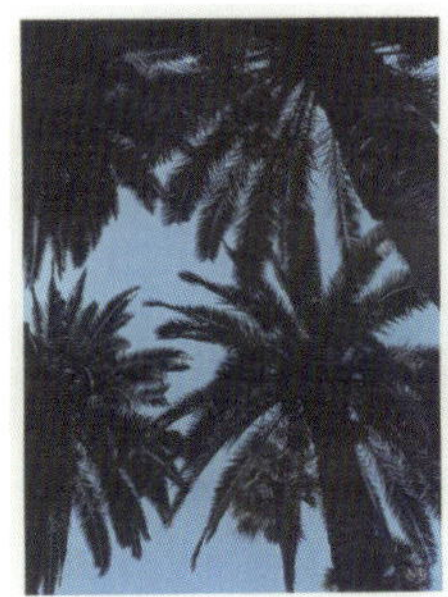

Plate 181
(Cliché of Palm Trees) II

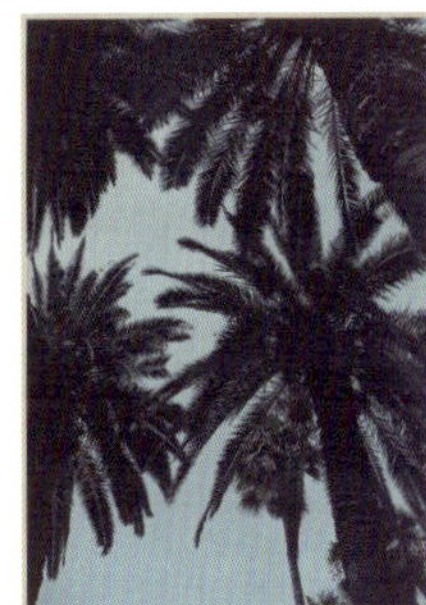

Plate 182
(Cliché of Palm Trees) II

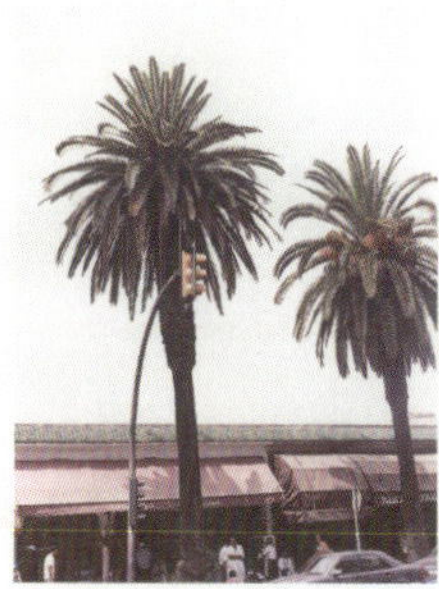

Plate 183
(Cliché of Palm Trees) III

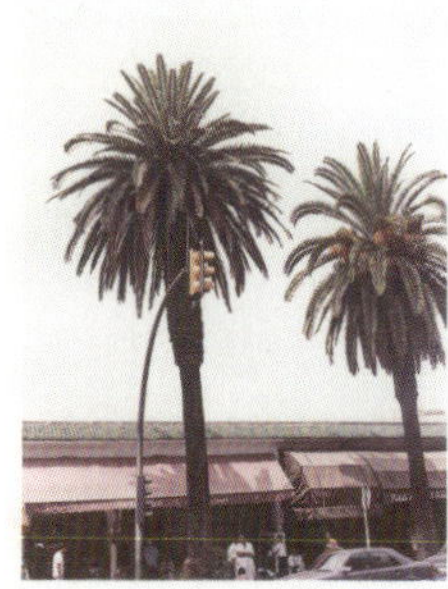

Plate 184
(Cliché of Palm Trees) III

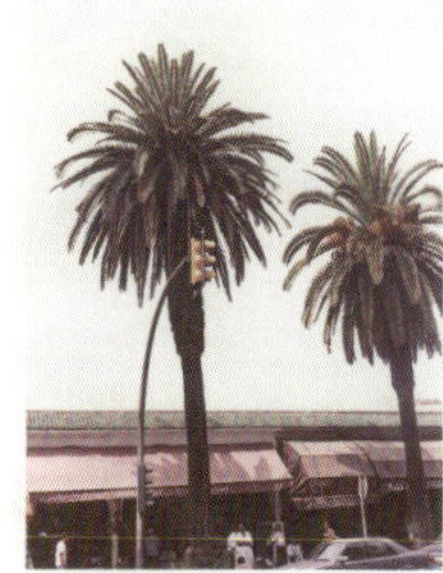

Plate 185
(Cliché of a Plant, Palm Trees) III

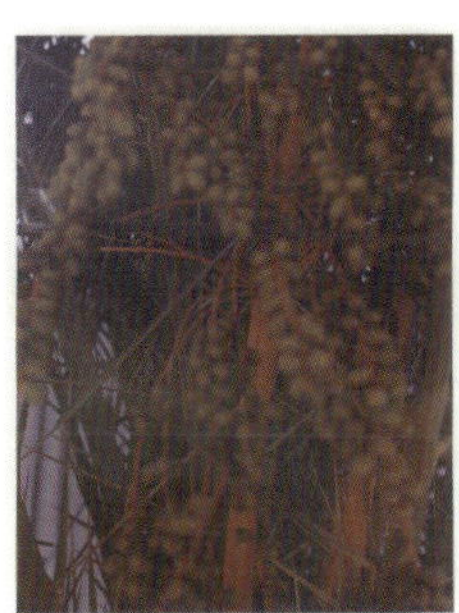

Plate 186
(Cliché of a Palm Tree, Close Up)

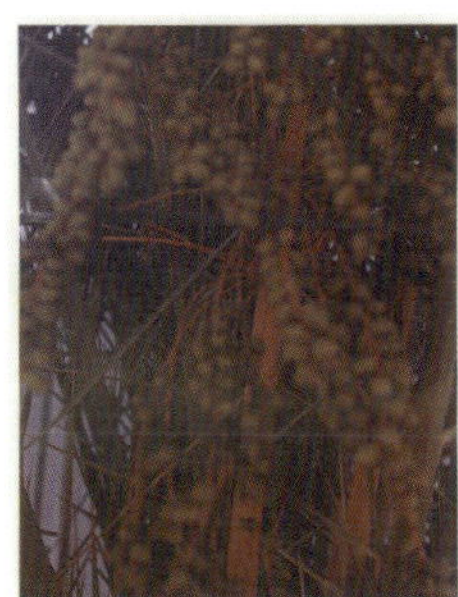

Plate 187
(Cliché of a Palm Tree, Close Up)

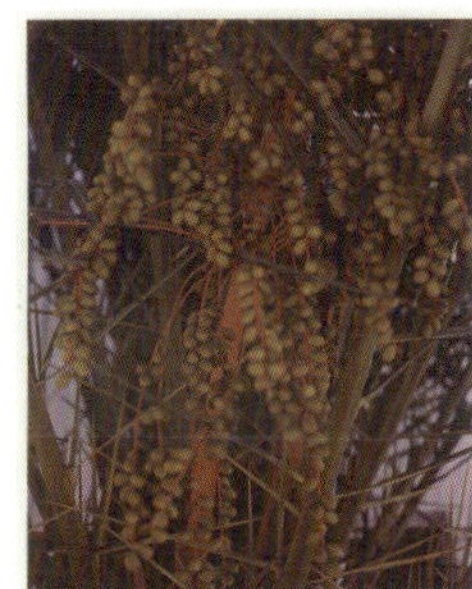

Plate 188
(Cliché of a Palm Tree, Close Up)

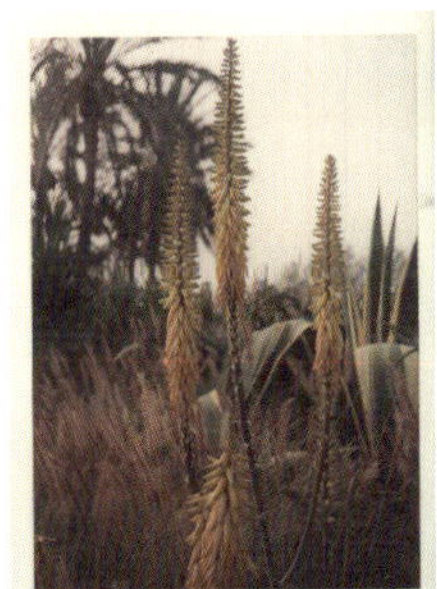

Plate 189
(Cliché of a Plant)

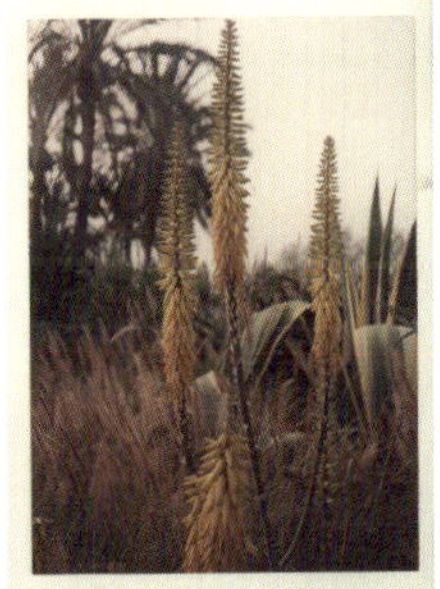

Plate 190
(Cliché of a Plant)

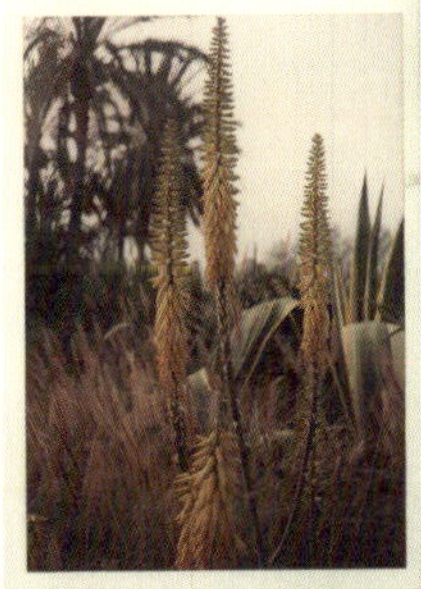

Plate 191
(Cliché of a Plant)

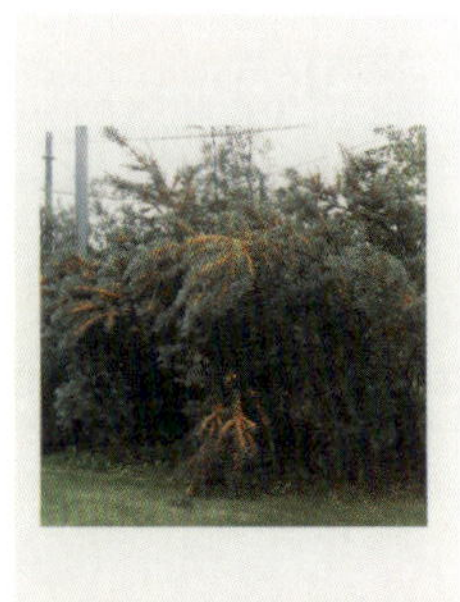

Plate 192
(Cliché of a Bush) I

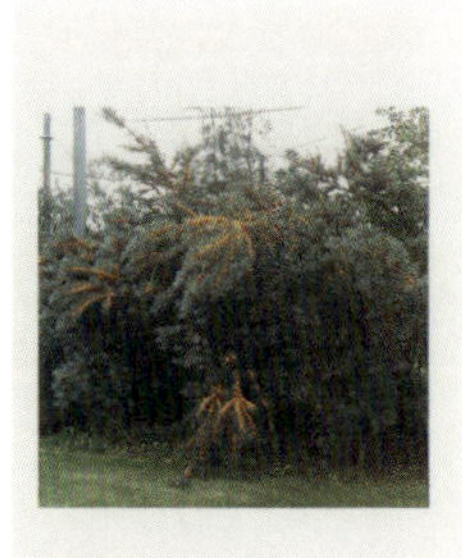

Plate 193
(Cliché of a Bush) I

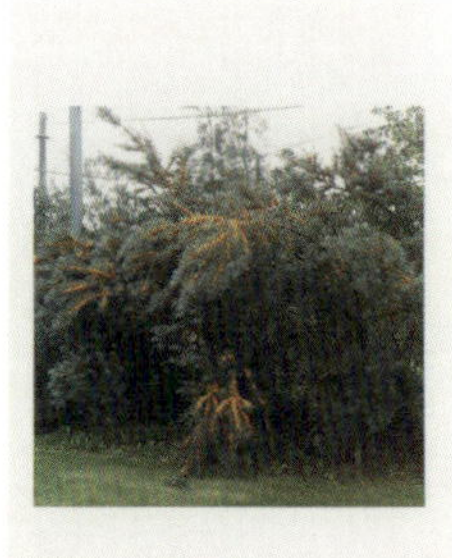

Plate 194
(Cliché of a Bush) I

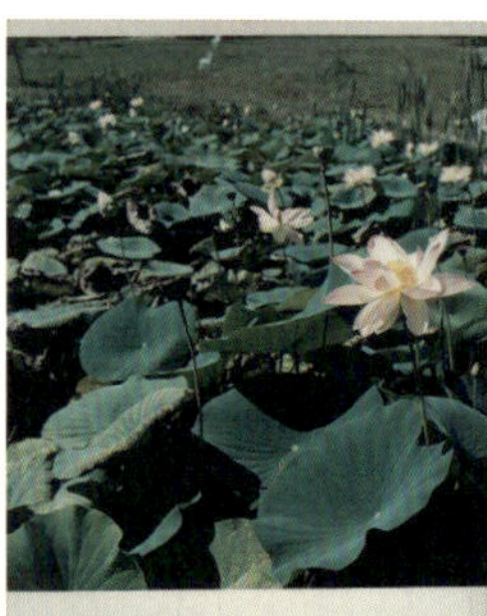

Plate 195
(Cliché of a Plant, Lotus)

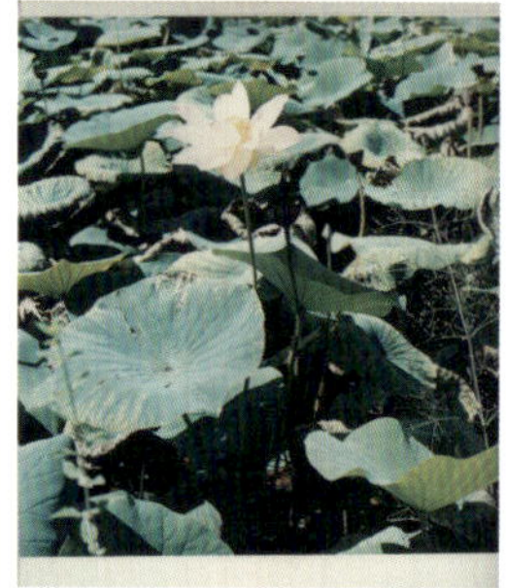

Plate 196
(Cliché of a Plant, Lotus)

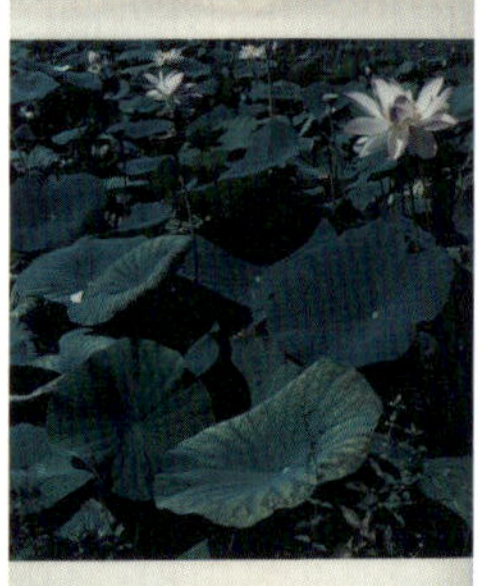

Plate 197
(Cliché of a Plant, Lotus)

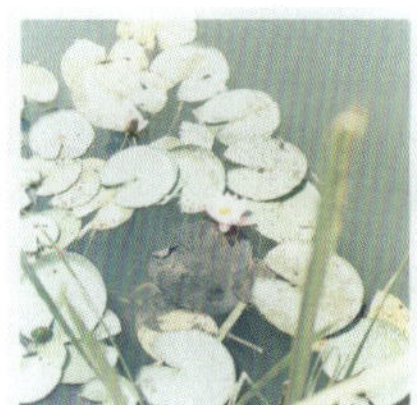

Plate 198
(Cliché of a Plant, Water Lilies)

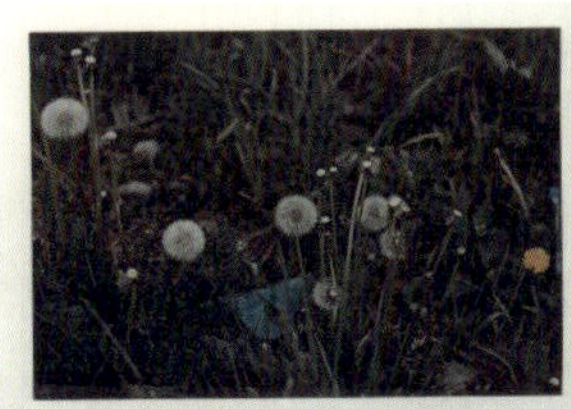

Plate 203
(Cliché of Plants, Dandelion)

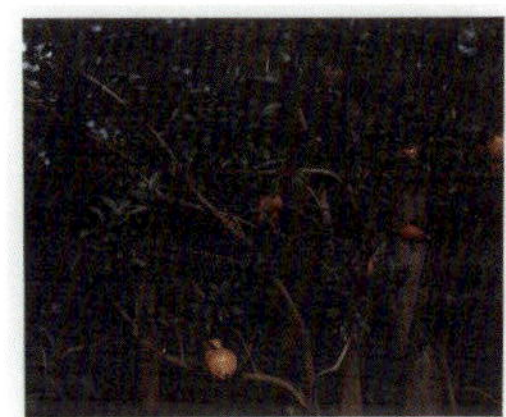

Plate 206
(Cliché of a Tree) I

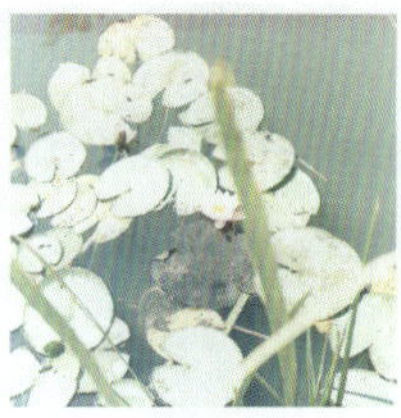

Plate 199
(Cliché of a Plant, Water Lilies)

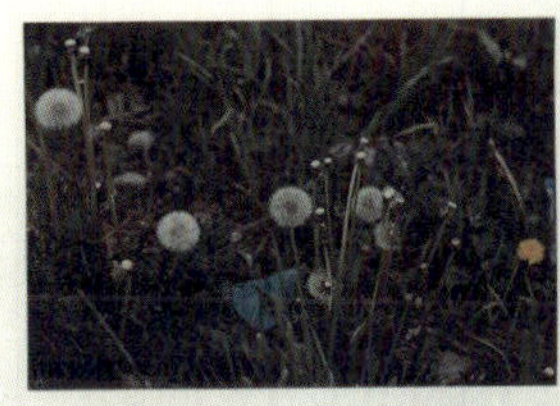

Plate 204
(Cliché of Plants, Dandelion)

Plate 207
(Cliché of a Tree) I

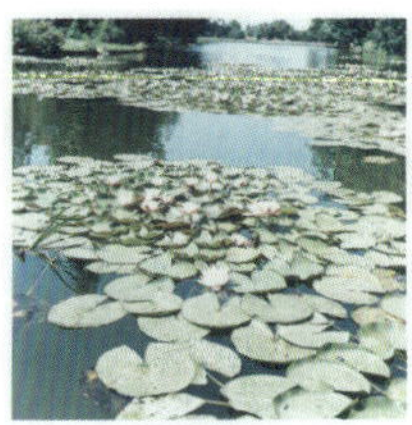

Plate 200
(Cliché of a Plant, Water Lilies)

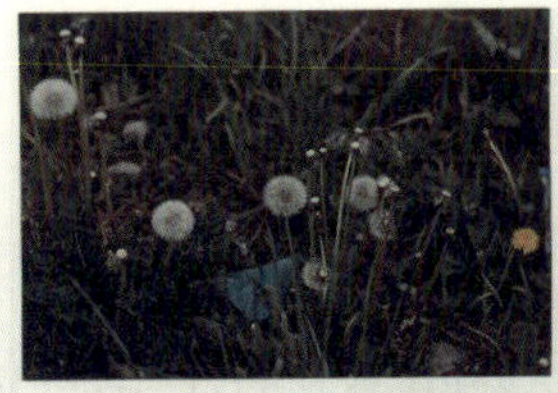

Plate 205
(Cliché of Plants, Dandelion)

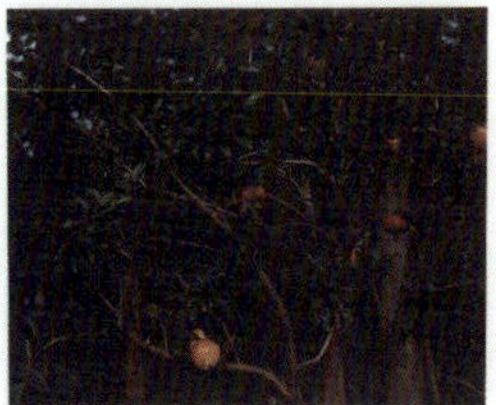

Plate 208
(Cliché of a Tree) I

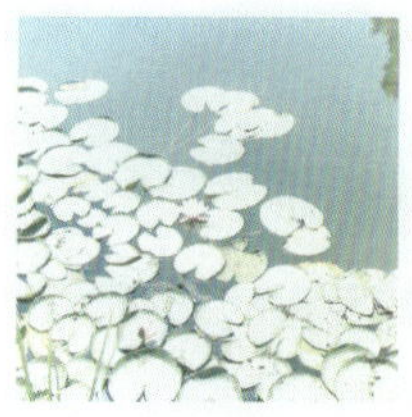

Plate 201
(Cliché of a Plant, Water Lilies)

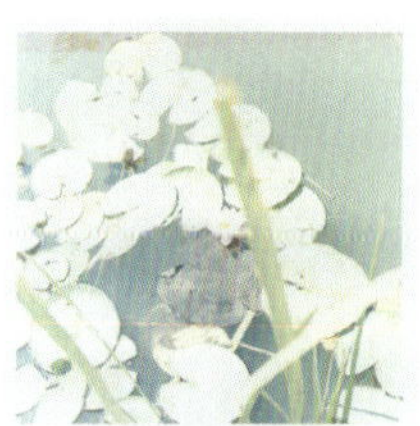

Plate 202
(Cliché of a Plant, Water Lilies)

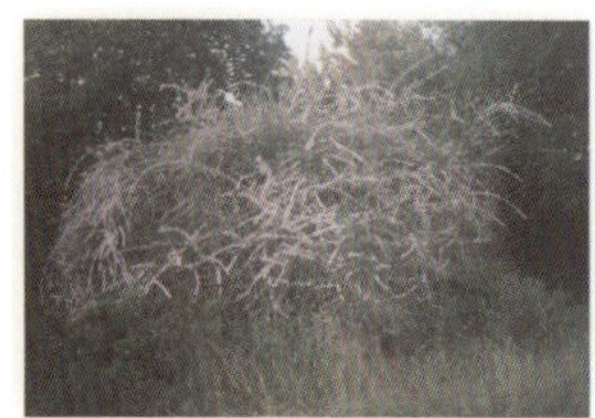

Plate 209
(Cliché of a Bush) II

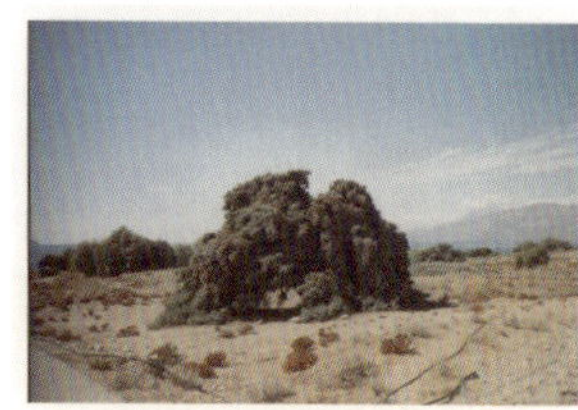

Plate 212
(Cliché of a Tree) II

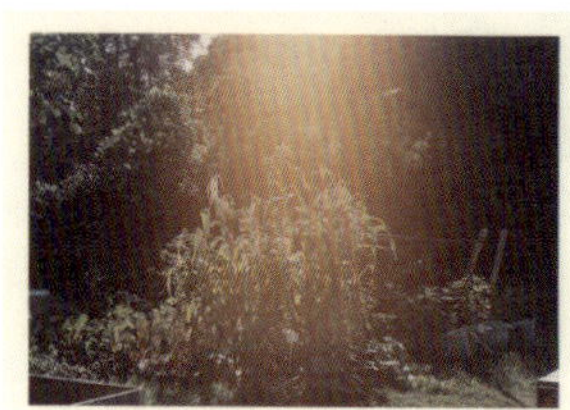

Plate 215
(Cliché of an Acre)

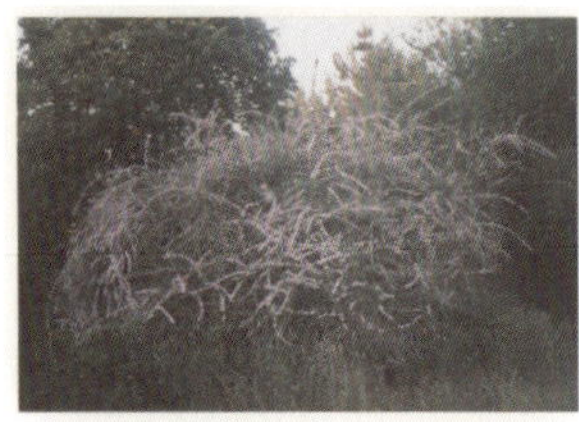

Plate 210
(Cliché of a Bush) II

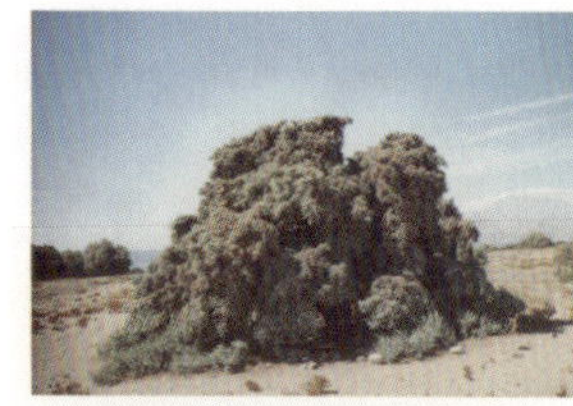

Plate 213
(Cliché of a Tree) II

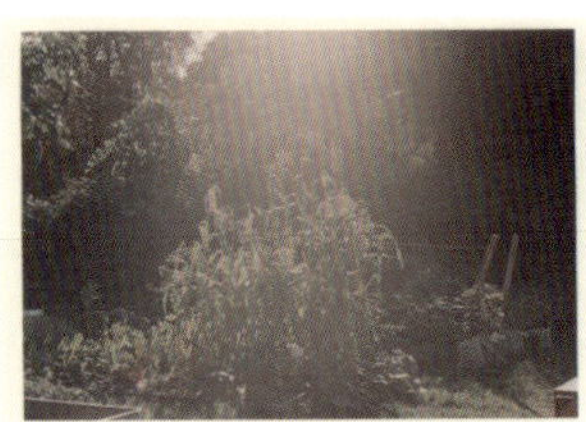

Plate 216
(Cliché of an Acre)

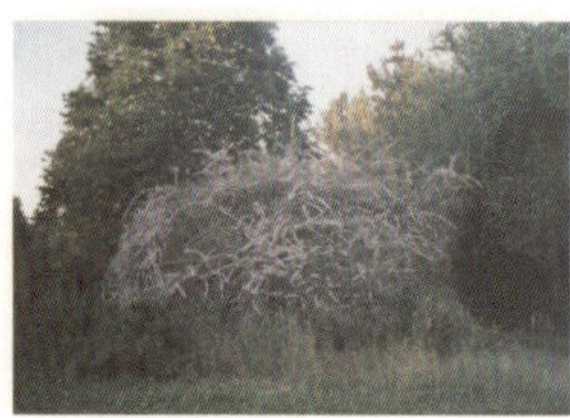

Plate 211
(Cliché of a Bush) II

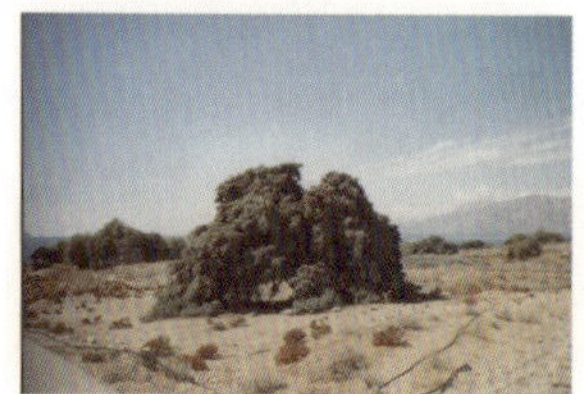

Plate 214
(Cliché of a Tree) II

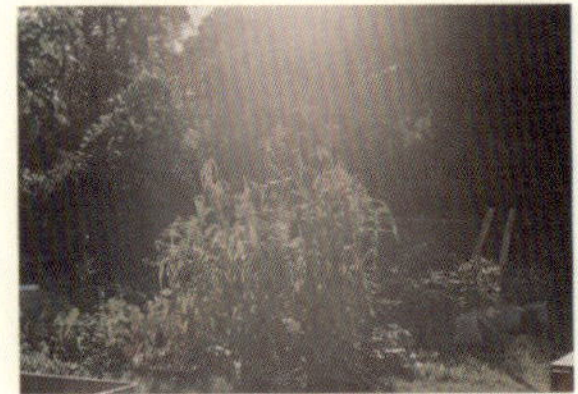

Plate 217
(Cliché of an Acre)

V

MEN

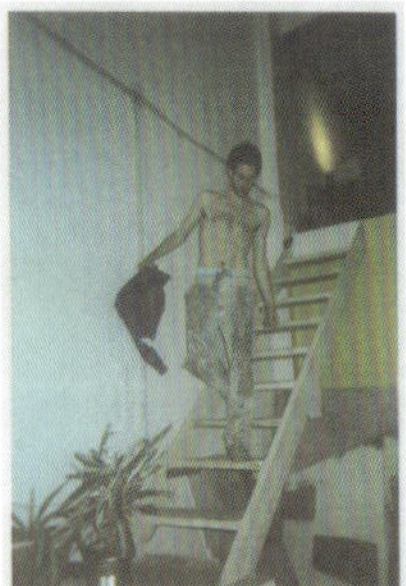

Plate 218
(Cliché of a Man, Nude Torso,
Descending a Staircase)

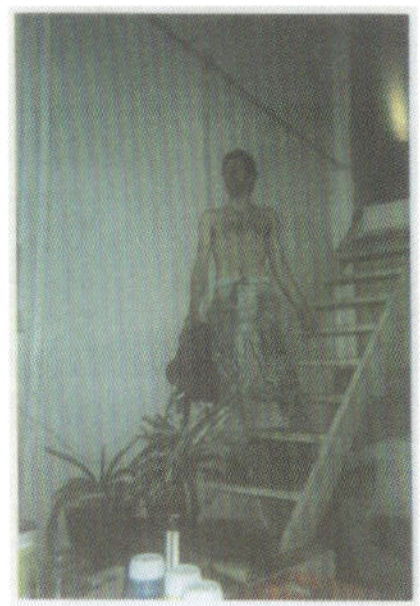

Plate 219
(Cliché of a Man, Nude Torso,
Descending a Staircase)

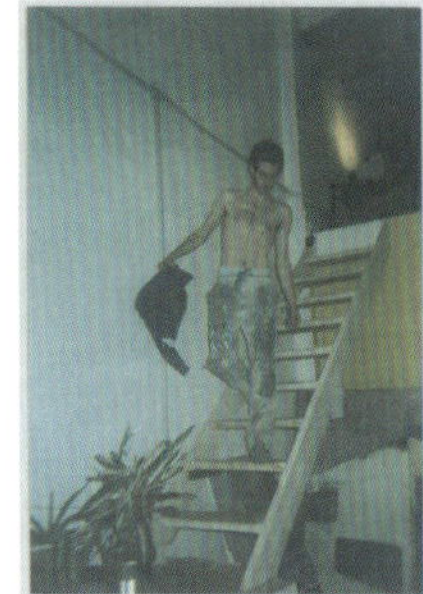

Plate 220
(Cliché of a Man, Nude Torso,
Descending a Staircase)

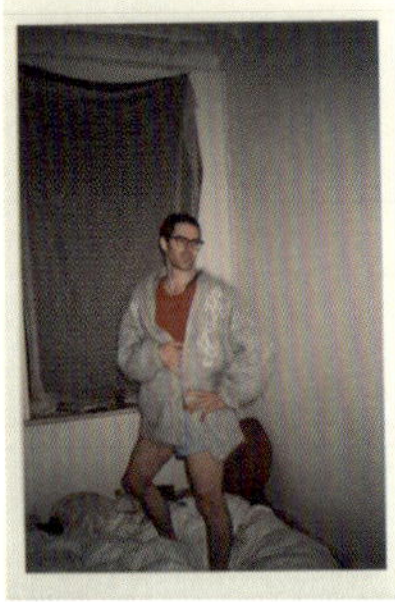

Plate 223
(Cliché of a Man, Standing Figure) I

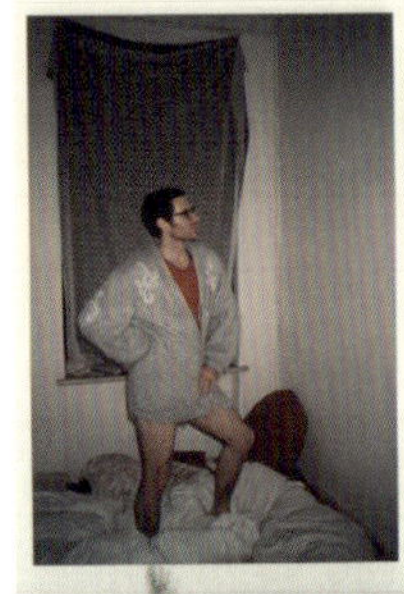

Plate 224
(Cliché of a Man, Standing Figure) I

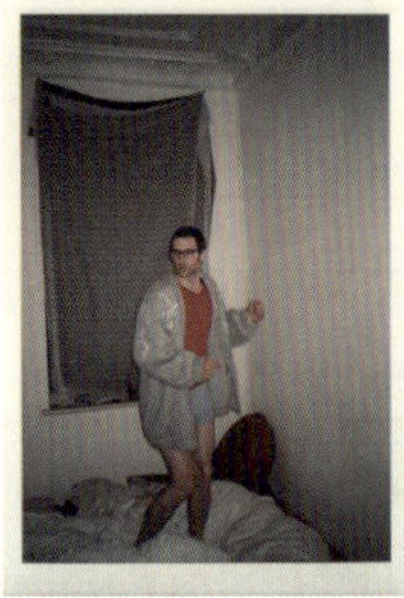

Plate 225
(Cliché of a Man, Standing Figure) I

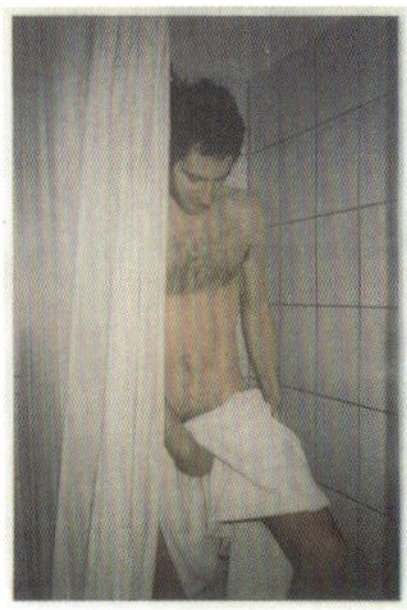

Plate 226
(Cliché of a Man, Nude Torso) I

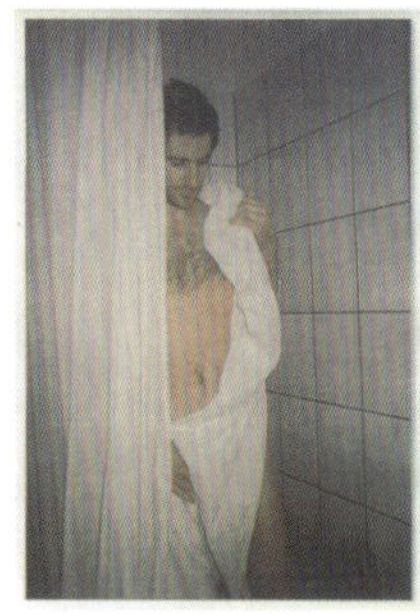

Plate 227
(Cliché of a Man, Nude Torso) I

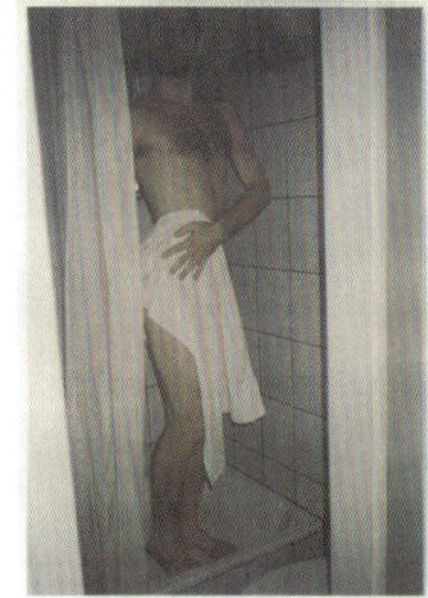

Plate 228
(Cliché of a Man, Nude Torso) I

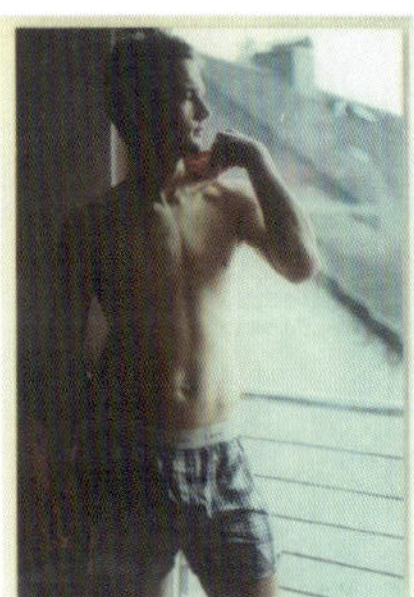

Plate 229
(Cliché of a Man, Nude Torso) II

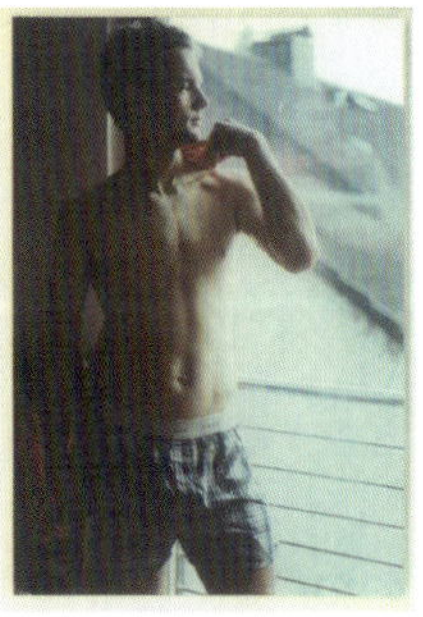

Plate 230
(Cliché of a Man, Nude Torso) II

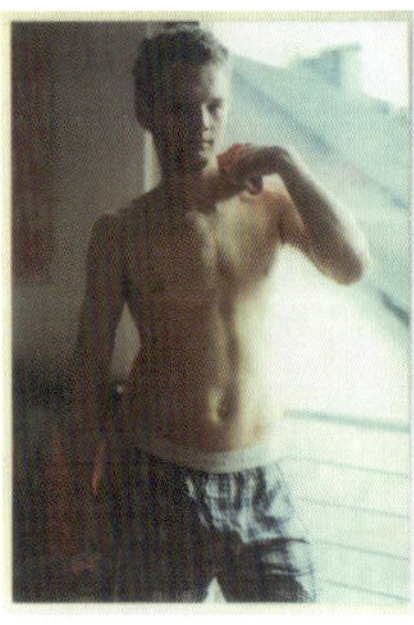

Plate 231
(Cliché of a Man, Nude Torso) II

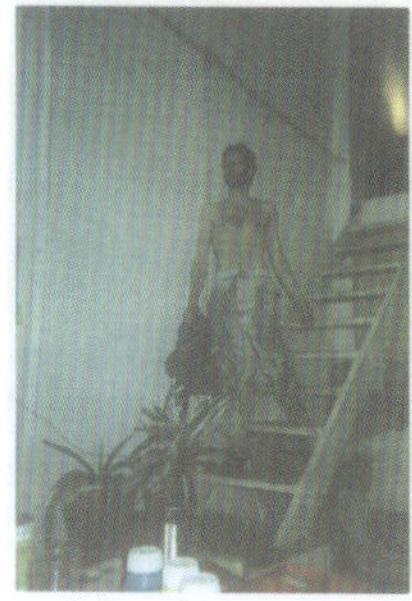

Plate 221
(Cliché of a Man, Nude Torso,
Descending a Staircase)

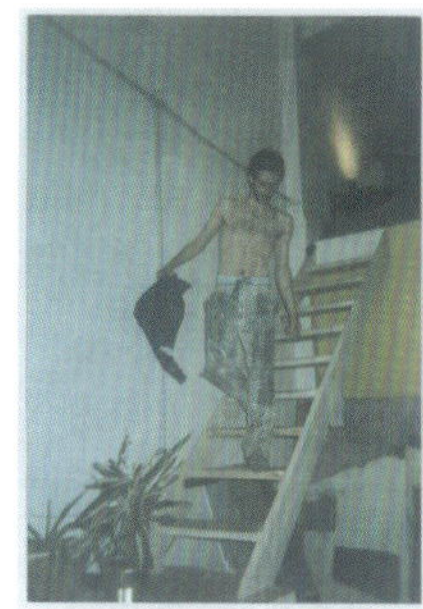

Plate 222
(Cliché of a Man, Nude Torso,
Descending a Staircase)

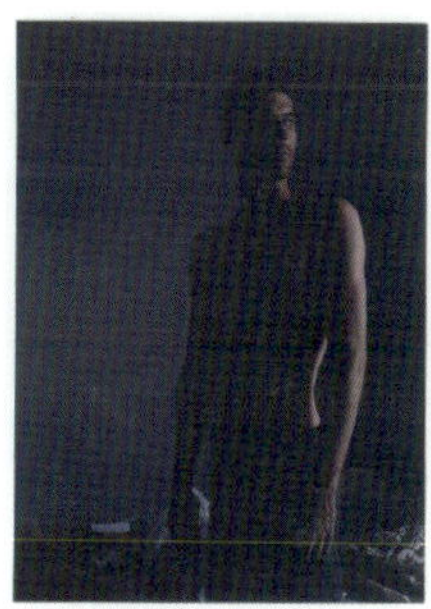

Plate 232
(Cliché of a Man, Nude Torso) III

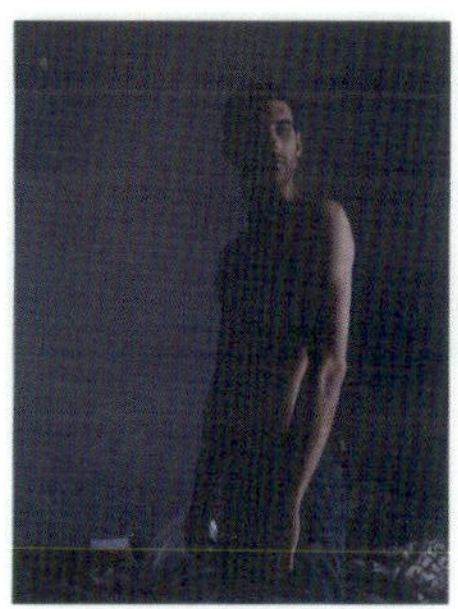

Plate 233
(Cliché of a Man, Nude Torso) III

Plate 234
(Cliché of a Man, Nude Torso) III

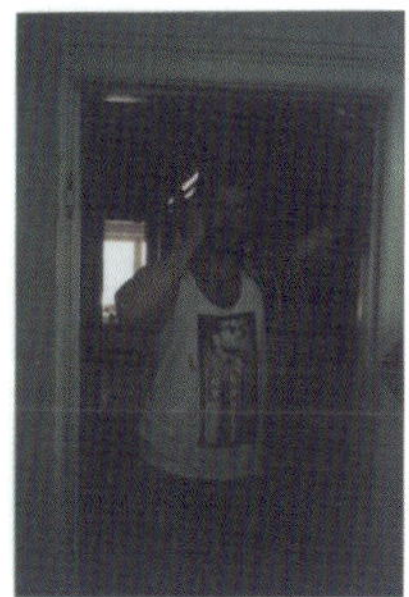

Plate 235
(Cliché of a Man, Semi Nude Torso)

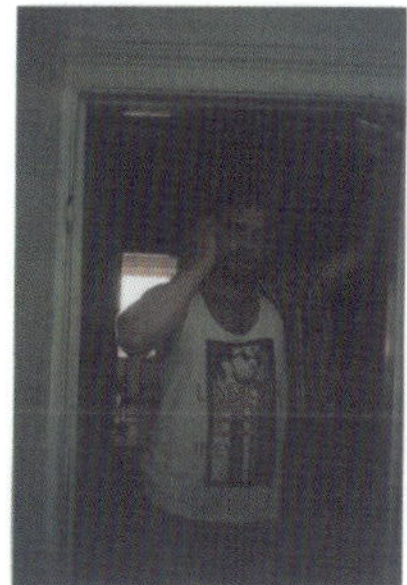

Plate 236
(Cliché of a Man, Semi Nude Torso)

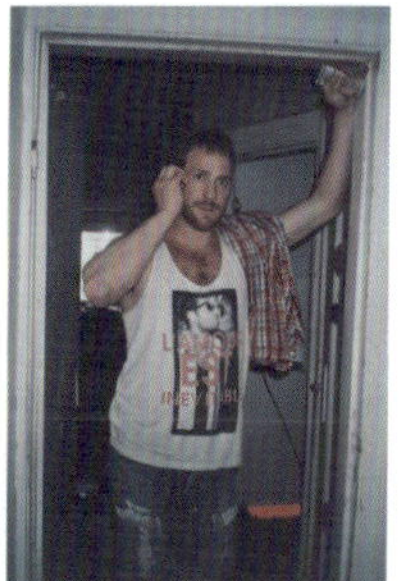

Plate 237
(Cliché of a Man, Semi Nude Torso)

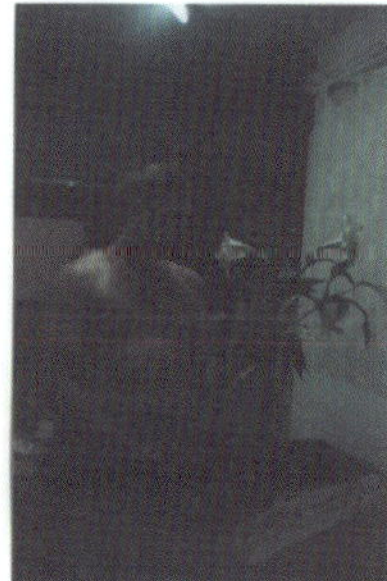

Plate 238
(Cliché of a Man, Nude Torso,
with Flowers)

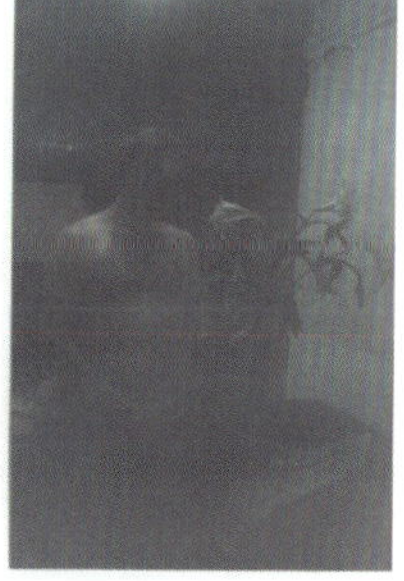

Plate 239
(Cliché of a Man, Nude Torso,
with Flowers)

Plate 240
(Cliché of a Man, Nude Torso,
with Flowers)

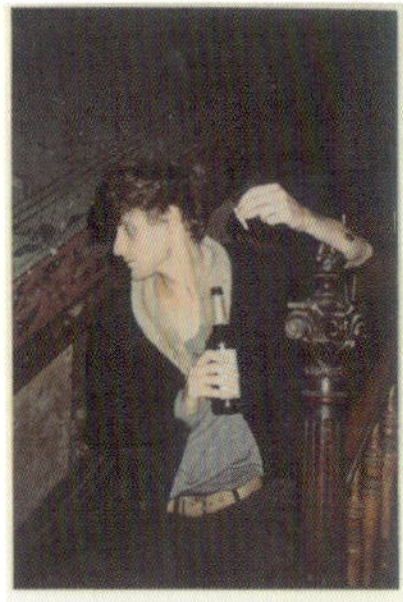

Plate 241
(Cliché of a Man, Torso) I

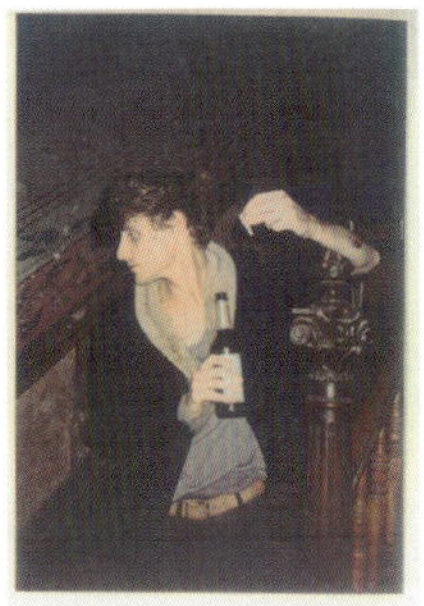

Plate 242
(Cliché of a Man, Torso) I

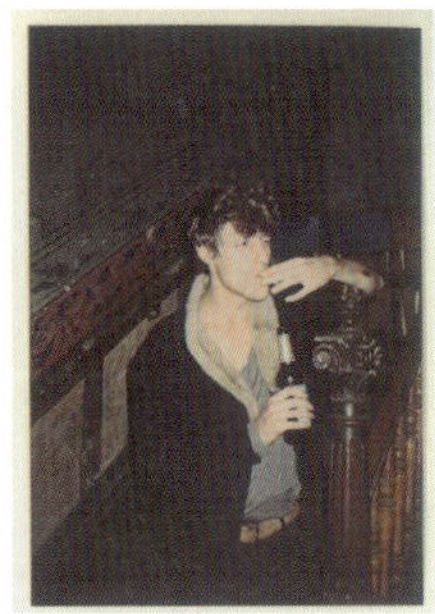

Plate 243
(Cliché of a Man, Torso) I

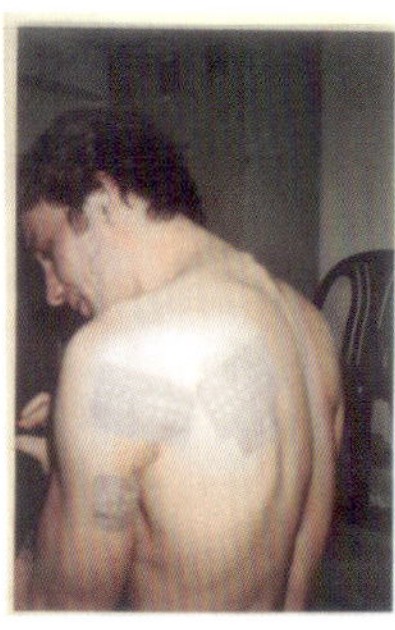

Plate 244
(Cliché of a Man, Nude Torso) IV

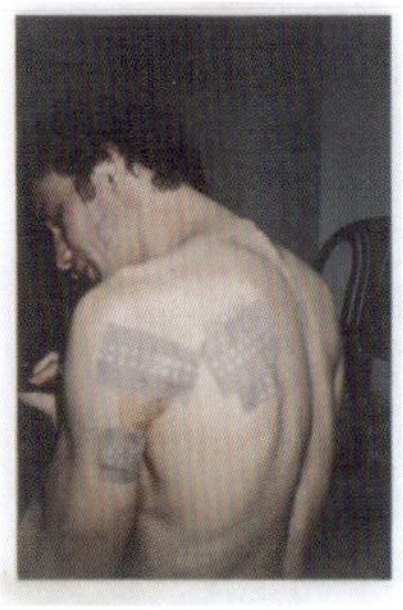

Plate 245
(Cliché of a Man, Nude Torso) IV

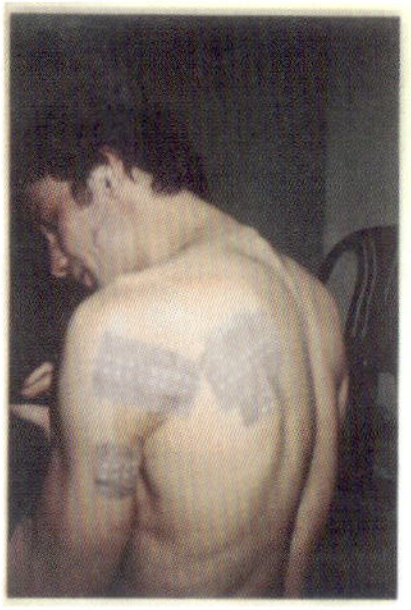

Plate 246
(Cliché of a Man, Nude Torso) IV

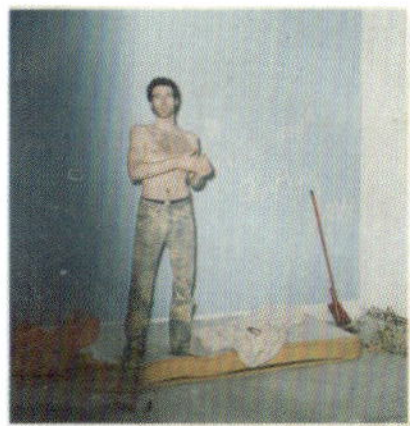

Plate 247
(Cliché of a Man, Nude Torso,
Standing Figure)

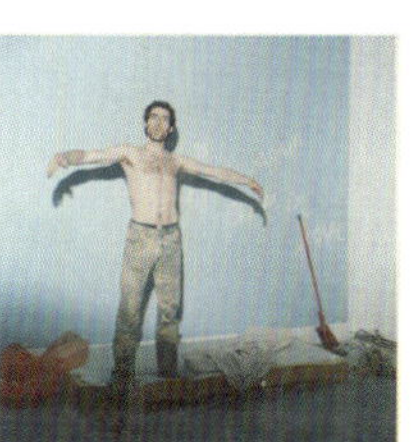

Plate 248
(Cliché of a Man, Nude Torso,
Standing Figure)

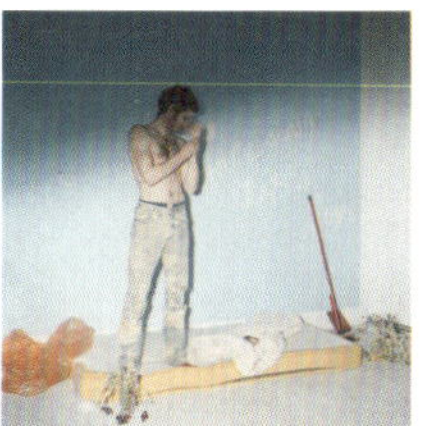

Plate 249
(Cliché of a Man, Nude Torso,
Standing Figure)

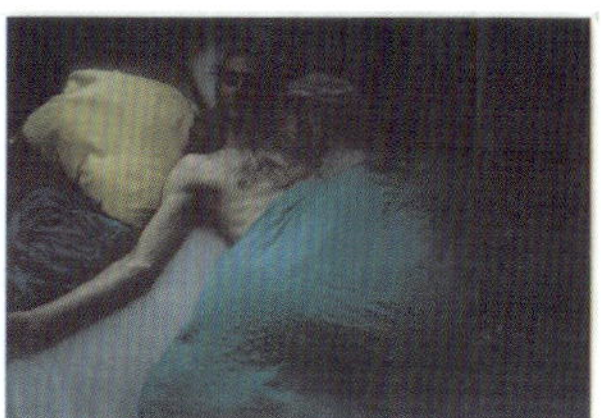

Plate 250
(Cliché of a Man, Lying Figure, Nude
Torso) I

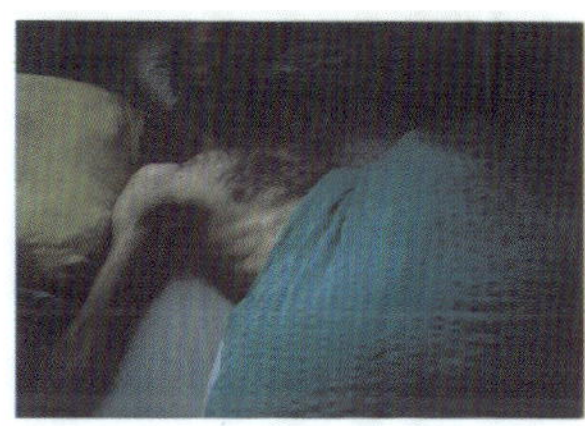

Plate 251
(Cliché of a Man, Lying Figure, Nude
Torso) I

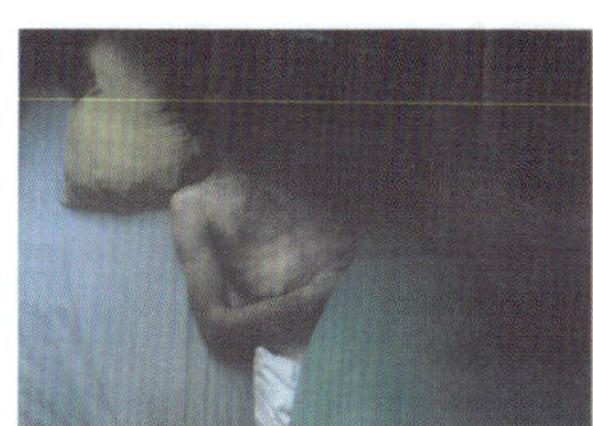

Plate 252
(Cliché of a Man, Lying Figure, Nude
Torso) I

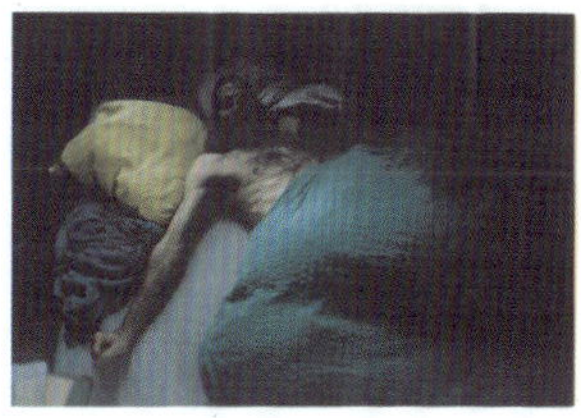

Plate 253
(Cliché of a Man, Lying Figure, Nude
Torso) I

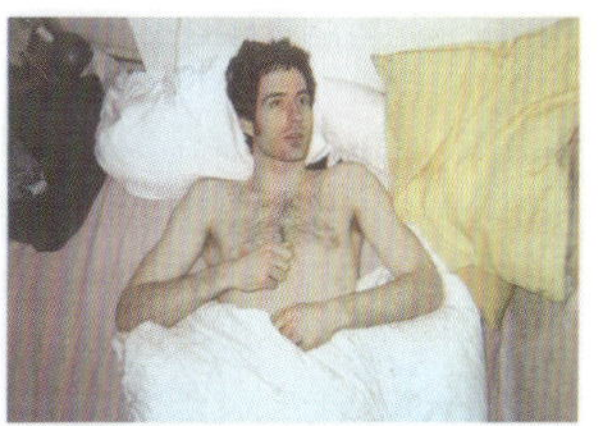

Plate 254
(Cliché of a Man, Lying Figure, Nude
Torso) II

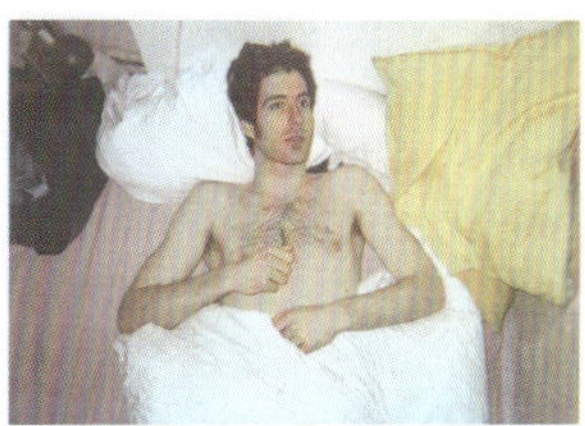

Plate 255
(Cliché of a Man, Lying Figure, Nude
Torso) II

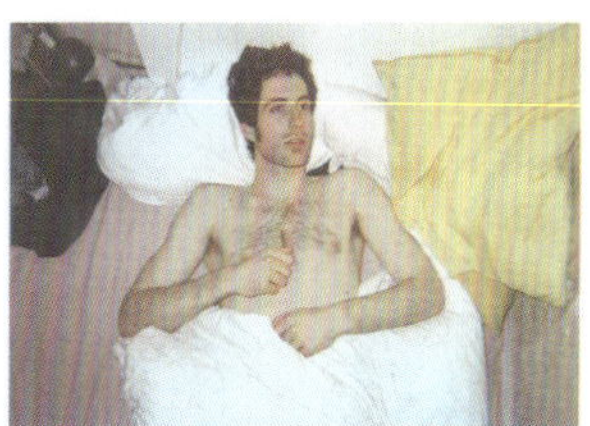

Plate 256
(Cliché of a Man, Lying Figure, Nude
Torso) II

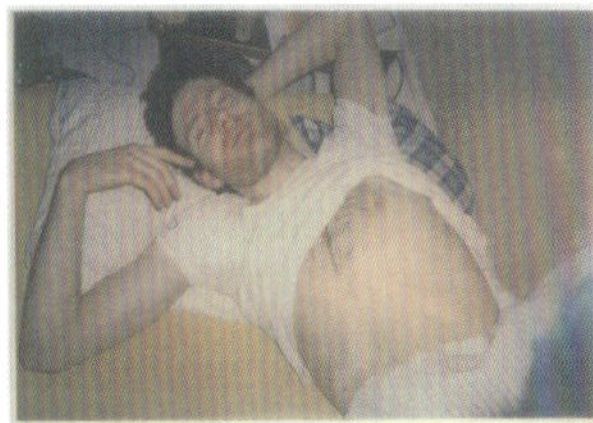

Plate 257
(Cliché of a Man, Lying Figure, Nude
Torso) III

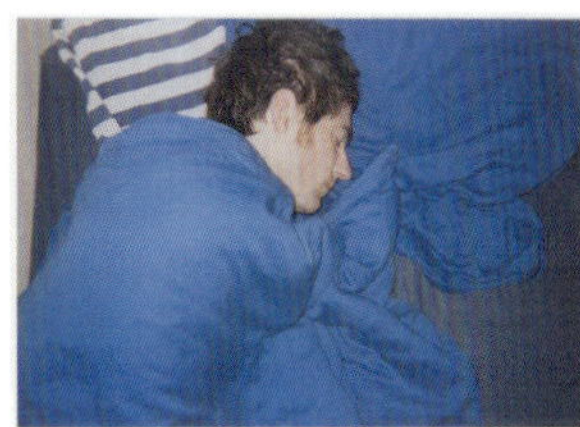

Plate 260
(Cliché of a Man, Lying Figure, Torso) I

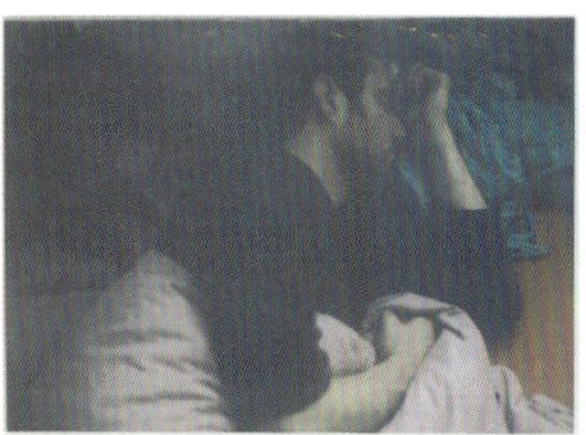

Plate 263
(Cliché of a Man, Lying Figure, Torso) II

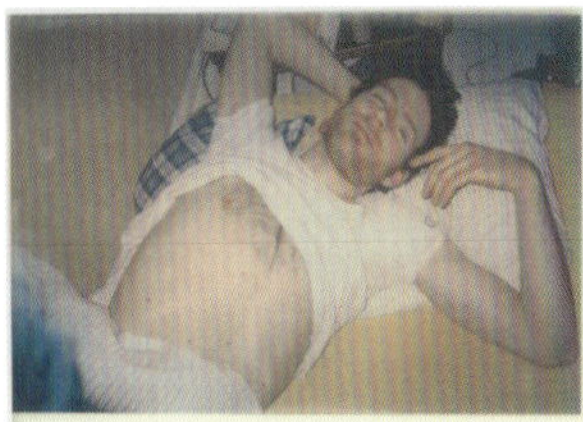

Plate 258
(Cliché of a Man, Lying Figure, Nude
Torso) III

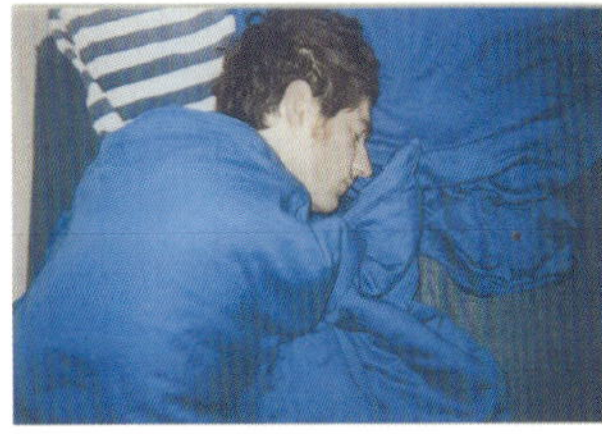

Plate 261
(Cliché of a Man, Lying Figure, Torso) I

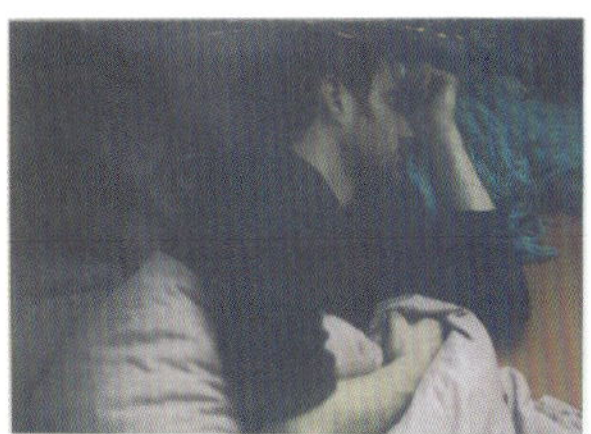

Plate 264
(Cliché of a Man, Lying Figure, Torso) II

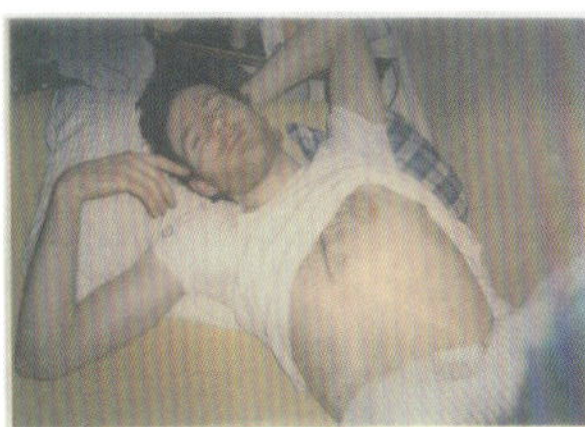

Plate 259
(Cliché of a Man, Lying Figure, Nude
Torso) III

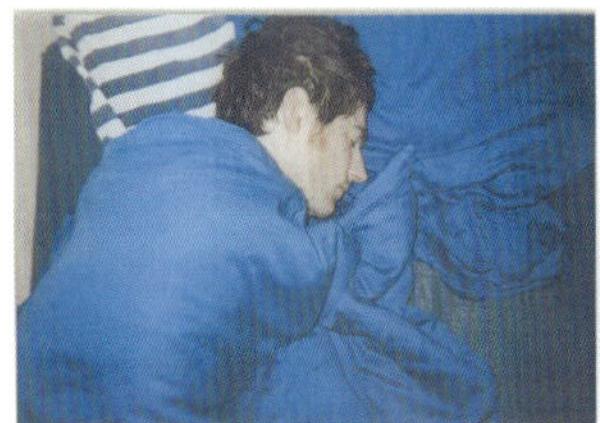

Plate 262
(Cliché of a Man, Lying Figure, Torso) I

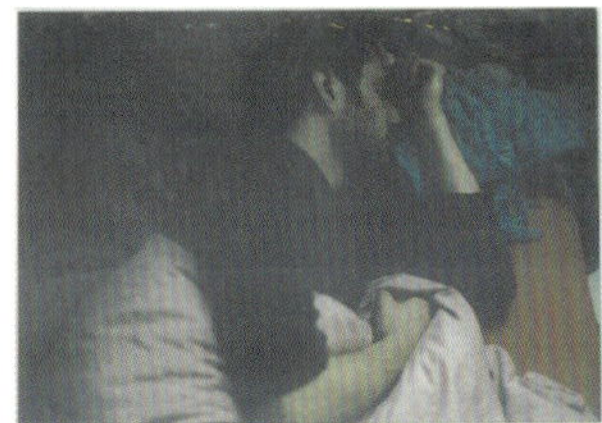

Plate 265
(Cliché of a Man, Lying Figure, Torso) II

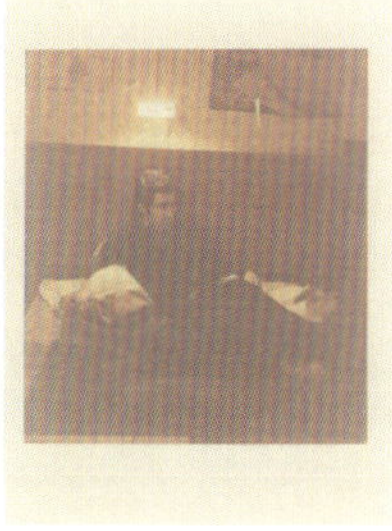

Plate 266
(Cliché of a Man, Lying Figure) I

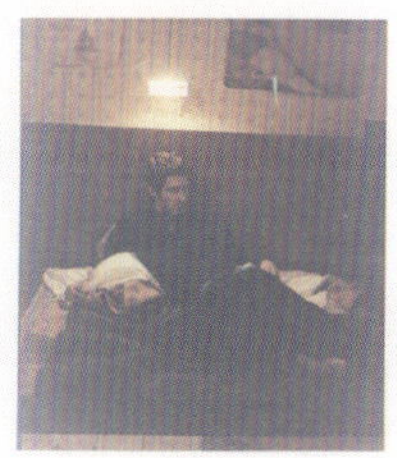

Plate 267
(Cliché of a Man, Lying Figure) I

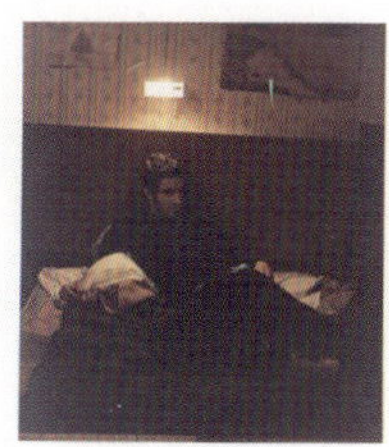

Plate 268
(Cliché of a Man, Lying Figure) I

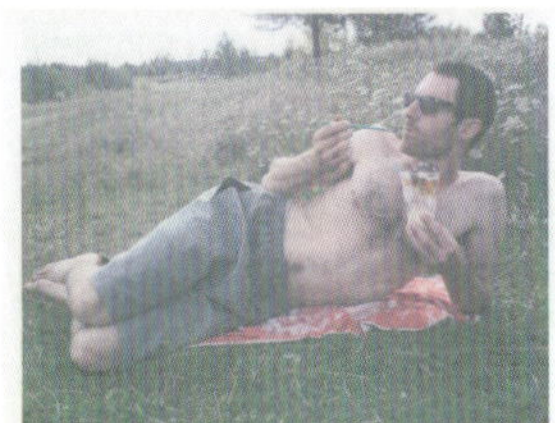

Plate 269
(Cliché of a Man, Lying Figure, in
Green Grass) I

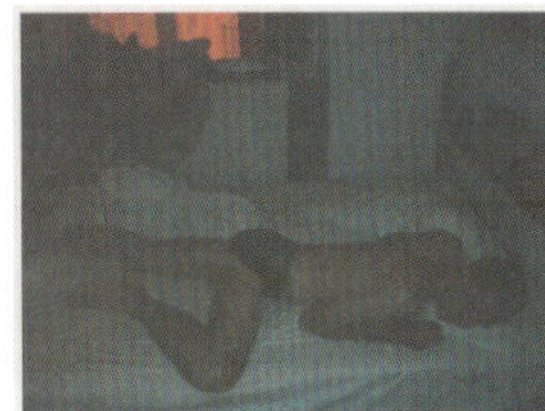

Plate 274
(Cliché of a Man, Lying Figure) II

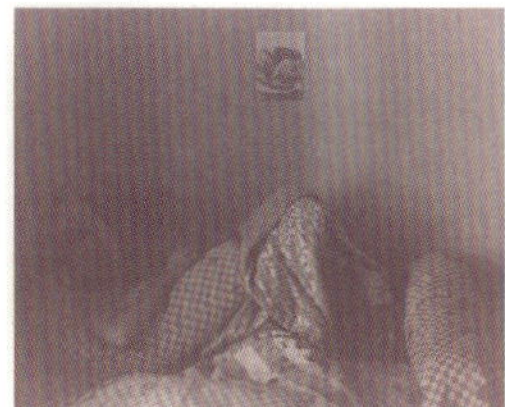

Plate 277
(Cliché of a Man, Lying Figure) III

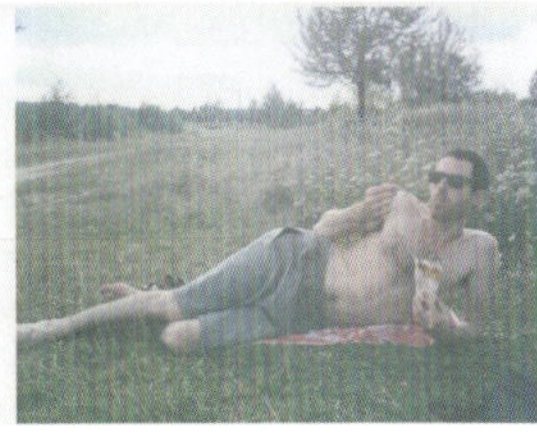

Plate 270
(Cliché of a Man, Lying Figure, in
Green Grass) I

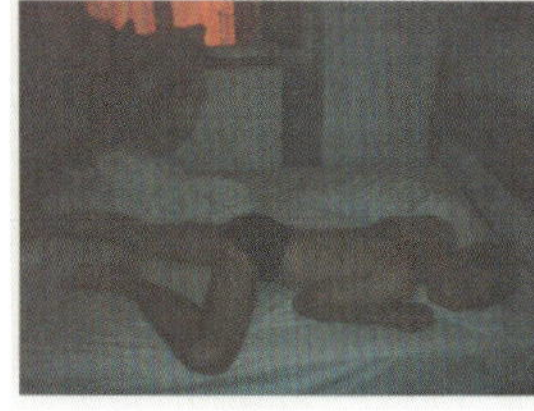

Plate 275
(Cliché of a Man, Lying Figure) II

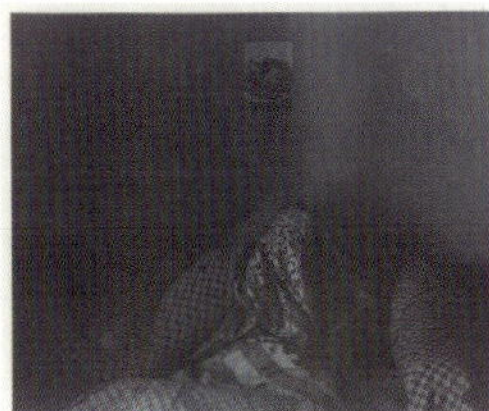

Plate 278
(Cliché of a Man, Lying Figure) III

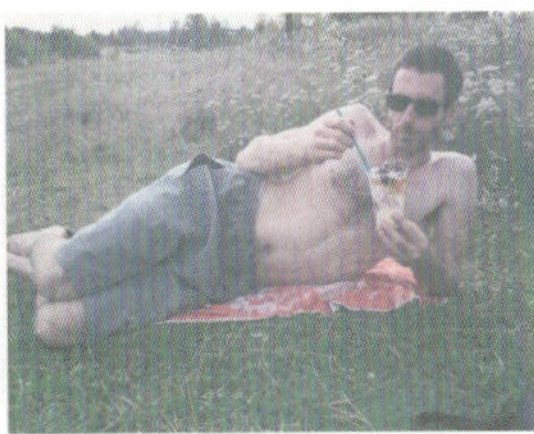

Plate 271
(Cliché of a Man, Lying Figure, in
Green Grass) I

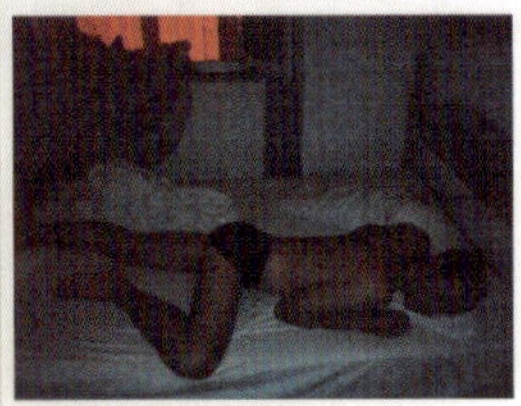

Plate 276
(Cliché of a Man, Lying Figure) II

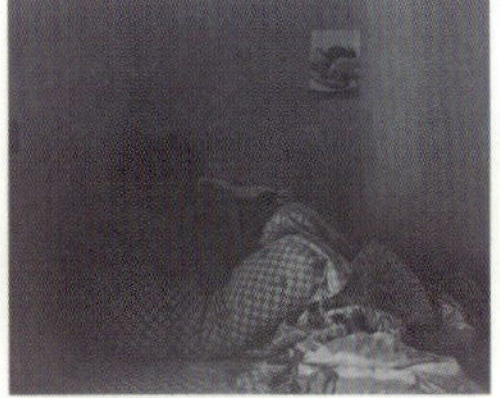

Plate 279
(Cliché of a Man, Lying Figure) III

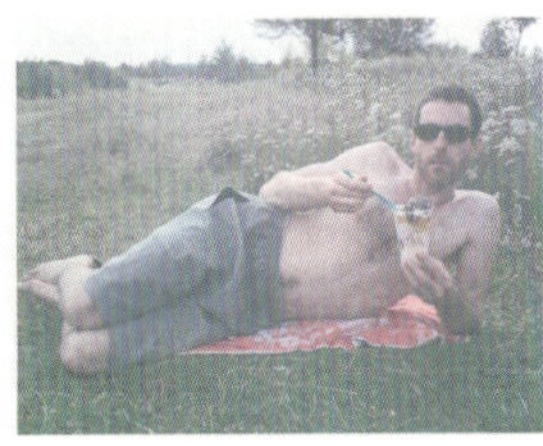

Plate 272
(Cliché of a Man, Lying Figure, in
Green Grass) I

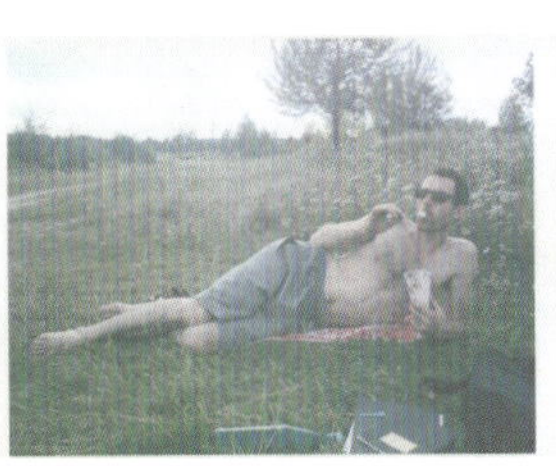

Plate 273
(Cliché of a Man, Lying Figure, in
Green Grass) I

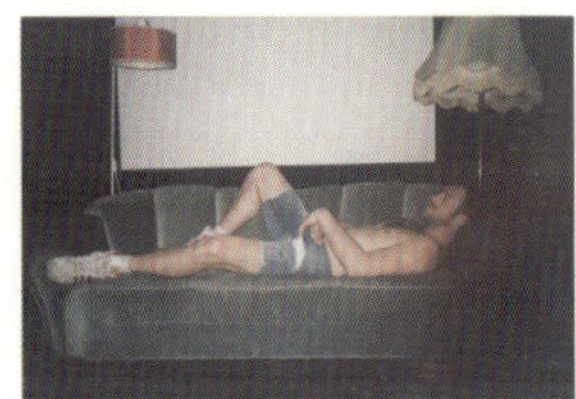

Plate 280
(Cliché of a Man, Lying Figure) IV

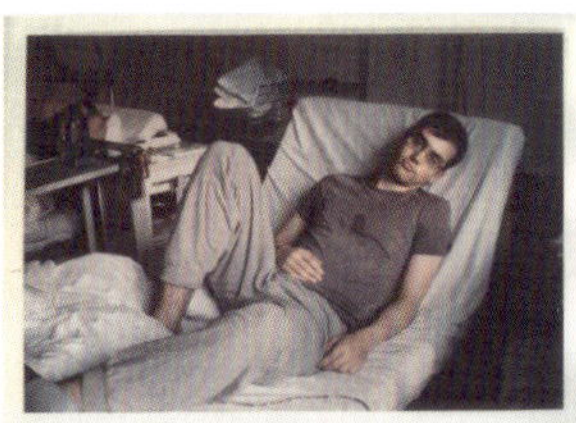

Plate 283
(Cliché of a Man, Lying Figure) V

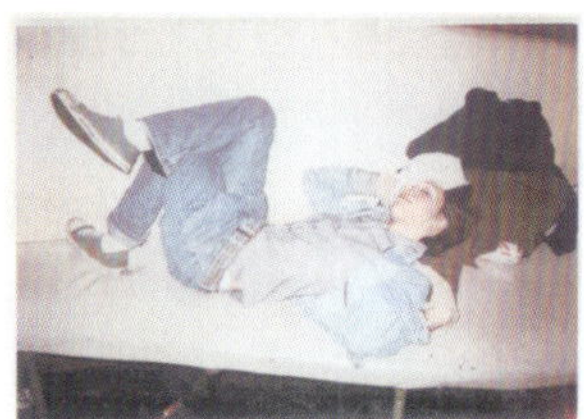

Plate 286
(Cliché of a Man, Lying Figure) VI

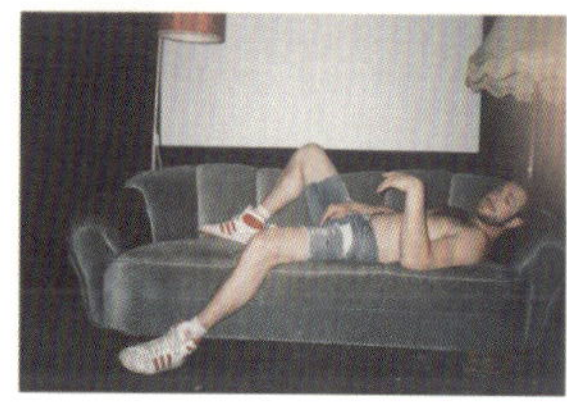

Plate 281
(Cliché of a Man, Lying Figure) IV

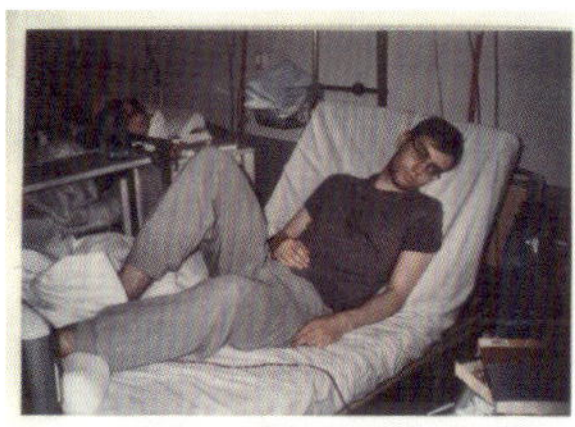

Plate 284
(Cliché of a Man, Lying Figure) V

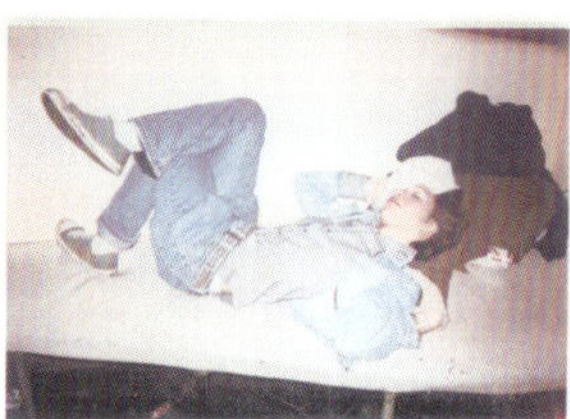

Plate 287
(Cliché of a Man, Lying Figure) VI

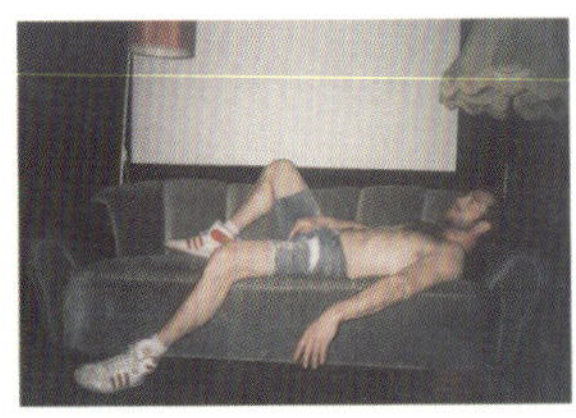

Plate 282
(Cliché of a Man, Lying Figure) IV

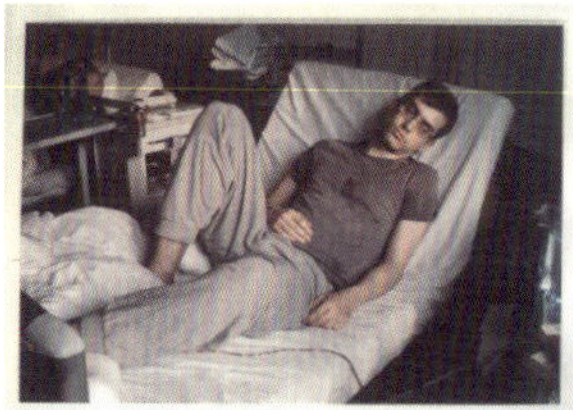

Plate 285
(Cliché of a Man, Lying Figure) V

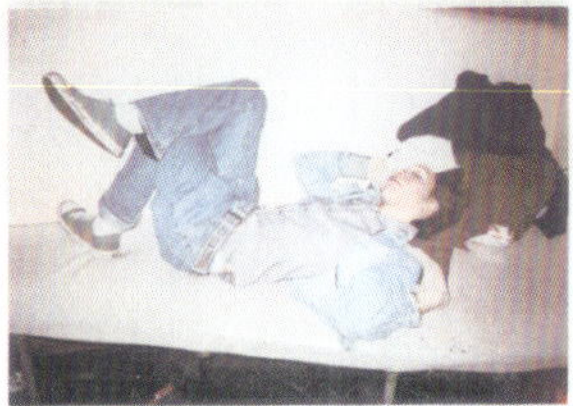

Plate 288
(Cliché of a Man, Lying Figure) VI

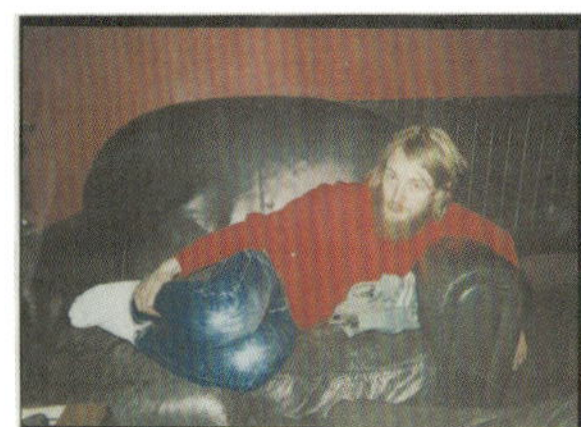

Plate 289
(Cliché of a Man, Lying Figure) VII

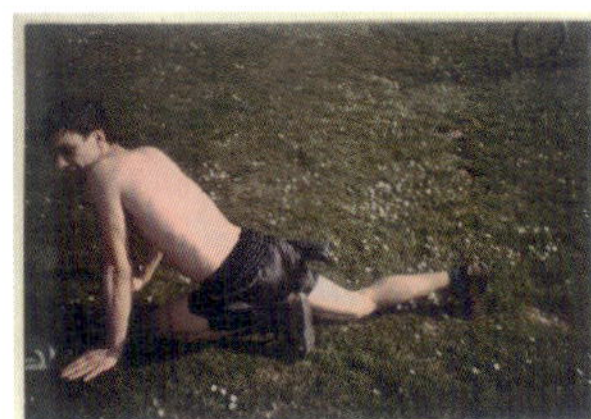

Plate 292
(Cliché of a Man, Lying Figure, in
Green Grass) II

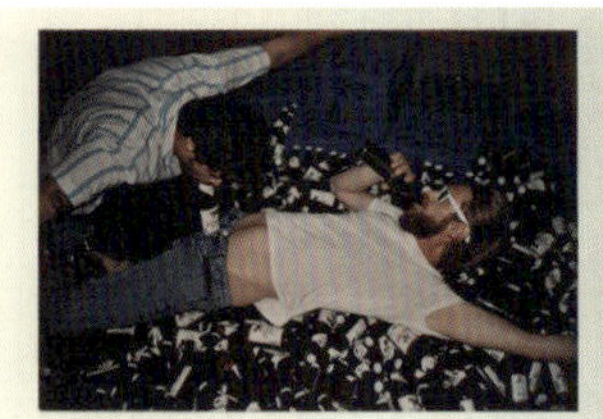

Plate 295
(Cliché of a Man, Lying Figure) VIII

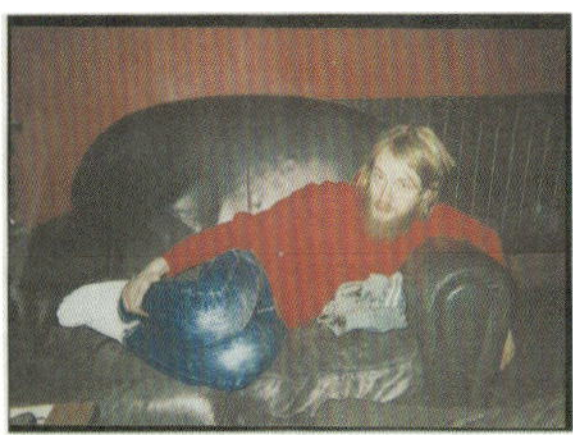

Plate 290
(Cliché of a Man, Lying Figure) VII

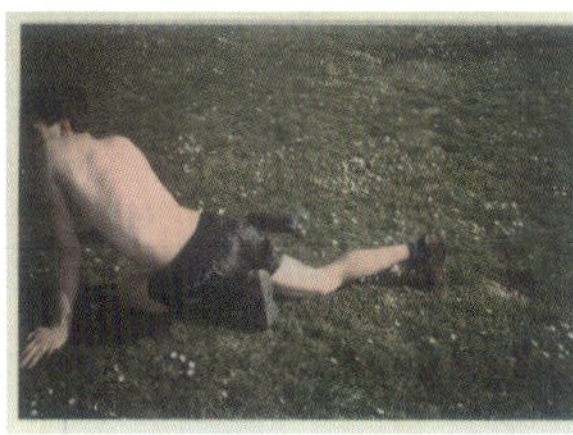

Platé 293
(Cliché of a Man, Lying Figure, in
Green Grass) II

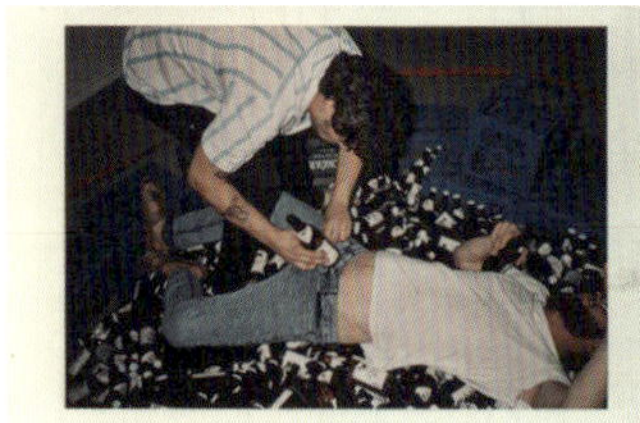

Plate 296
(Cliché of a Man, Lying Figure) VIII

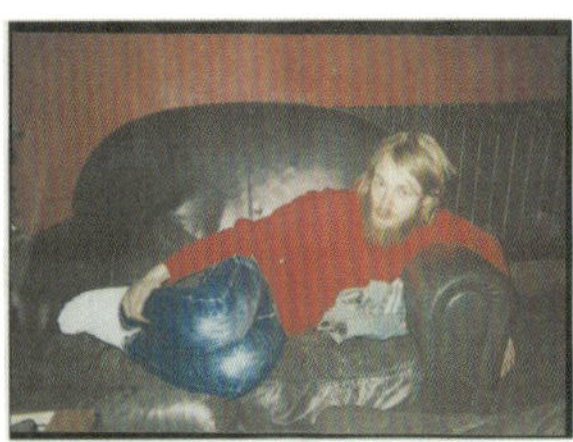

Plate 291
(Cliché of a Man, Lying Figure) VII

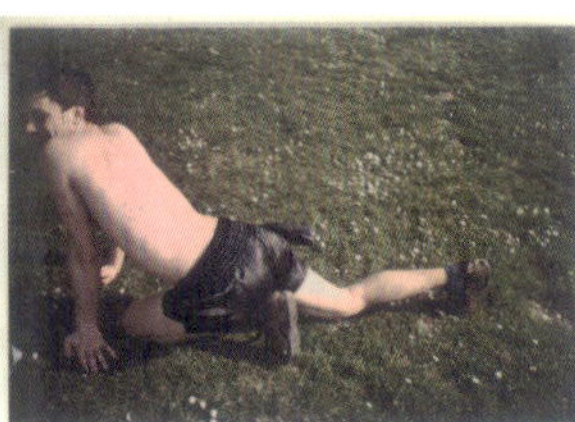

Plate 294
(Cliché of a Man, Lying Figure, in
Green Grass) II

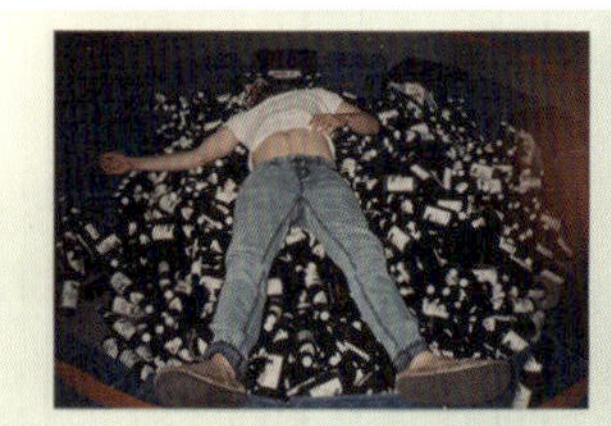

Plate 297
(Cliché of a Man, Lying Figure) VIII

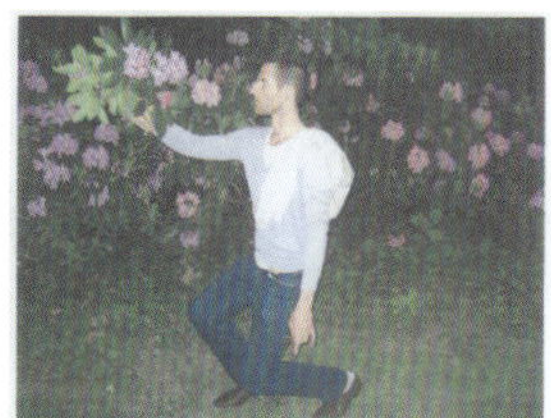

Plate 298
(Cliché of a Man, Crouching Figure,
with Flowers)

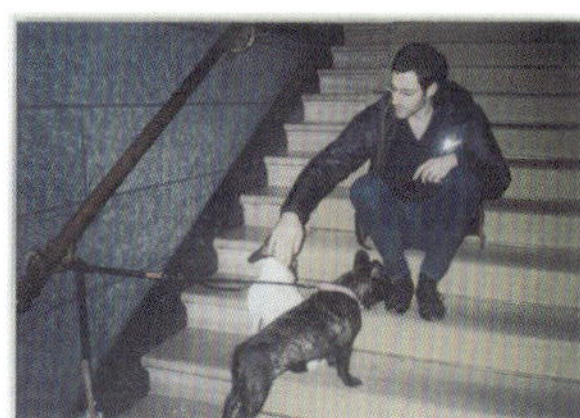

Plate 301
(Cliché of a Man, with Dogs) I

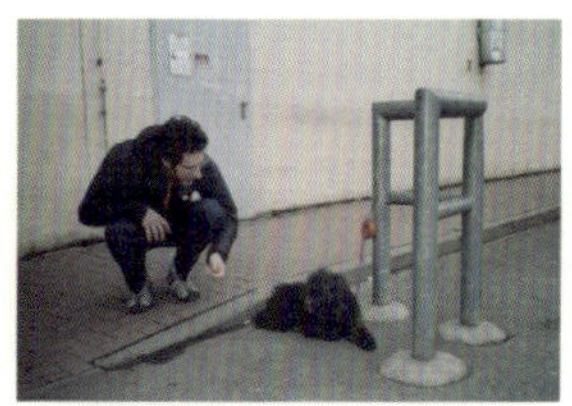

Plate 304
(Cliché of a Man, with Dogs) II

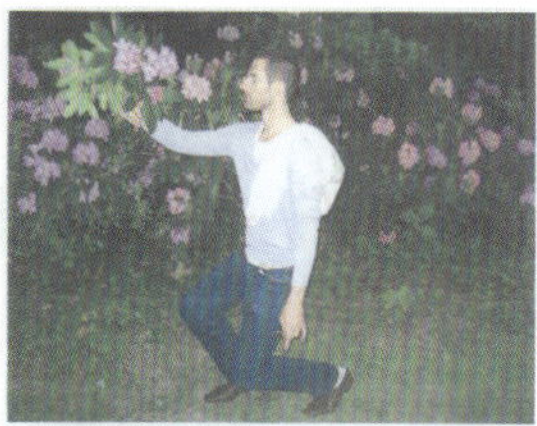

Plate 299
(Cliché of a Man, Crouching Figure,
with Flowers)

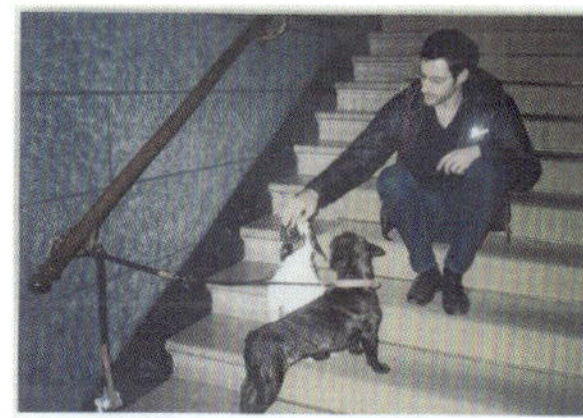

Plate 302
(Cliché of a Man, with Dogs) I

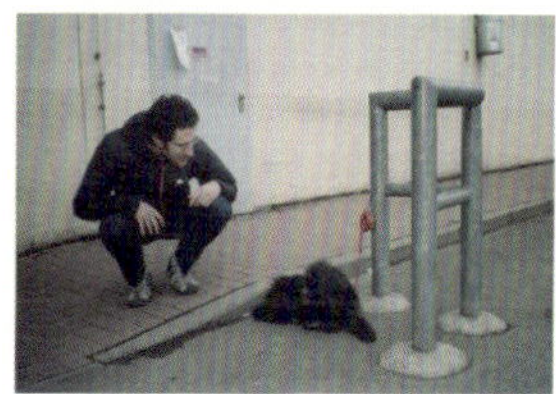

Plate 305
(Cliché of a Man, with Dogs) II

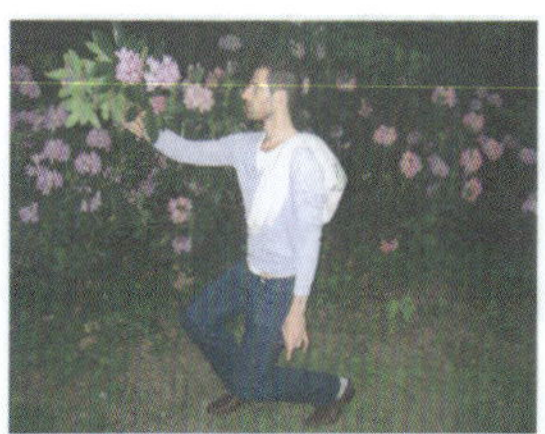

Plate 300
(Cliché of a Man, Crouching Figure,
with Flowers)

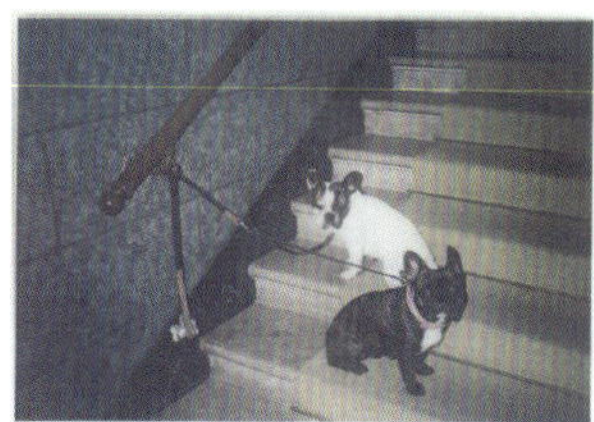

Plate 303
(Cliché of a Man, with Dogs) I

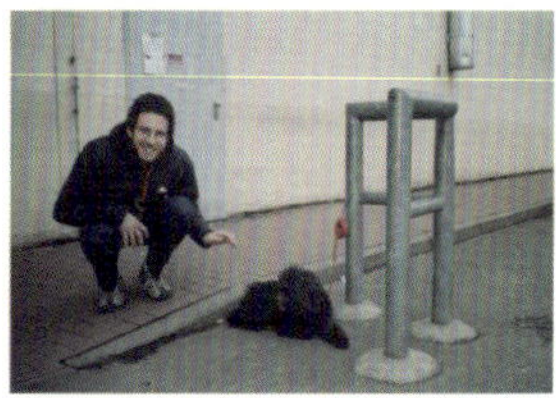

Plate 306
(Cliché of a Man, with Dogs) II

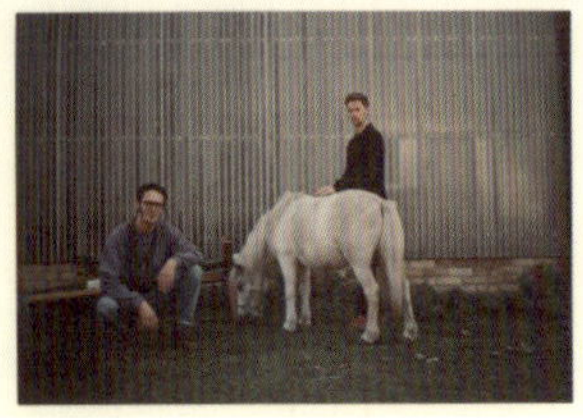

Plate 307
(Cliché of Two Men, with Pony)

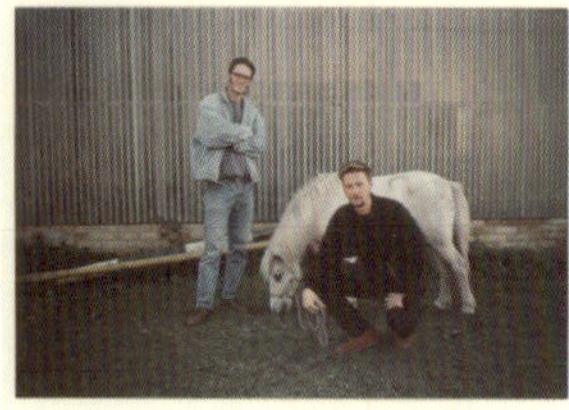

Plate 308
(Cliché of Two Men, with Pony)

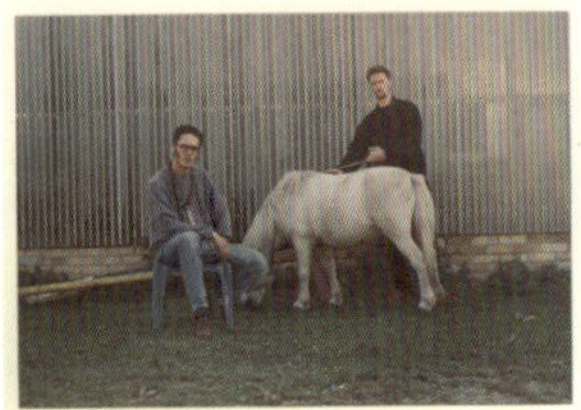

Plate 309
(Cliché of Two Men, with Pony)

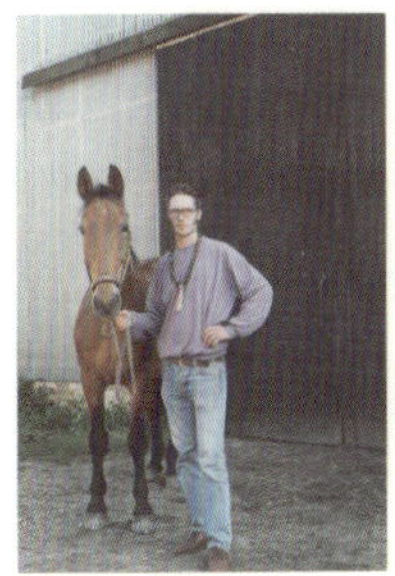

Plate 310
(Cliché of a Men, with Horse)

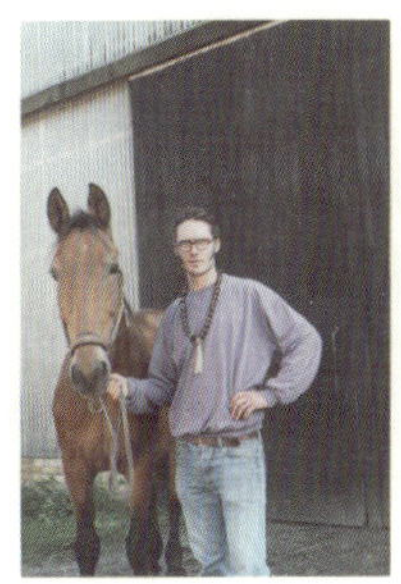

Plate 311
(Cliché of a Men, with Horse)

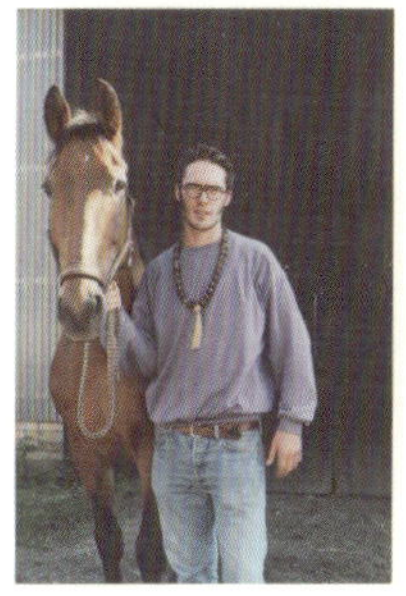

Plate 312
(Cliché of a Men, with Horse)

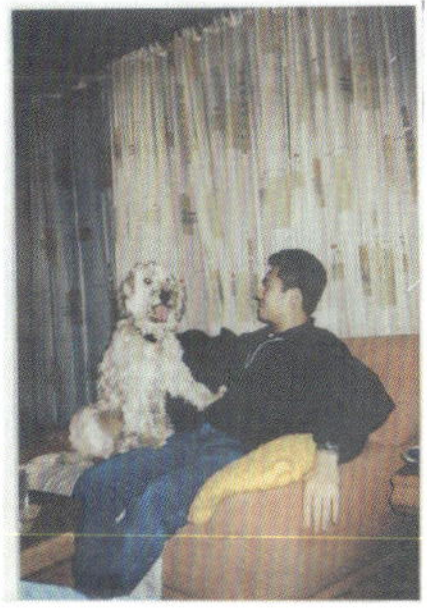

Plate 313
(Cliché of a Man, Sitting Figure,
with Dog)

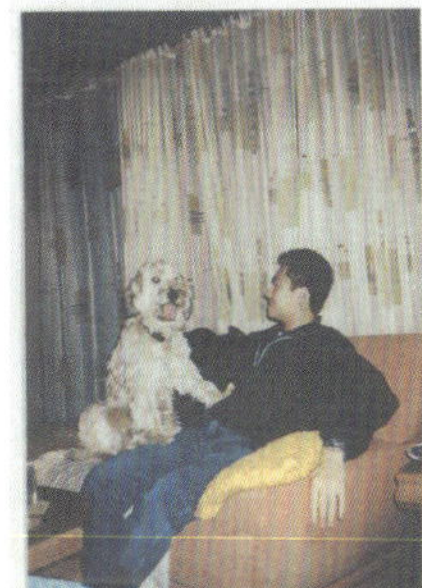

Plate 314
(Cliché of a Man, Sitting Figure,
with Dog)

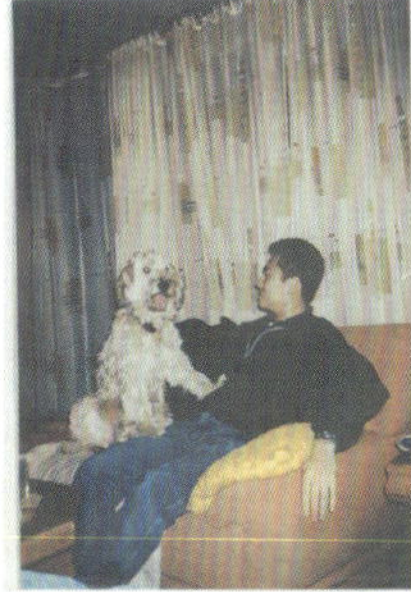

Plate 315
(Cliché of a Man, Sitting Figure,
with Dog)

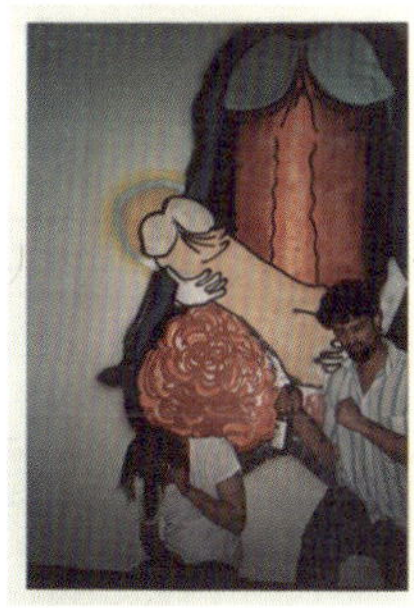

Plate 316
(Cliché of Two Men, Sitting Figures)

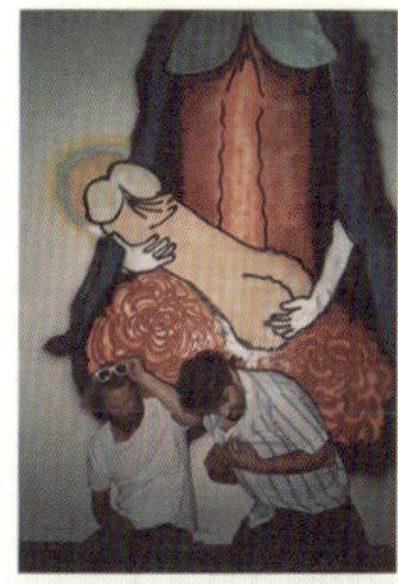

Plate 317
(Cliché of Two Men, Sitting Figures)

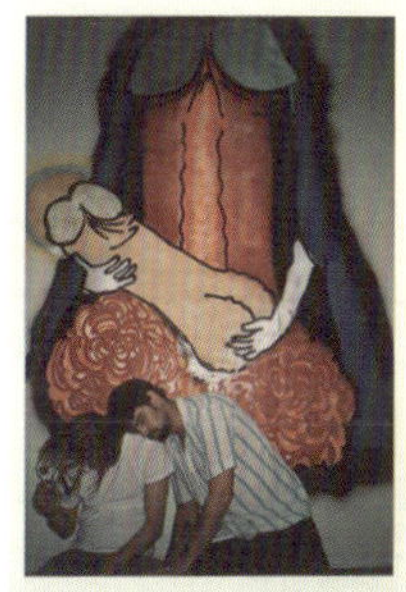

Plate 318
(Cliché of Two Men, Sitting Figures)

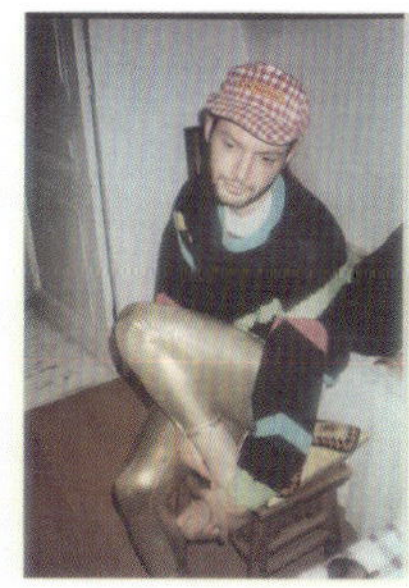

Plate 319
(Cliché of a Man, Sitting Figure)

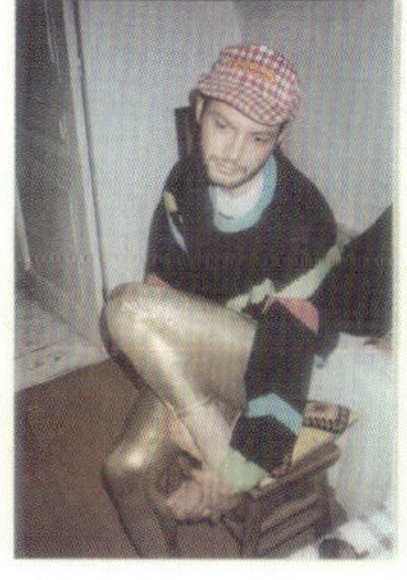

Plate 320
(Cliché of a Man, Sitting Figure)

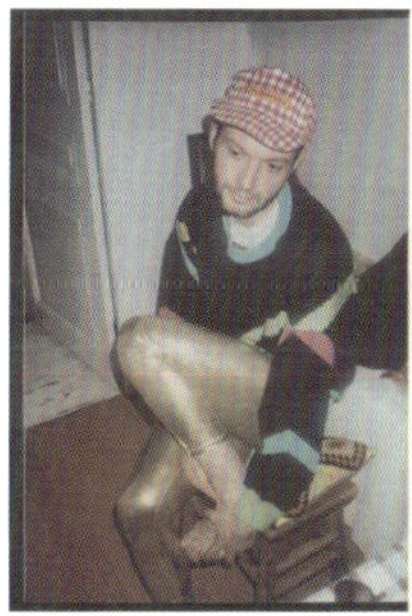

Plate 321
(Cliché of a Man, Sitting Figure)

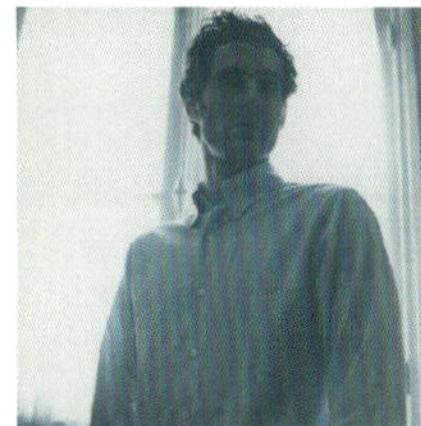

Plate 322
(Cliché of a Man, Portait,
with Torso) I

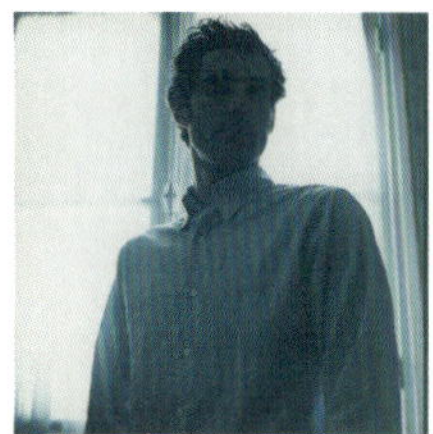

Plate 323
(Cliché of a Man, Portait,
with Torso) I

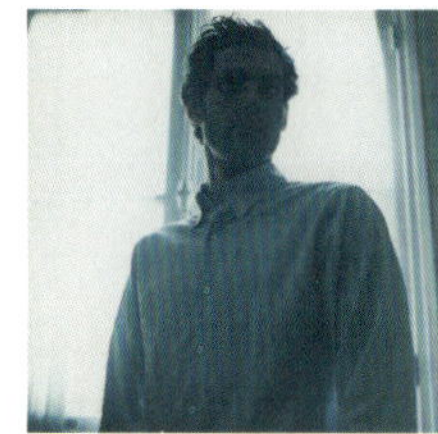

Plate 324
(Cliché of a Man, Portait,
with Torso) I

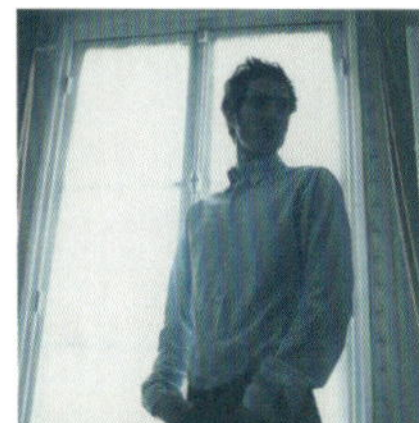

Plate 325
(Cliché of a Man, Portait,
with Torso) II

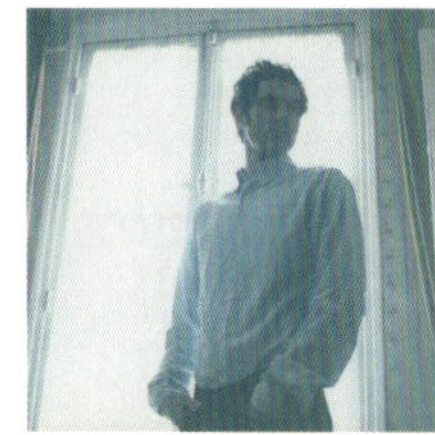

Plate 326
(Cliché of a Man, Portait,
with Torso) II

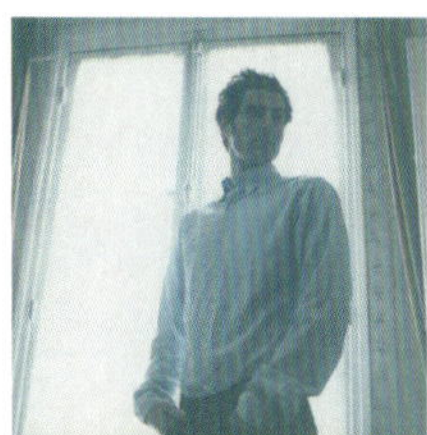

Plate 327
(Cliché of a Man, Portait,
with Torso) II

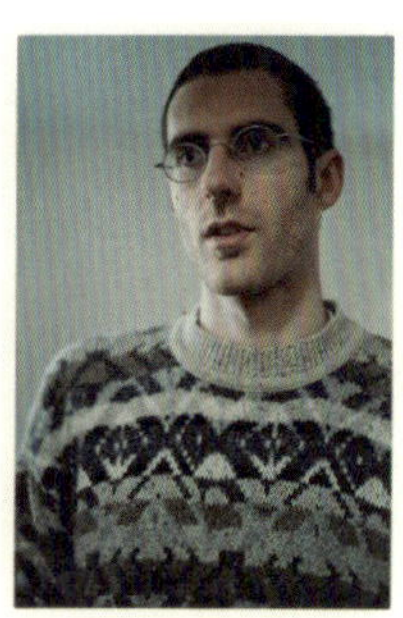

Plate 328
(Cliché of a Man, Portrait)

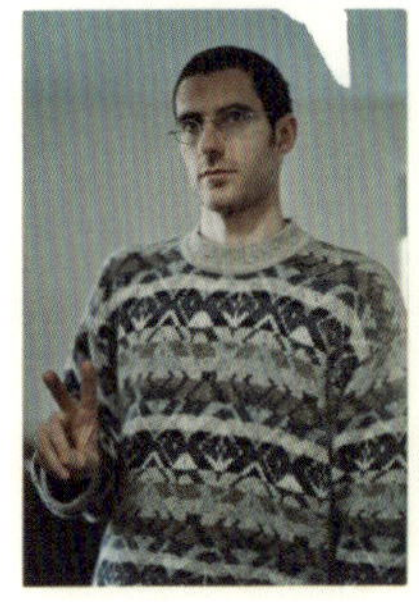

Plate 329
(Cliché of a Man, Portrait)

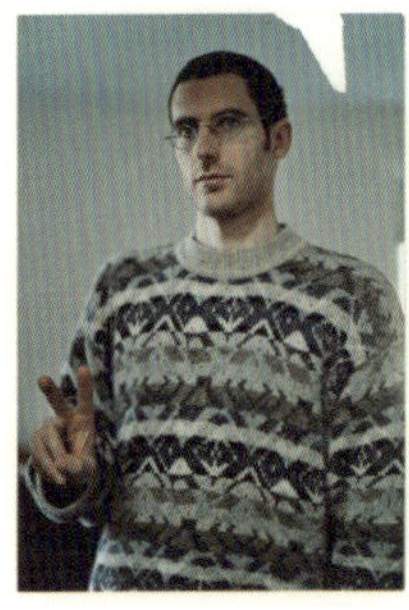

Plate 330
(Cliché of a Man, Portrait)

VI

WOMEN

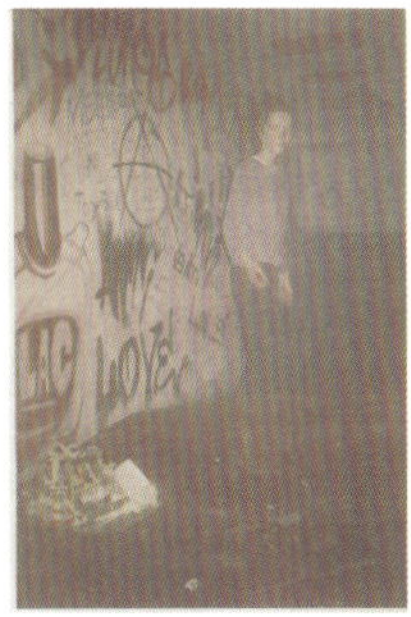

Plate 331
(Cliché of a Woman, Standing Figure) I

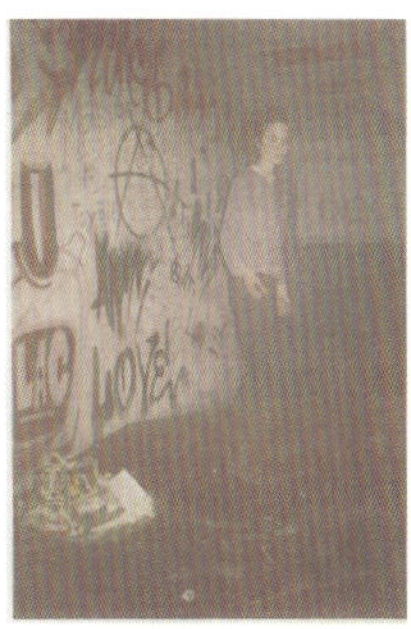

Plate 332
(Cliché of a Woman, Standing Figure) I

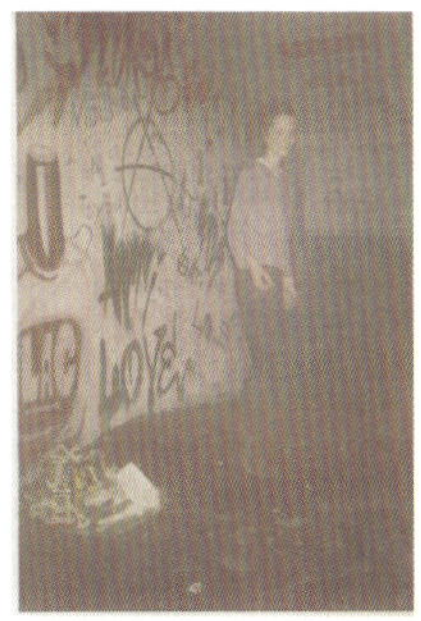

Plate 333
(Cliché of a Woman, Standing Figure) I

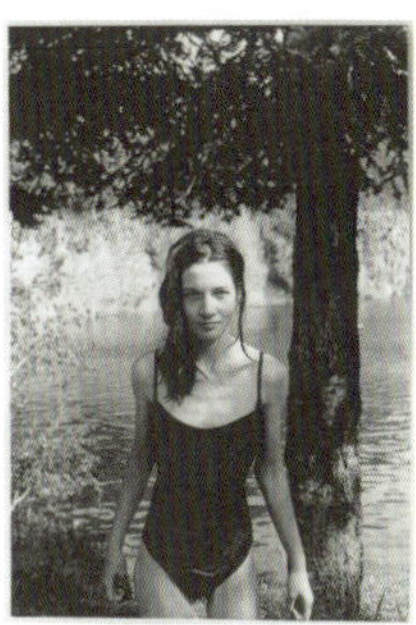

Plate 334
(Cliché of a Woman, Standing Figure, at the Lake)

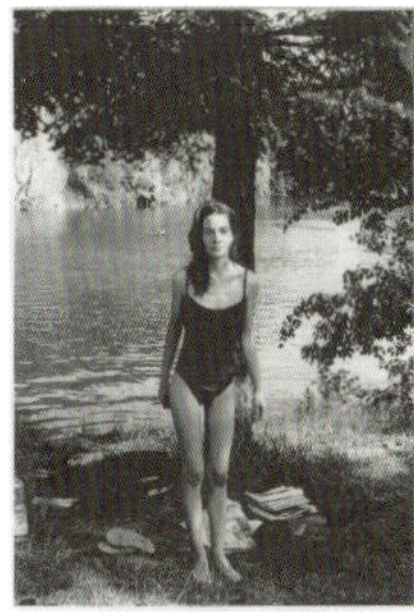

Plate 335
(Cliché of a Woman, Standing Figure, at the Lake)

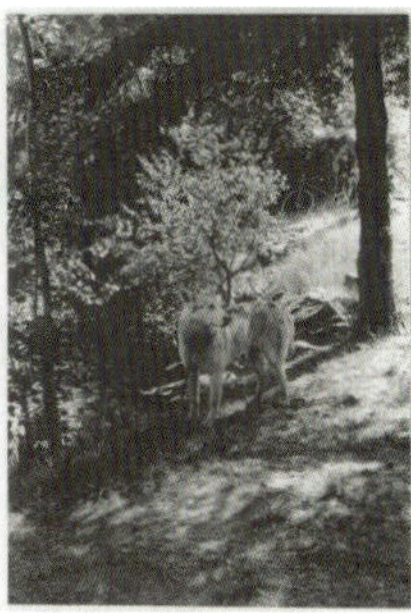

Plate 336
(Cliché of a Woman, Standing Figure, at the Lake)

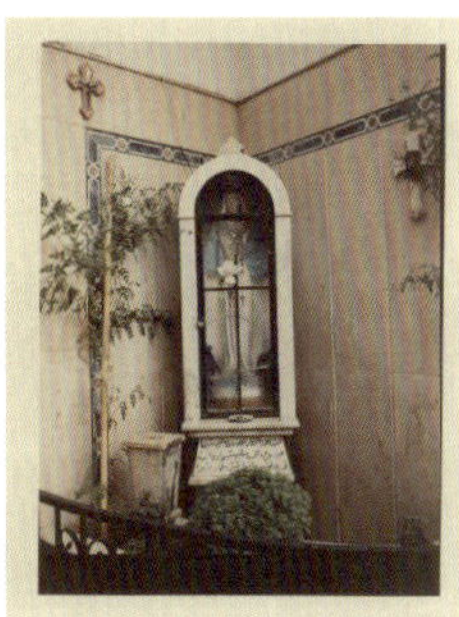

Plate 337
(Cliché of a Woman, Mary) I

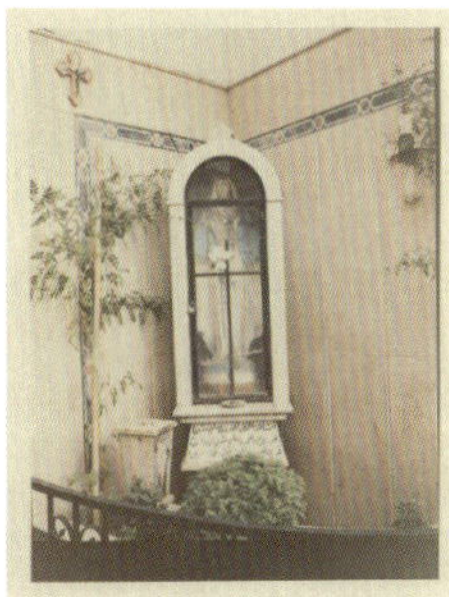

Plate 338
(Cliché of a Woman, Mary) I

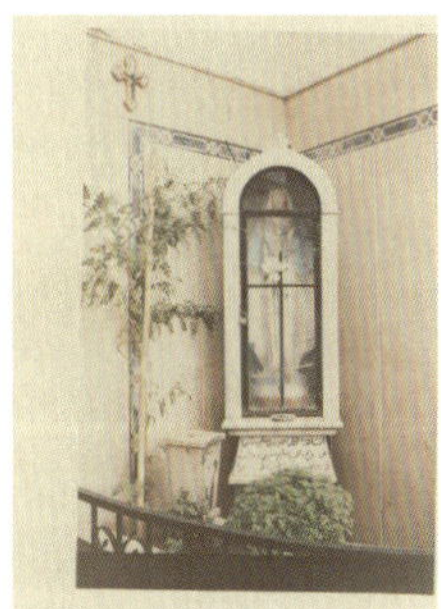

Plate 339
(Cliché of a Woman, Mary) I

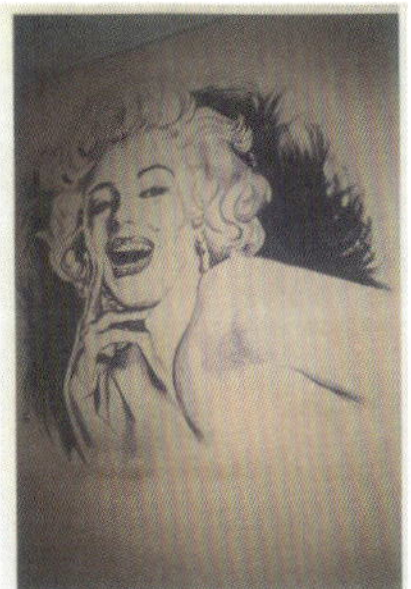

Plate 340
(Cliché of a Woman, Marilyn)

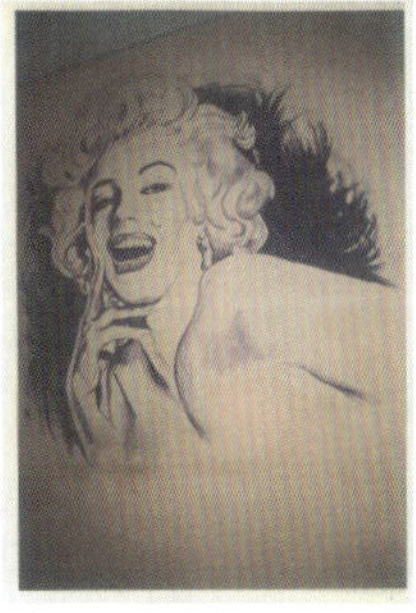

Plate 341
(Cliché of a Woman, Marilyn)

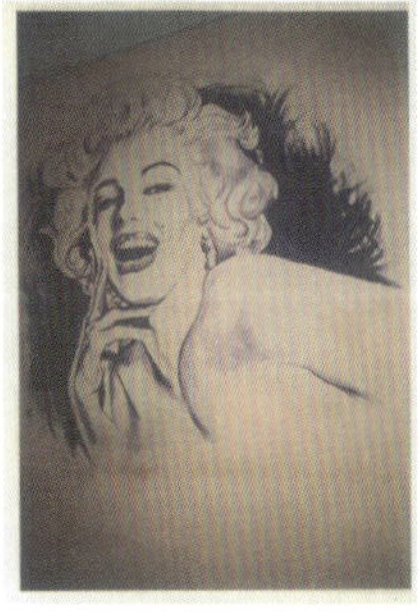

Plate 342
(Cliché of a Woman, Marilyn)

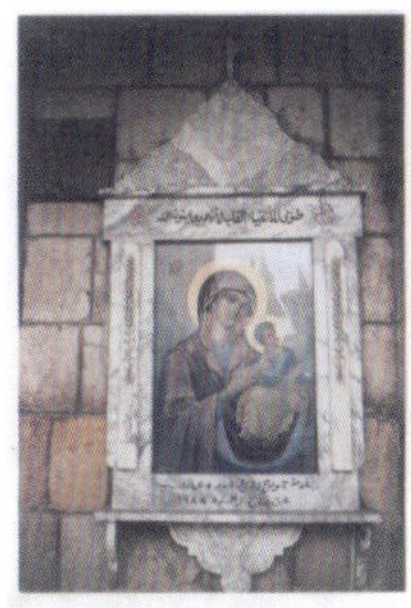

Plate 343
(Cliché of a Woman, Icon)

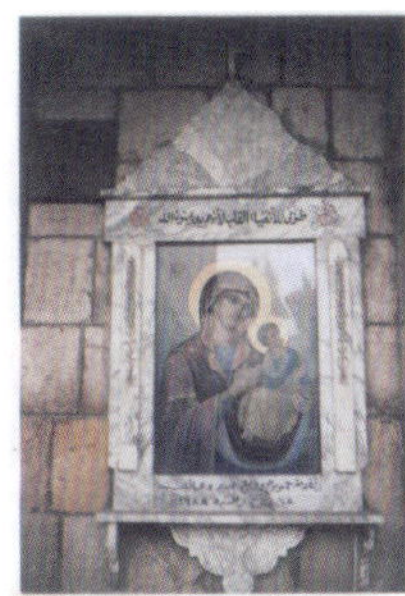

Plate 344
(Cliché of a Woman, Icon)

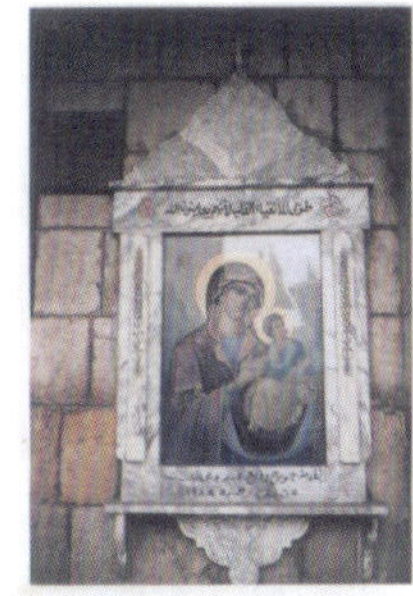

Plate 345
(Cliché of a Woman, Icon)

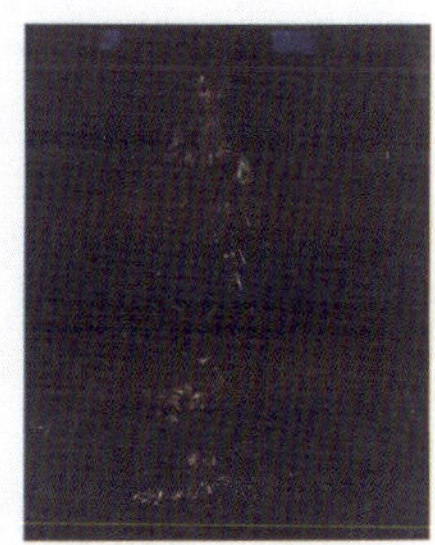

Plate 346
(Cliché of a Woman, Mary) II

Plate 347
(Cliché of a Woman, Mary) II

Plate 348
(Cliché of a Woman, Mary) II

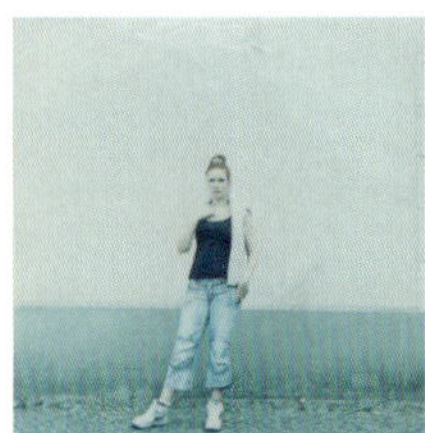

Plate 349
(Cliché of a Woman, Standing Figure) II

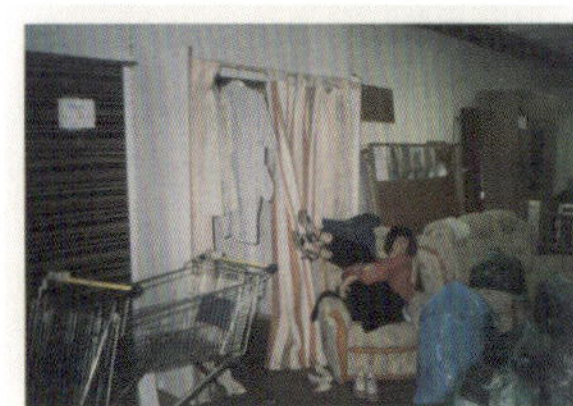

Plate 352
(Cliché of a Woman, Standing Figure,
in a Shop)

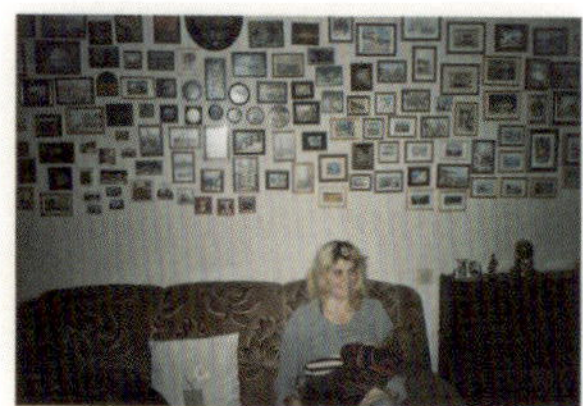

Plate 355
(Cliché of a Woman, Sitting Figure)

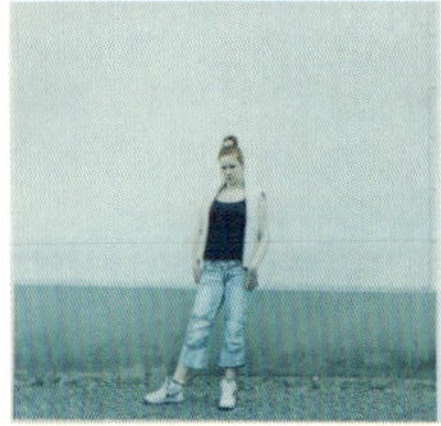

Plate 350
(Cliché of a Woman, Standing Figure) II

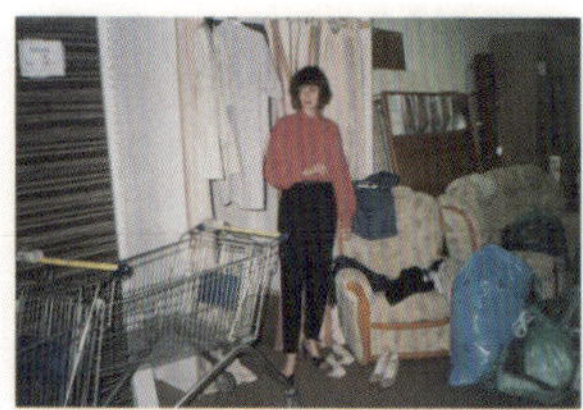

Plate 353
(Cliché of a Woman, Standing Figure,
in a Shop)

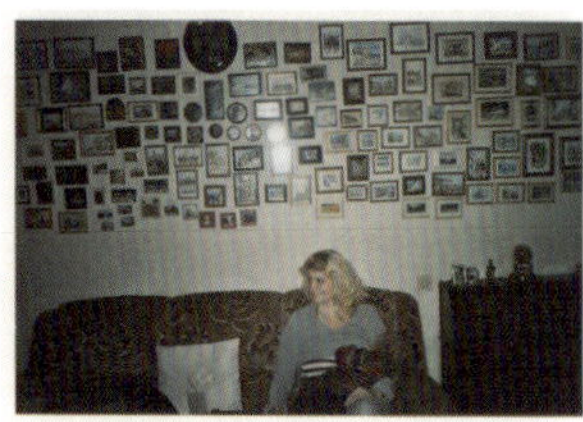

Plate 356
(Cliché of a Woman, Sitting Figure)

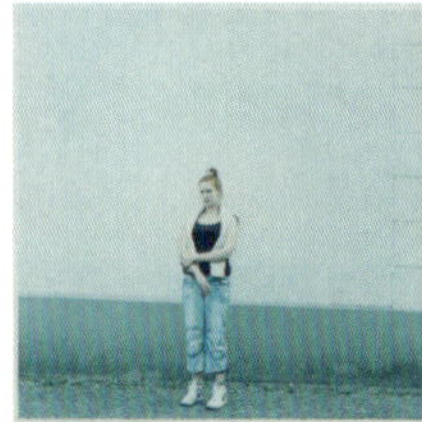

Plate 351
(Cliché of a Woman, Standing Figure) II

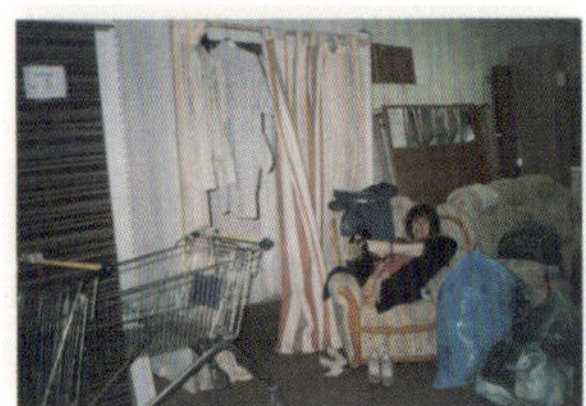

Plate 354
(Cliché of a Woman, Standing Figure,
in a Shop)

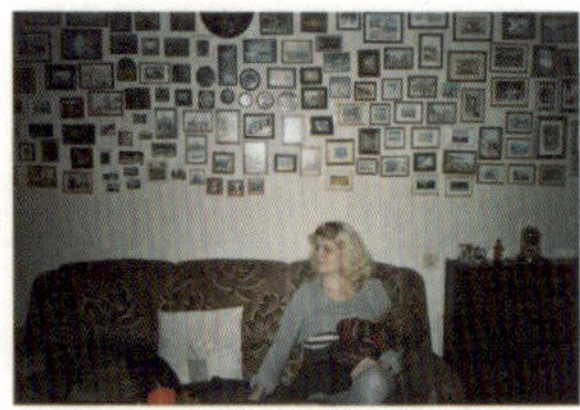

Plate 357
(Cliché of a Woman, Sitting Figure)

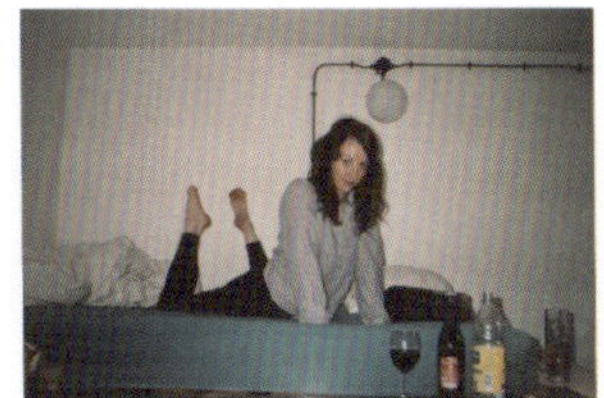

Plate 358
(Cliché of a Woman, Lying Figure)

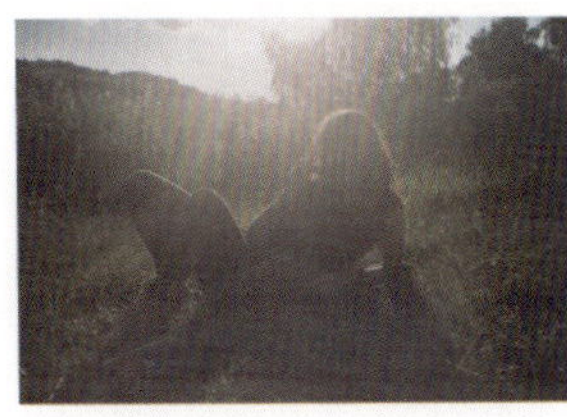

Plate 361
(Cliché of a Woman, Lying Figure,
in Green Grass)

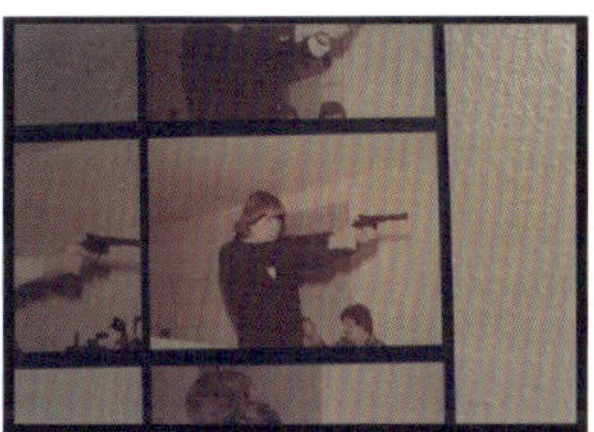

Plate 364
(Cliché of a Woman, Shooting)

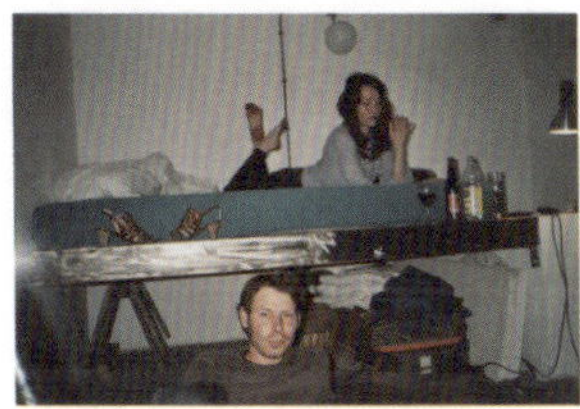

Plate 359
(Cliché of a Woman, Lying Figure)

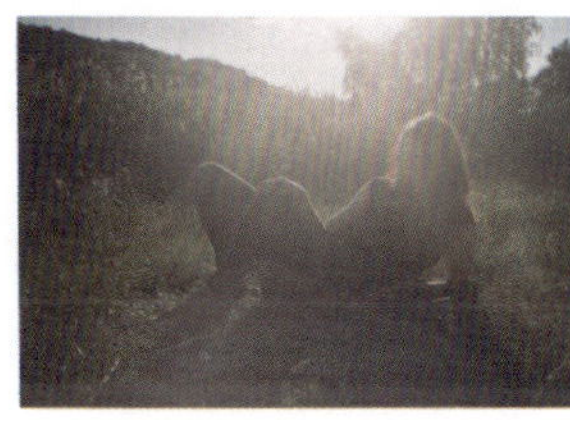

Plate 362
(Cliché of a Woman, Lying Figure,
in Green Grass)

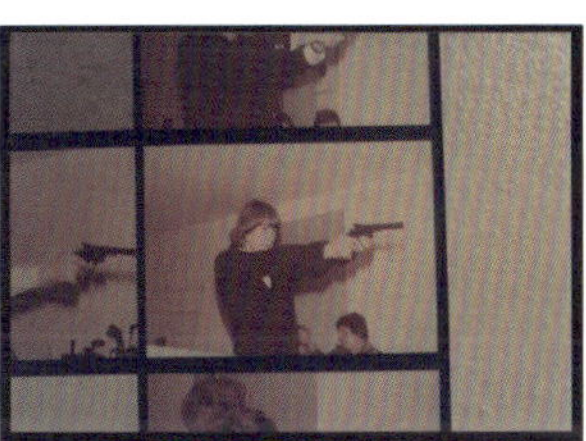

Plate 365
(Cliché of a Woman, Shooting)

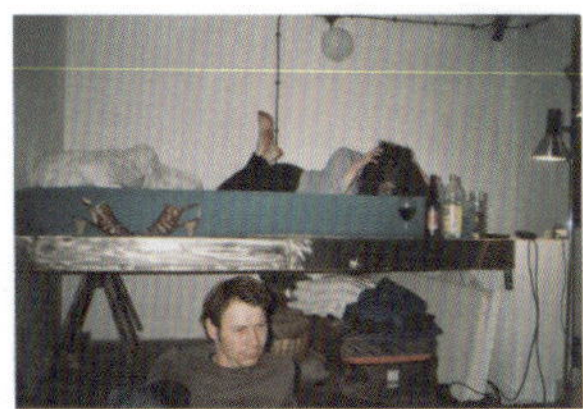

Plate 360
(Cliché of a Woman, Lying Figure)

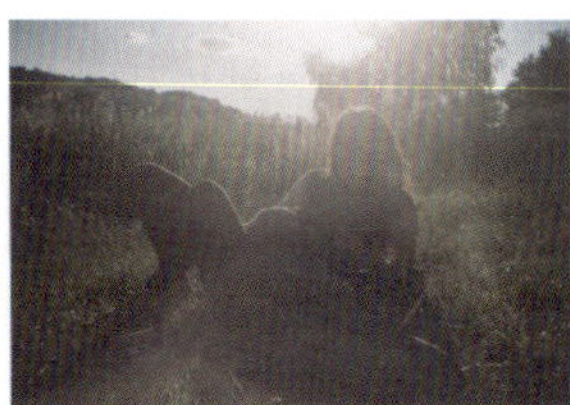

Plate 363
(Cliché of a Woman, Lying Figure,
in Green Grass)

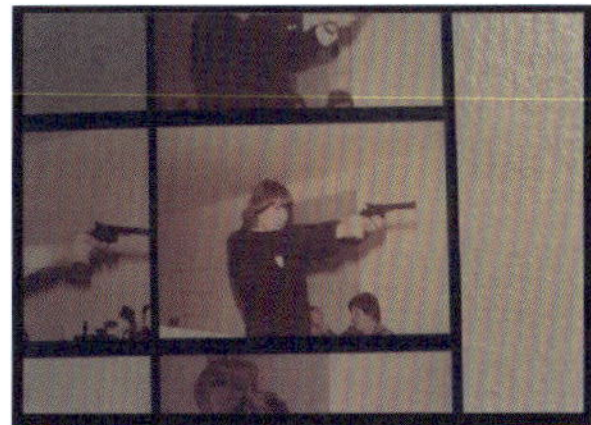

Plate 366
(Cliché of a Woman, Shooting)

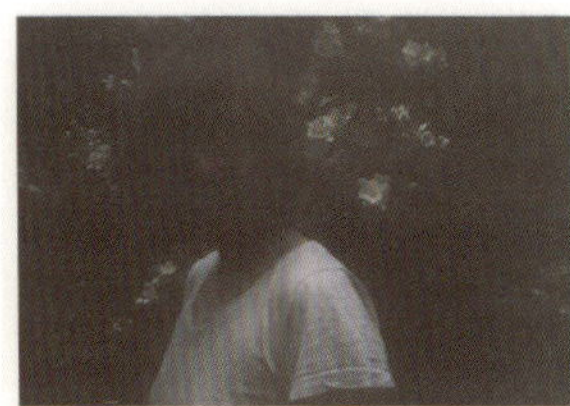

Plate 367
(Cliché of a Woman, Portrait, under
a Bush)

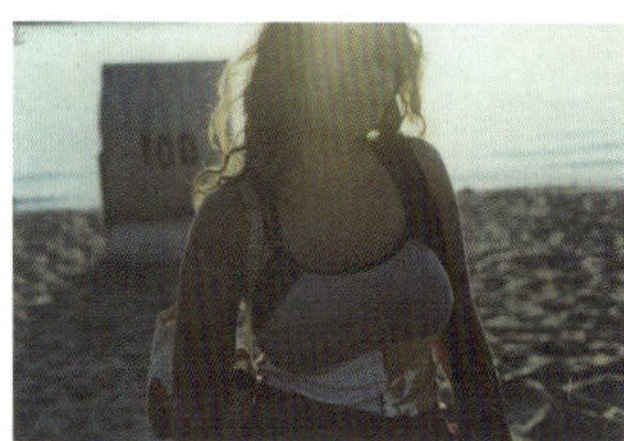

Plate 370
(Cliché of a Woman, on the Beach)

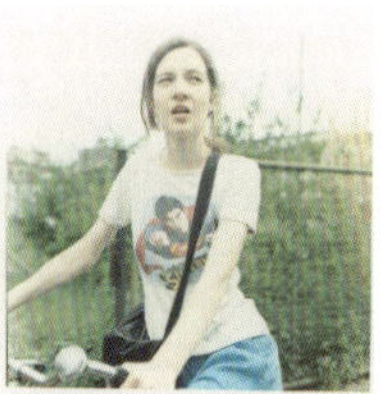

Plate 373
(Cliché of a Woman)

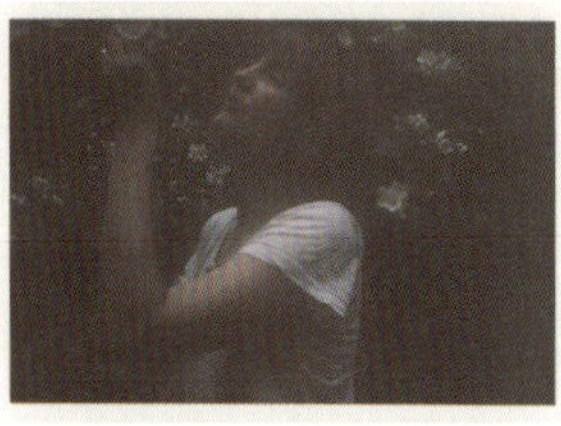

Plate 368
(Cliché of a Woman, Portrait, under
a Bush)

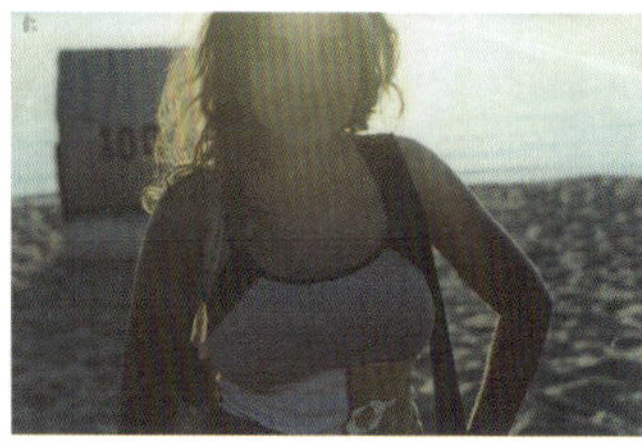

Plate 371
(Cliché of a Woman, on the Beach)

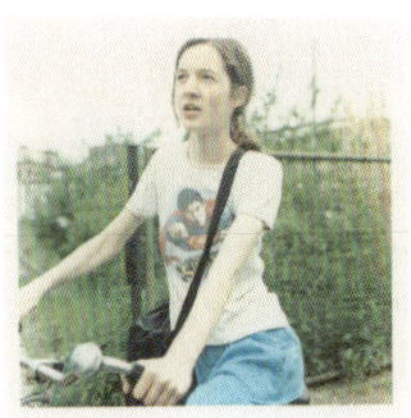

Plate 374
(Cliché of a Woman)

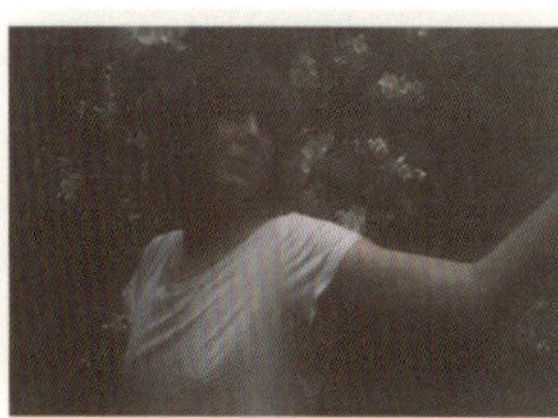

Plate 369
(Cliché of a Woman, Portrait, under
a Bush)

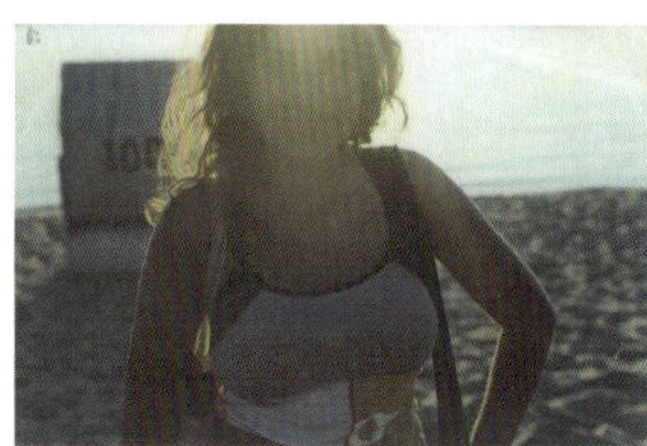

Plate 372
(Cliché of a Woman, on the Beach)

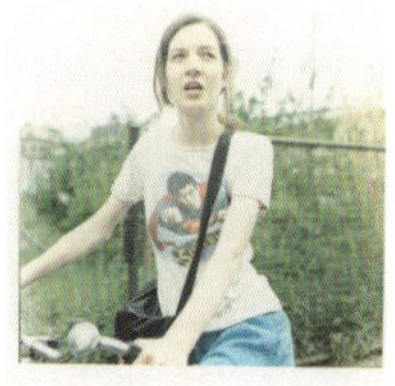

Plate 375
(Cliché of a Woman)

VII

CITY

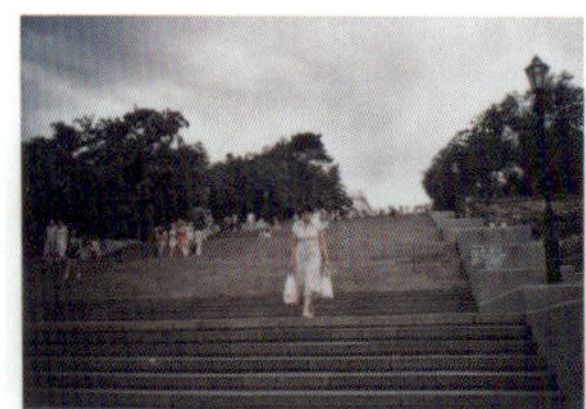

Plate 376
(Cliché of a City) I

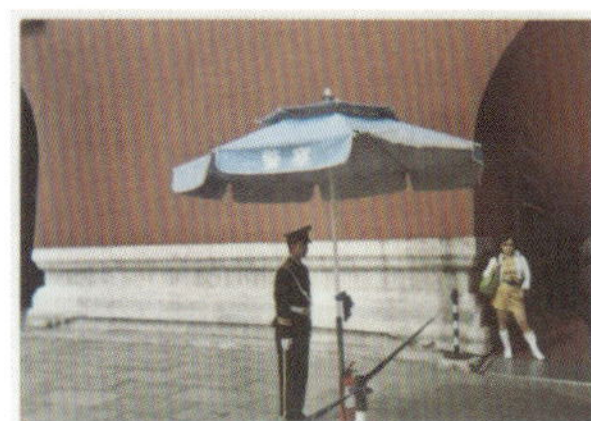

Plate 379
(Cliché of a City) II

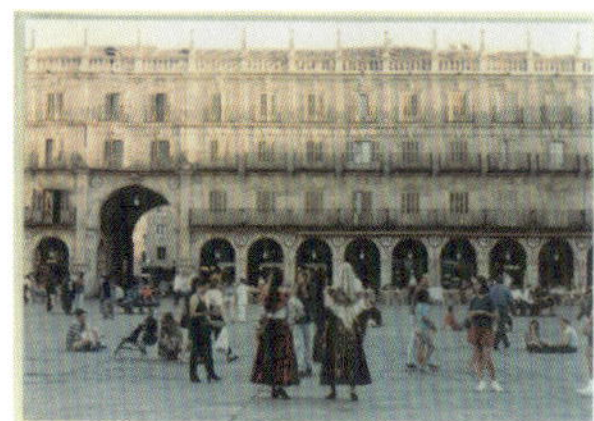

Plate 382
(Cliché of a City) III

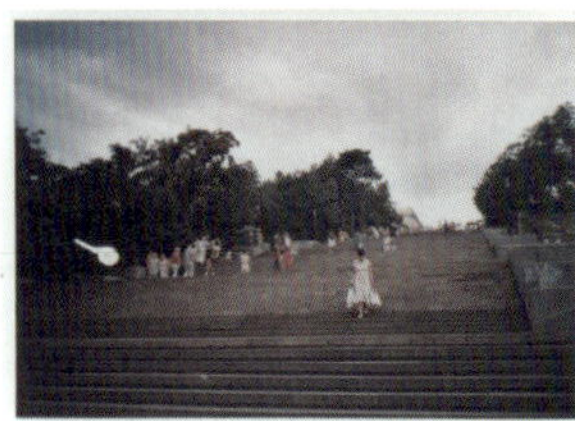

Plate 377
(Cliché of a City) I

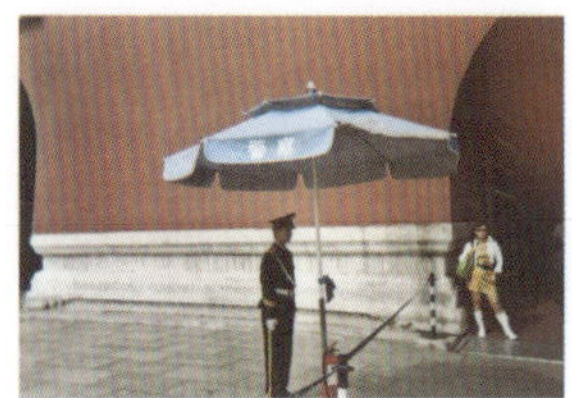

Plate 380
(Cliché of a City) II

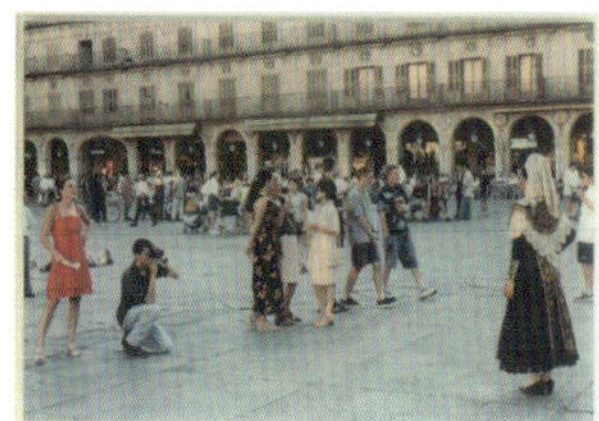

Plate 383
(Cliché of a City) III

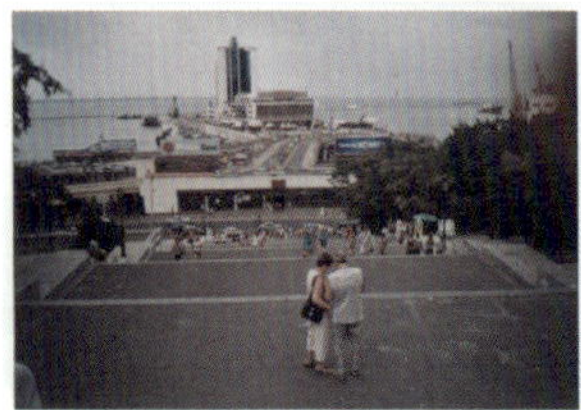

Plate 378
(Cliché of a City) I

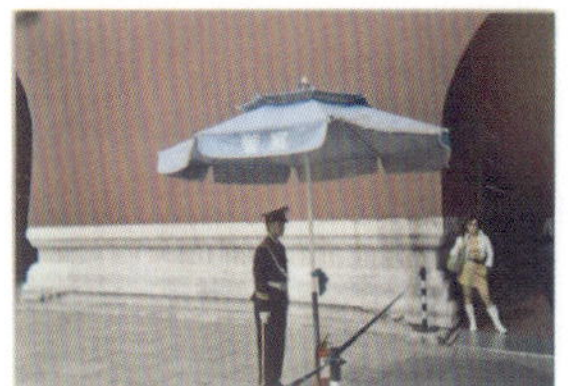

Plate 381
(Cliché of a City) II

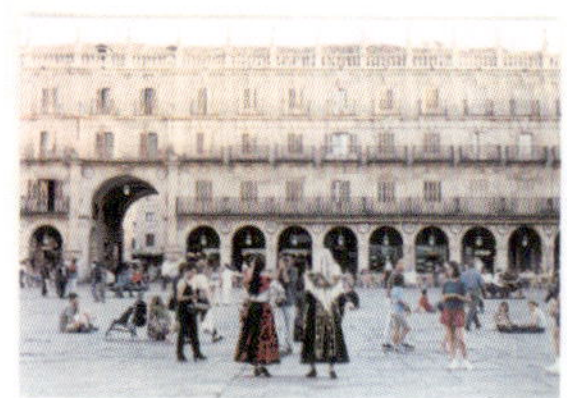

Plate 384
(Cliché of a City) III

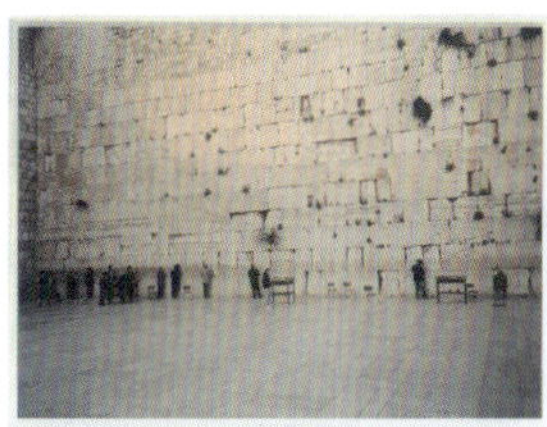

Plate 385
(Cliché of a City) IV

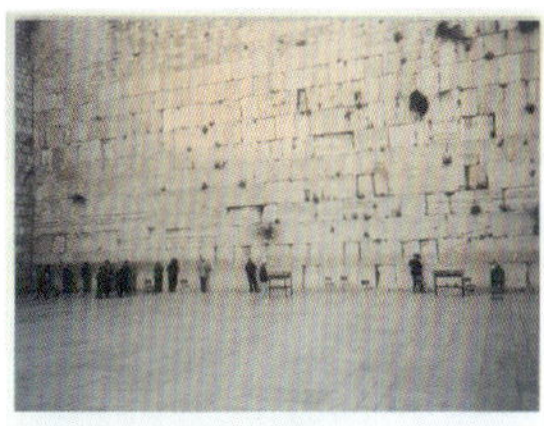

Plate 386
(Cliché of a City) IV

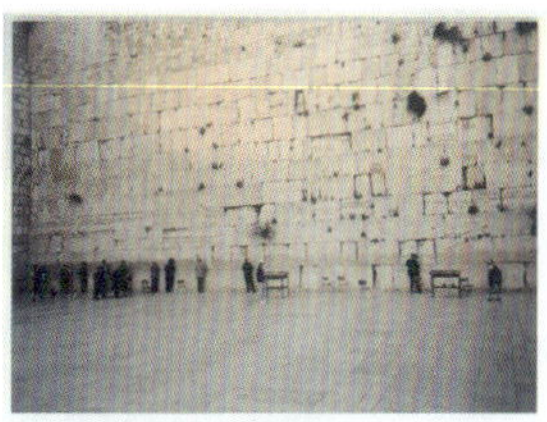

Plate 387
(Cliché of a City) IV

VIII

CIRCUS

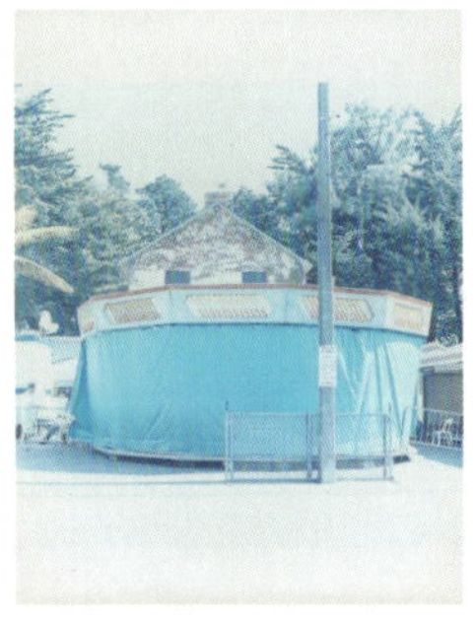
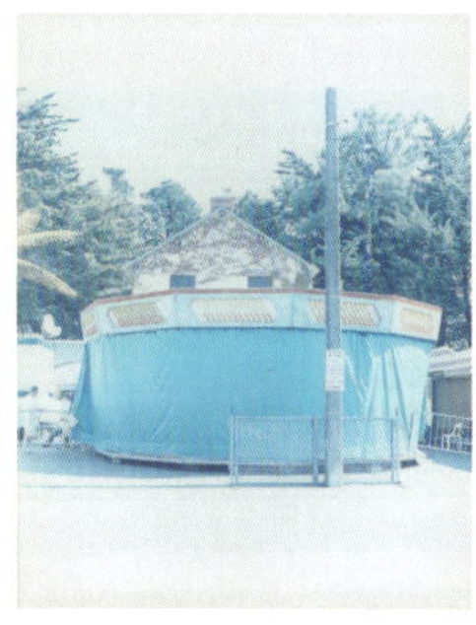
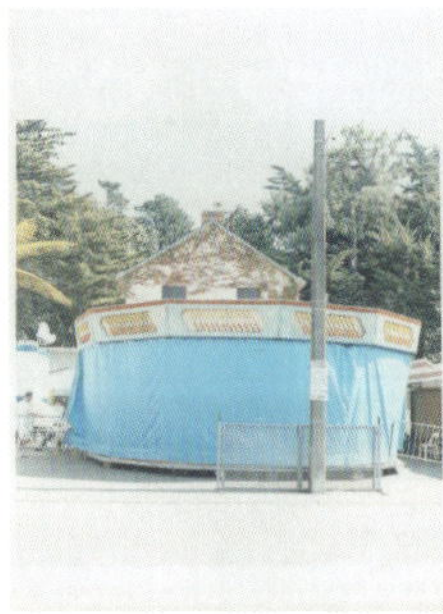

Plate 388
(Cliché of a Caroussel) I

Plate 389
(Cliché of a Caroussel) I

Plate 390
(Cliché of a Caroussel) I

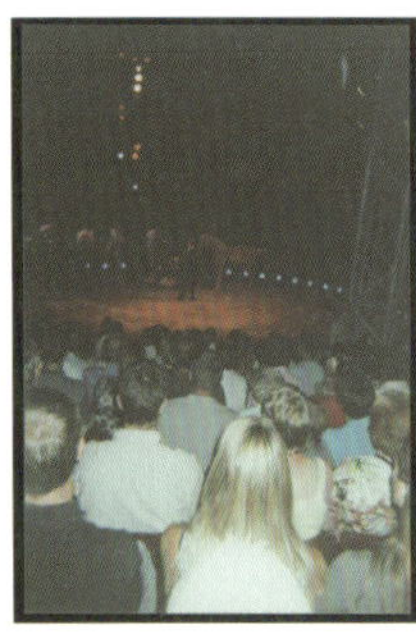
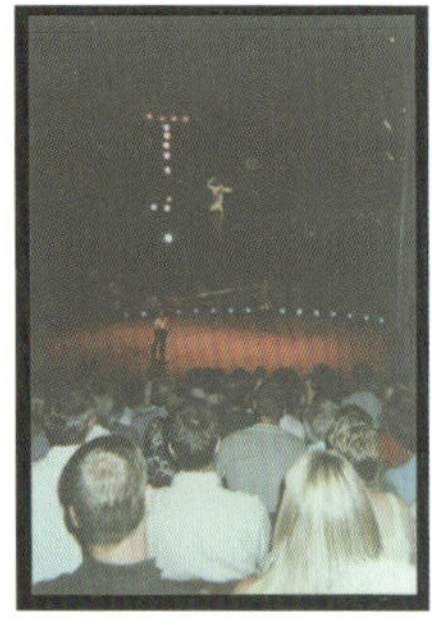
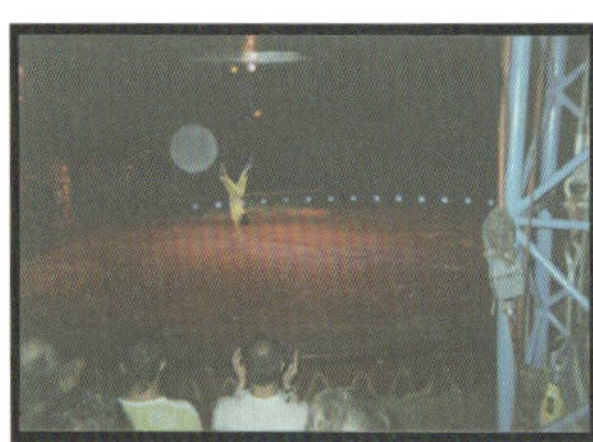

Plate 391
(Cliché of a Circus) I

Plate 392
(Cliché of a Circus) I

Plate 393
(Cliché of a Circus) I

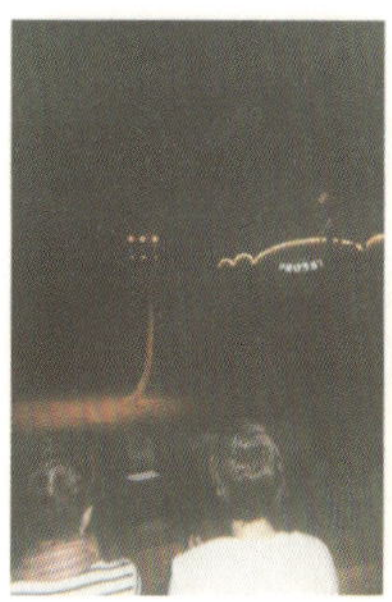

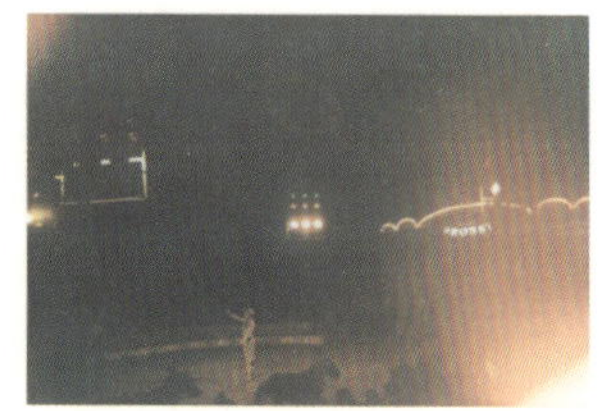

Plate 394
(Cliché of a Circus) II

Plate 395
(Cliché of a Circus) II

Plate 396
(Cliché of a Circus) II

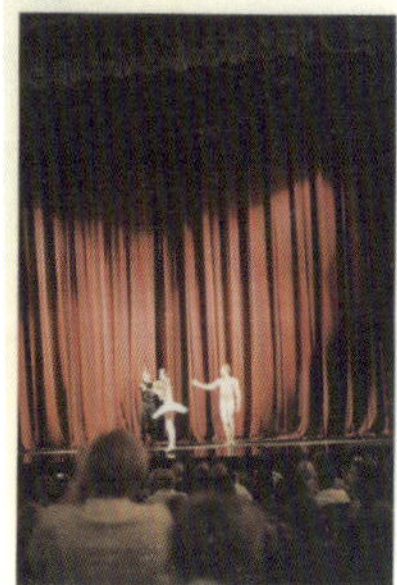

Plate 397
(Cliché of a Ballet) I

Plate 398
(Cliché of a Ballet) I

Plate 399
(Cliché of a Ballet) I

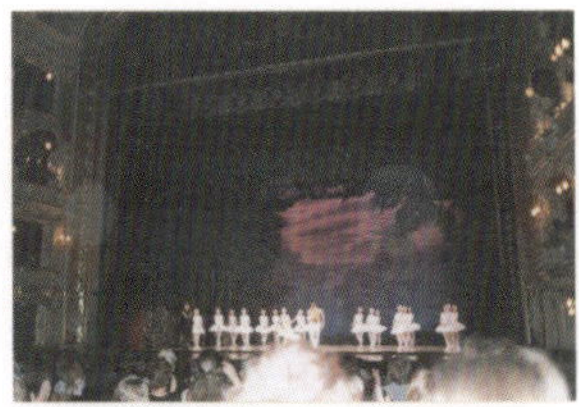

Plate 400
(Cliché of a Ballet) II

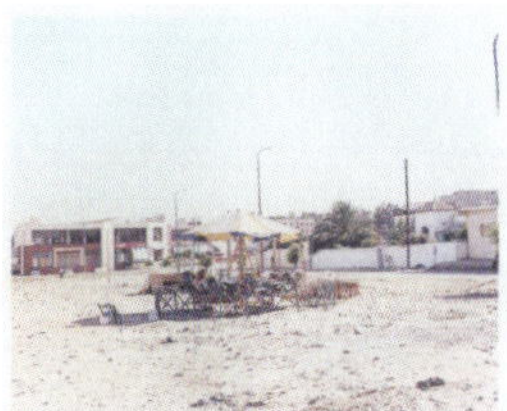

Plate 403
(Cliché of a Caroussel) II

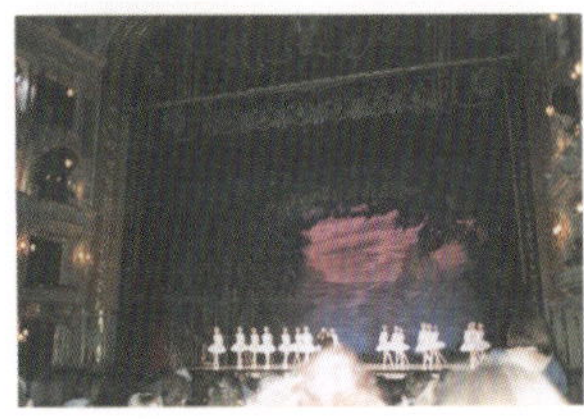

Plate 401
(Cliché of a Ballet) II

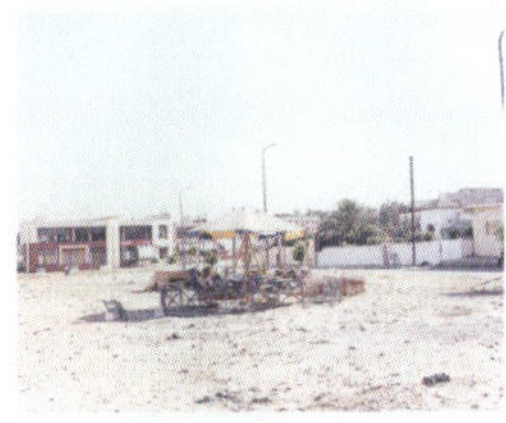

Plate 404
(Cliché of a Caroussel) II

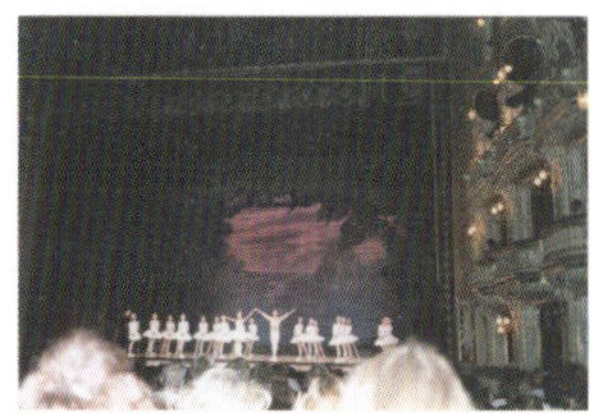

Plate 402
(Cliché of a Ballet) II

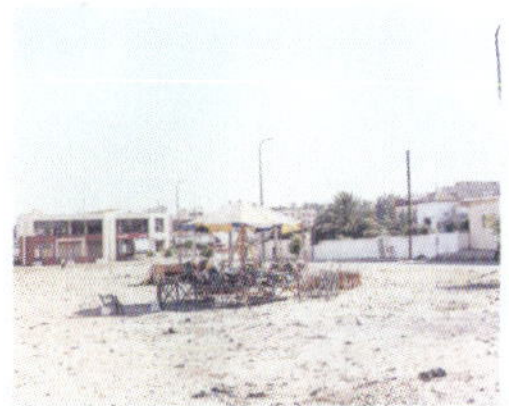

Plate 405
(Cliché of a Caroussel) II

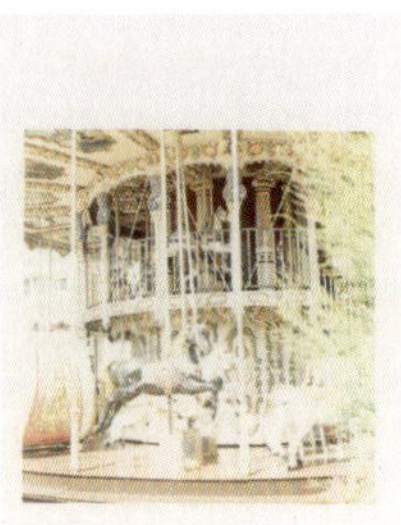

Plate 406
(Cliché of a Caroussel) III

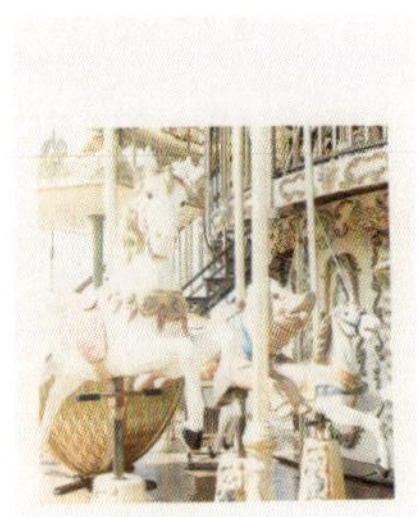

Plate 407
(Cliché of a Caroussel) III

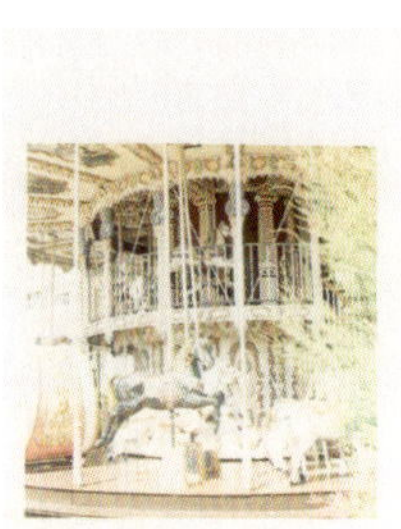

Plate 408
(Cliché of a Caroussel) III

IX

GROUPS / PAIRS

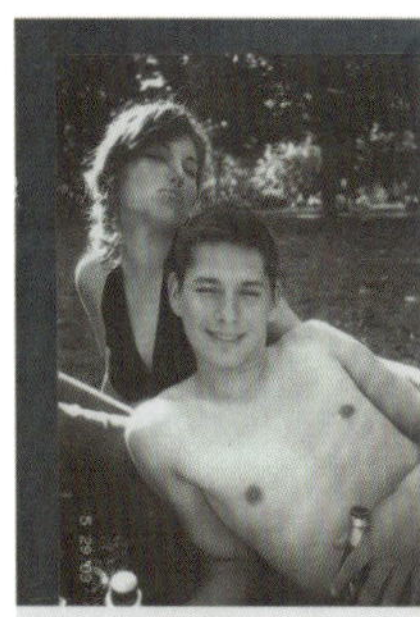

Plate 409
(Cliché of a Couple) I

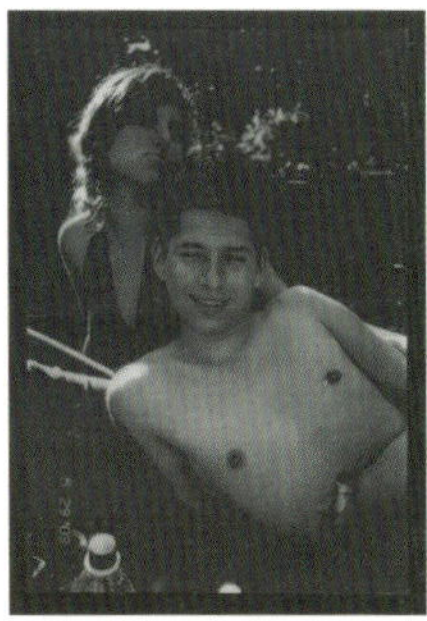

Plate 410
(Cliché of a Couple) I

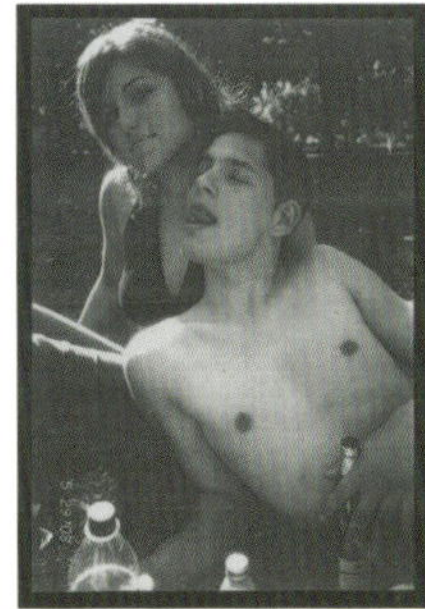

Plate 411
(Cliché of a Couple) I

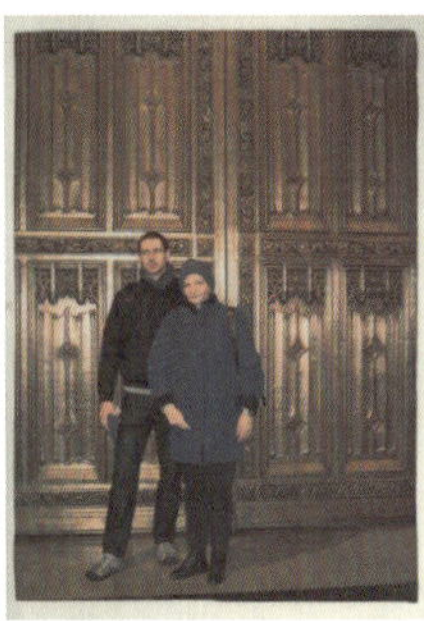

Plate 412
(Cliché of a Couple) II

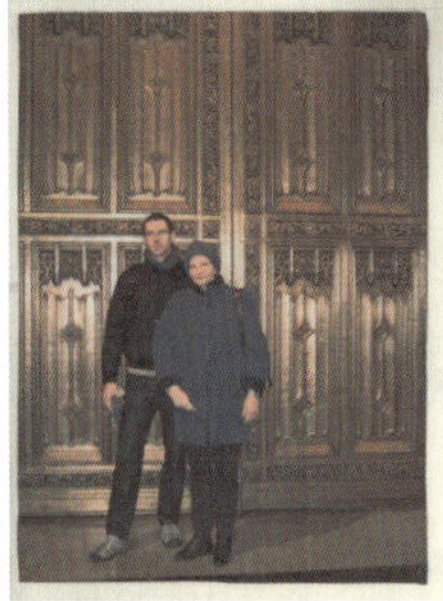

Plate 413
(Cliché of a Couple) II

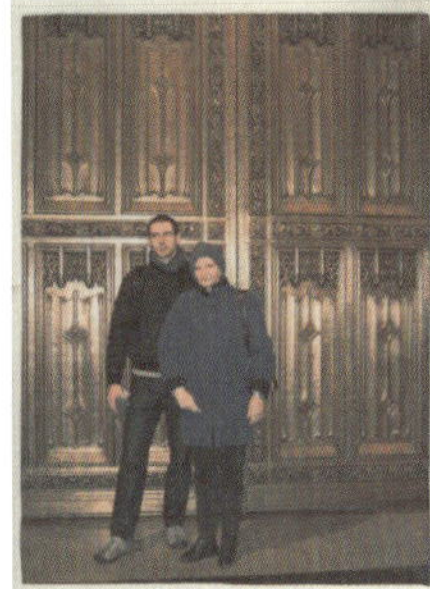

Plate 414
(Cliché of a Couple) II

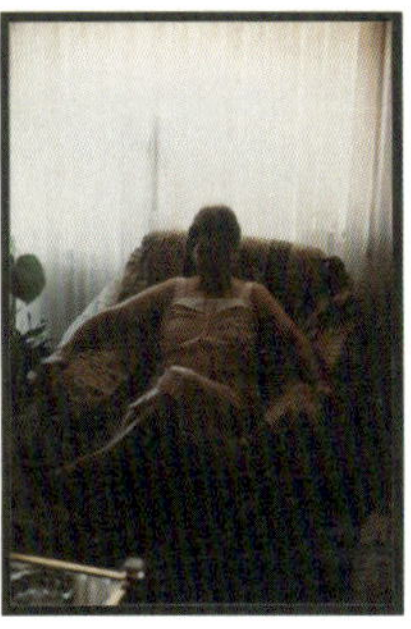

Plate 415
(Cliché of a Group, Family)

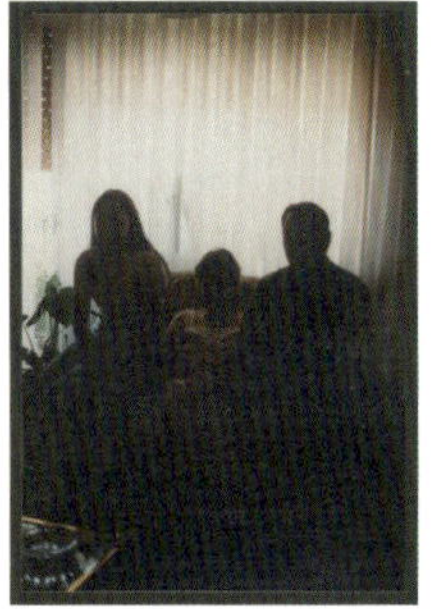

Plate 416
(Cliché of a Group, Family)

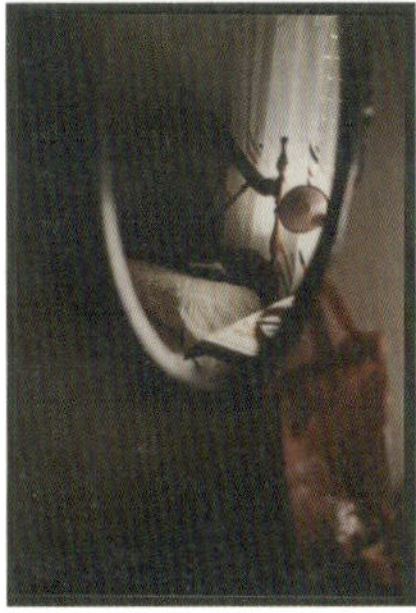

Plate 417
(Cliché of a Group, Family)

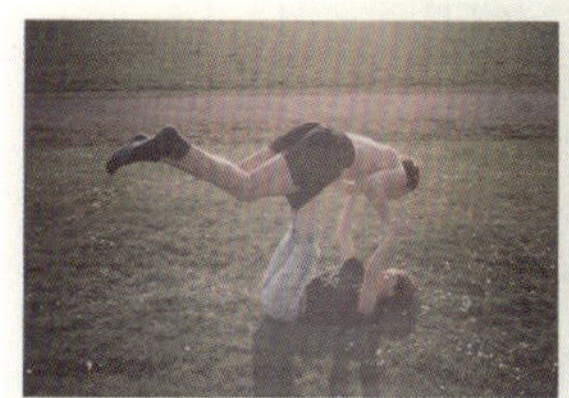

Plate 418
(Cliché of a Couple) III

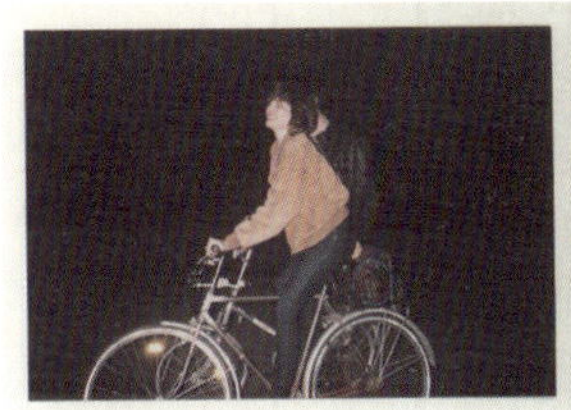

Plate 421
(Cliché of a Couple) IV

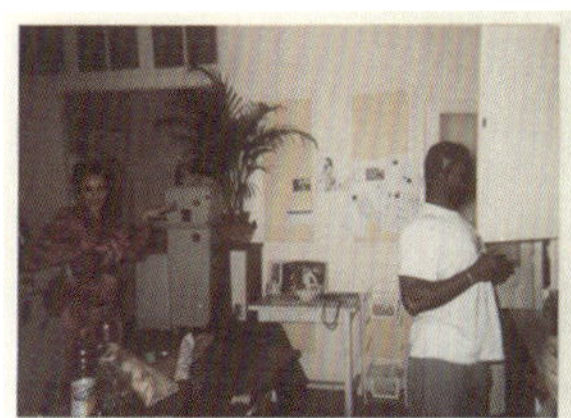

Plate 424
(Cliché of a Couple) V

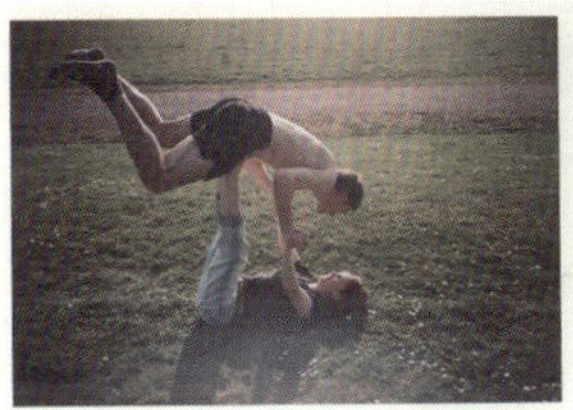

Plate 419
(Cliché of a Couple) III

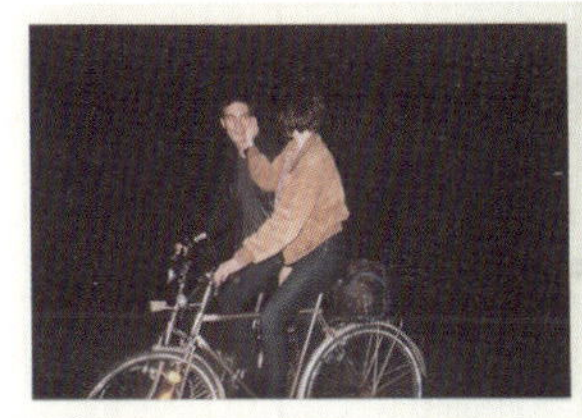

Plate 422
(Cliché of a Couple) IV

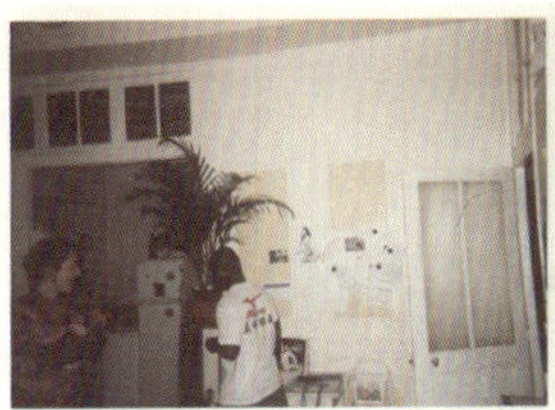

Plate 425
(Cliché of a Couple) V

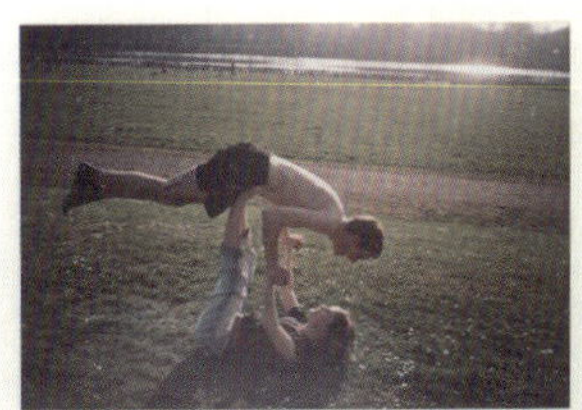

Plate 420
(Cliché of a Couple) III

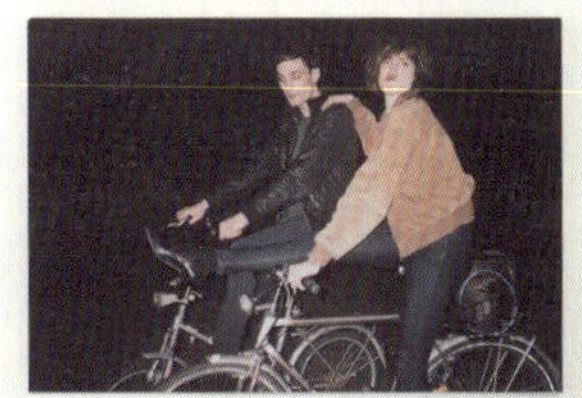

Plate 423
(Cliché of a Couple) IV

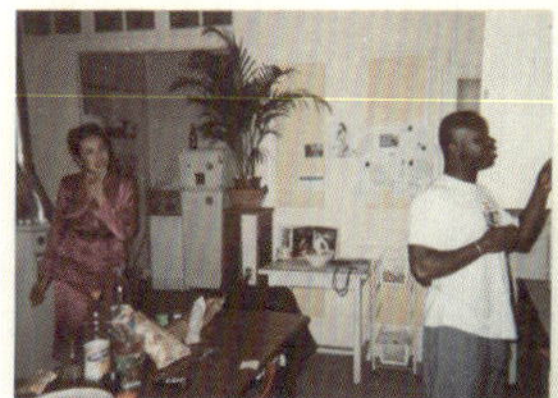

Plate 426
(Cliché of a Couple) V

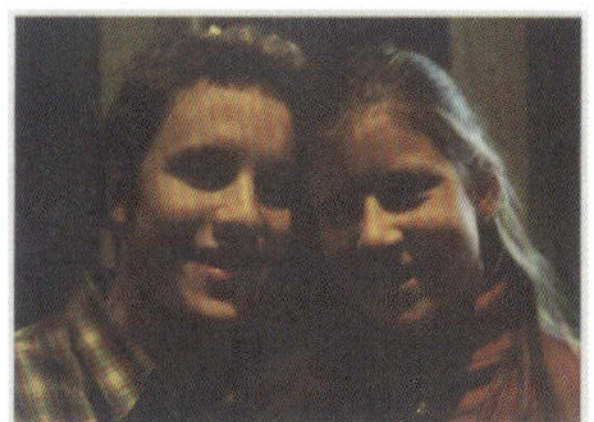

Plate 427
(Cliché of a Couple) VI

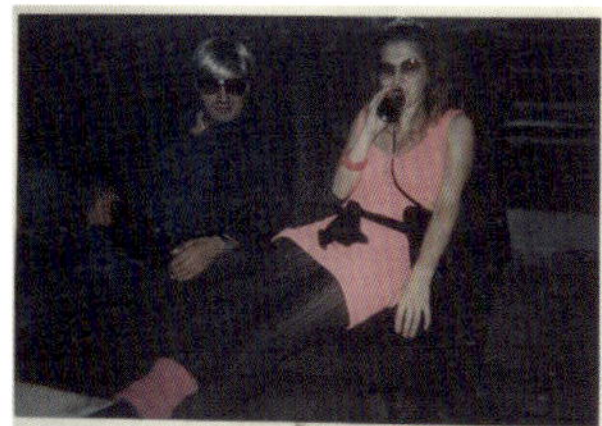

Plate 430
(Cliché of a Couple) VII

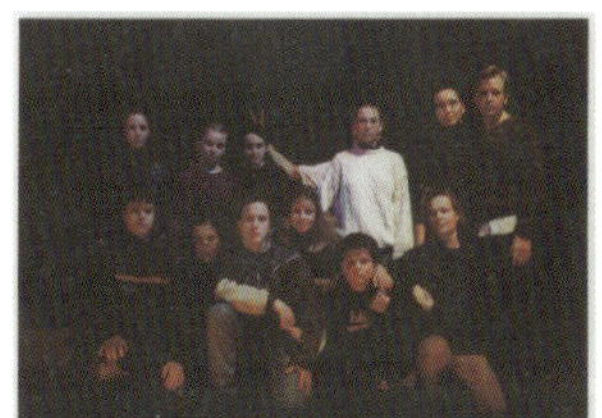

Plate 433
(Cliché of a Group)

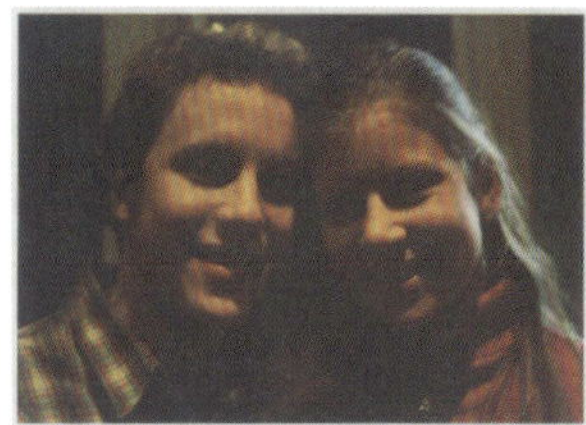

Plate 428
(Cliché of a Couple) VI

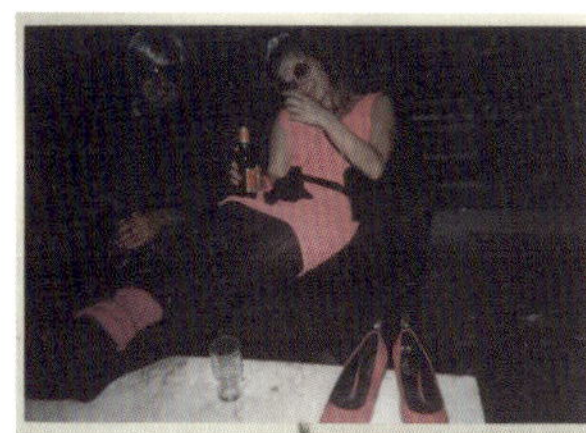

Plate 431
(Cliché of a Couple) VII

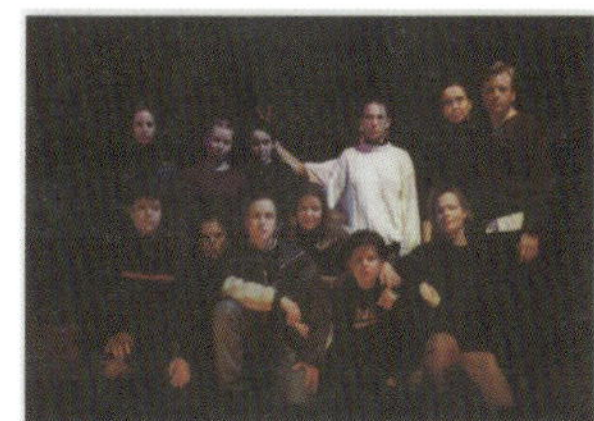

Plate 434
(Cliché of a Group)

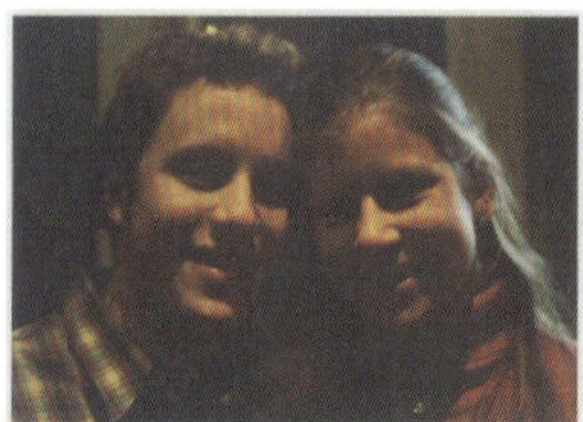

Plate 429
(Cliché of a Couple) VI

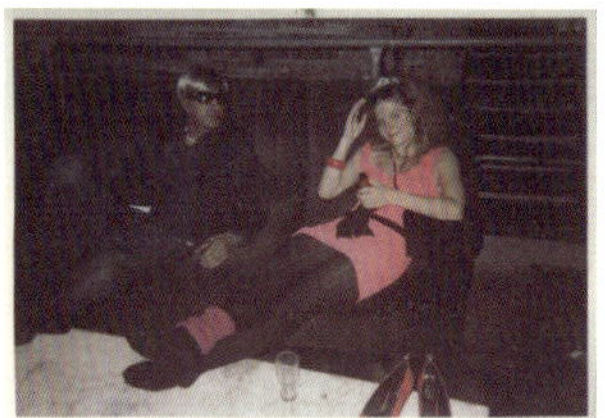

Plate 432
(Cliché of a Couple) VII

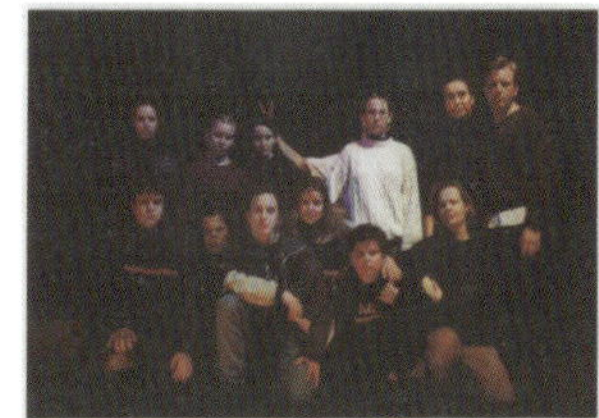

Plate 435
(Cliché of a Group)

X

CHILDREN

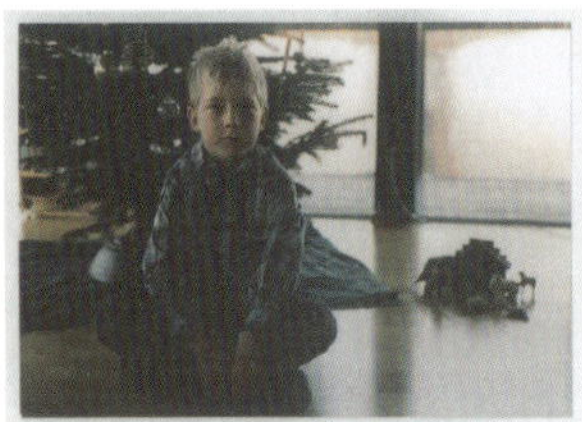

Plate 436
(Cliché of a Child, Little Boy, under a Christmas Tree)

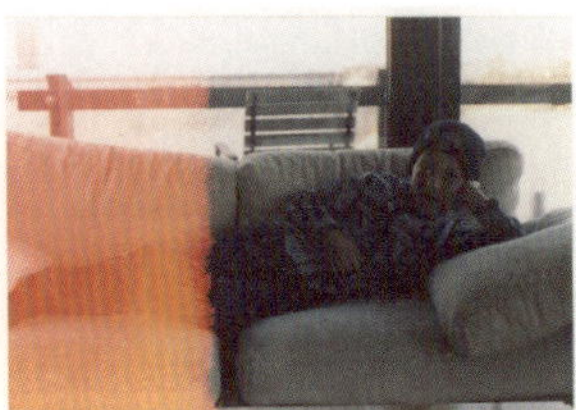

Plate 439
(Cliché of a Child, Little Boy, Lying Figure)

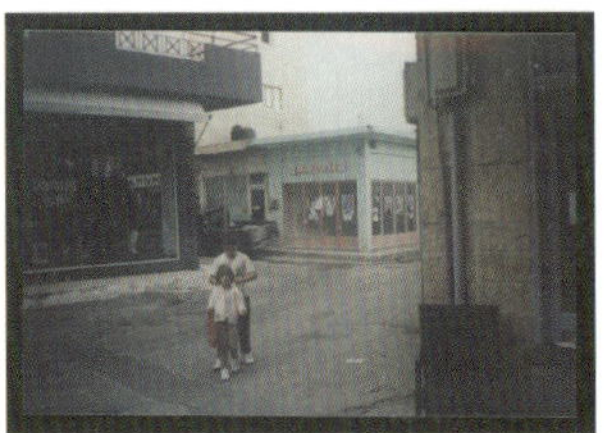

Plate 442
(Cliché of Two Children, Little Girl and Boy)

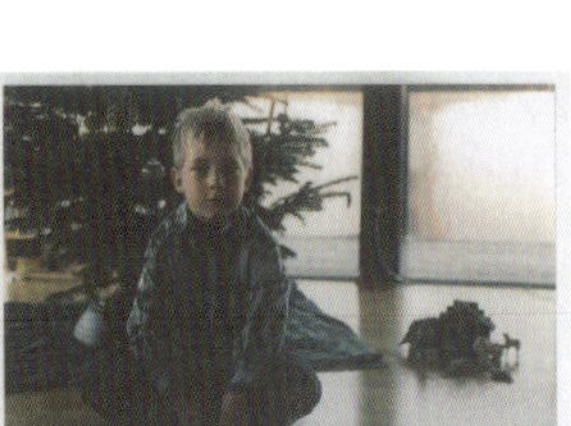

Plate 437
(Cliché of a Child, Little Boy, under a Christmas Tree)

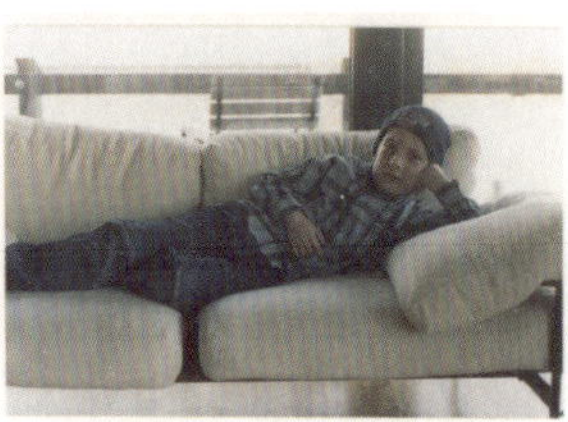

Plate 440
(Cliché of a Child, Little Boy, Lying Figure)

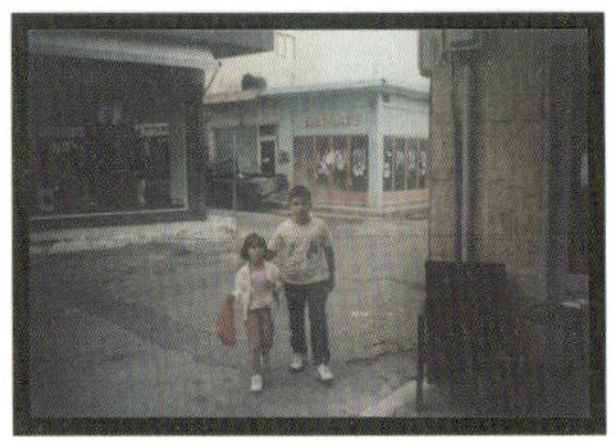

Plate 443
(Cliché of Two Children, Little Girl and Boy)

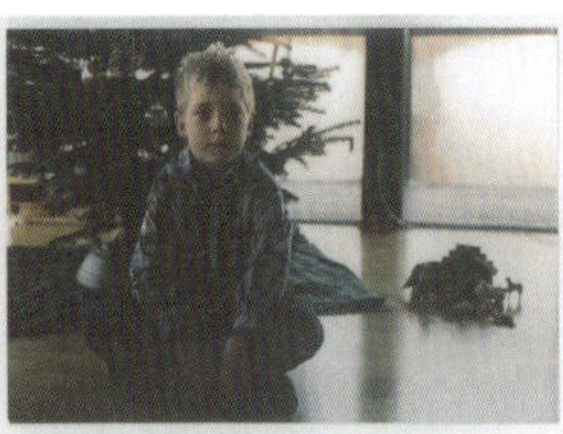

Plate 438
(Cliché of a Child, Little Boy, under a Christmas Tree)

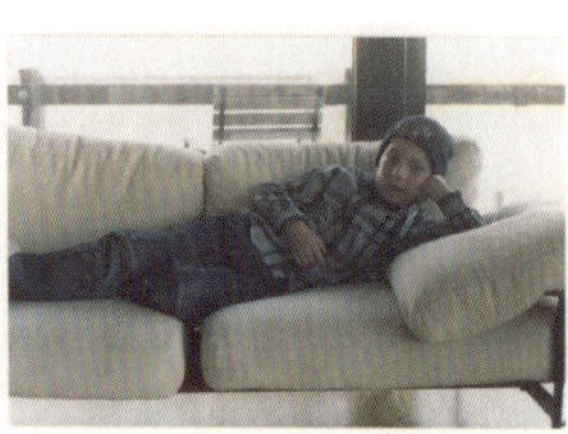

Plate 441
(Cliché of a Child, Little Boy, Lying Figure)

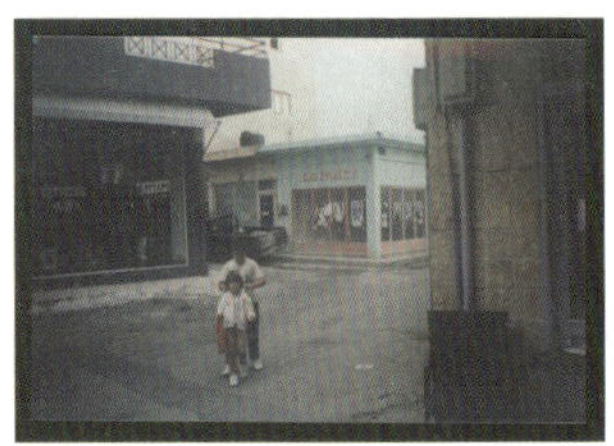

Plate 444
(Cliché of Two Children, Little Girl and Boy)

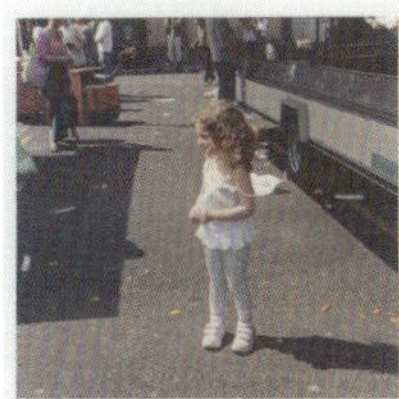

Plate 445
(Cliché of a Child, Little Girl) I

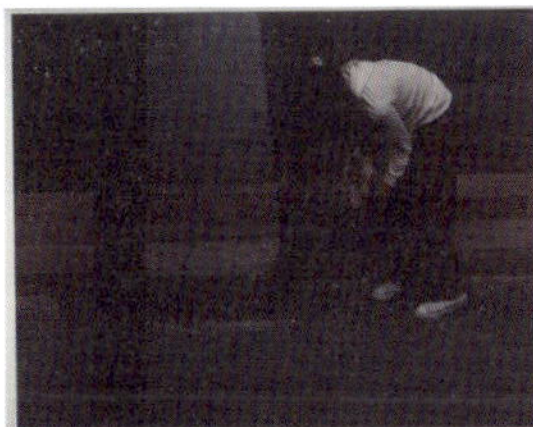

Plate 449
(Cliché of a Child, Girl, with Rabbit)

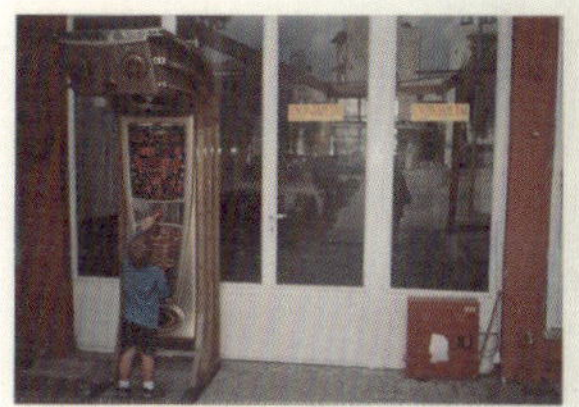

Plate 452
(Cliché of a Child, Little Boy, with
Automat)

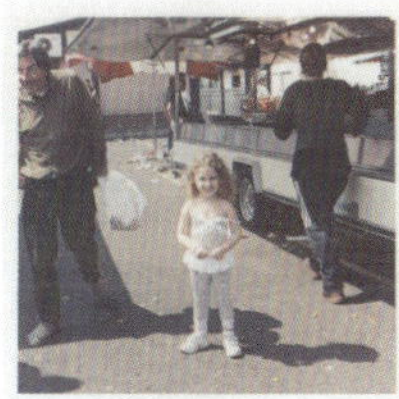

Plate 446
(Cliché of a Child, Little Girl) I

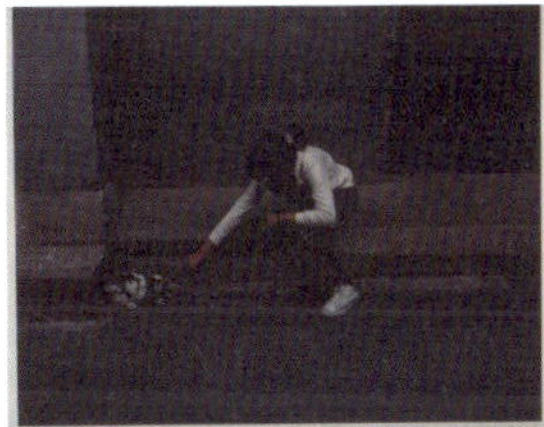

Plate 450
(Cliché of a Child, Girl, with Rabbit)

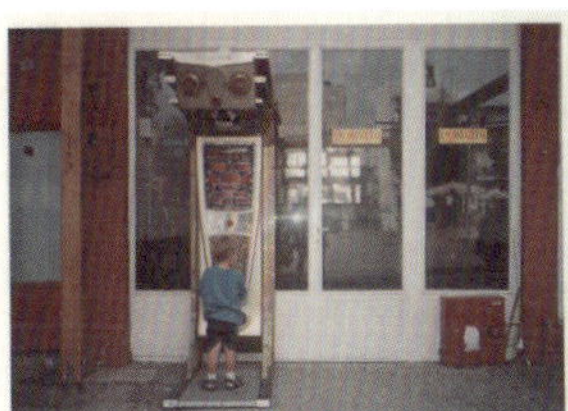

Plate 453
(Cliché of a Child, Little Boy, with
Automat)

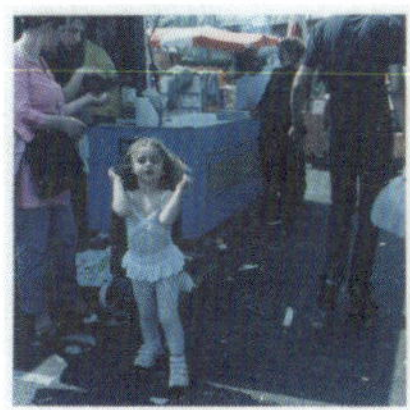

Plate 447
(Cliché of a Child, Little Girl) I

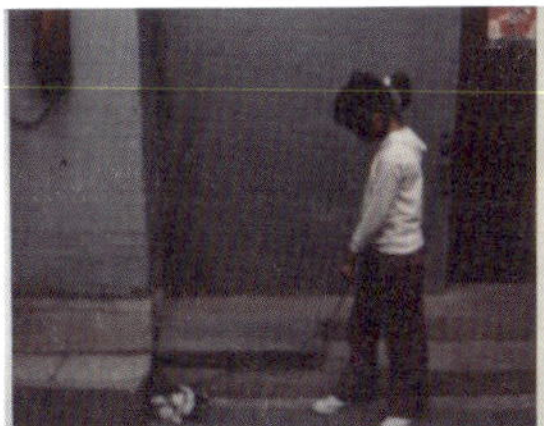

Plate 451
(Cliché of a Child, Girl, with Rabbit)

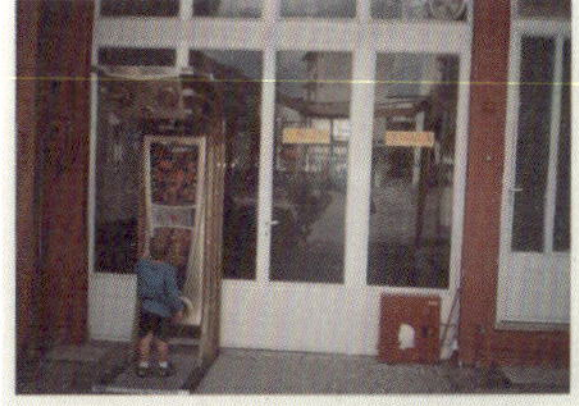

Plate 454
(Cliché of a Child, Little Boy, with
Automat)

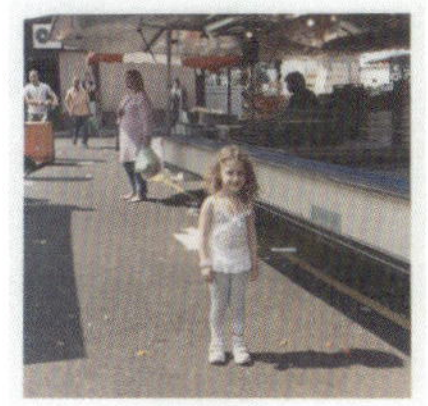

Plate 448
(Cliché of a Child, Little Girl) I

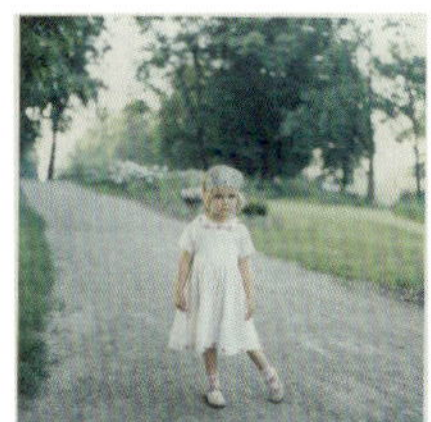

Plate 455
(Cliché of a Child, Littlle Girl) II

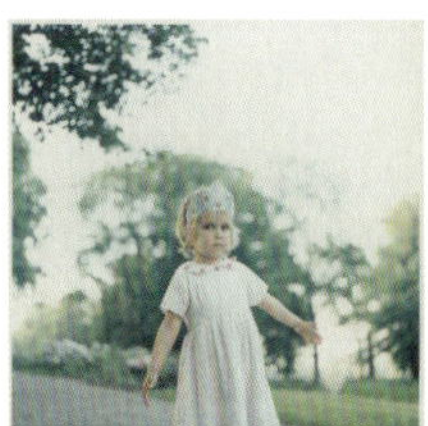

Plate 456
(Cliché of a Child, Littlle Girl) II

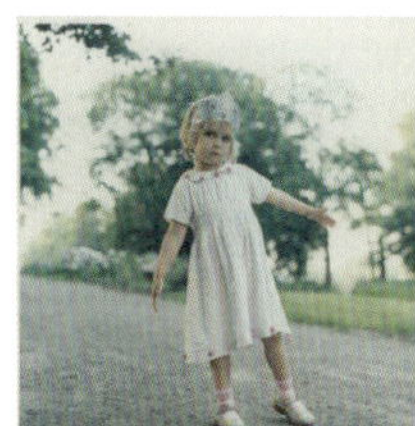

Plate 457
(Cliché of a Child, Littlle Girl) II

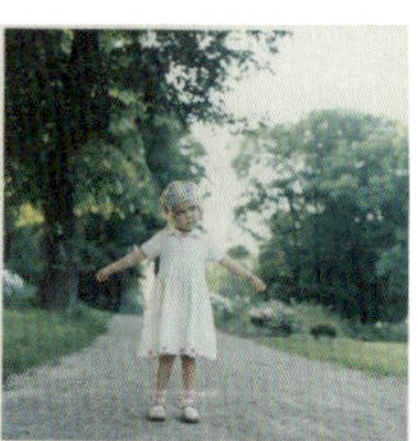

Plate 458
(Cliché of a Child, Littlle Girl) II

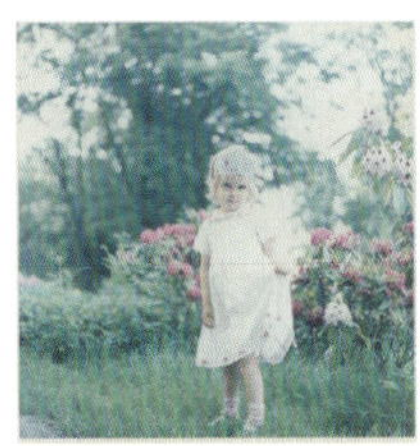

Plate 462
(Cliché of a Child, Littlle Girl) III

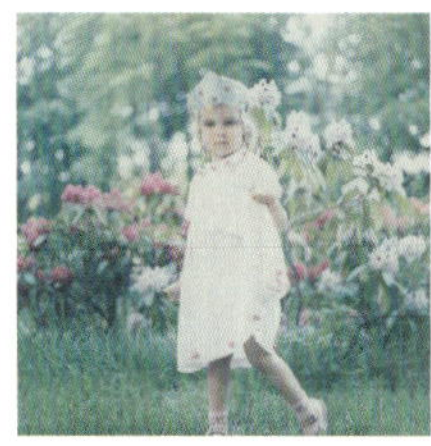

Plate 463
(Cliché of a Child, Littlle Girl) III

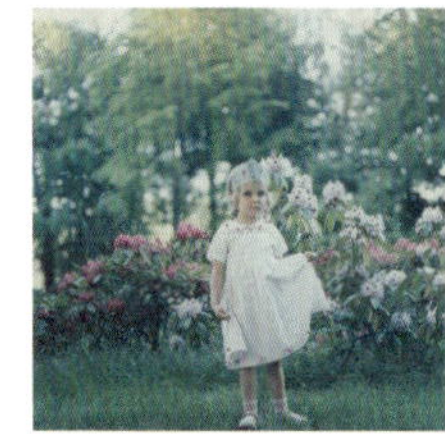

Plate 464
(Cliché of a Child, Littlle Girl) III

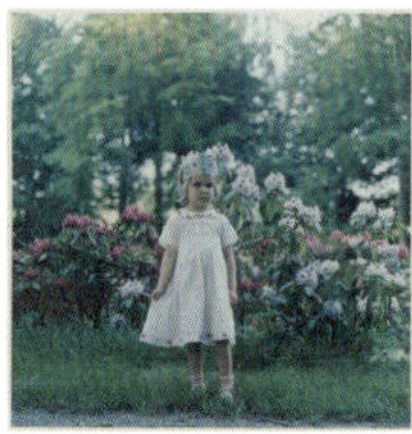

Plate 465
(Cliché of a Child, Littlle Girl) III

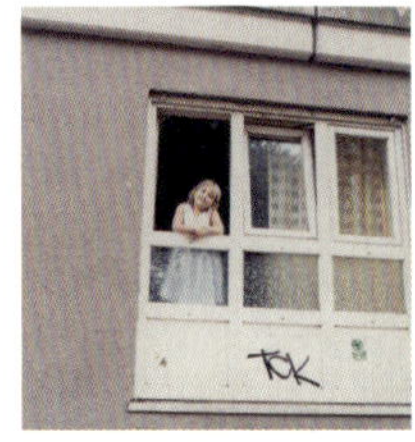

Plate 469
(Cliché of a Child, Littlle Girl) IV

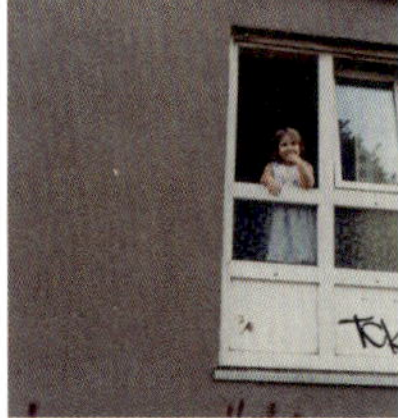

Plate 470
(Cliché of a Child, Littlle Girl) IV

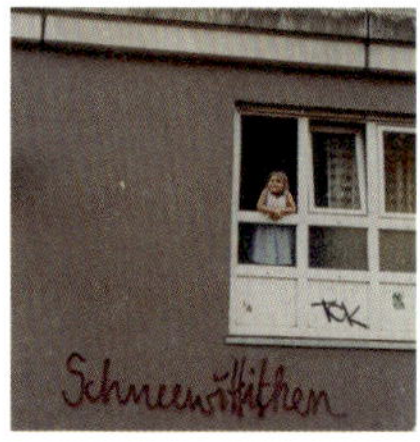

Plate 471
(Cliché of a Child, Littlle Girl) IV

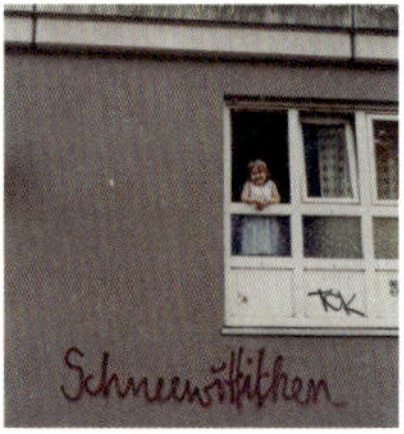

Plate 472
(Cliché of a Child, Littlle Girl) IV

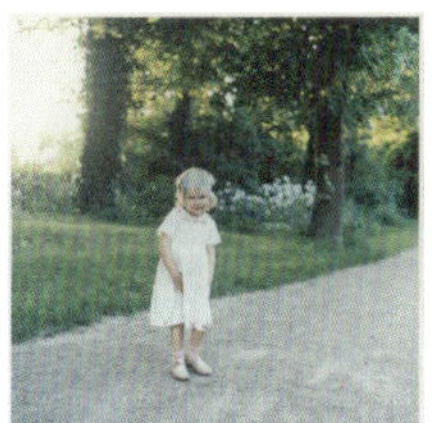

Plate 459
(Cliché of a Child, Littlle Girl) II

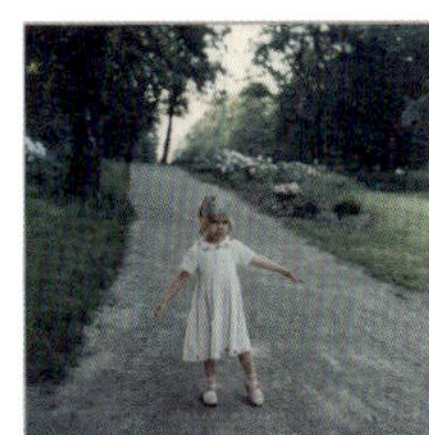

Plate 460
(Cliché of a Child, Littlle Girl) II

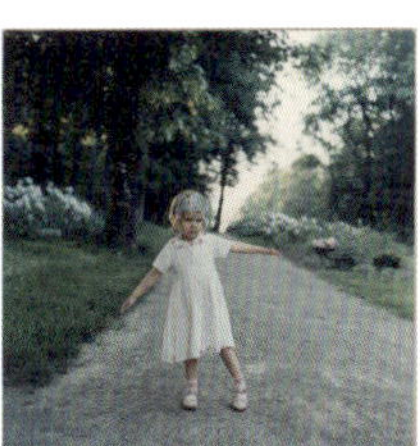

Plate 461
(Cliché of a Child, Littlle Girl) II

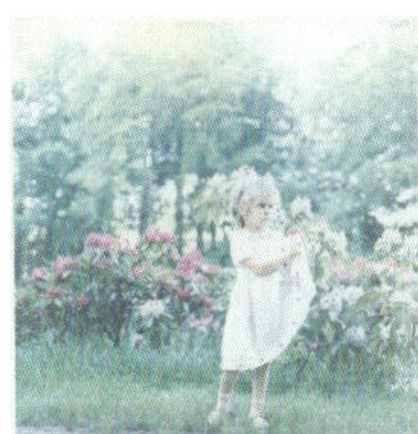

Plate 466
(Cliché of a Child, Littlle Girl) III

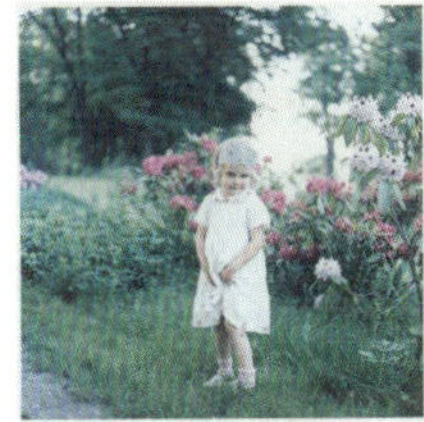

Plate 467
(Cliché of a Child, Littlle Girl) III

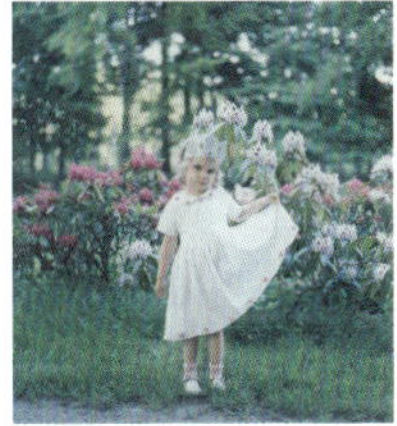

Plate 468
(Cliché of a Child, Littlle Girl) III

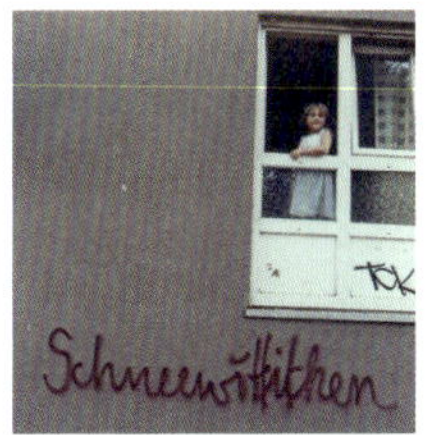

Plate 473
(Cliché of a Child, Littlle Girl) IV

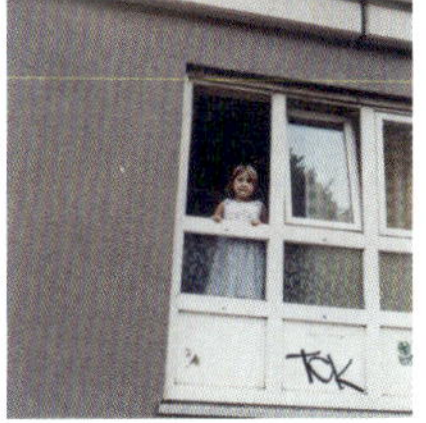

Plate 474
(Cliché of a Child, Littlle Girl) IV

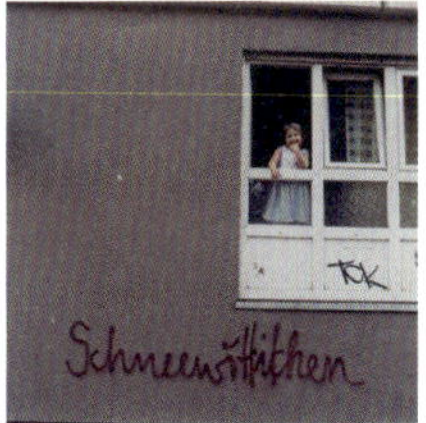

Plate 475
(Cliché of a Child, Littlle Girl) IV

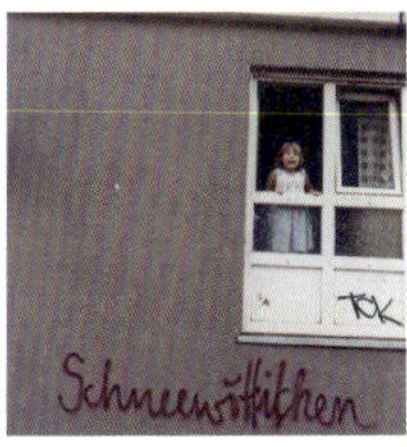

Plate 476
(Cliché of a Child, Littlle Girl) IV

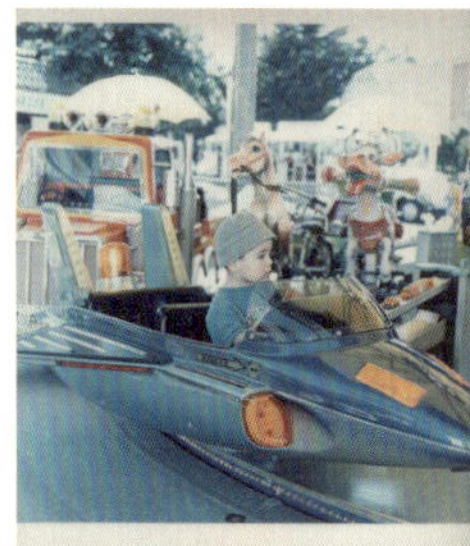

Plate 477
(Cliché of a Child, Little Boy,
in a Caroussel)

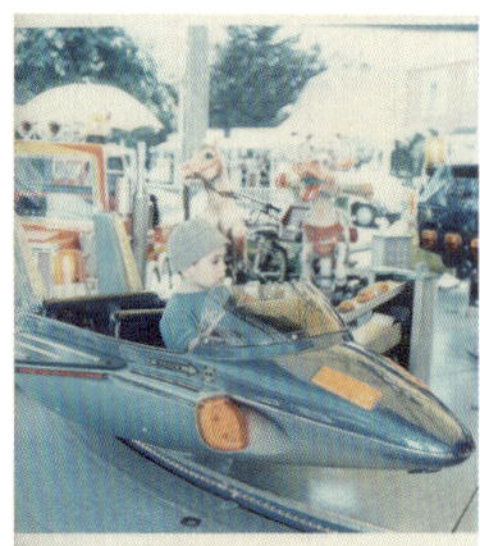

Plate 478
(Cliché of a Child, Little Boy,
in a Caroussel)

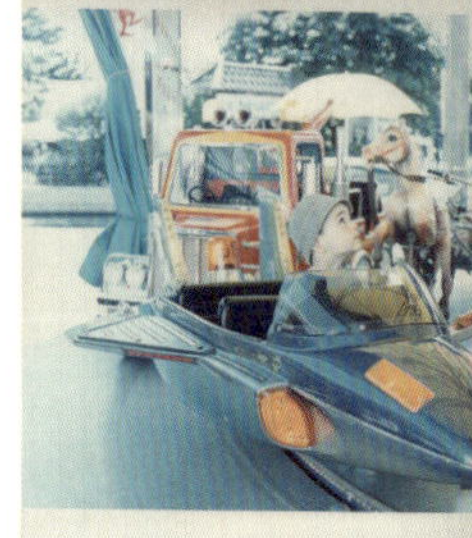

Plate 479
(Cliché of a Child, Little Boy,
in a Caroussel)

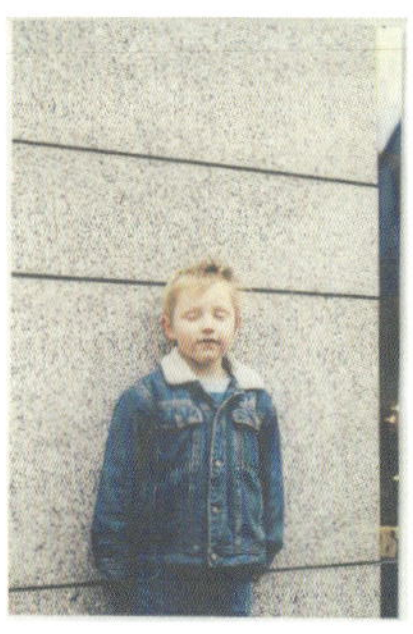

Plate 480
(Cliché of a Child, Little Boy) I

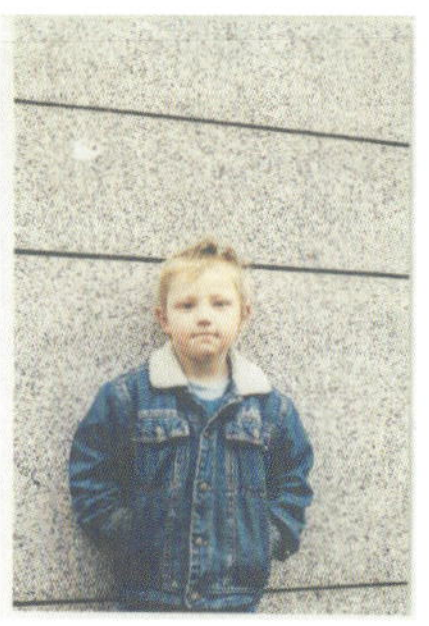

Plate 481
(Cliché of a Child, Little Boy) I

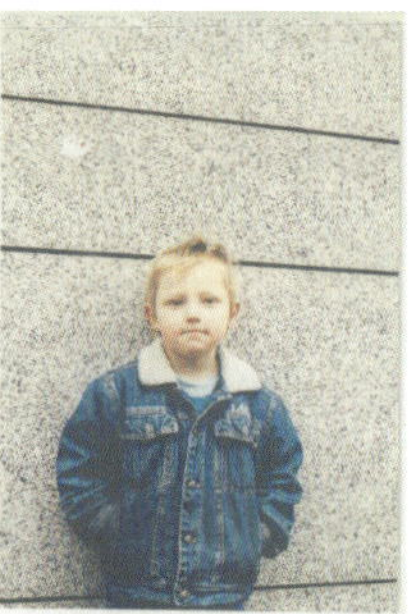

Plate 482
(Cliché of a Child, Little Boy) I

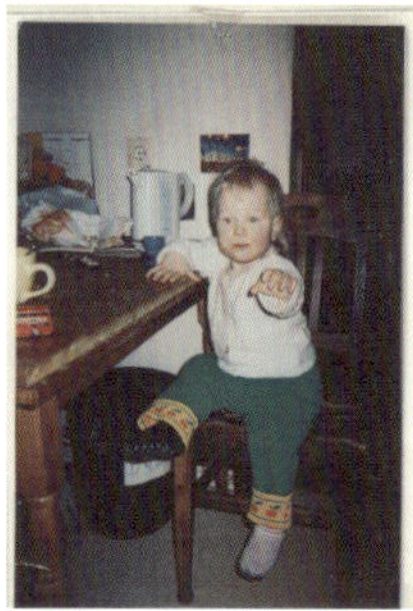

Plate 483
(Cliché of a Child) I

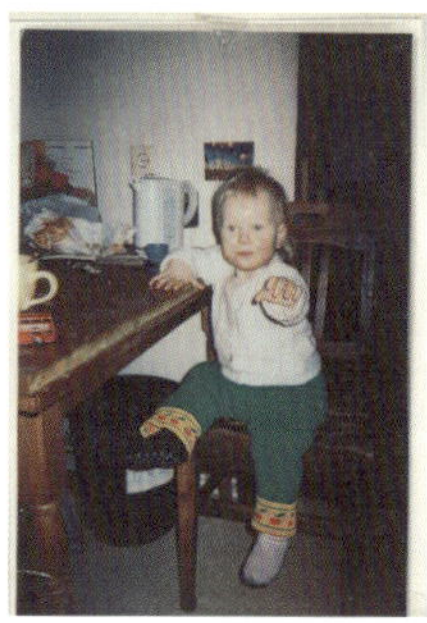

Plate 484
(Cliché of a Child) I

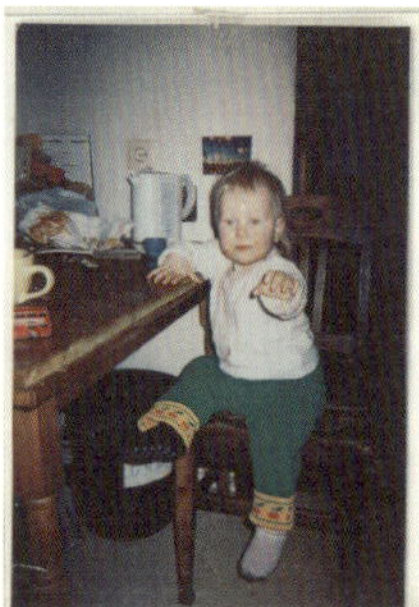

Plate 485
(Cliché of a Child) I

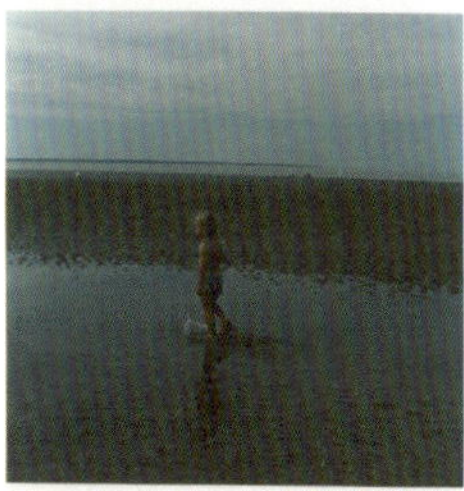

Plate 486
(Cliché of a Child, Littlle Girl) V

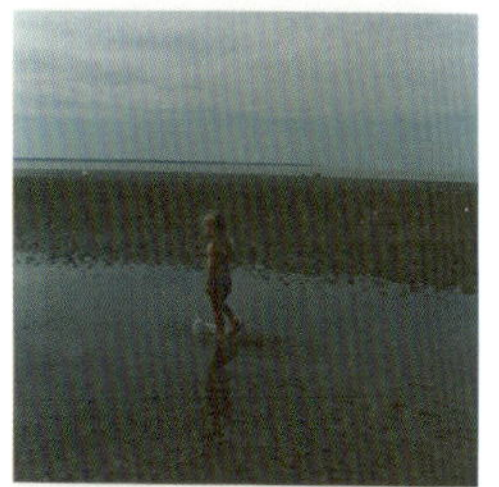

Plate 487
(Cliché of a Child, Littlle Girl) V

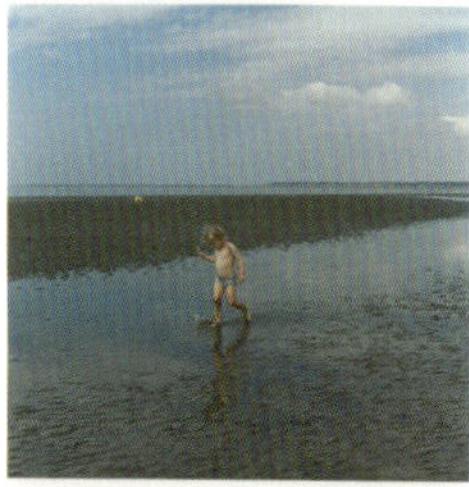

Plate 488
(Cliché of a Child, Littlle Girl) V

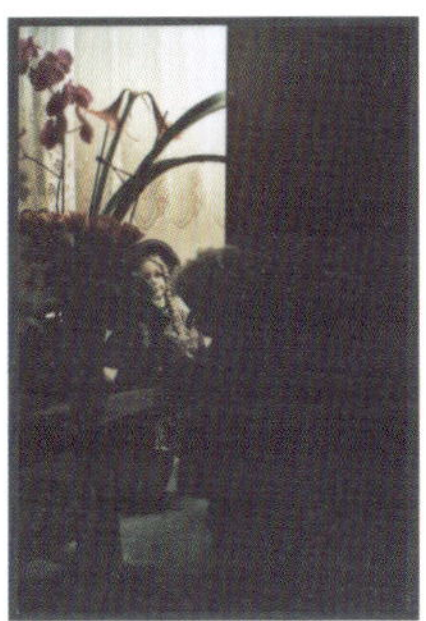

Plate 489
(Cliché of a Child, Littlle Girl) VI

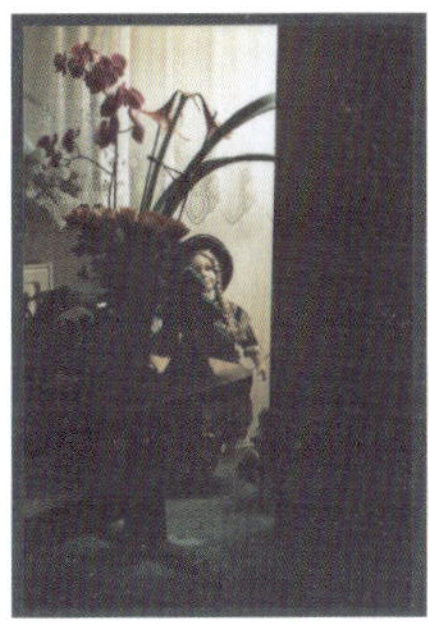

Plate 490
(Cliché of a Child, Littlle Girl) VI

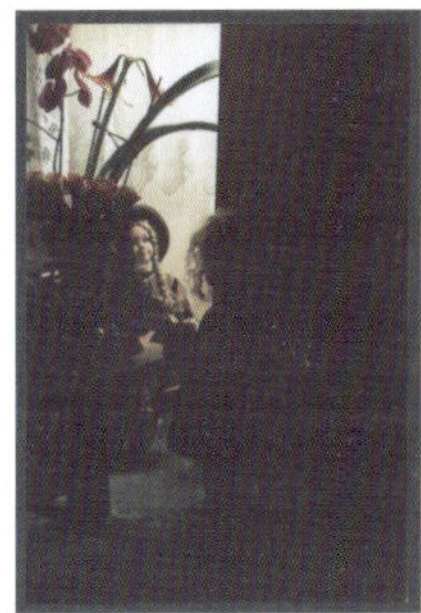

Plate 491
(Cliché of a Child, Littlle Girl) VI

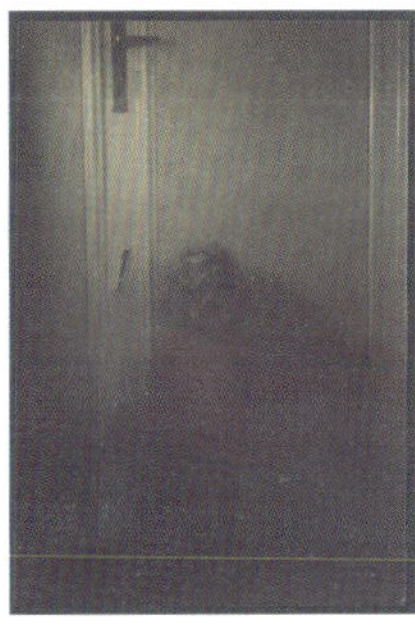

Plate 492
(Cliché of a Child, Littlle Girl) VII

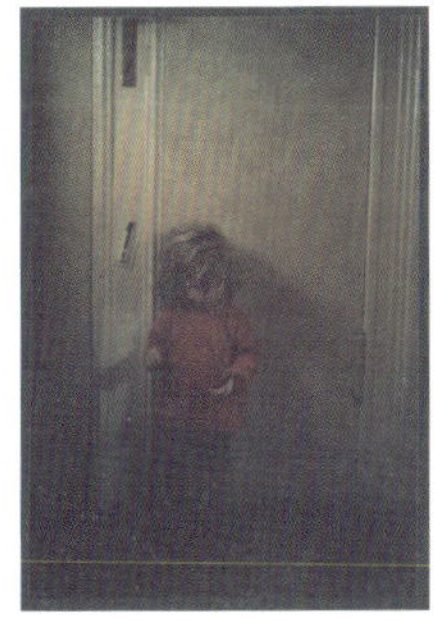

Plate 493
(Cliché of a Child, Littlle Girl) VII

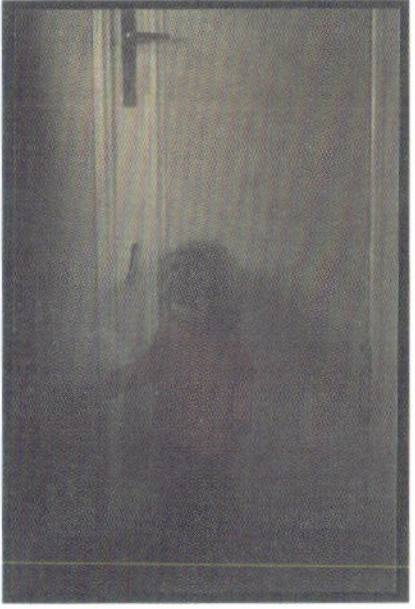

Plate 494
(Cliché of a Child, Littlle Girl) VII

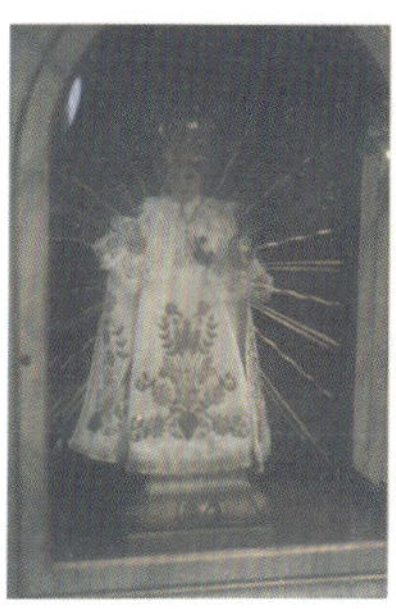

Plate 495
(Cliché of a Child) II

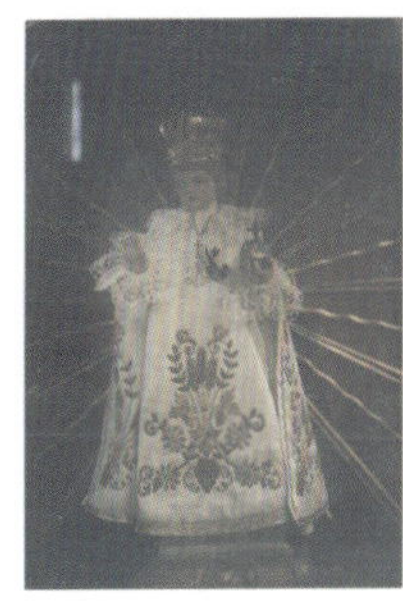

Plate 496
(Cliché of a Child) II

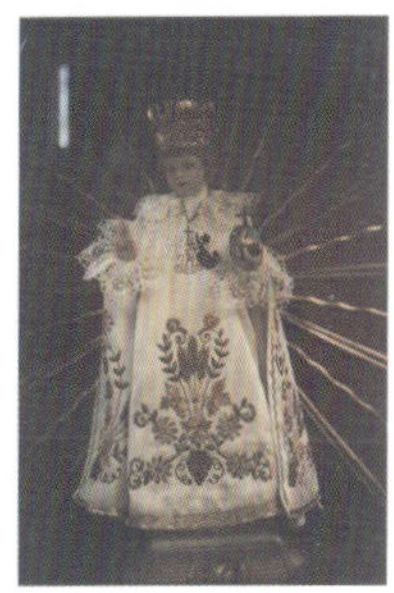

Plate 497
(Cliché of a Child) II

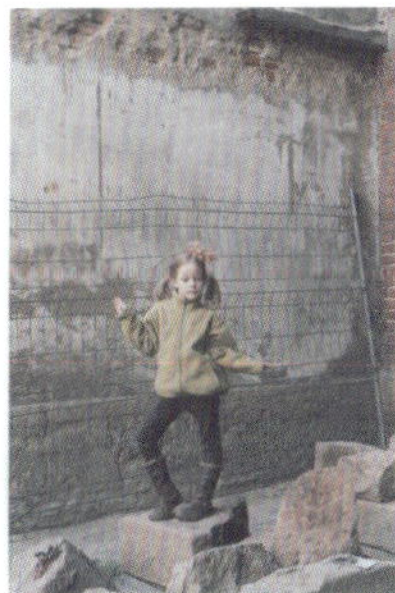

Plate 498
(Cliché of a Child, Girl)

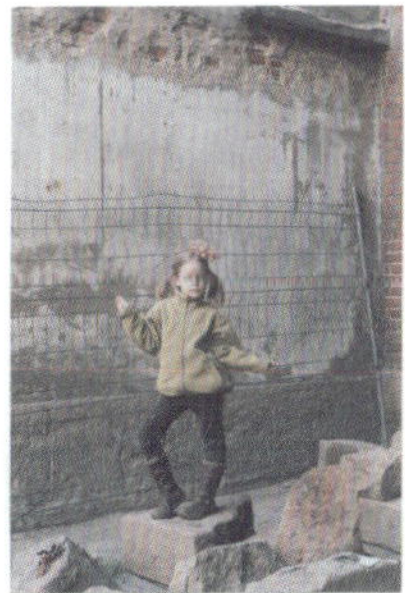

Plate 499
(Cliché of a Child, Girl)

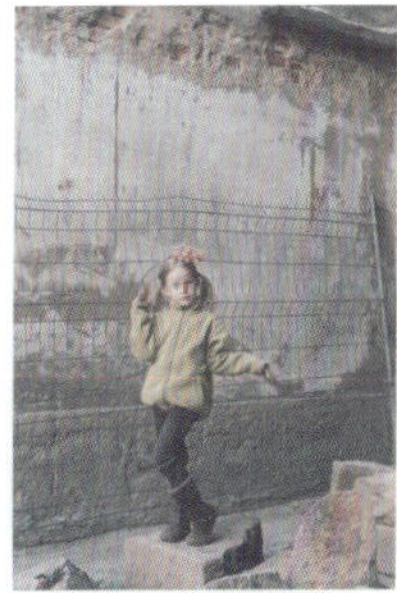

Plate 500
(Cliché of a Child, Girl)

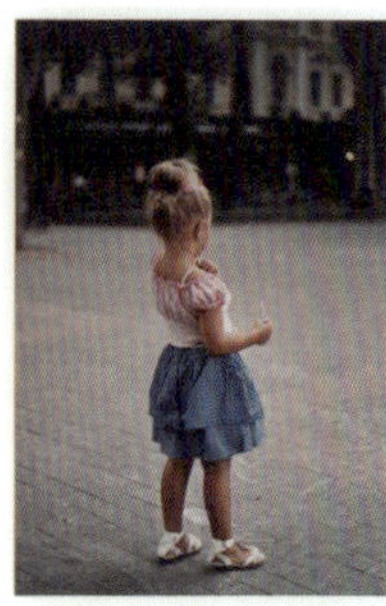

Plate 501
(Cliché of a Child, Littlle Girl) VIII

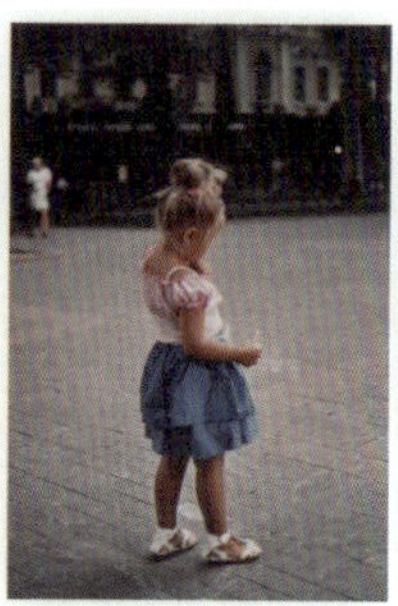

Plate 502
(Cliché of a Child, Littlle Girl) VIII

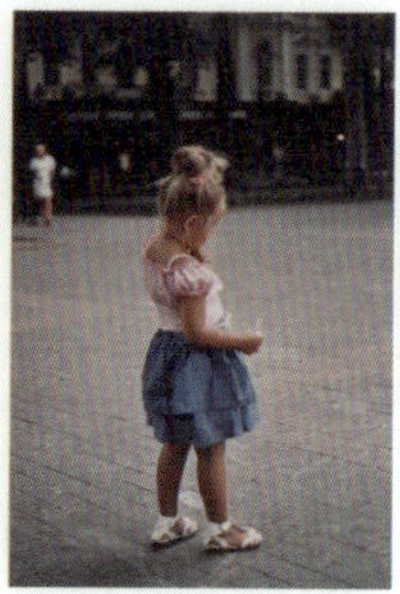

Plate 503
(Cliché of a Child, Littlle Girl) VIII

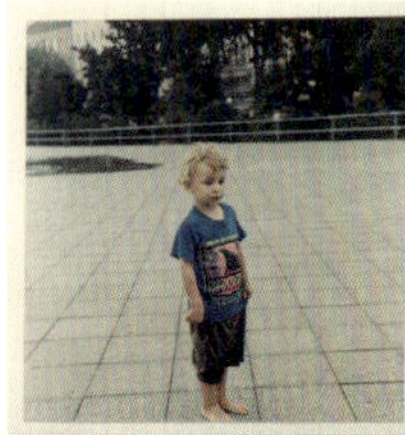

Plate 504
(Cliché of a Child, Little Boy) II

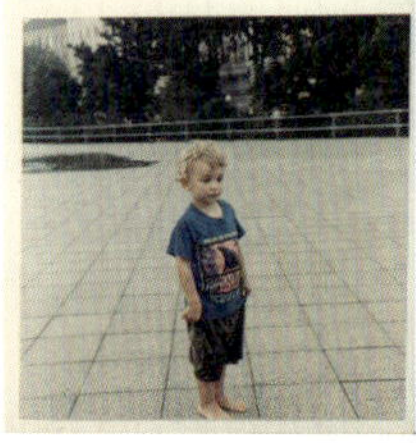

Plate 505
(Cliché of a Child, Little Boy) II

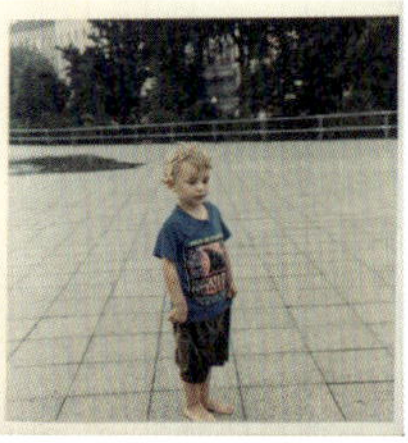

Plate 506
(Cliché of a Child, Little Boy) II

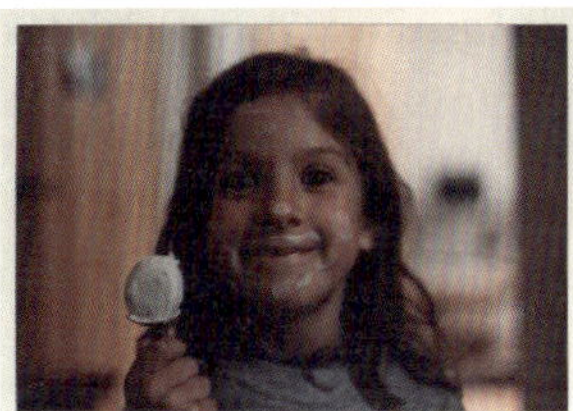
Plate 507
(Cliché of a Child, Littlle Girl) IX

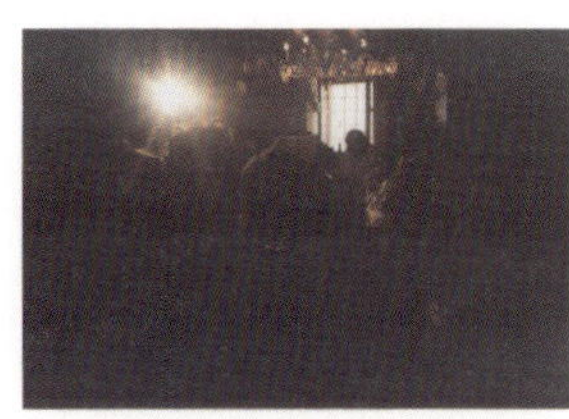
Plate 510
(Cliché of a Child, Baptism)

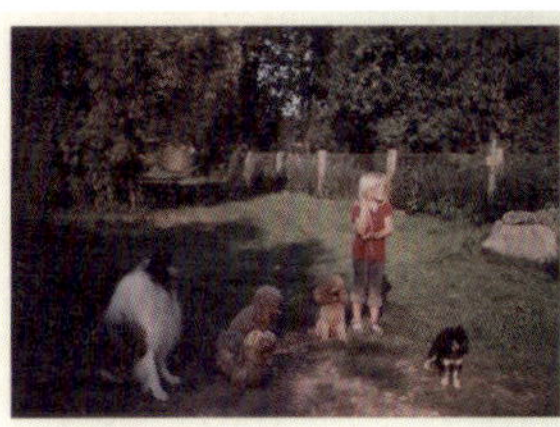
Plate 513
(Cliché of a Child, Little Girl, with Dogs)

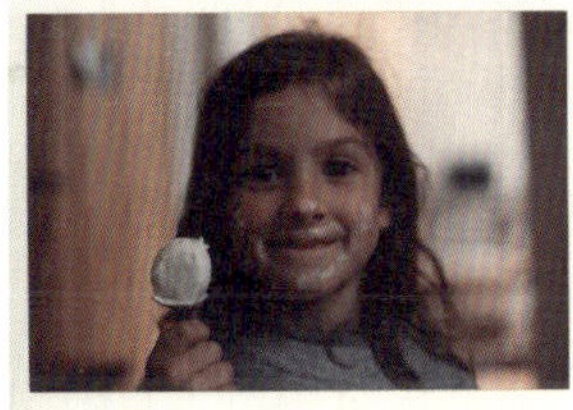
Plate 508
(Cliché of a Child, Littlle Girl) IX

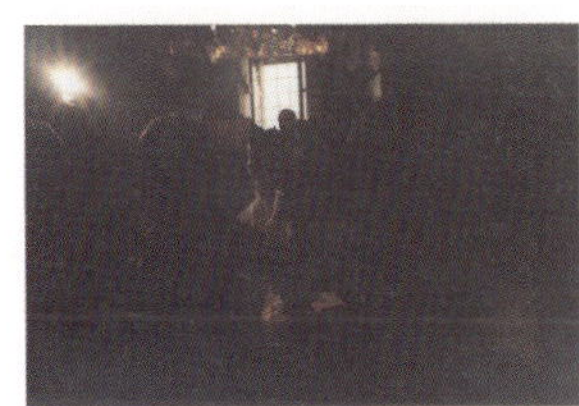
Plate 511
(Cliché of a Child, Baptism)

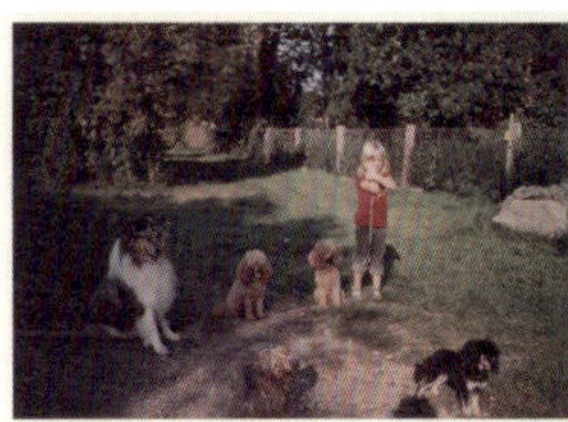
Plate 514
(Cliché of a Child, Little Girl, with Dogs)

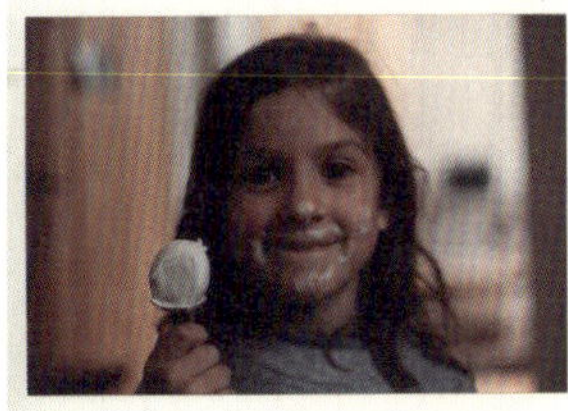
Plate 509
(Cliché of a Child, Littlle Girl) IX

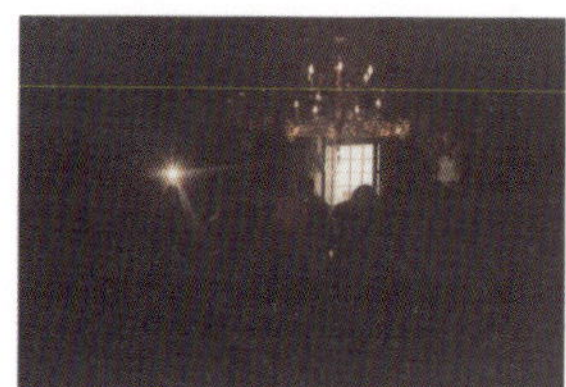
Plate 512
(Cliché of a Child, Baptism)

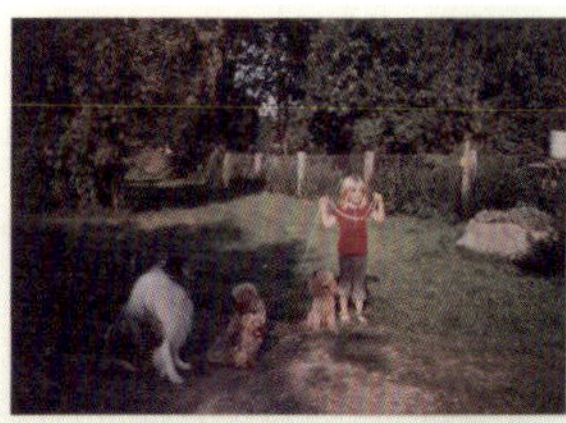
Plate 515
(Cliché of a Child, Little Girl, with Dogs)

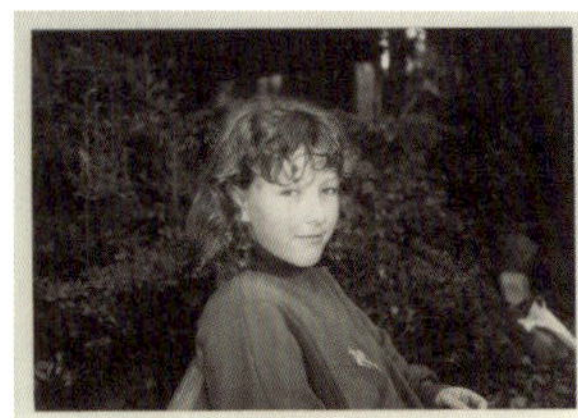

Plate 516
(Cliché of a Child, Young Girl)

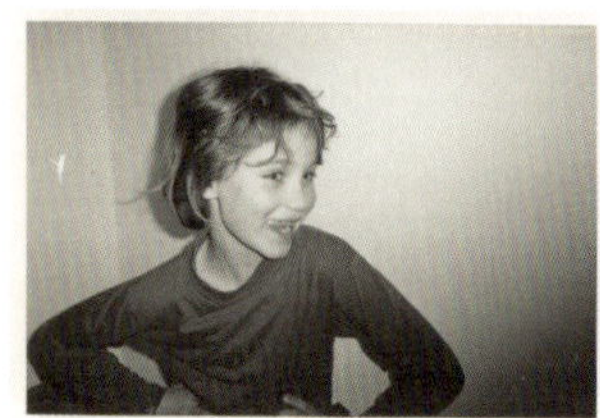

Plate 519
(Cliché of a Child, Little Girl)

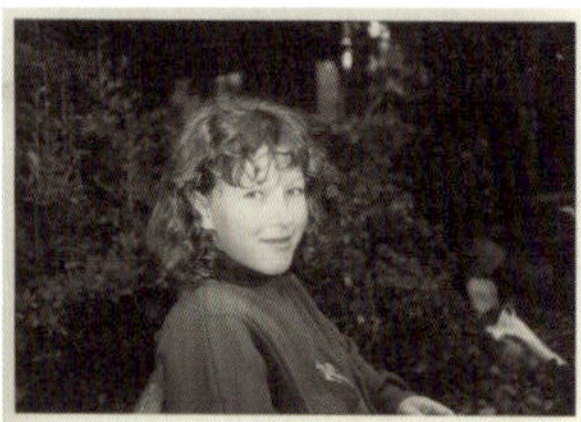

Plate 517
(Cliché of a Child, Young Girl)

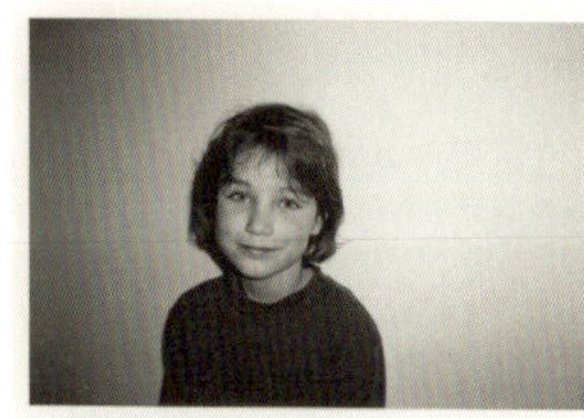

Plate 520
(Cliché of a Child, Little Girl)

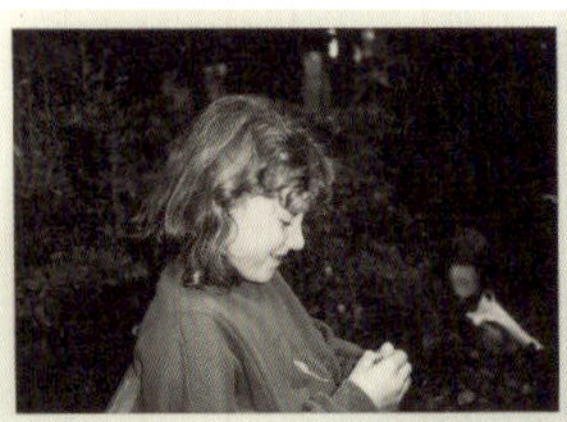

Plate 518
(Cliché of a Child, Young Girl)

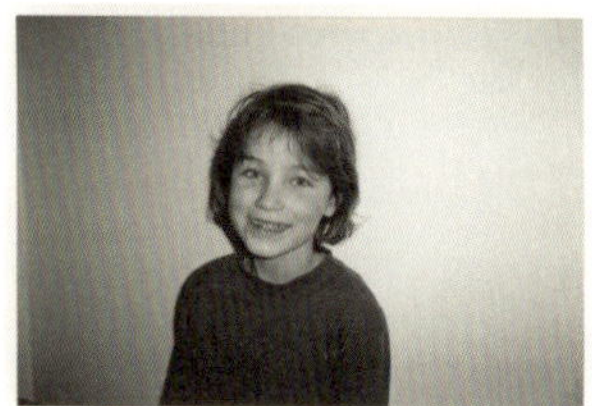

Plate 521
(Cliché of a Child, Little Girl)

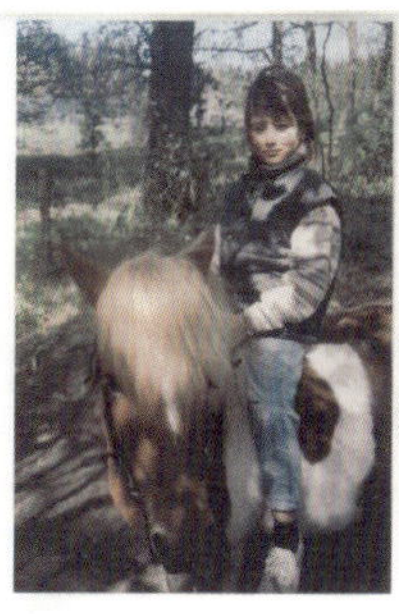

Plate 522
(Cliché of a Child, Little Girl,
on a Pony)

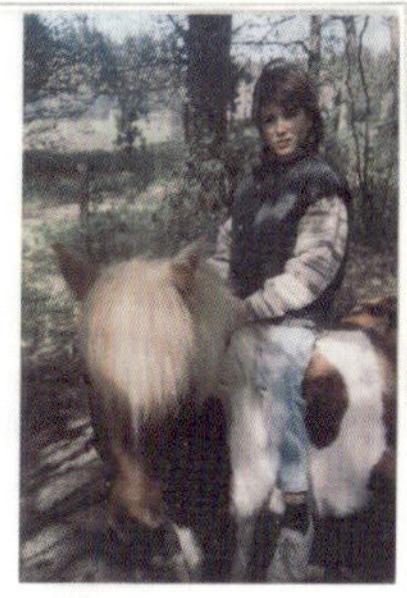

Plate 523
(Cliché of a Child, Little Girl,
on a Pony)

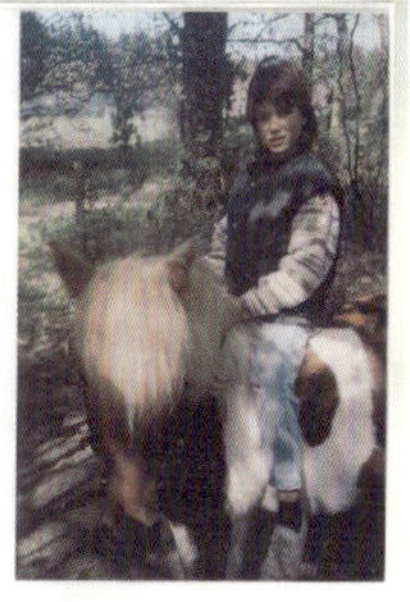

Plate 524
(Cliché of a Child, Little Girl,
on a Pony)

XI

ANIMALS

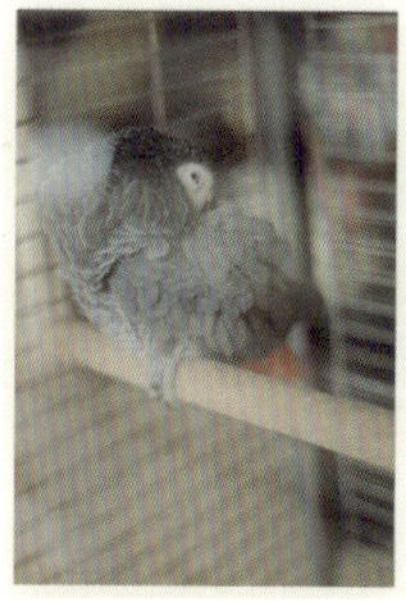

Plate 525
(Cliché of an Animal, Parrot) I

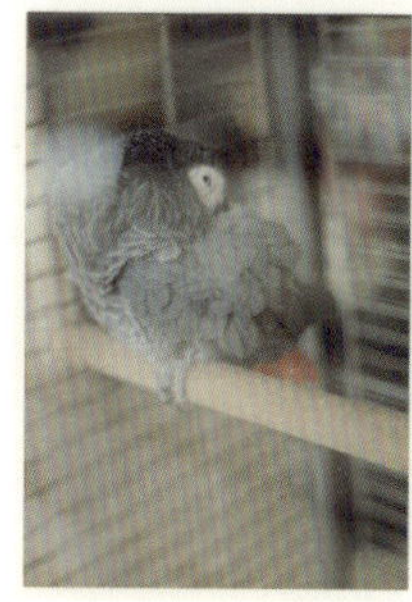

Plate 526
(Cliché of an Animal, Parrot) I

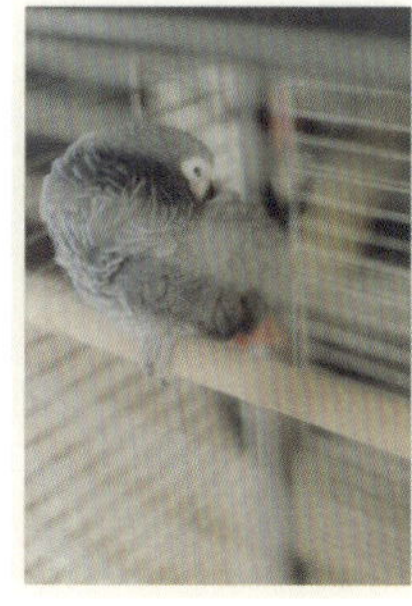

Plate 527
(Cliché of an Animal, Parrot) I

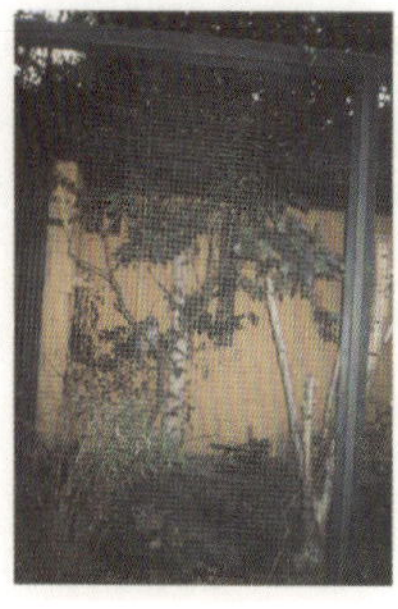

Plate 528
(Cliché of an Animal, Wild Bird)

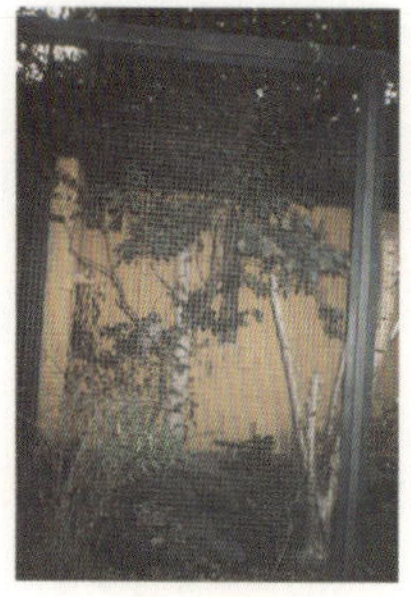

Plate 529
(Cliché of an Animal, Wild Bird)

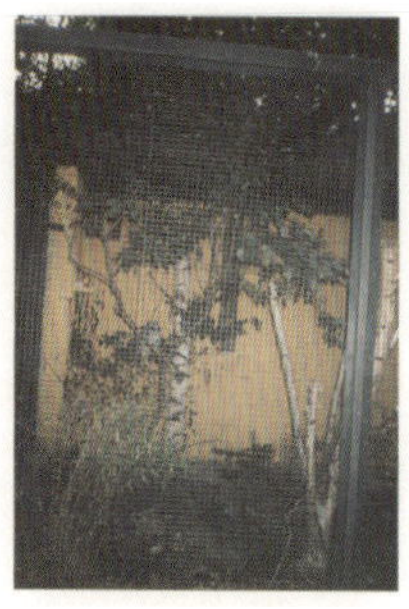

Plate 530
(Cliché of an Animal, Wild Bird)

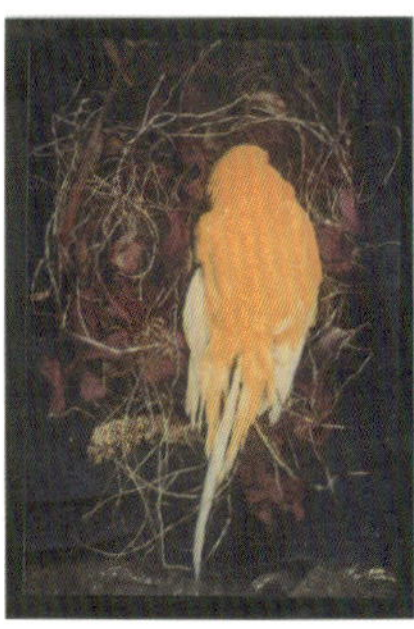

Plate 531
(Cliché of an Animal, Dead Bird)

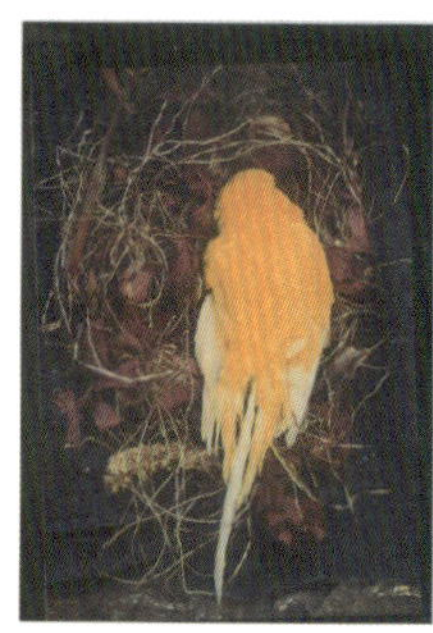

Plate 532
(Cliché of an Animal, Dead Bird)

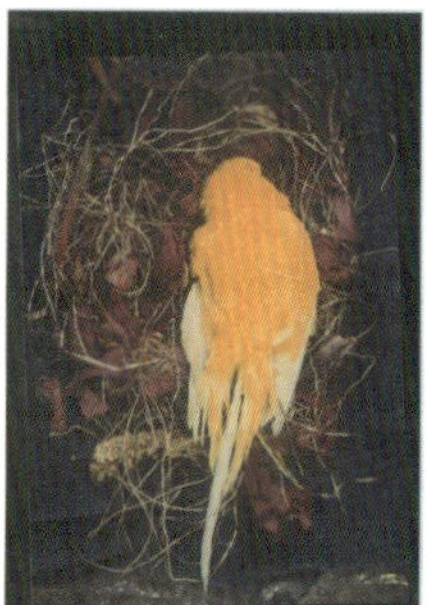

Plate 533
(Cliché of an Animal, Dead Bird)

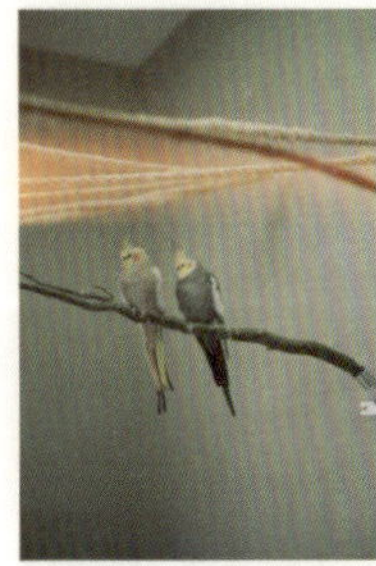

Plate 534
(Cliché of an Animal, Parrot) II

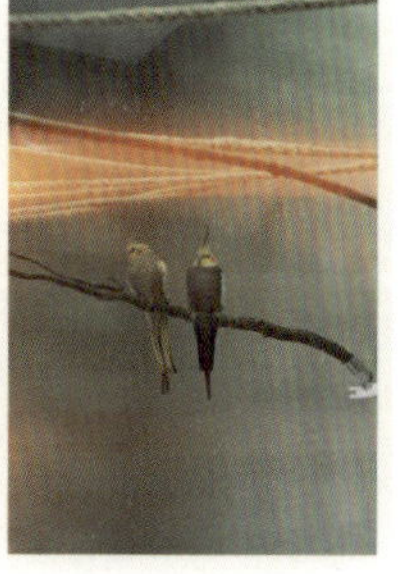

Plate 535
(Cliché of an Animal, Parrot) II

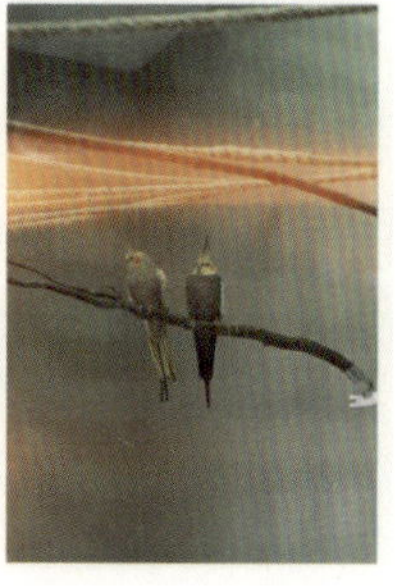

Plate 536
(Cliché of an Animal, Parrot) II

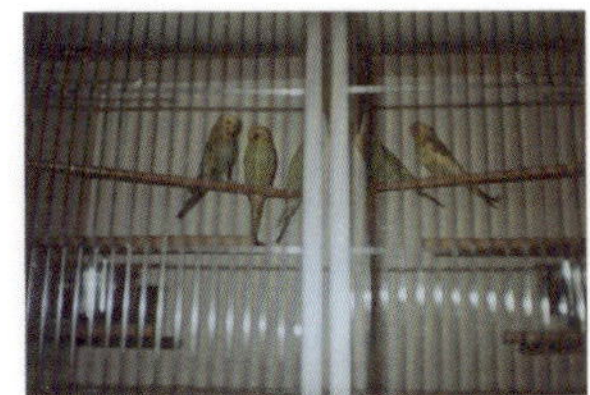

Plate 537
(Cliché of Animals, Parrots) I

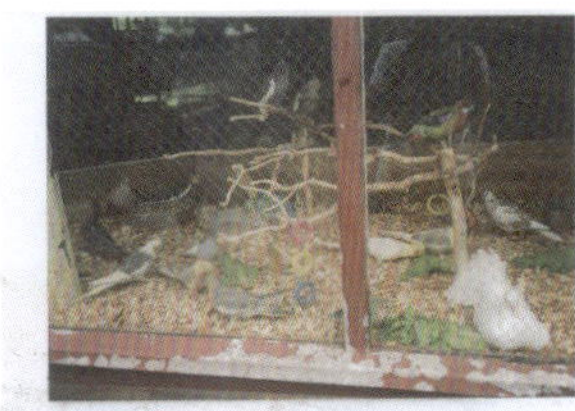

Plate 540
(Cliché of Animals, Parrots) II

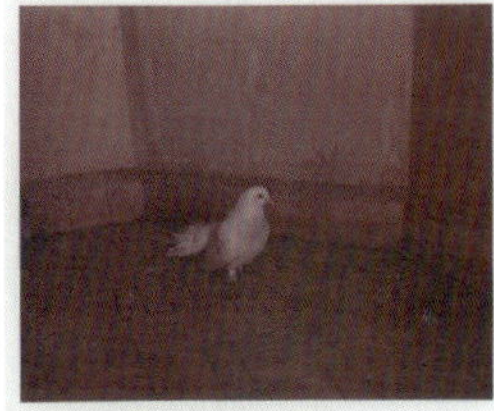

Plate 543
(Cliché of an Animal, Dove)

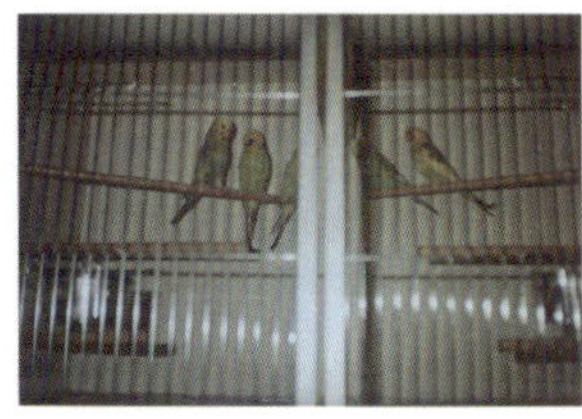

Plate 538
(Cliché of Animals, Parrots) I

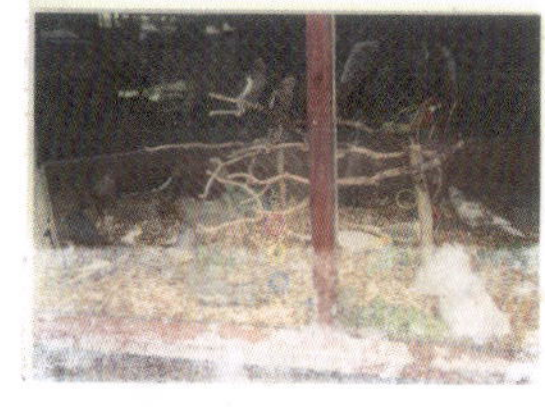

Plate 541
(Cliché of Animals, Parrots) II

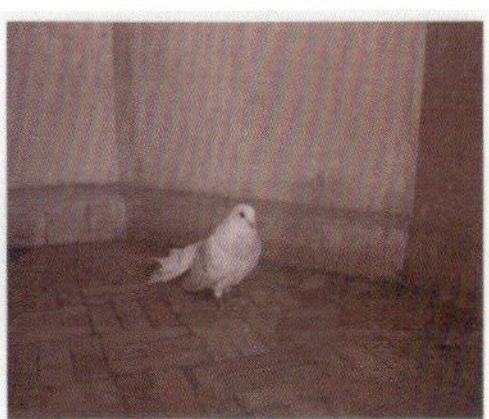

Plate 544
(Cliché of an Animal, Dove)

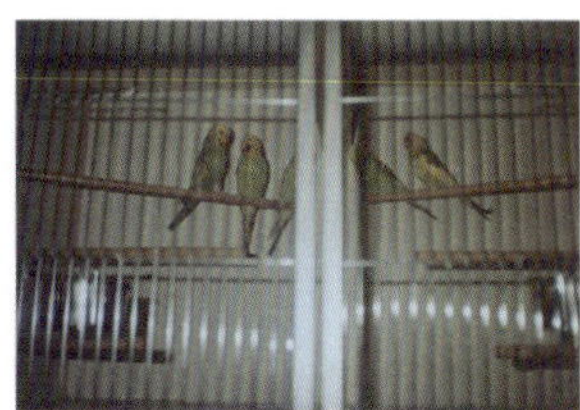

Plate 539
(Cliché of Animals, Parrots) I

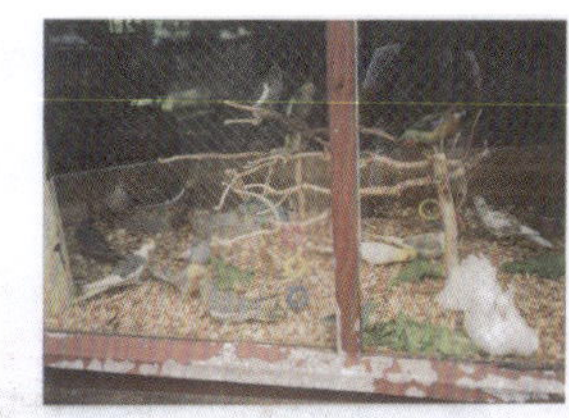

Plate 542
(Cliché of Animals, Parrots) II

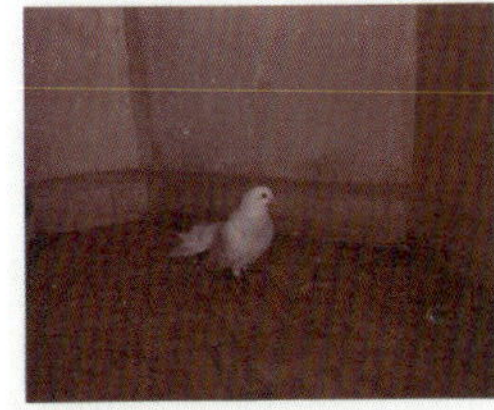

Plate 545
(Cliché of an Animal, Dove)

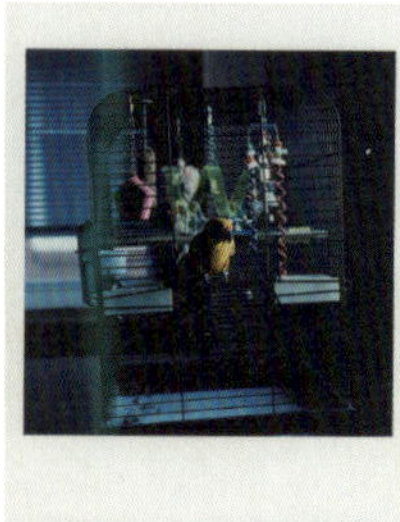

Plate 546
(Cliché of an Animal, Parrot) III

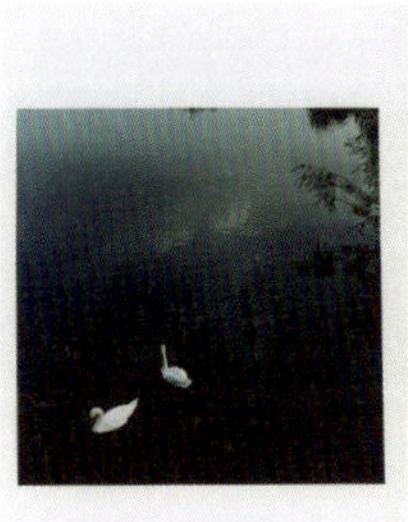

Plate 549
(Cliché of Animals, White Swans)

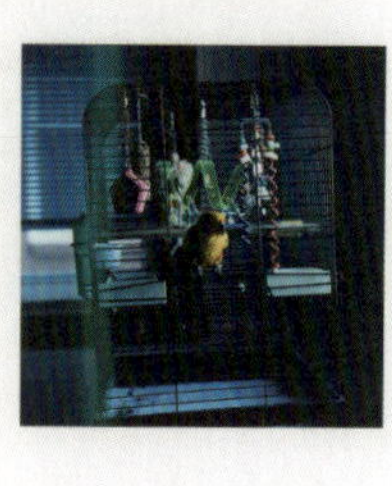

Plate 547
(Cliché of an Animal, Parrot) III

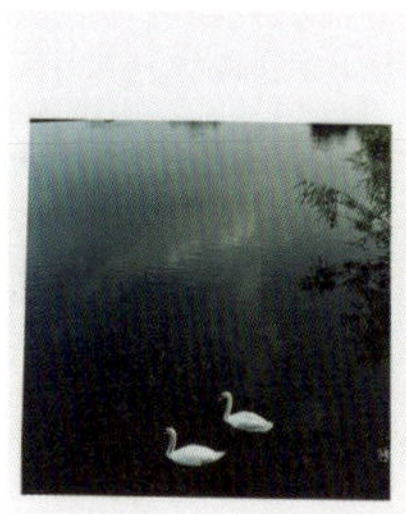

Plate 550
(Cliché of Animals, White Swans)

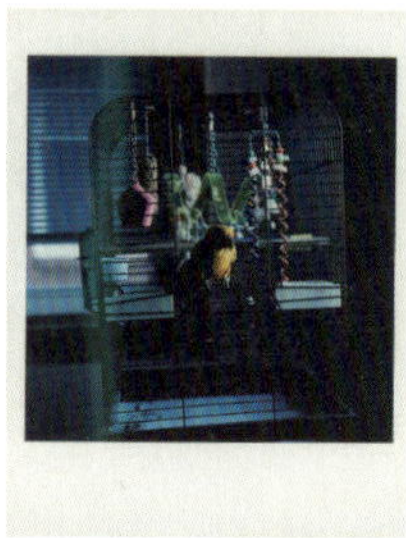

Plate 548
(Cliché of an Animal, Parrot) III

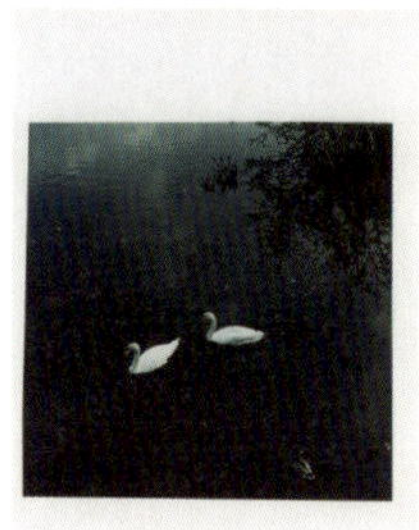

Plate 551
(Cliché of Animals, White Swans)

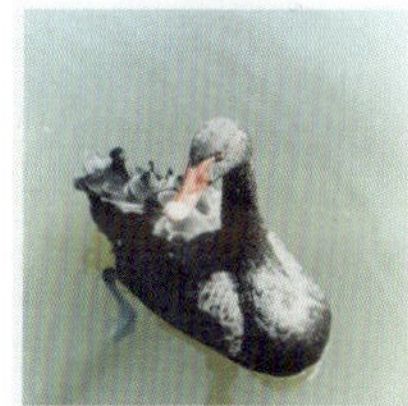

Plate 552
(Cliché of an Animal, Black Swan)

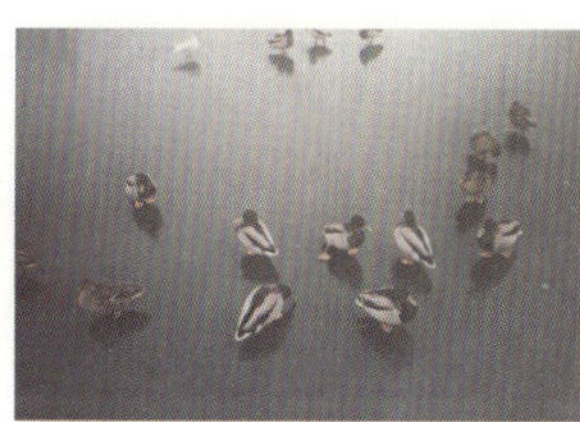

Plate 557
(Cliché of Animals, Ducks)

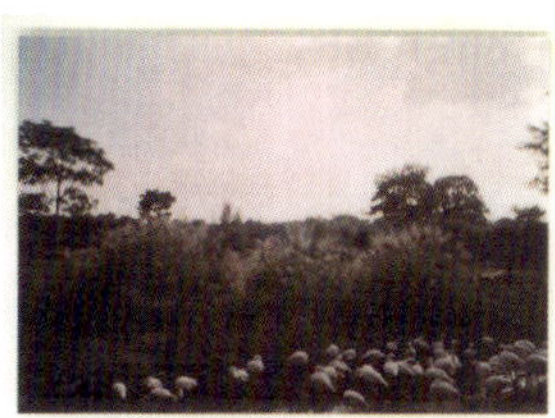

Plate 560
(Cliché of Animals, Flamingos)

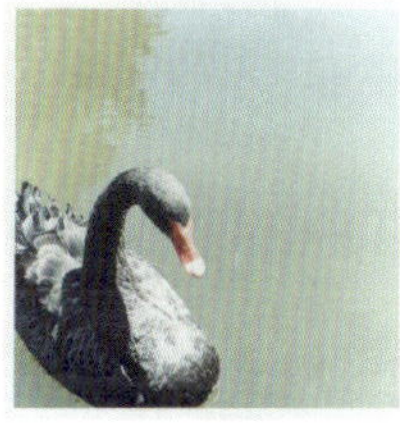

Plate 553
(Cliché of an Animal, Black Swan)

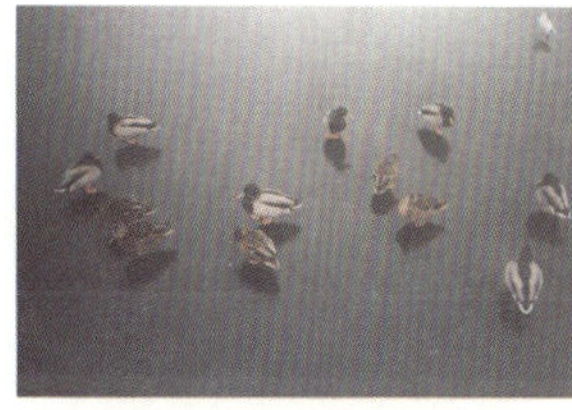

Plate 558
(Cliché of Animals, Ducks)

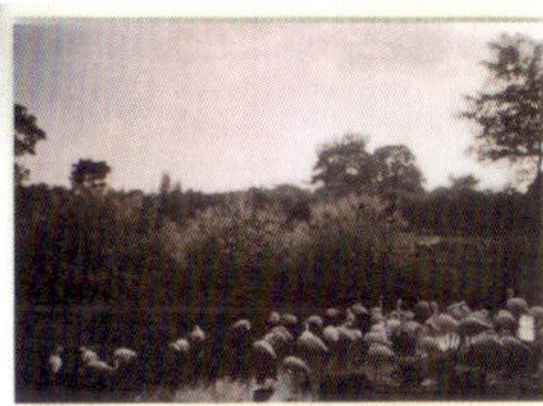

Plate 561
(Cliché of Animals, Flamingos)

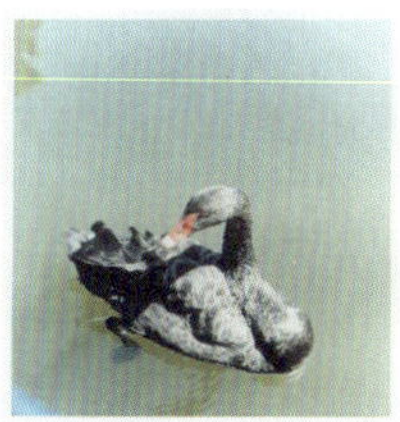

Plate 554
(Cliché of an Animal, Black Swan)

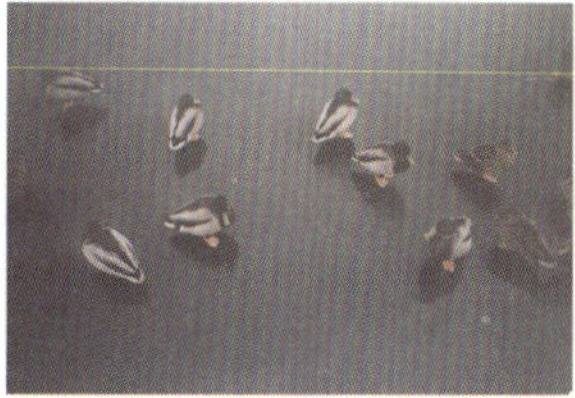

Plate 559
(Cliché of Animals, Ducks)

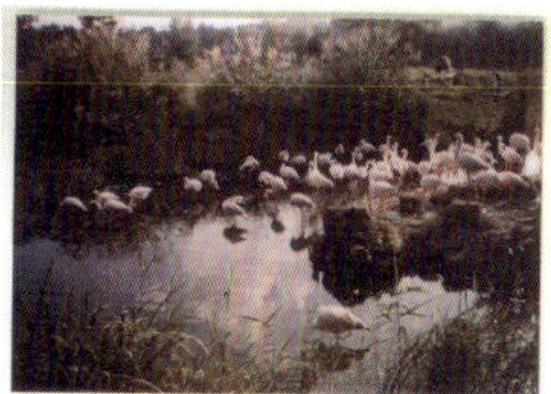

Plate 562
(Cliché of Animals, Flamingos)

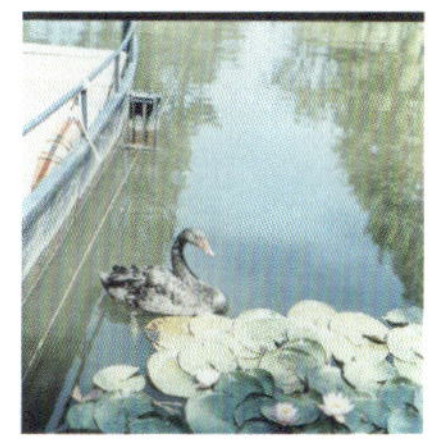

Plate 555
(Cliché of an Animal, Black Swan)

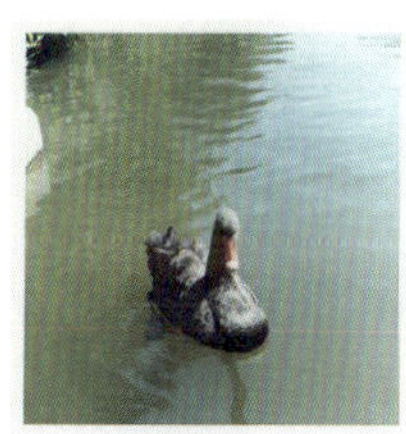

Plate 566
(Cliché of an Animal, Black Swan)

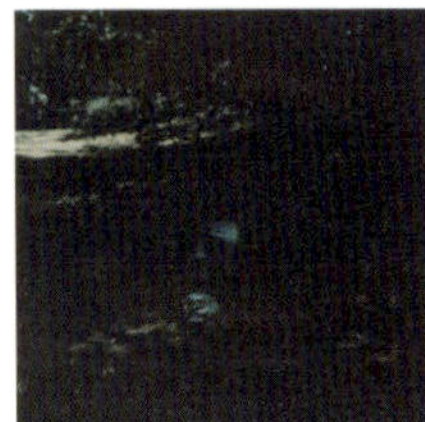

Plate 563
(Cliché of an Animal, Peacock) I

Plate 564
(Cliché of an Animal, Peacock) I

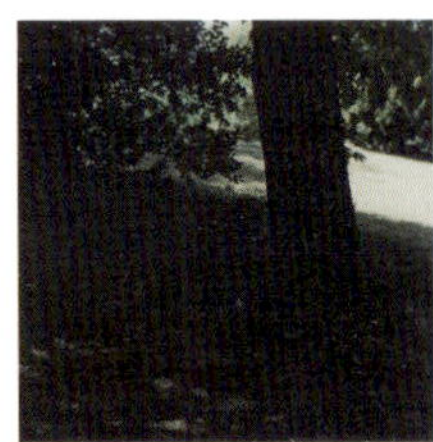

Plate 565
(Cliché of an Animal, Peacock) I

Plate 569
(Cliché of an Animal, Peacock) II

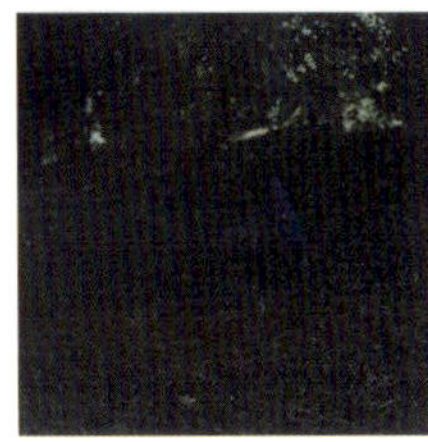

Plate 570
(Cliché of an Animal, Peacock) II

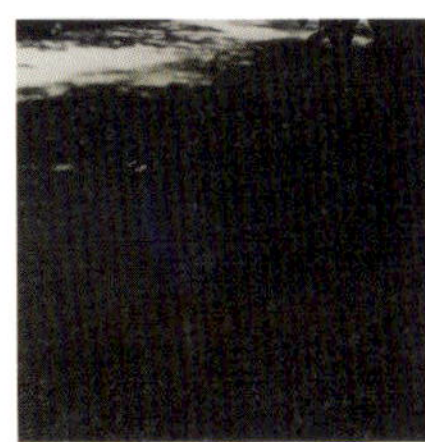

Plate 571
(Cliché of an Animal, Peacock) II

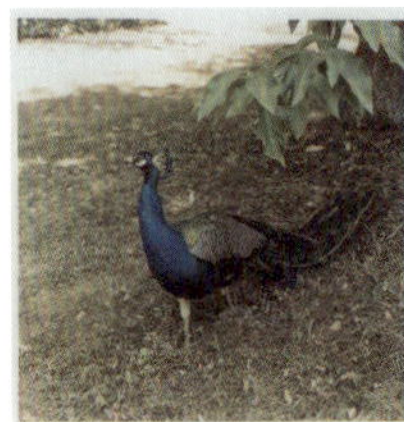

Plate 575
(Cliché of an Animal, Peacock) III

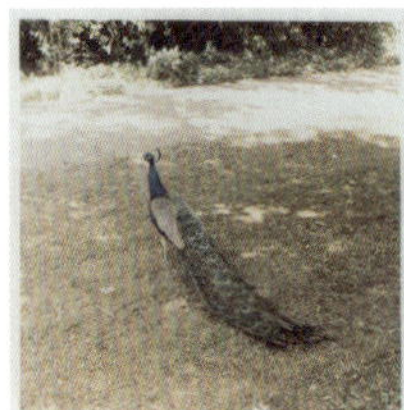

Plate 576
(Cliché of an Animal, Peacock) III

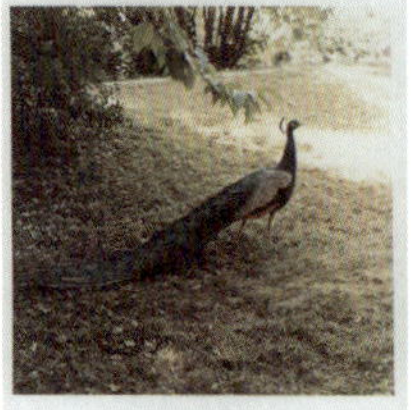

Plate 577
(Cliché of an Animal, Peacock) III

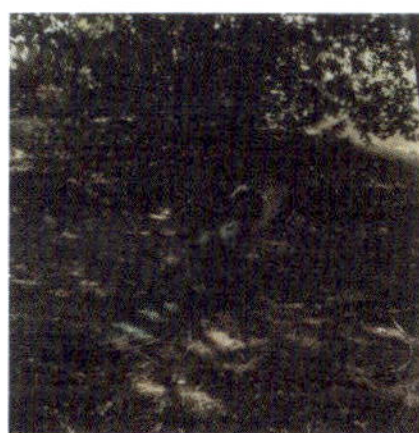

Plate 566
(Cliché of an Animal, Peacock) I

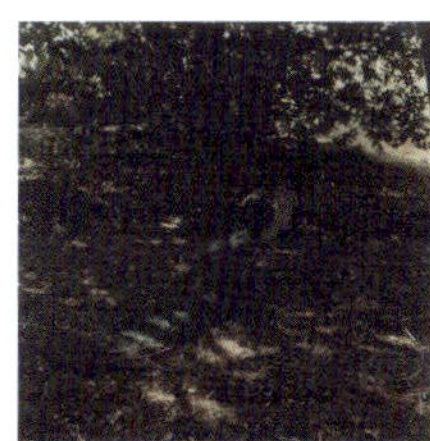

Plate 567
(Cliché of an Animal, Peacock) I

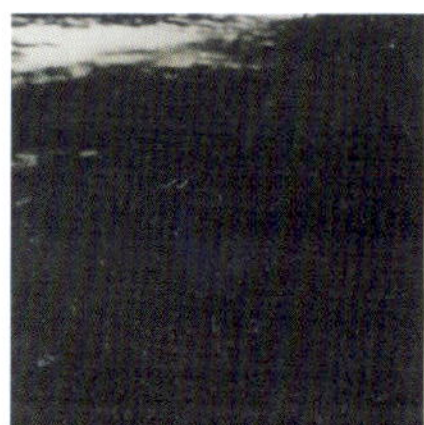

Plate 568
(Cliché of an Animal, Peacock) I

Plate 572
(Cliché of an Animal, Peacock) II

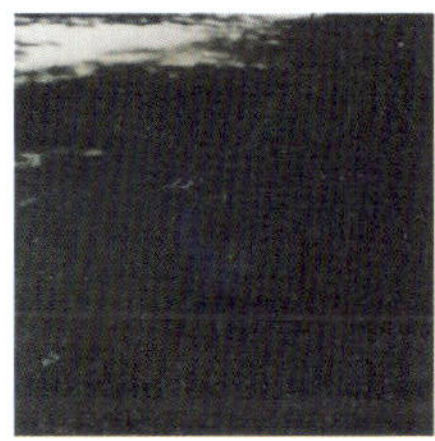

Plate 573
(Cliché of an Animal, Peacock) II

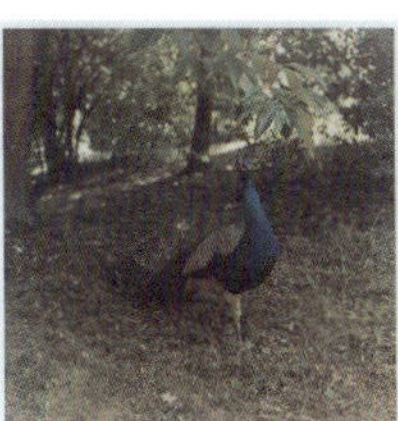

Plate 574
(Cliché of an Animal, Peacock) II

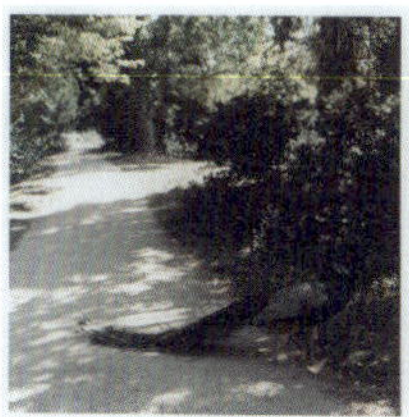

Plate 578
(Cliché of an Animal, Peacock) III

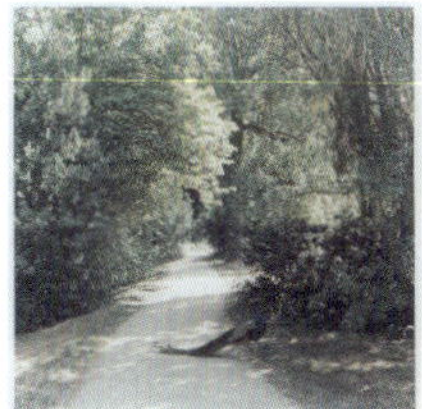

Plate 579
(Cliché of an Animal, Peacock) III

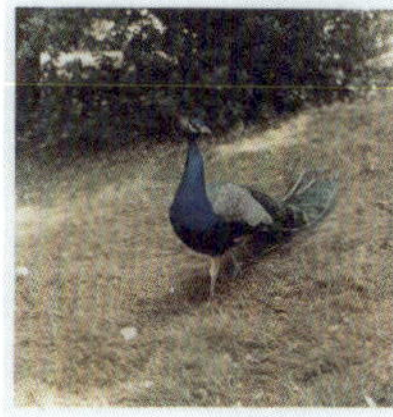

Plate 580
(Cliché of an Animal, Peacock) III

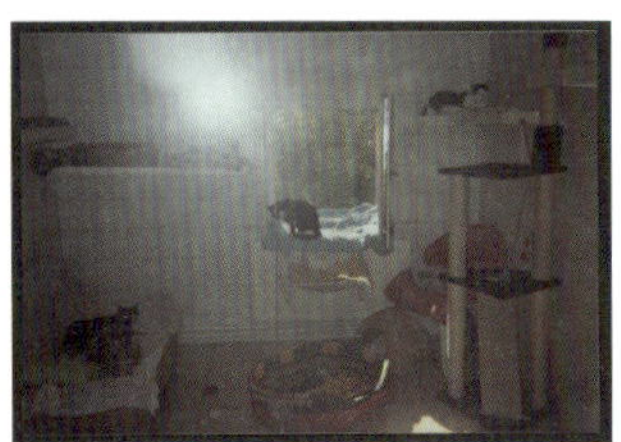

Plate 581
(Cliché of Animals, Cats) I

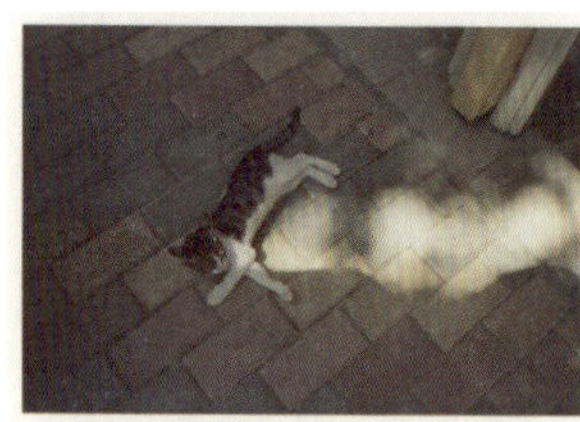

Plate 584
(Cliché of an Animal, Young Cat) I

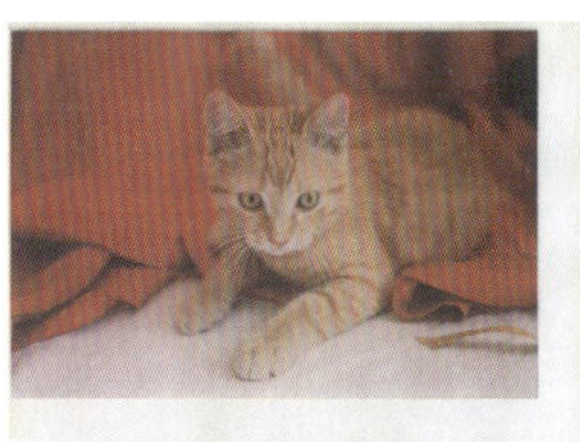

Plate 587
(Cliché of an Animal, Young Cat) II

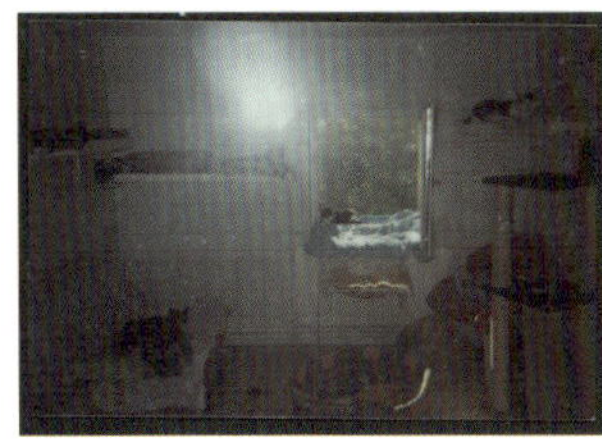

Plate 582
(Cliché of Animals, Cats) I

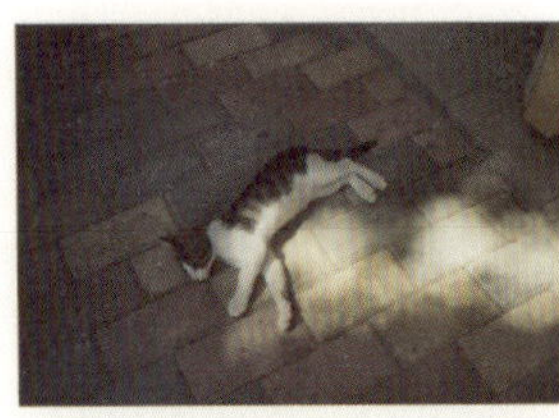

Plate 585
(Cliché of an Animal, Young Cat) I

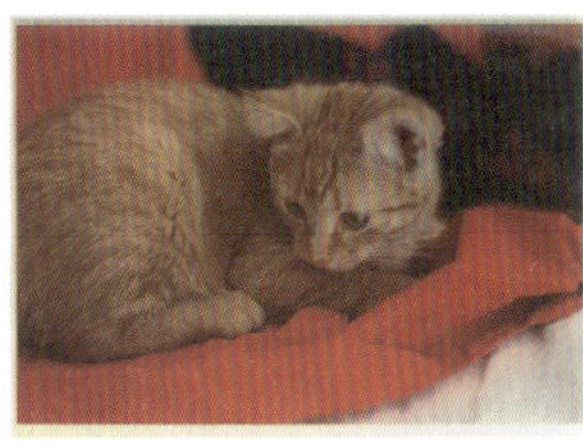

Plate 588
(Cliché of an Animal, Young Cat) II

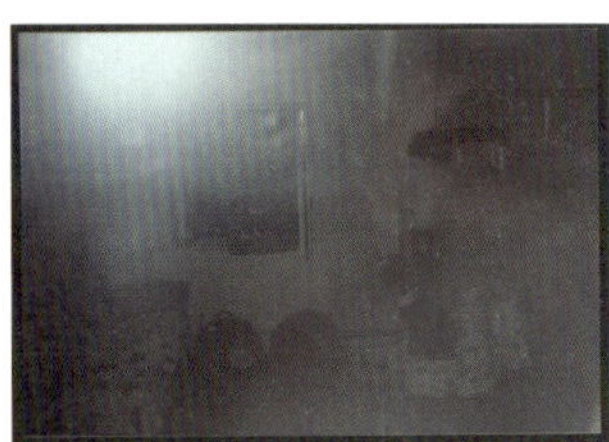

Plate 583
(Cliché of Animals, Cats) I

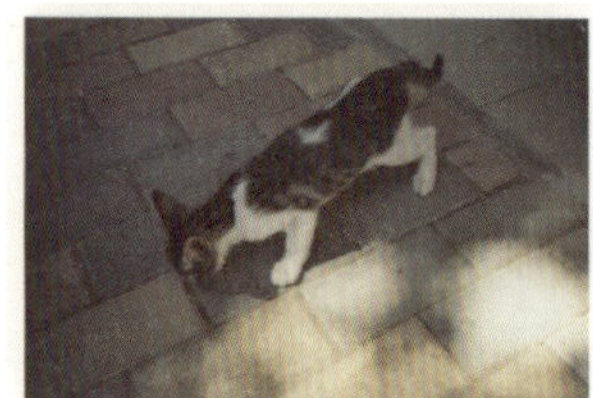

Plate 586
(Cliché of an Animal, Young Cat) I

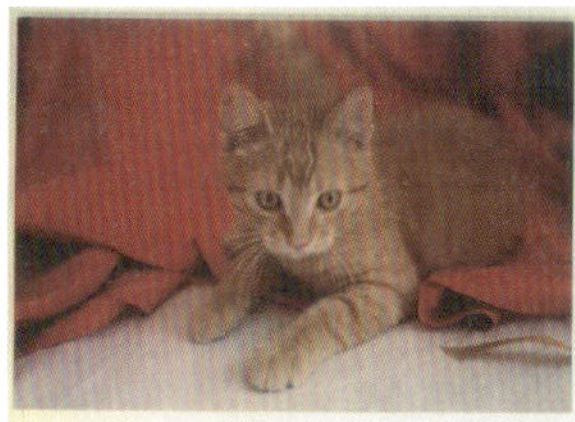

Plate 589
(Cliché of an Animal, Young Cat) II

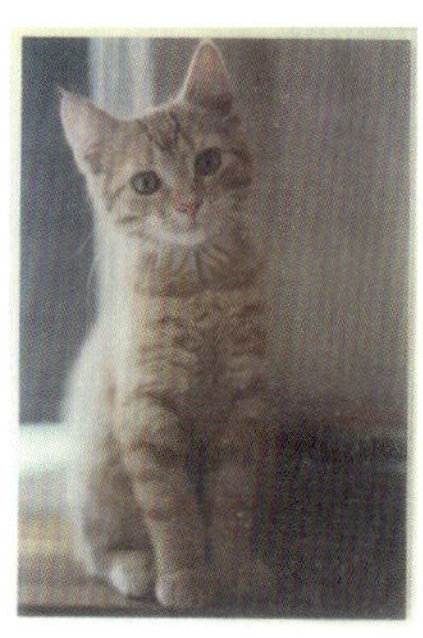

Plate 590
(Cliché of an Animal, Young Cat) III

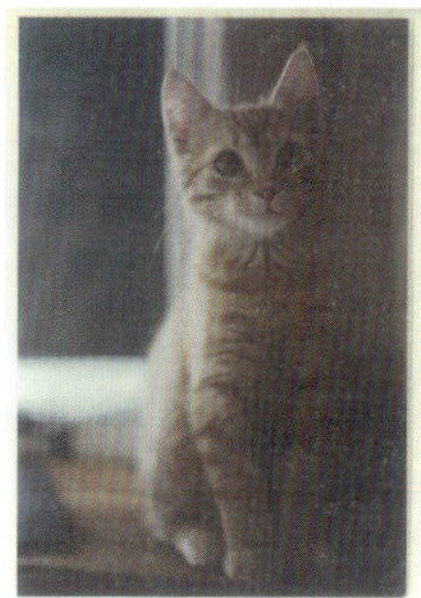

Plate 591
(Cliché of an Animal, Young Cat) III

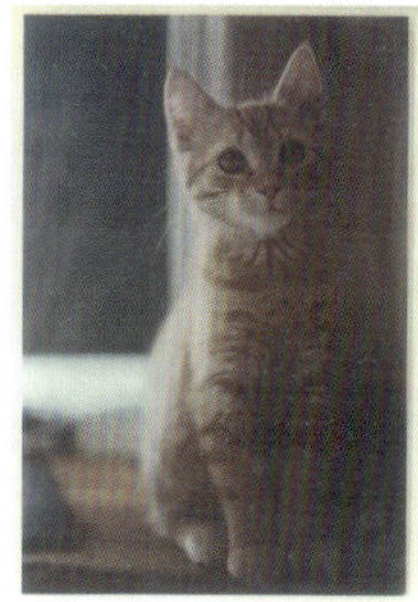

Plate 592
(Cliché of an Animal, Young Cat) III

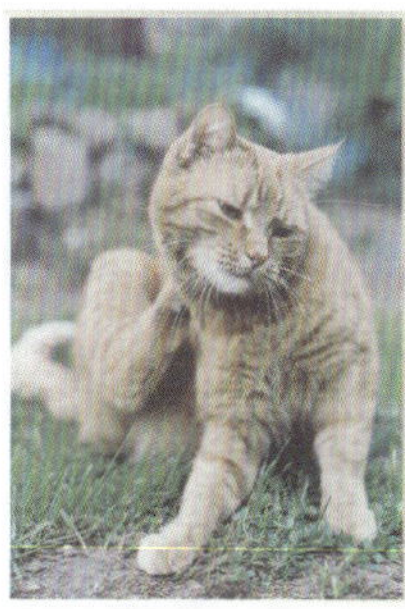

Plate 593
(Cliché of an Animal, Cat)

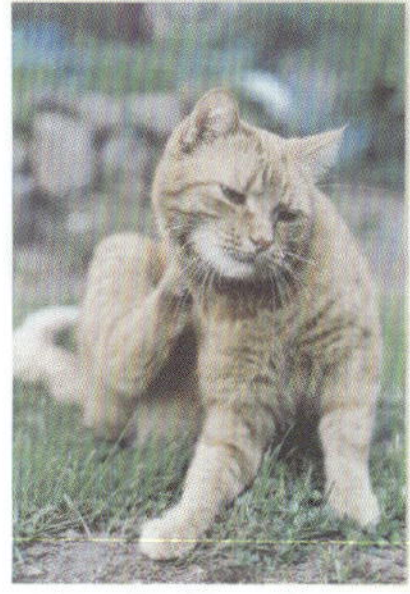

Plate 594
(Cliché of an Animal, Cat)

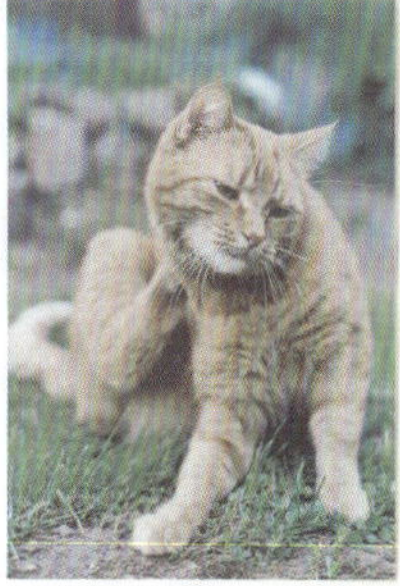

Plate 595
(Cliché of an Animal, Cat)

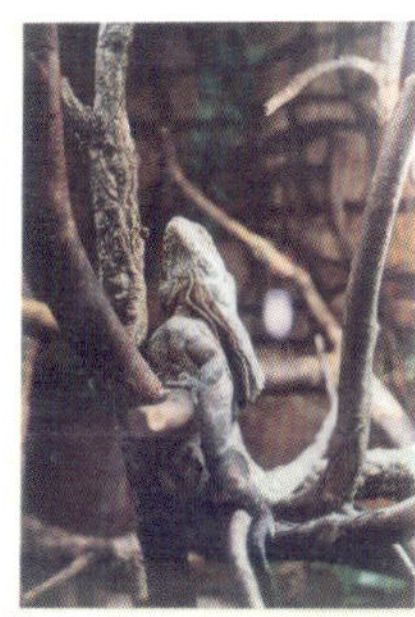

Plate 596
(Cliché of an Animal, Reptile) I

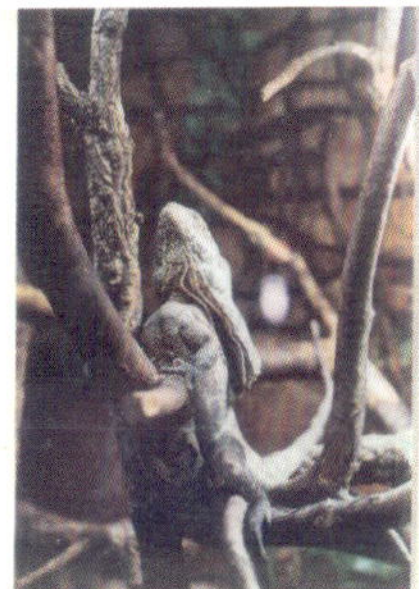

Plate 597
(Cliché of an Animal, Reptile) I

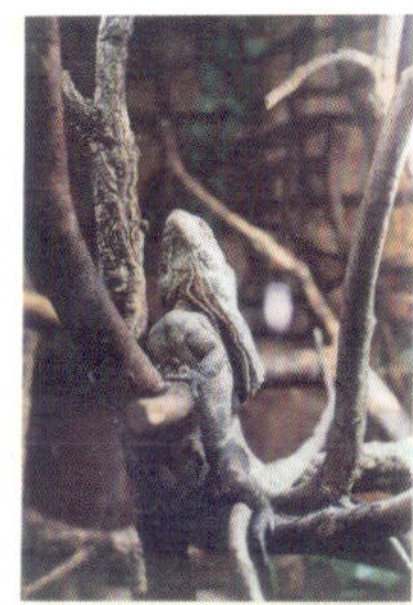

Plate 598
(Cliché of an Animal, Reptile) I

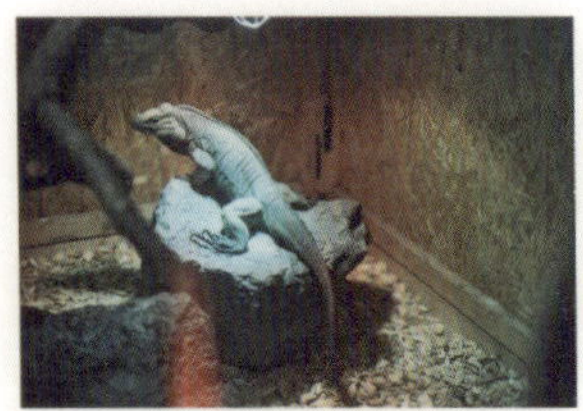

Plate 599
(Cliché of an Animal, Reptile) II

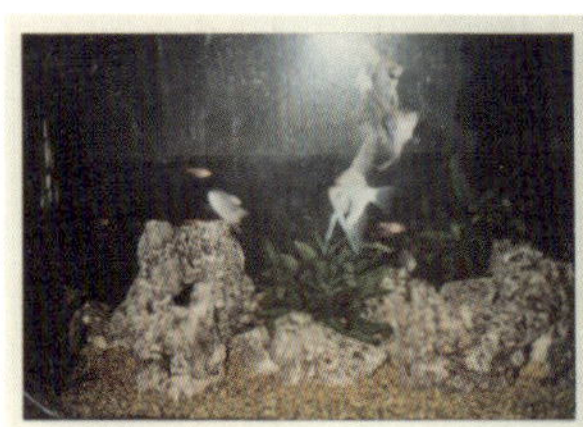

Plate 602
(Cliché of Animals, Fish, Aquarium) I

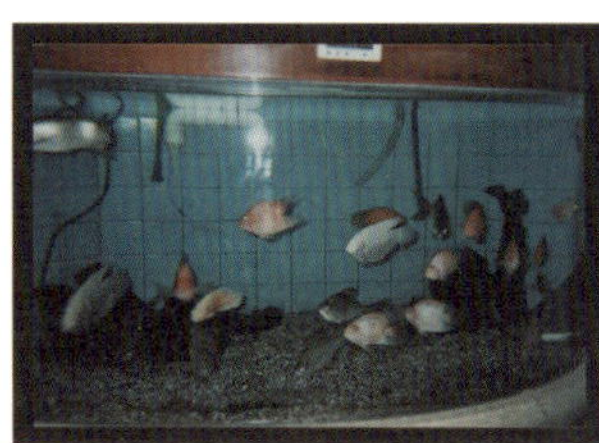

Plate 605
(Cliché of Animals, Fish, Aquarium) II

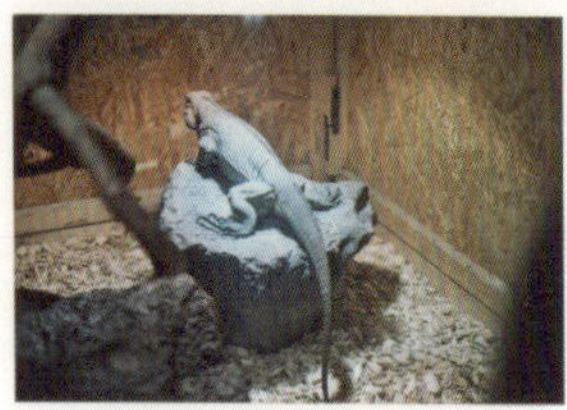

Plate 600
(Cliché of an Animal, Reptile) II

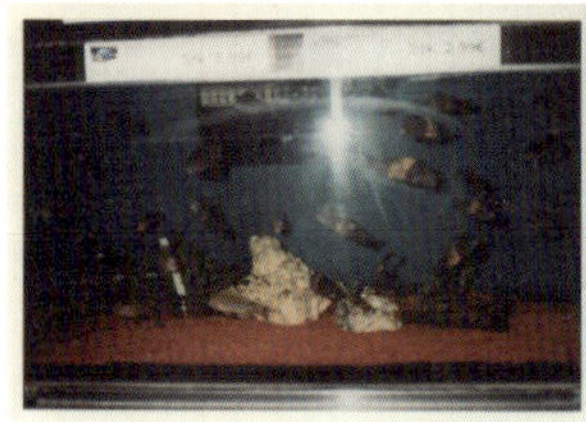

Plate 603
(Cliché of Animals, Fish, Aquarium) I

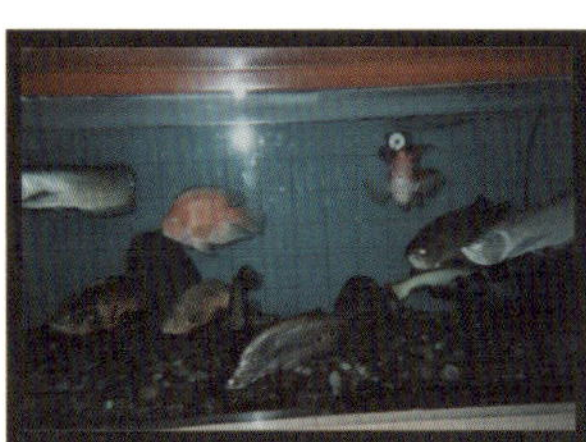

Plate 606
(Cliché of Animals, Fish, Aquarium) II

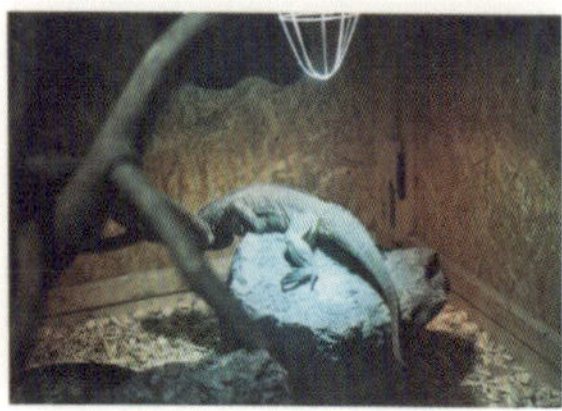

Plate 601
(Cliché of an Animal, Reptile) II

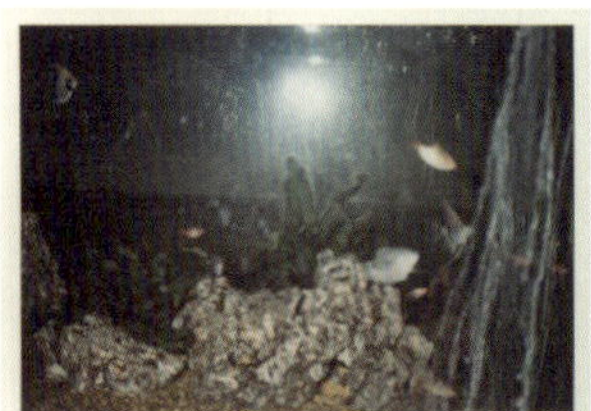

Plate 604
(Cliché of Animals, Fish, Aquarium) I

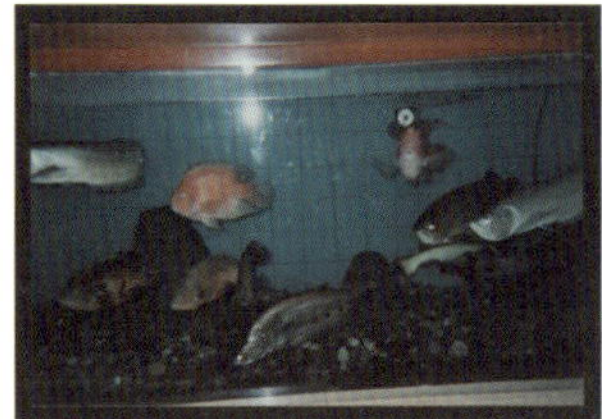

Plate 607
(Cliché of Animals, Fish, Aquarium) II

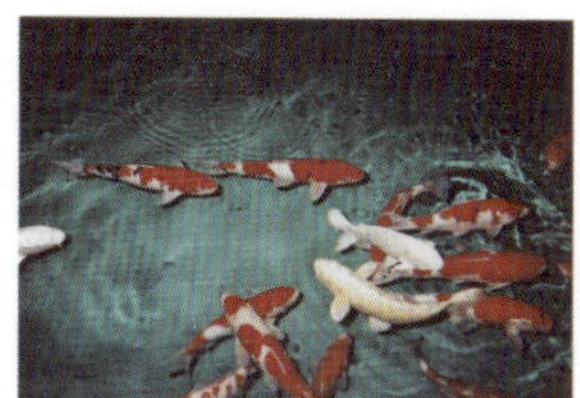

Plate 608
(Cliché of Animals, Fish)

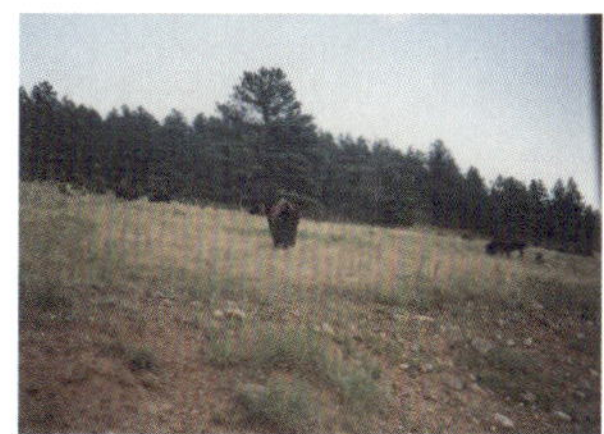

Plate 611
(Cliché of an Animal, Buffalo) I

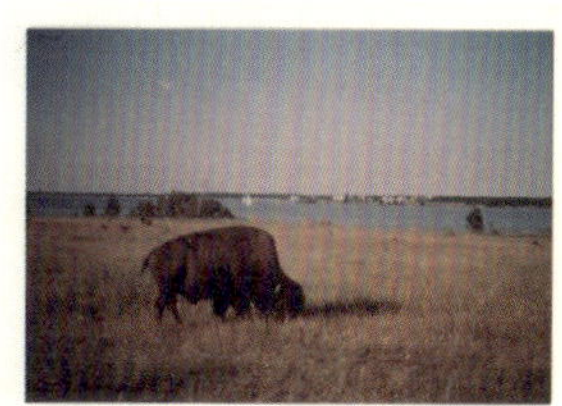

Plate 614
(Cliché of an Animal, Buffalo) II

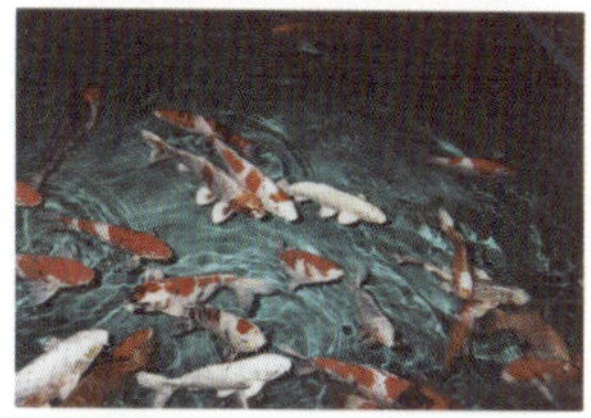

Plate 609
(Cliché of Animals, Fish)

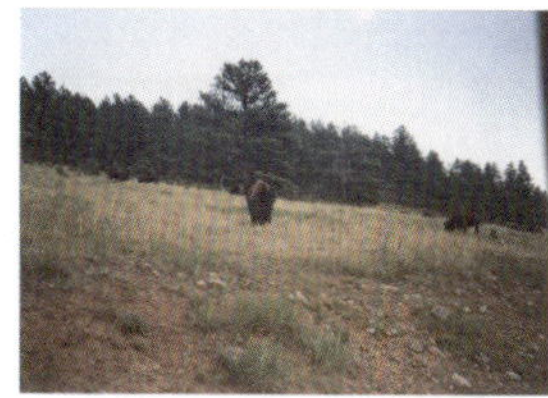

Plate 612
(Cliché of an Animal, Buffalo) I

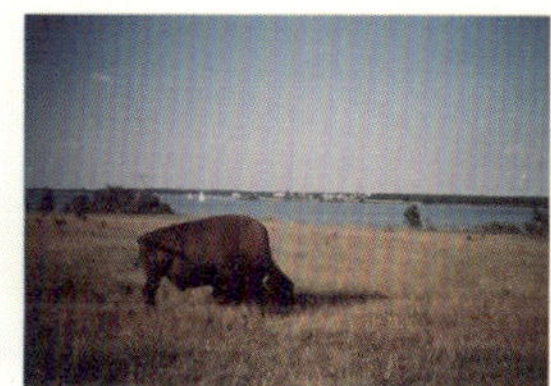

Plate 615
(Cliché of an Animal, Buffalo) II

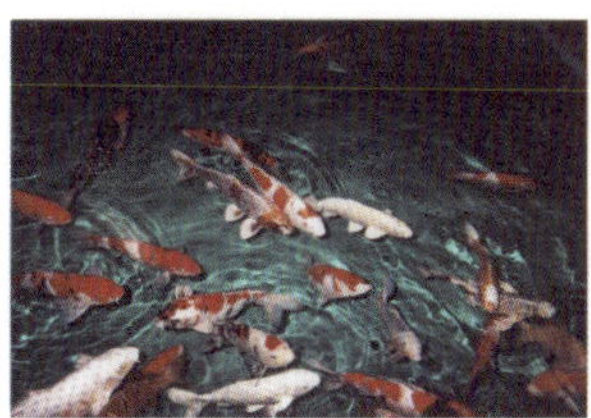

Plate 610
(Cliché of Animals, Fish)

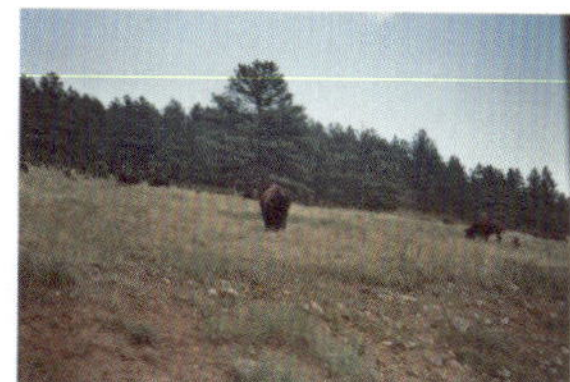

Plate 613
(Cliché of an Animal, Buffalo) I

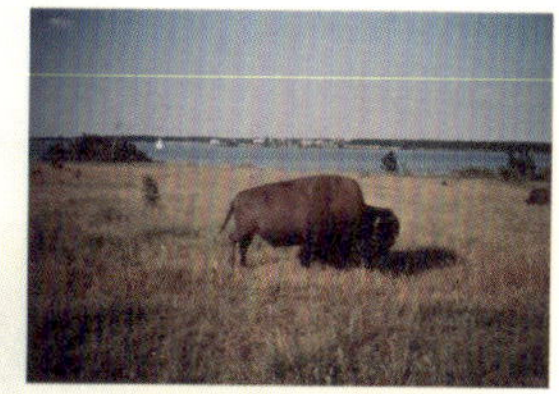

Plate 616
(Cliché of an Animal, Buffalo) II

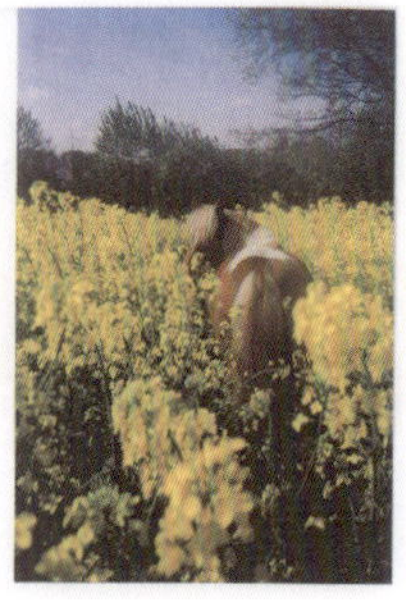

Plate 617
(Cliché of an Animal, Pony) I

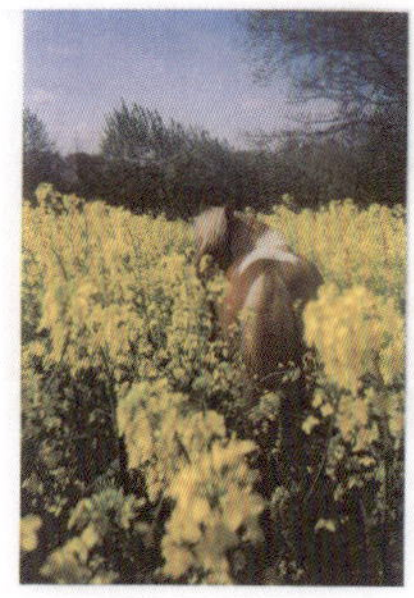

Plate 618
(Cliché of an Animal, Pony) I

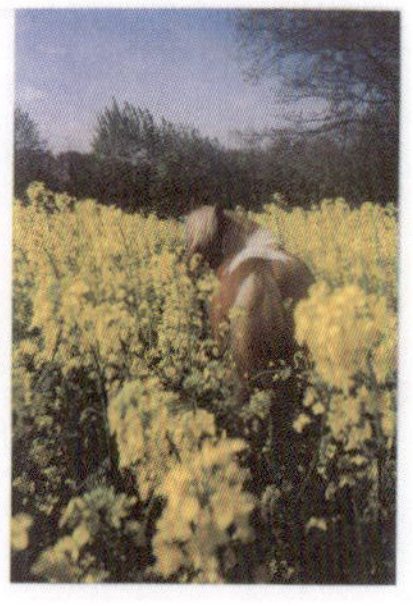

Plate 619
(Cliché of an Animal, Pony) I

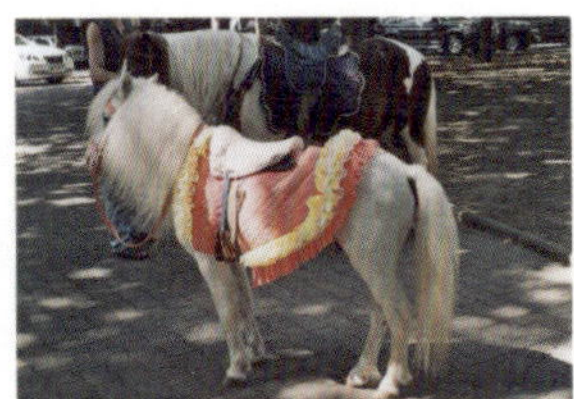

Plate 620
(Cliché of an Animal, Pony) II

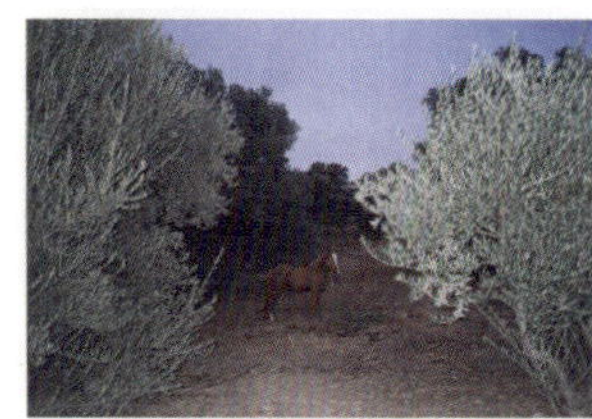

Plate 623
(Cliché of an Animal, Horse)

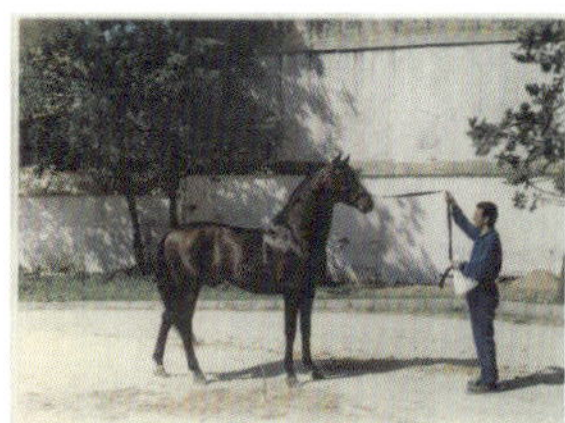

Plate 626
(Cliché of an Animal, Horse, Stallion)

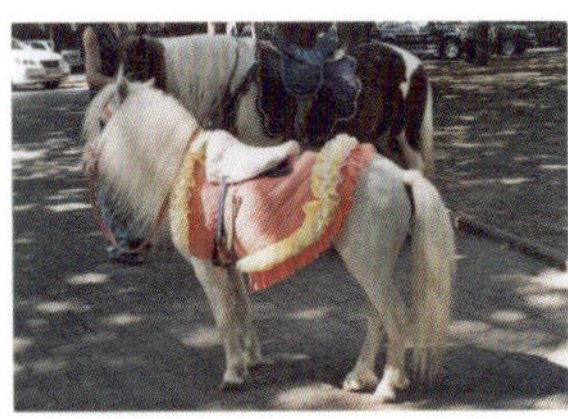

Plate 621
(Cliché of an Animal, Pony) II

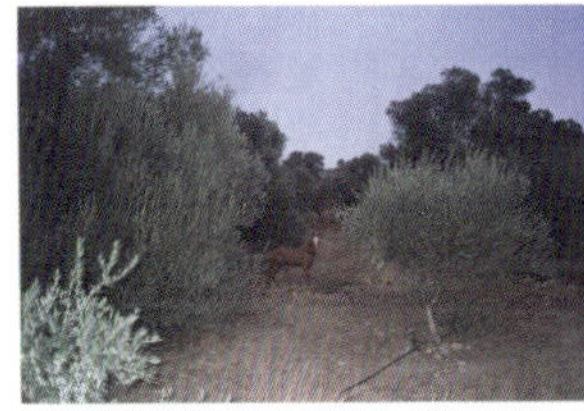

Plate 624
(Cliché of an Animal, Horse)

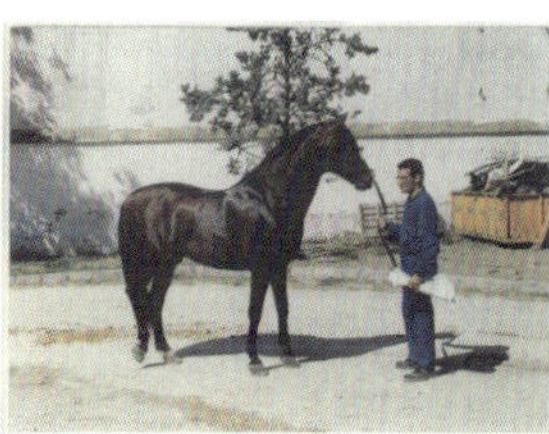

Plate 627
(Cliché of an Animal, Horse, Stallion)

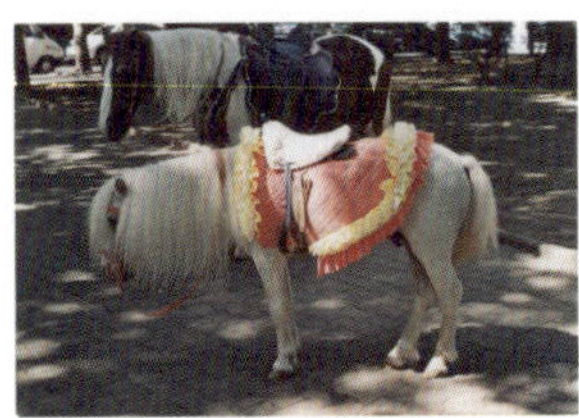

Plate 622
(Cliché of an Animal, Pony) II

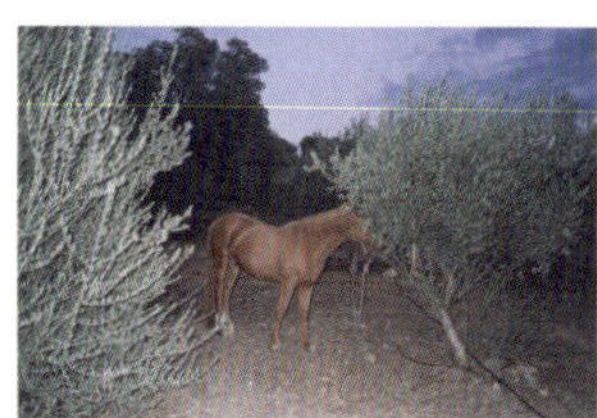

Plate 625
(Cliché of an Animal, Horse)

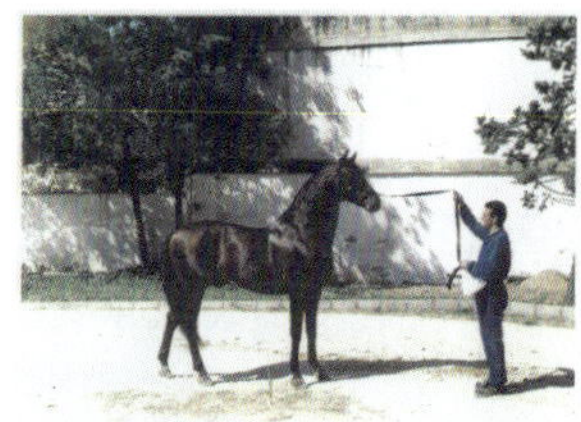

Plate 628
(Cliché of an Animal, Horse, Stallion)

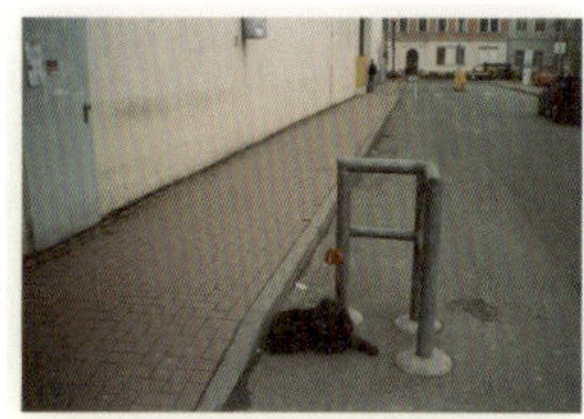

Plate 629
(Cliché of an Animal, Dog Waiting)

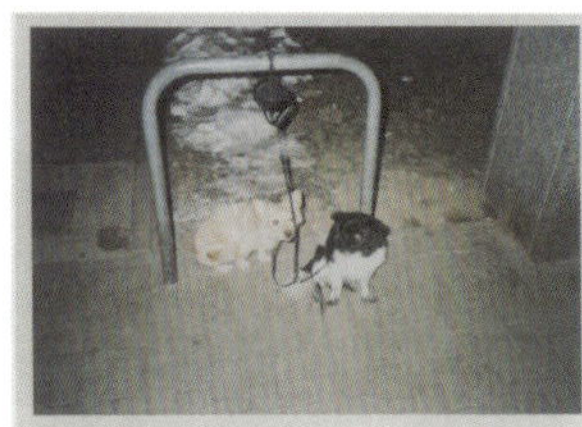

Plate 632
(Cliché of Animals, Two Dogs Waiting)

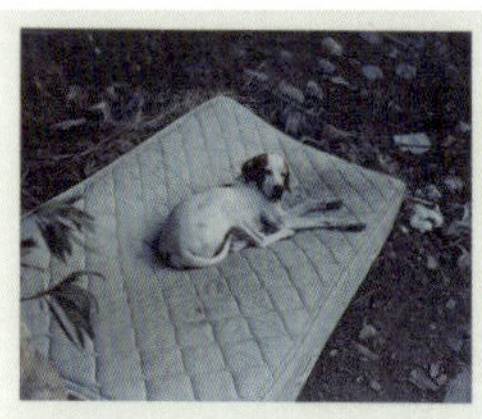

Plate 635
(Cliché of an Animal, Dog Lying) I

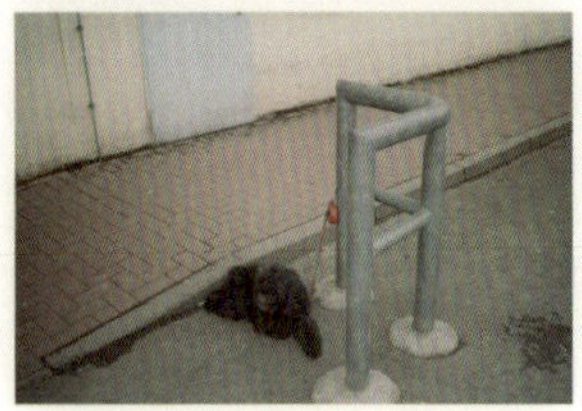

Plate 630
(Cliché of an Animal, Dog Waiting)

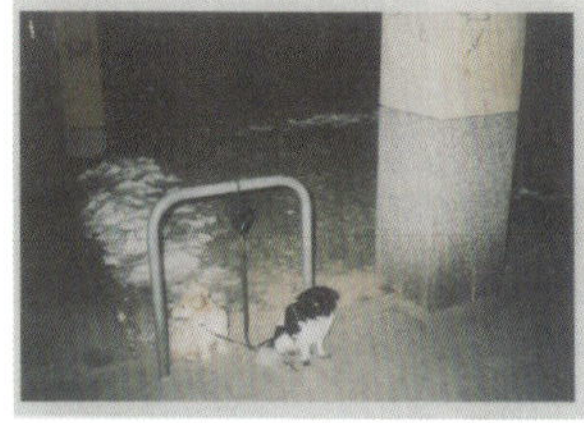

Plate 633
(Cliché of Animals, Two Dogs Waiting)

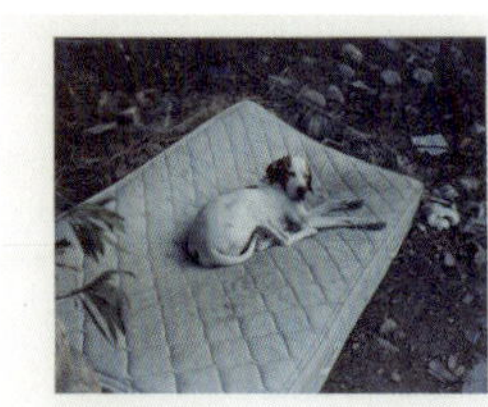

Plate 636
(Cliché of an Animal, Dog Lying) I

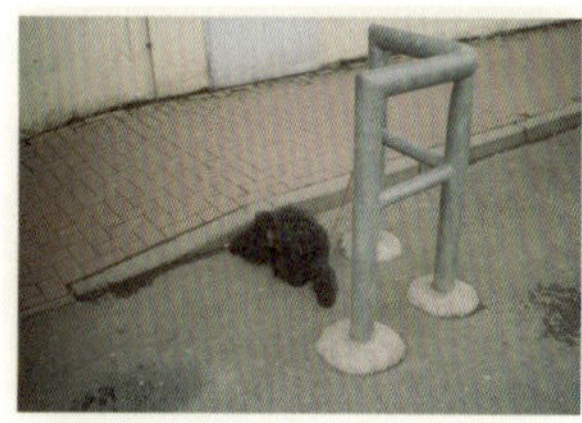

Plate 631
(Cliché of an Animal, Dog Waiting)

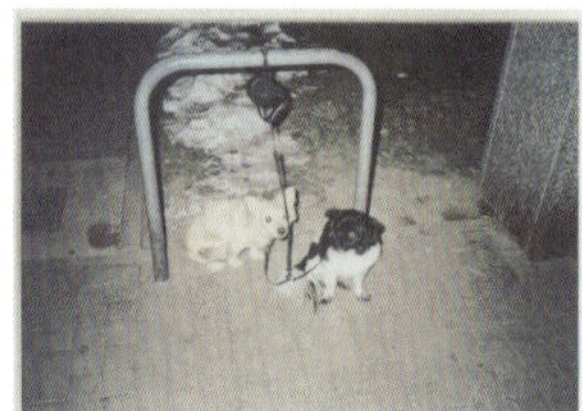

Plate 634
(Cliché of Animals, Two Dogs Waiting)

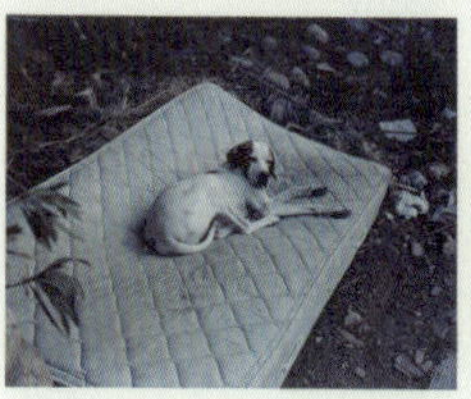

Plate 637
(Cliché of an Animal, Dog Lying) I

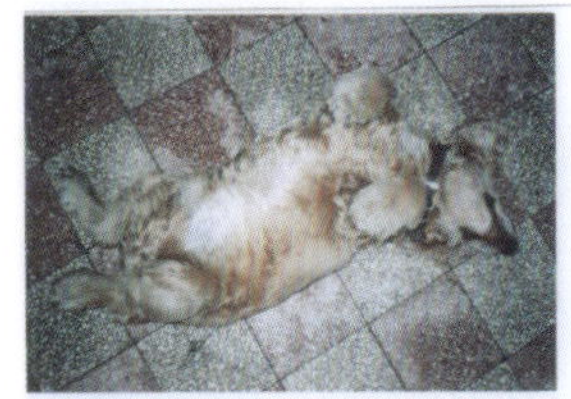

Plate 638
(Cliché of an Animal, Dog Lying) II

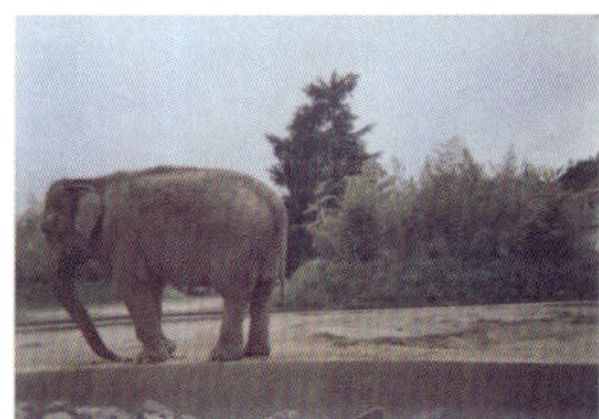

Plate 641
(Cliché of an Animal, Elephant)

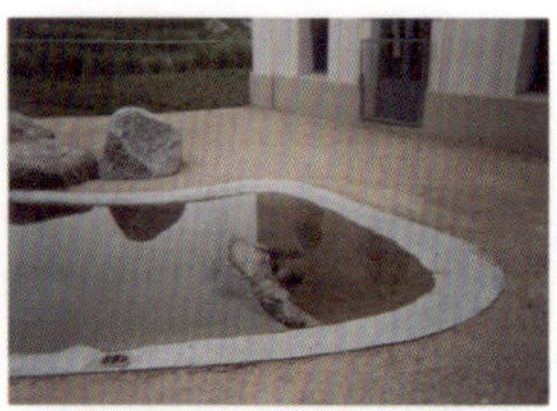

Plate 644
(Cliché of an Animal, Crocodile)

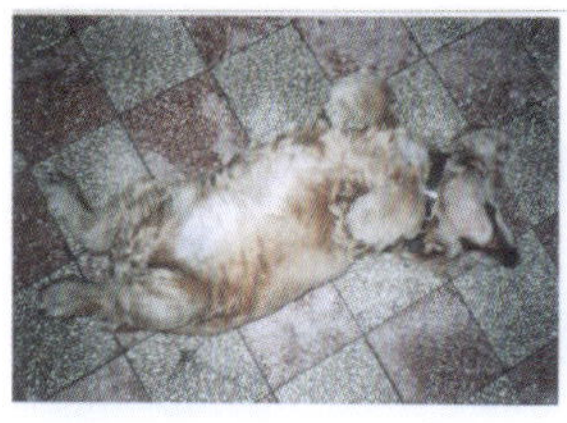

Plate 639
(Cliché of an Animal, Dog Lying) II

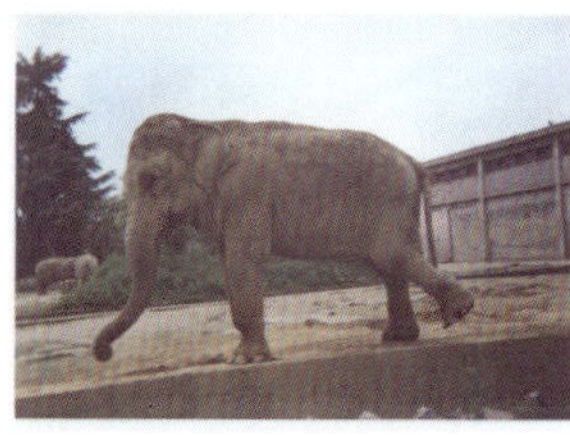

Plate 642
(Cliché of an Animal, Elephant)

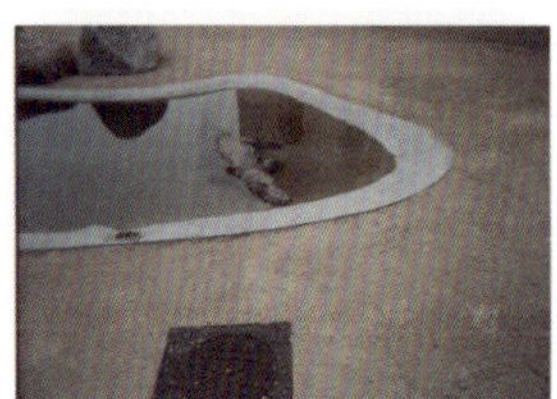

Plate 645
(Cliché of an Animal, Crocodile)

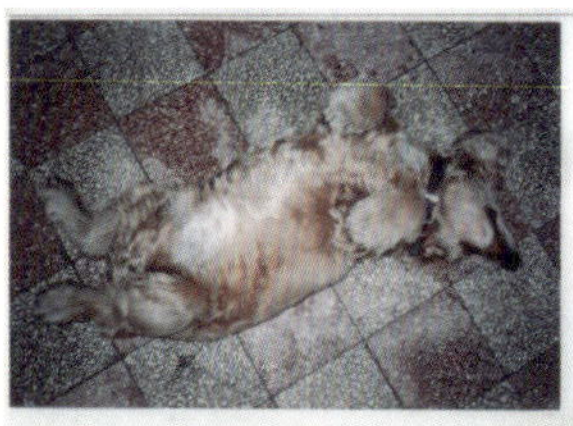

Plate 640
(Cliché of an Animal, Dog Lying) II

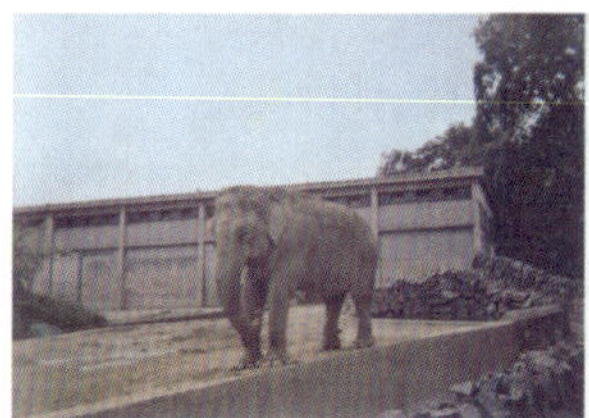

Plate 643
(Cliché of an Animal, Elephant)

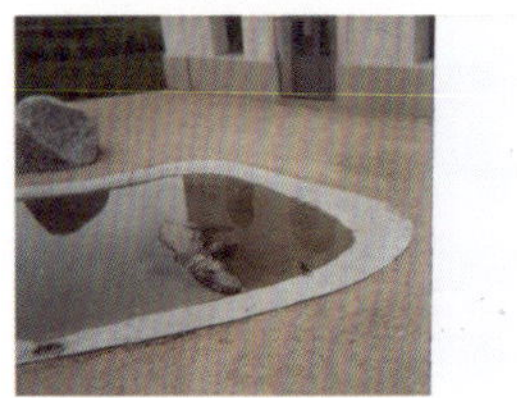

Plate 646
(Cliché of an Animal, Crocodile)

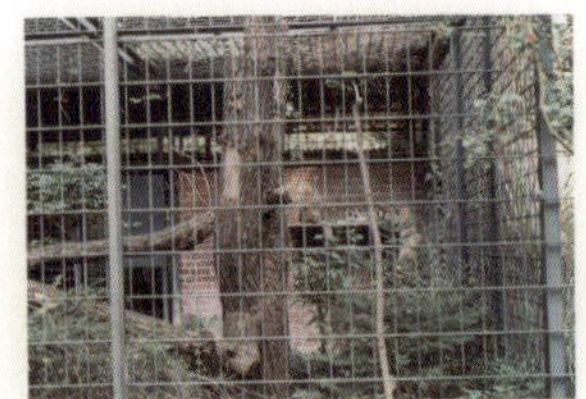

Plate 647
(Cliché of an Animal, Ocelot)

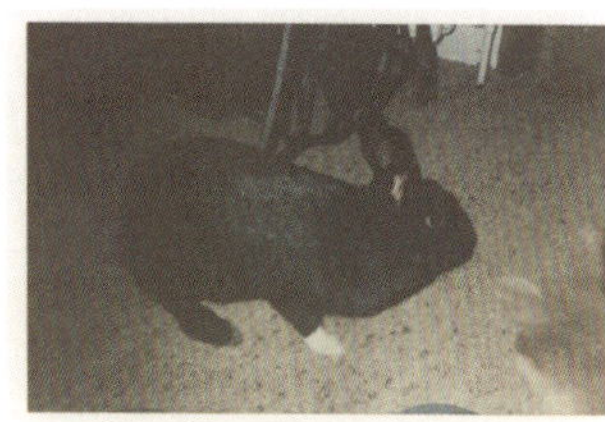

Plate 650
(Cliché of an Animal, Rabbit) I

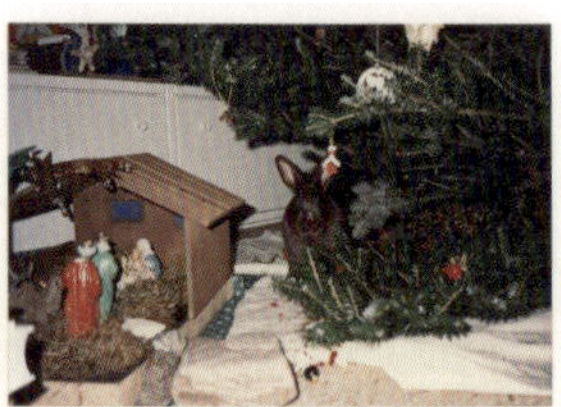

Plate 653
(Cliché of an Animal, Rabbit) II

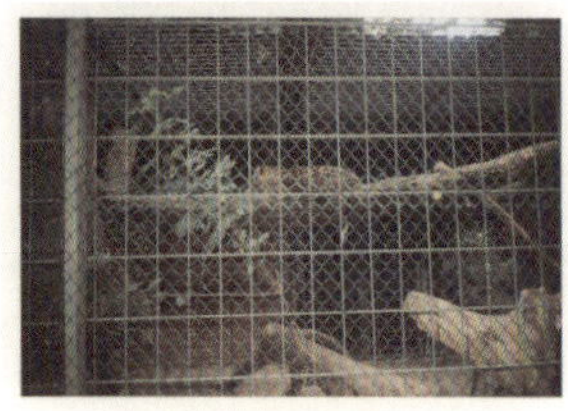

Plate 648
(Cliché of an Animal, Ocelot)

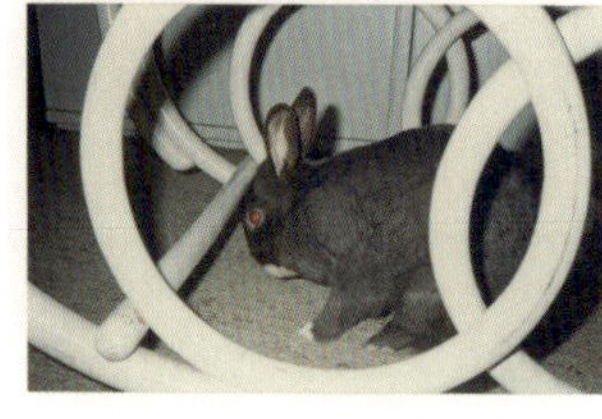

Plate 651
(Cliché of an Animal, Rabbit) I

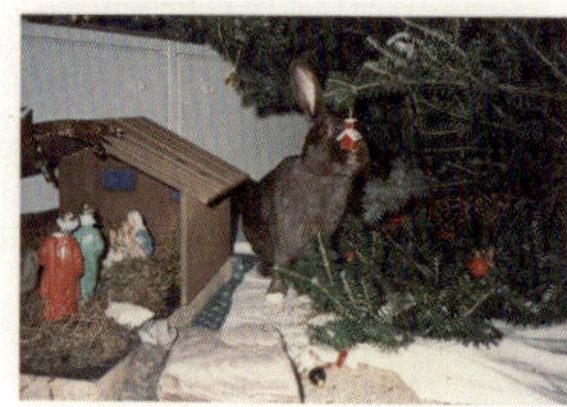

Plate 654
(Cliché of an Animal, Rabbit) II

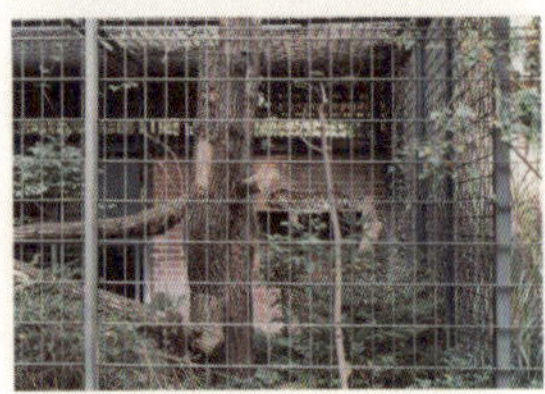

Plate 649
(Cliché of an Animal, Ocelot)

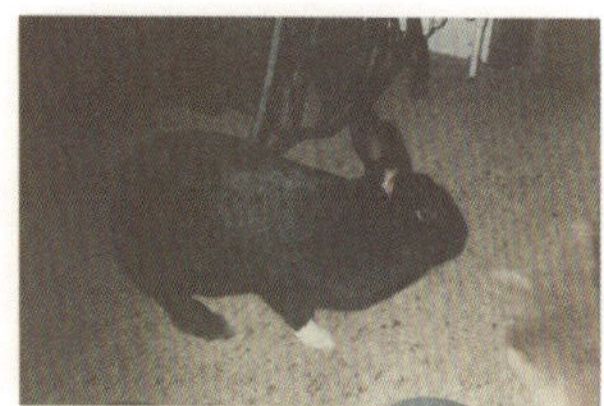

Plate 652
(Cliché of an Animal, Rabbit) I

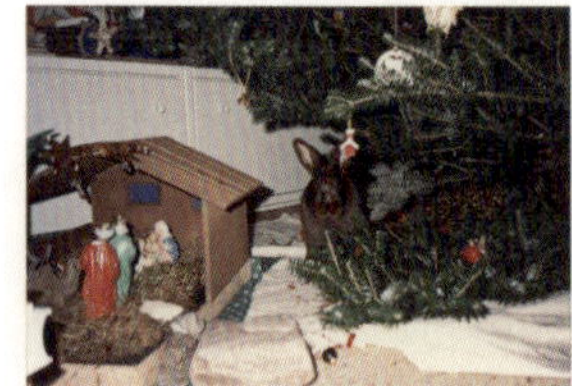

Plate 655
(Cliché of an Animal, Rabbit) II

A

PICTURE OF A PAINTER (P. OF A P.) I

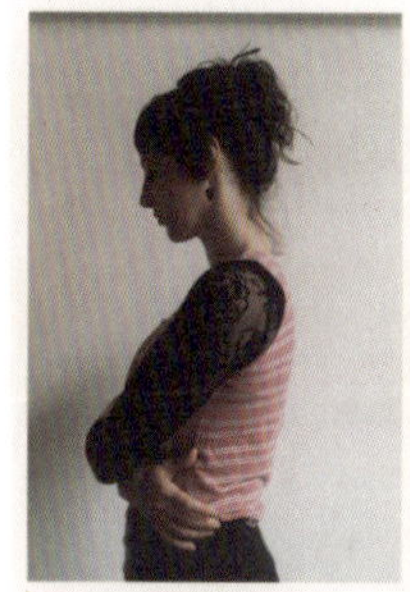

Plate 656
Corinne von Lebusa (P. of a P.) I

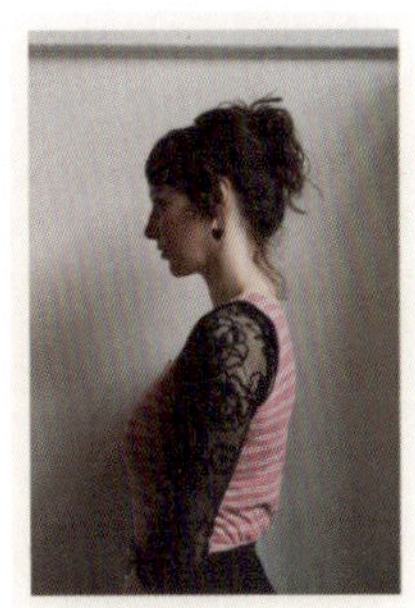

Plate 657
Corinne von Lebusa (P. of a P.) I

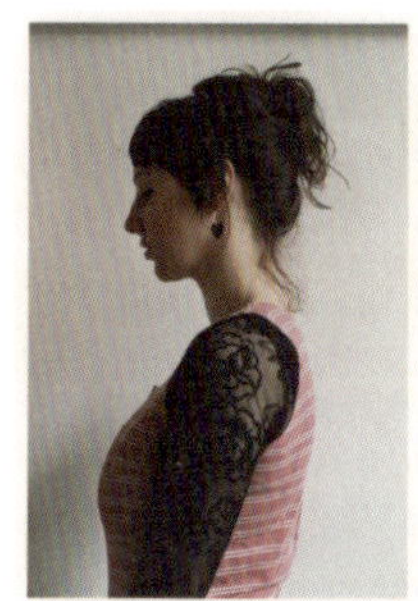

Plate 658
Corinne von Lebusa (P. of a P.) I

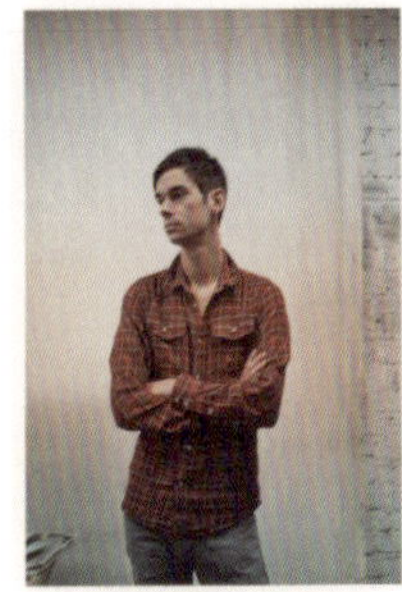

Plate 659
Johannes Rochhausen (P. of a P.) I

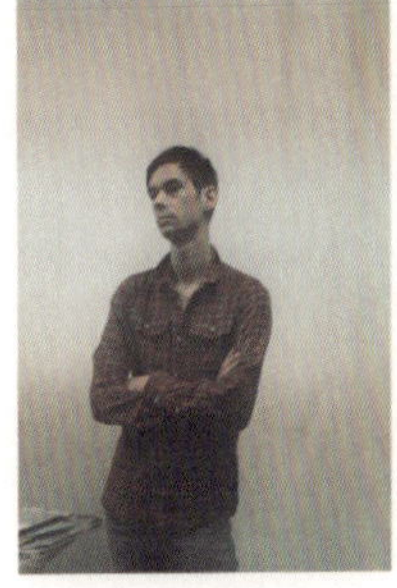

Plate 660
Johannes Rochhausen (P. of a P.) I

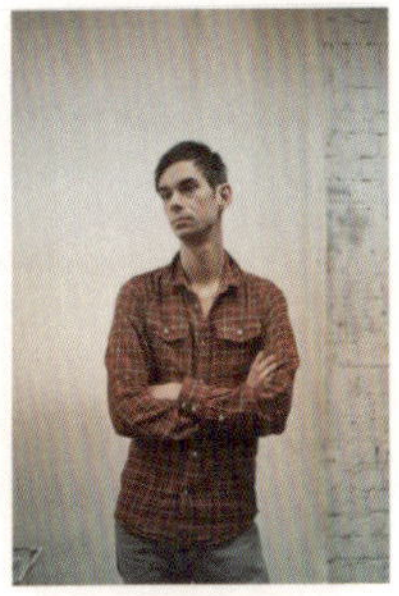

Plate 661
Johannes Rochhausen (P. of a P.) I

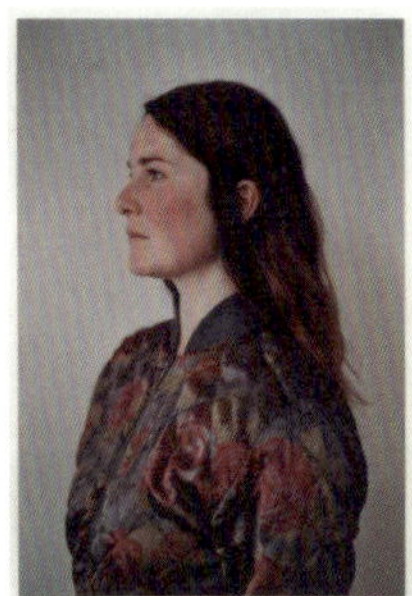

Plate 662
Kristina Schuldt (P. of a P.) I

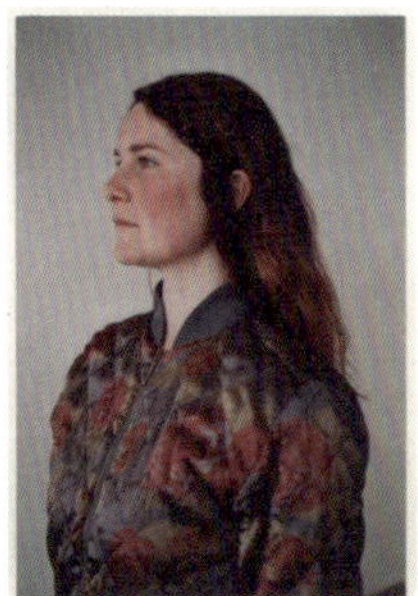

Plate 663
Kristina Schuldt (P. of a P.) I

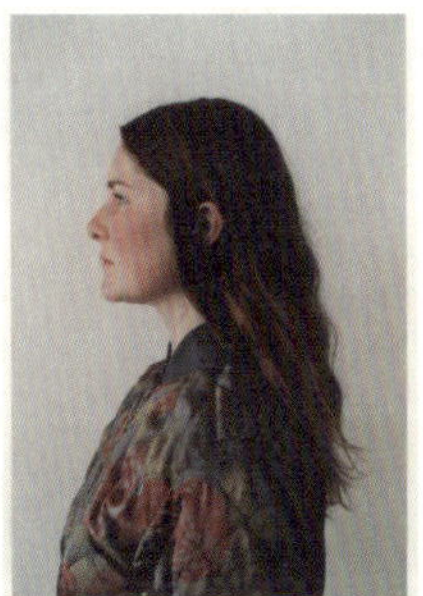

Plate 664
Kristina Schuldt (P. of a P.) I

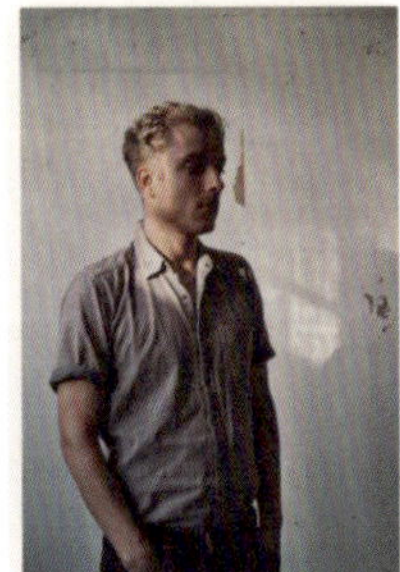

Plate 665
Valentin Just (P. of a P.) I

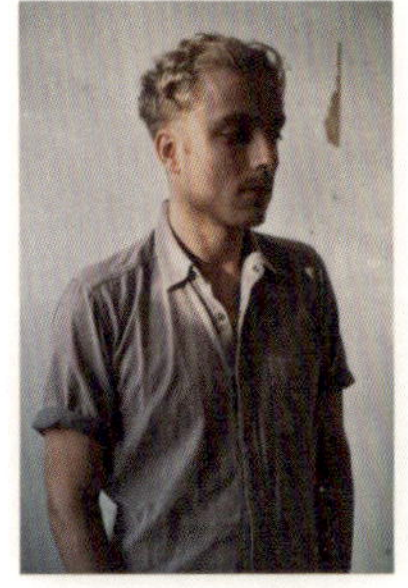

Plate 666
Valentin Just (P. of a P.) I

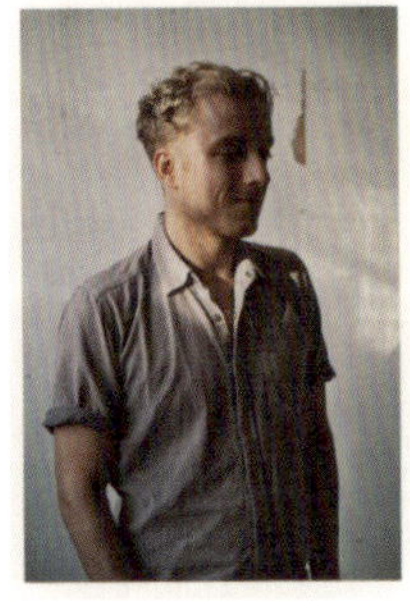

Plate 667
Valentin Just (P. of a P.) I

A

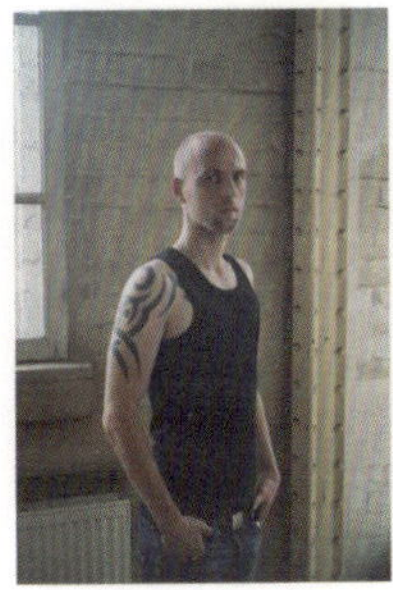
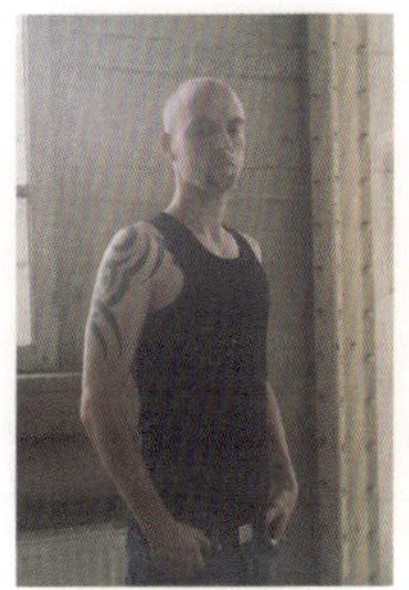
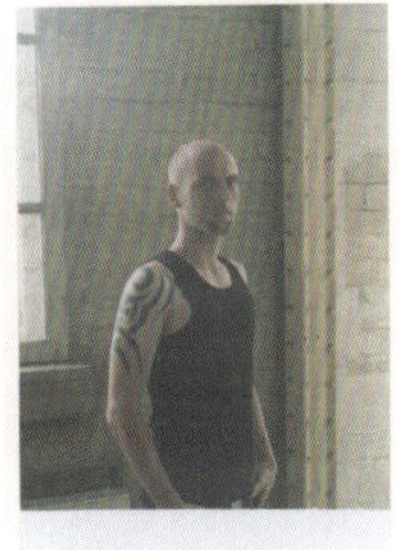

Plate 668
Sebastian Burger (P. of a P.) I

Plate 669
Sebastian Burger (P. of a P.) I

Plate 670
Sebastian Burger (P. of a P.) I

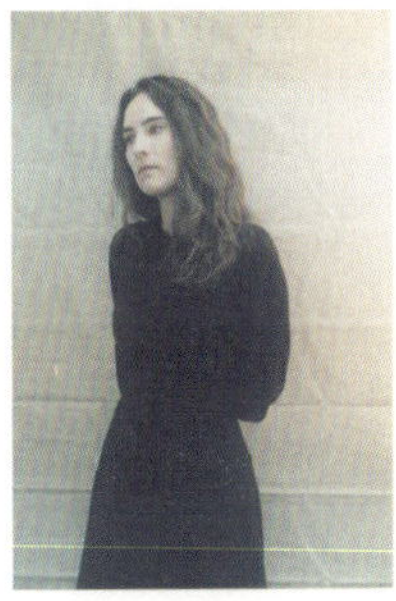
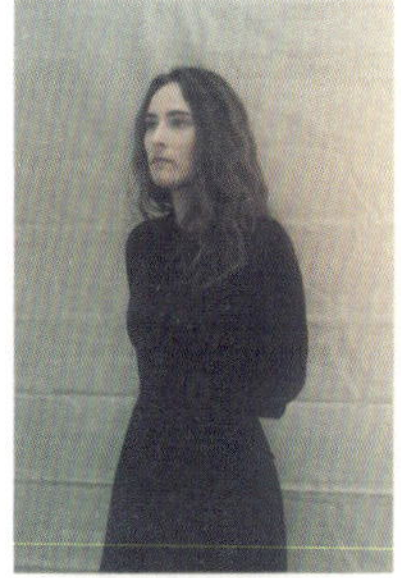
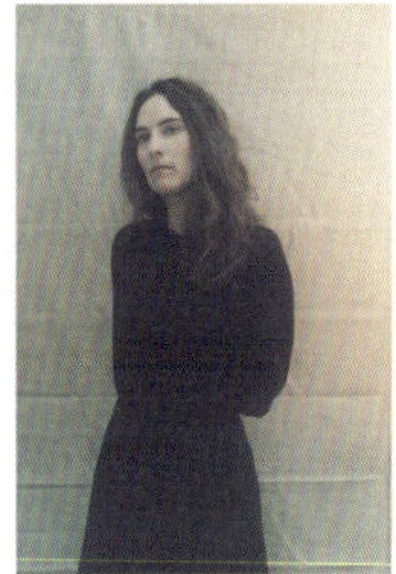

Plate 671
Isabelle Dutoit (P. of a P.) I

Plate 672
Isabelle Dutoit (P. of a P.) I

Plate 673
Isabelle Dutoit (P. of a P.) I

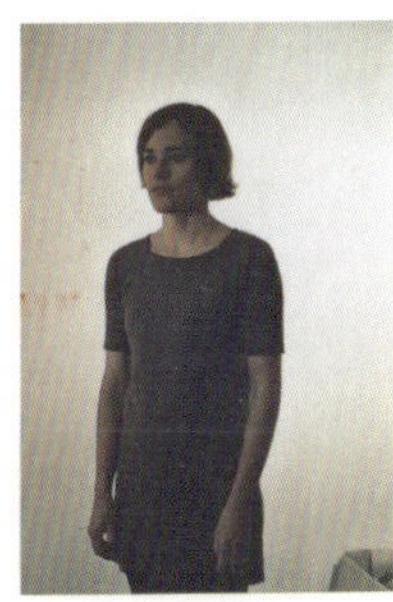
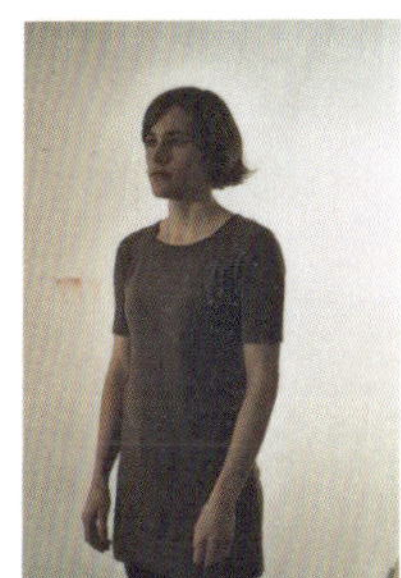
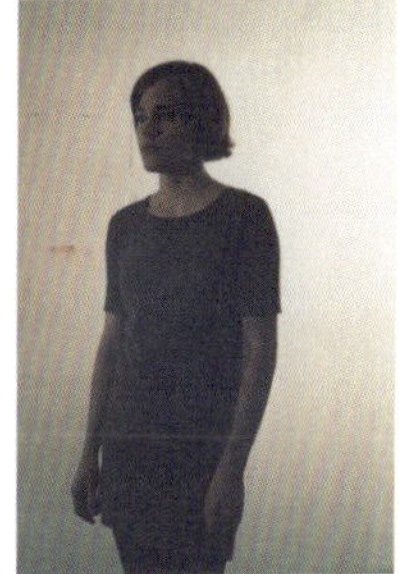

Plate 674
Katharina Schilling (P. of a P.) I

Plate 675
Katharina Schilling (P. of a P.) I

Plate 676
Katharina Schilling (P. of a P.) I

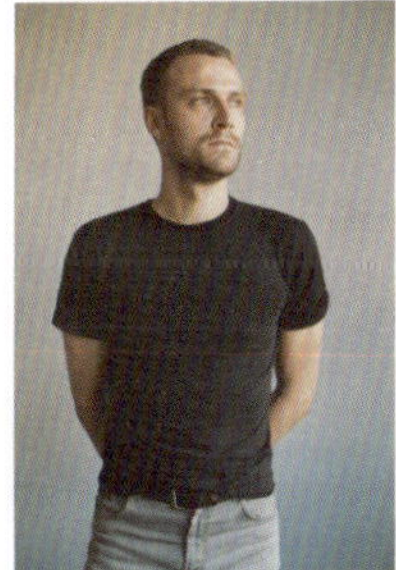
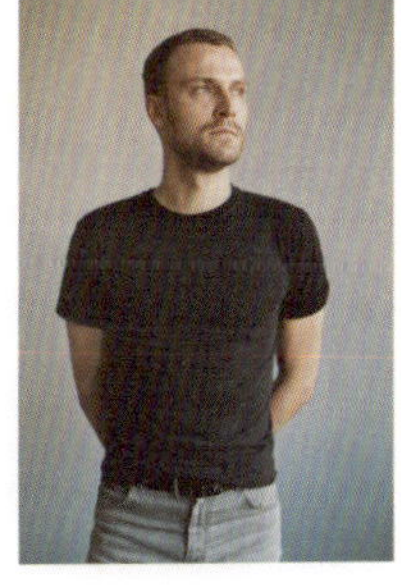
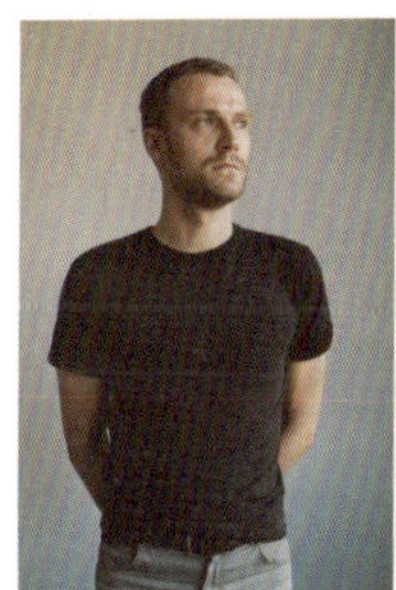

Plate 677
Robert Seidel (P. of a P.) I

Plate 678
Robert Seidel (P. of a P.) I

Plate 679
Robert Seidel (P. of a P.) I

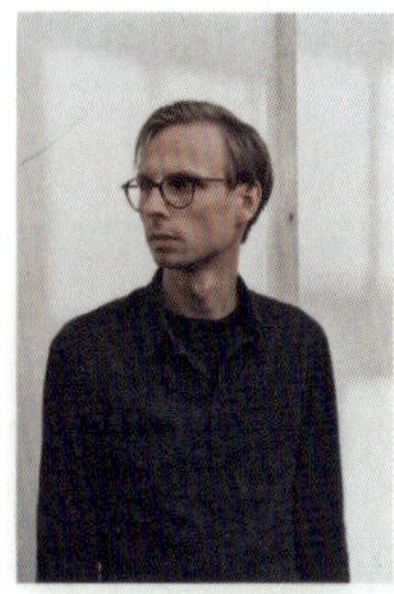

Plate 680
Sebastian Nebe (P. of a P.) I

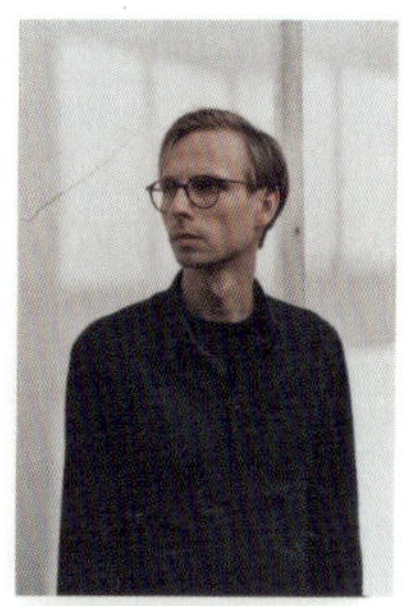

Plate 681
Sebastian Nebe (P. of a P.) I

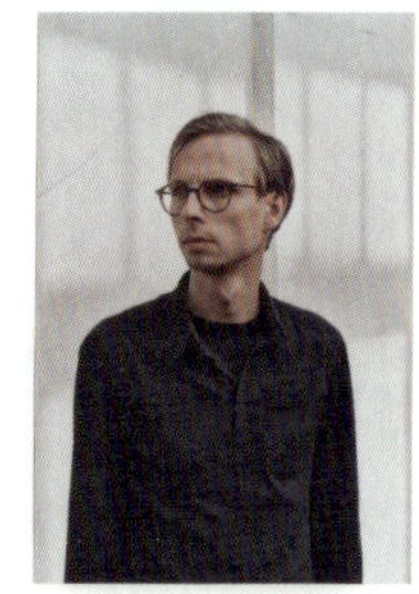

Plate 682
Sebastian Nebe (P. of a P.) I

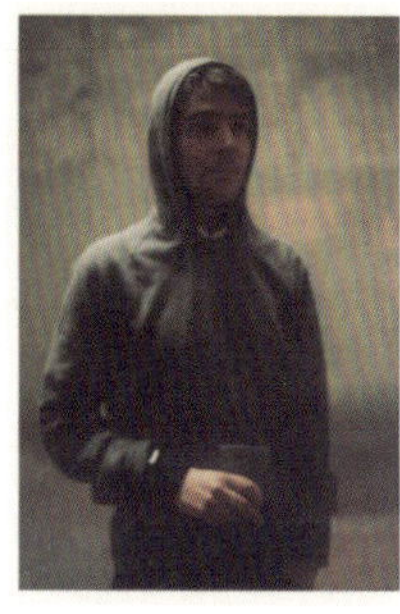

Plate 683
Johannes Tiepelmann (P. of a P.) I

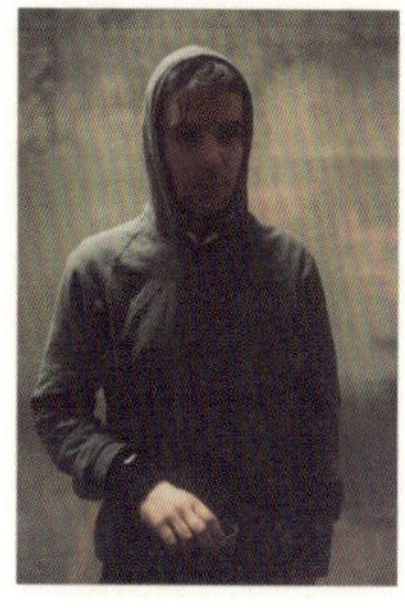

Plate 684
Johannes Tiepelmann (P. of a P.) I

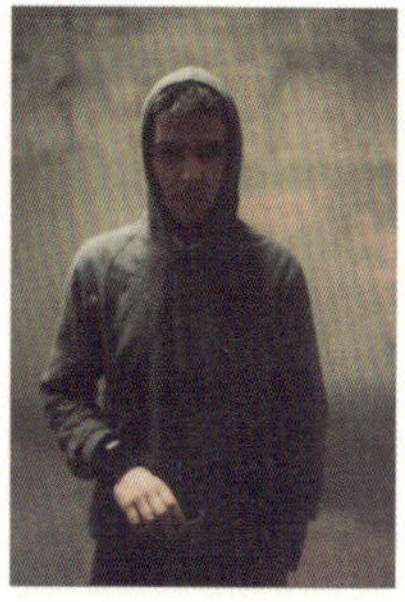

Plate 685
Johannes Tiepelmann (P. of a P.) I

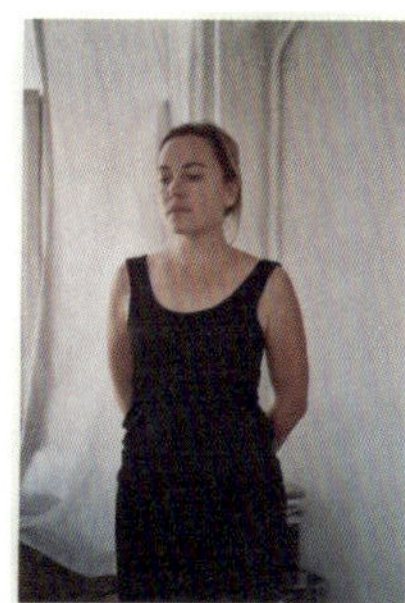

Plate 686
Yvette Kießling (P. of a P.) I

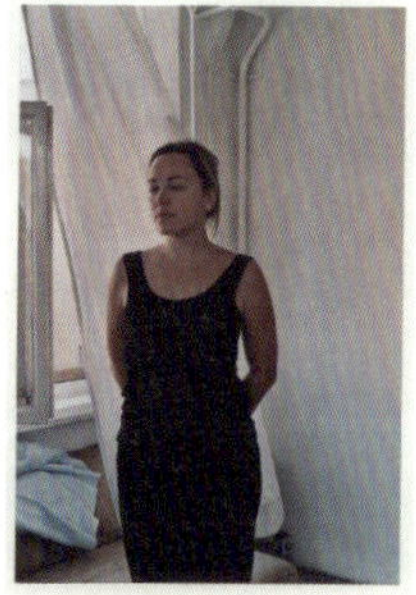

Plate 687
Yvette Kießling (P. of a P.) I

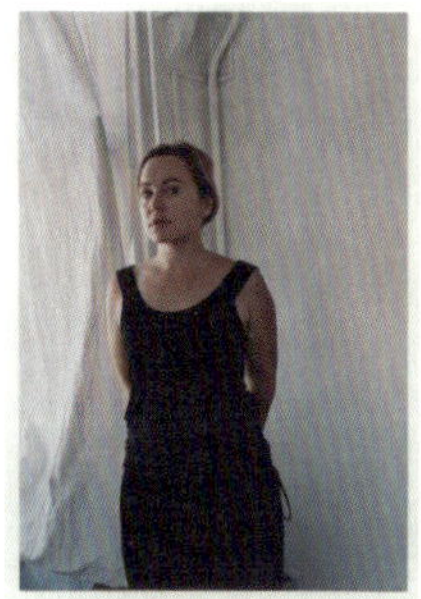

Plate 688
Yvette Kießling (P. of a P.) I

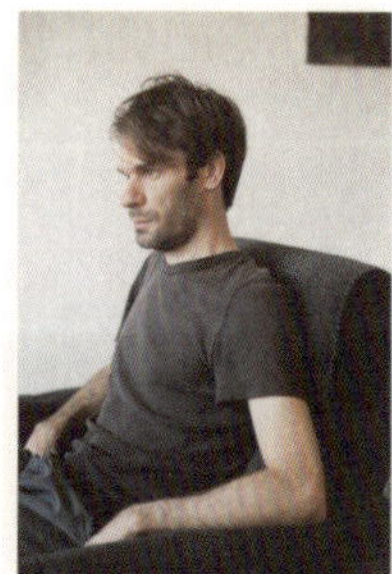

Plate 689
Steven Black (P. of a P.) I

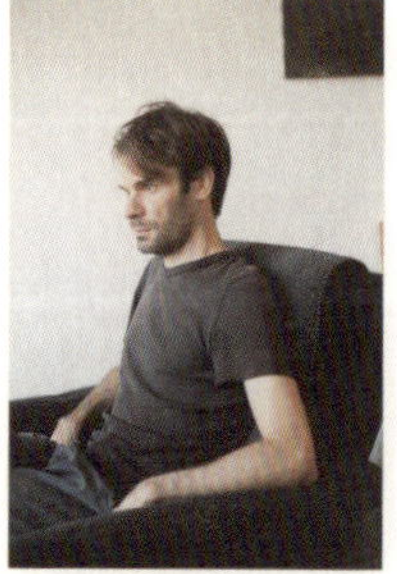

Plate 690
Steven Black (P. of a P.) I

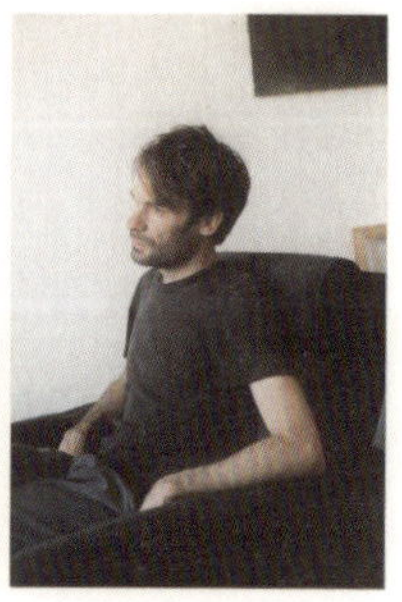

Plate 691
Steven Black (P. of a P.) I

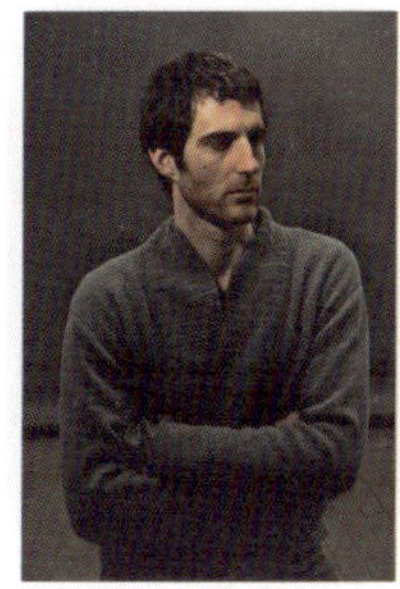

Plate 692
Jochen Plogsties (P. of a P.) I

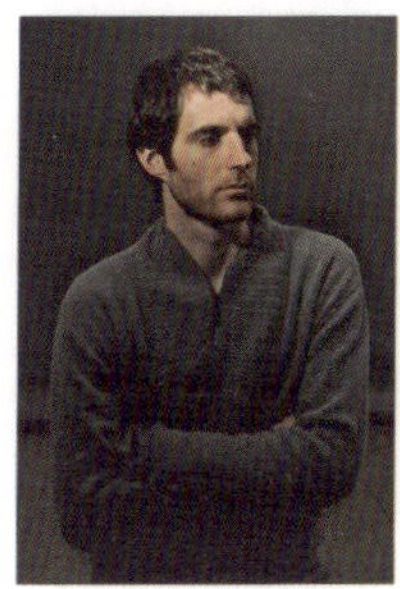

Plate 693
Jochen Plogsties (P. of a P.) I

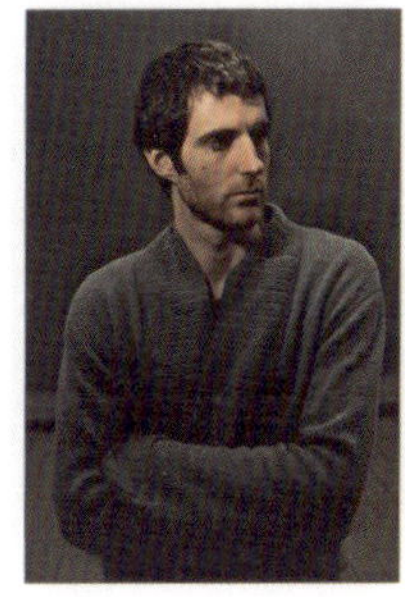

Plate 694
Jochen Plogsties (P. of a P.) I

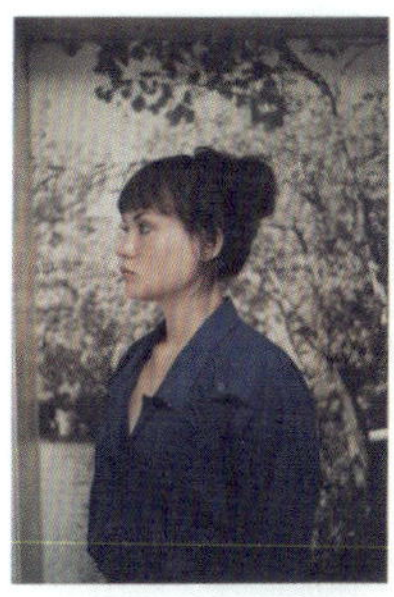

Plate 695
Julia Sie-Yong Fischer (P. of a P.) I

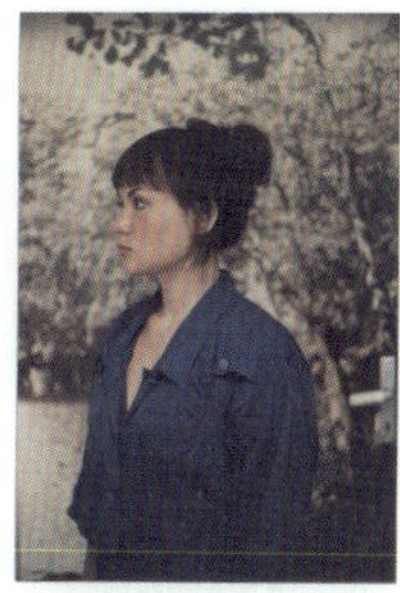

Plate 696
Julia Sie-Yong Fischer (P. of a P.) I

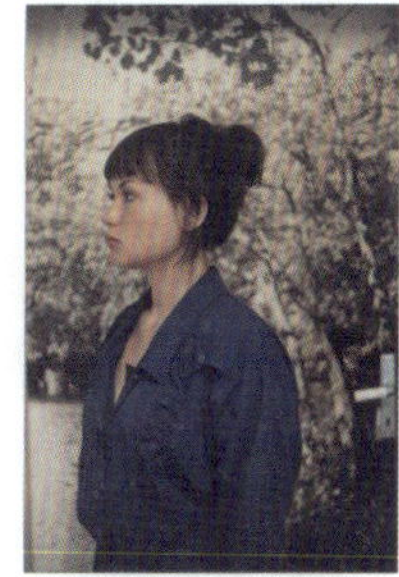

Plate 697
Julia Sie-Yong Fischer (P. of a P.) I

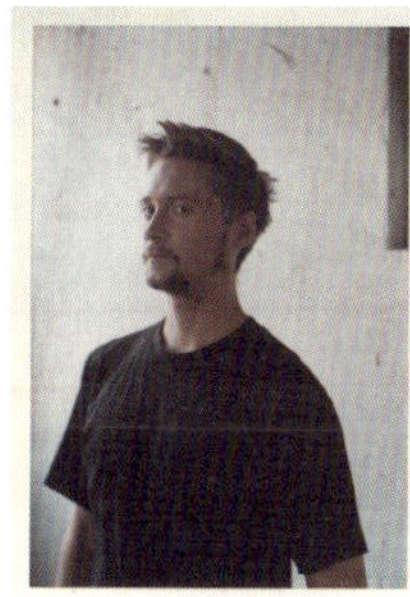

Plate 698
Matthias Sommerer (P. of a P.) I

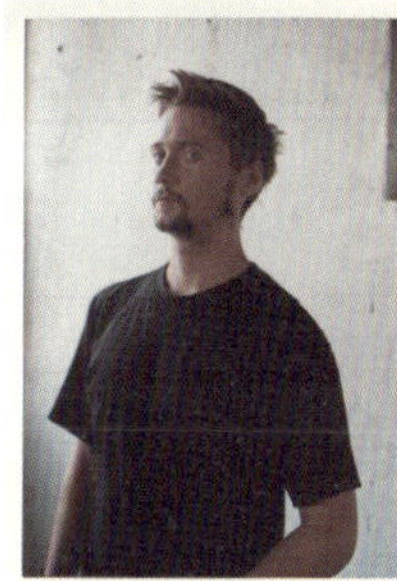

Plate 699
Matthias Sommerer (P. of a P.) I

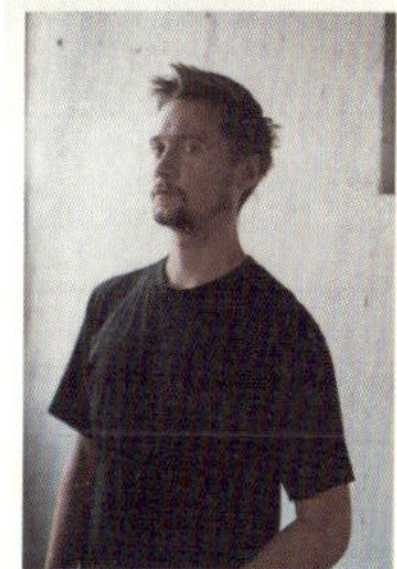

Plate 700
Matthias Sommerer (P. of a P.) I

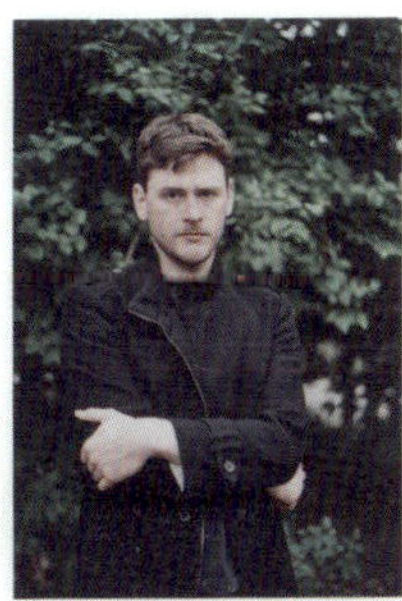

Plate 701
David O'Kane (P. of a P.) I

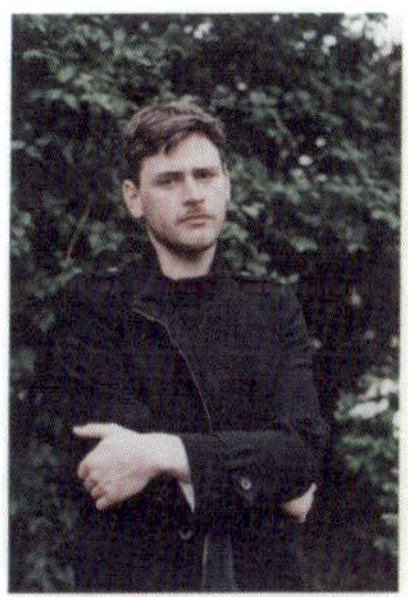

Plate 702
David O'Kane (P. of a P.) I

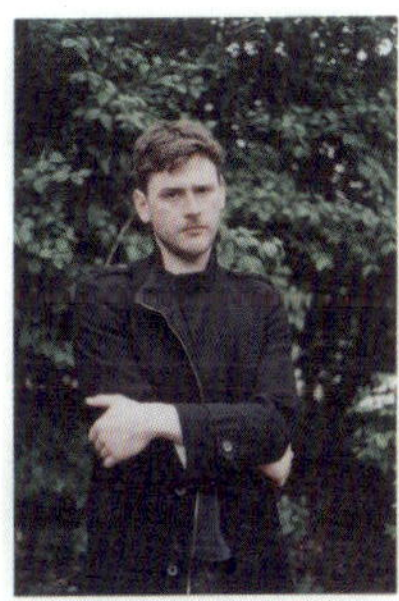

Plate 703
David O'Kane (P. of a P.) I

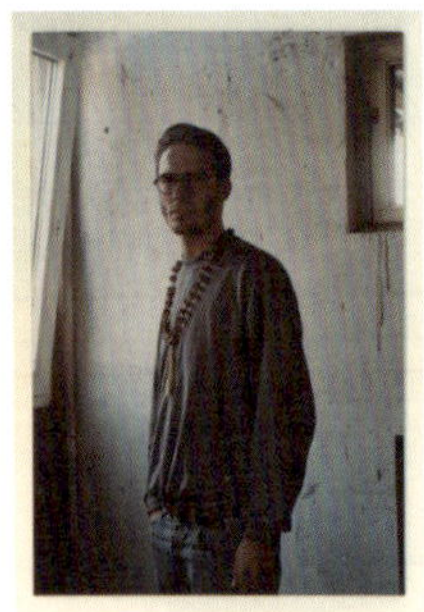

Plate 704
Maximilian Kirmse (P. of a P.) I

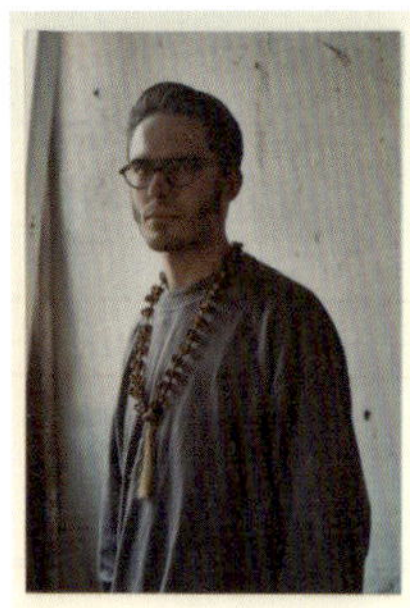

Plate 705
Maximilian Kirmse (P. of a P.) I

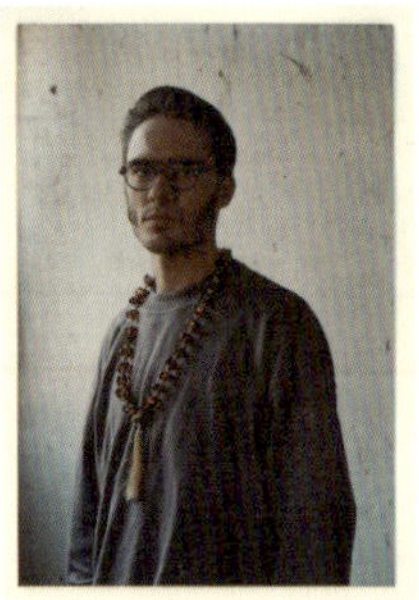

Plate 706
Maximilian Kirmse (P. of a P.) I

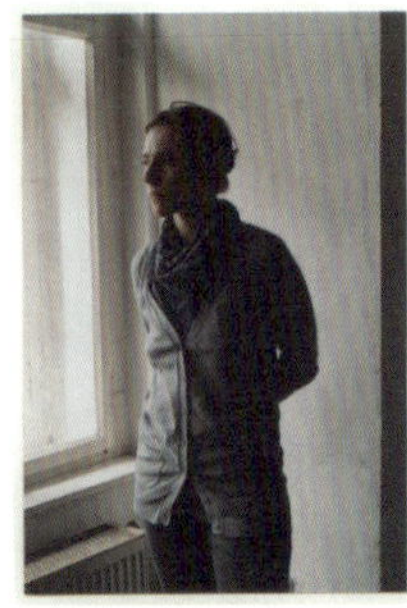

Plate 707
Friederike Jokisch (P. of a P.) I

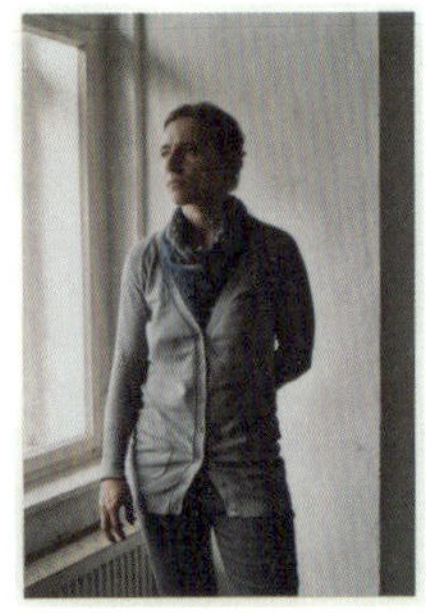

Plate 708
Friederike Jokisch (P. of a P.) I

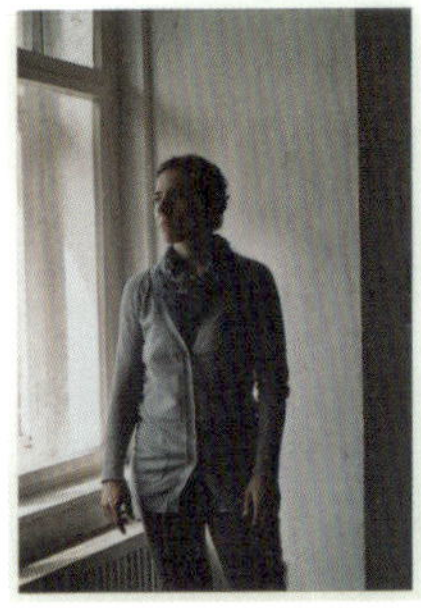

Plate 709
Friederike Jokisch (P. of a P.) I

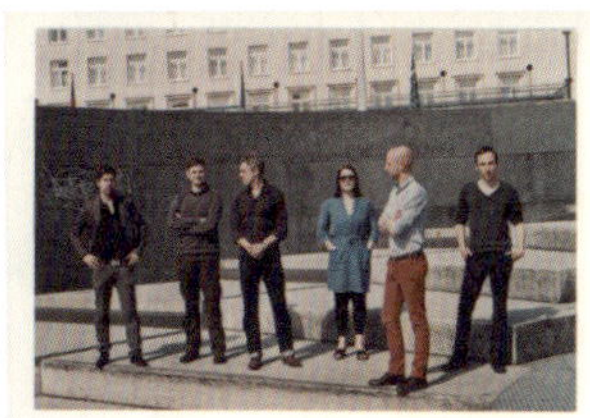

Plate 710
Meisterklasse Rauch (P. of a P.) I

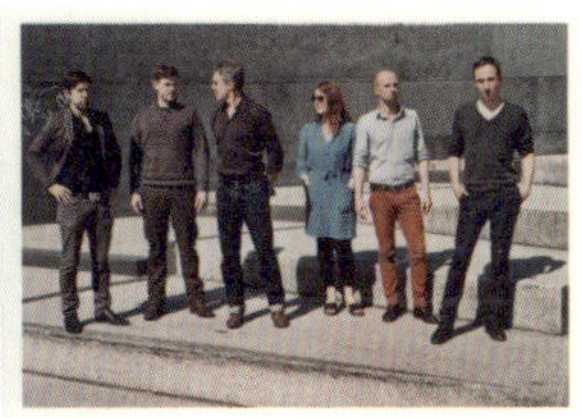

Plate 711
Meisterklasse Rauch (P. of a P.) I

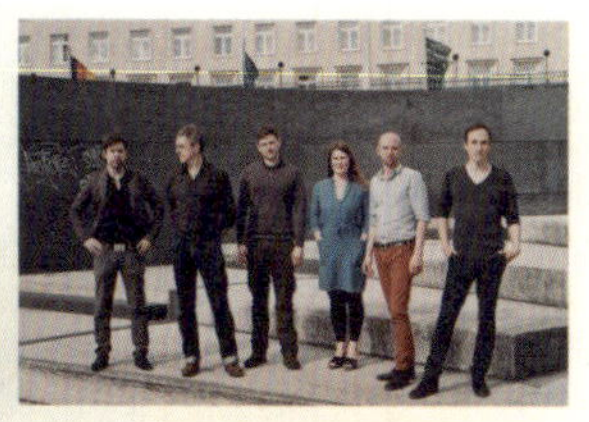

Plate 712
Meisterklasse Rauch (P. of a P.) I

B

DOUBLES (P. OF A P.) II

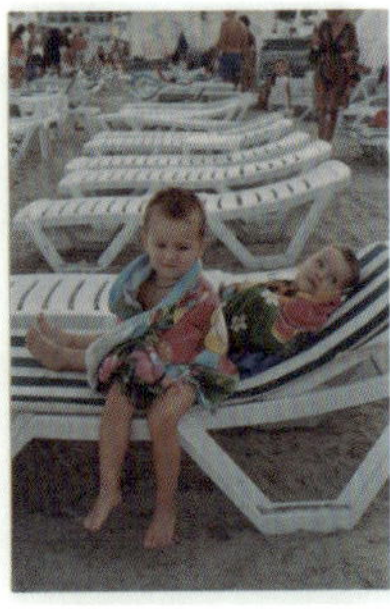

Plate 713
Odessa Beach (P. of a P.) II

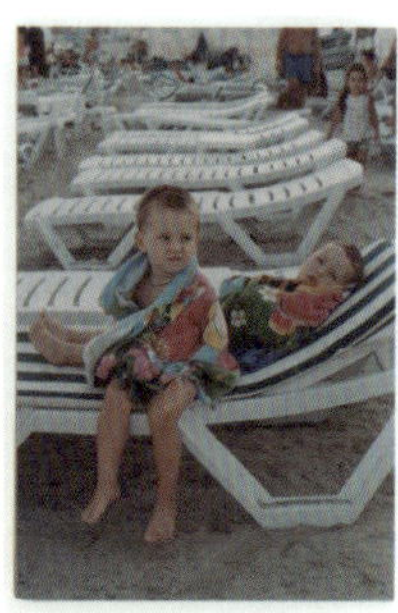

Plate 714
Odessa Beach (P. of a P.) II

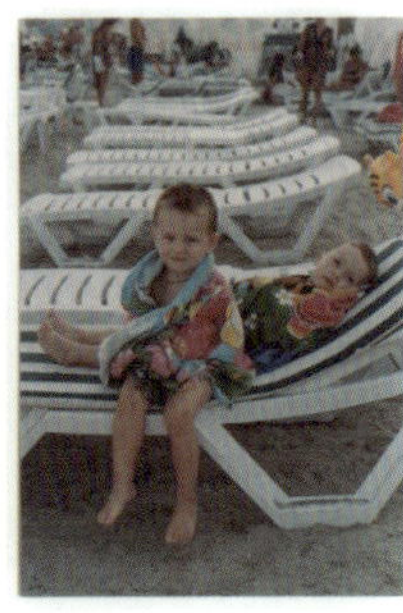

Plate 715
Odessa Beach (P. of a P.) II

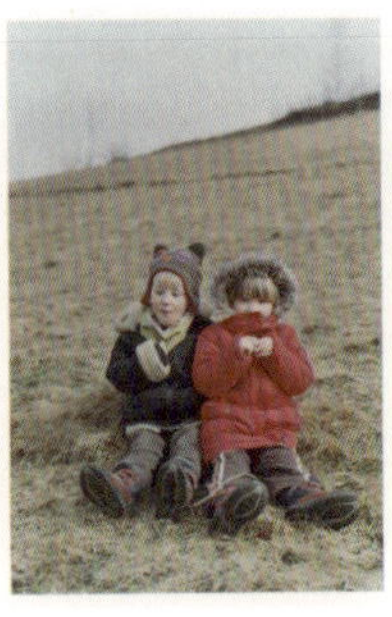

Plate 716
Mette and Amrai Hofmann
(P. of a P.) II

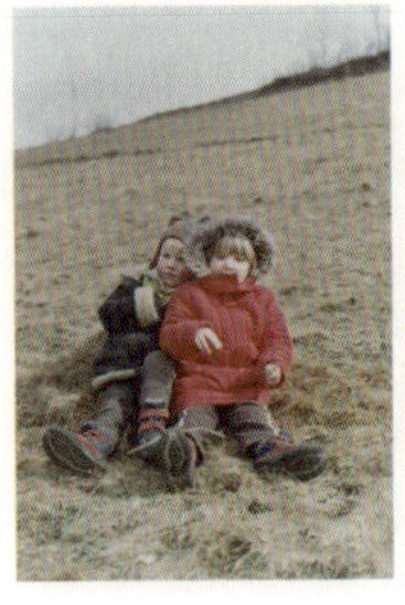

Plate 717
Mette and Amrai Hofmann
(P. of a P.) II

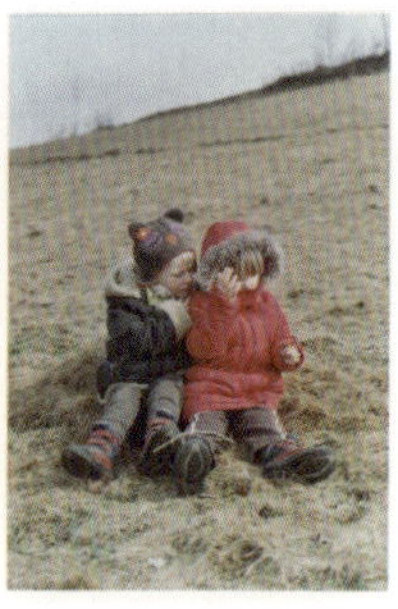

Plate 718
Mette and Amrai Hofmann
(P. of a P.) II

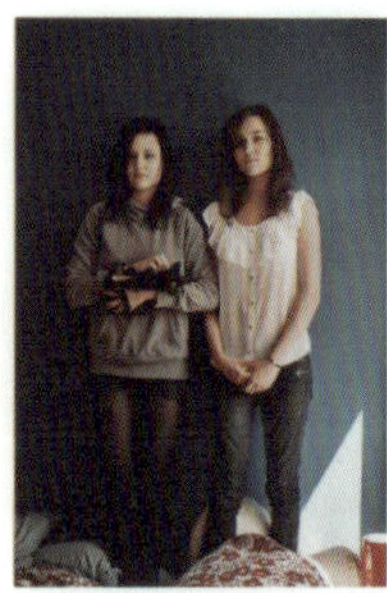

Plate 719
Luca and Madou Ghosh
(P. of a P.) II

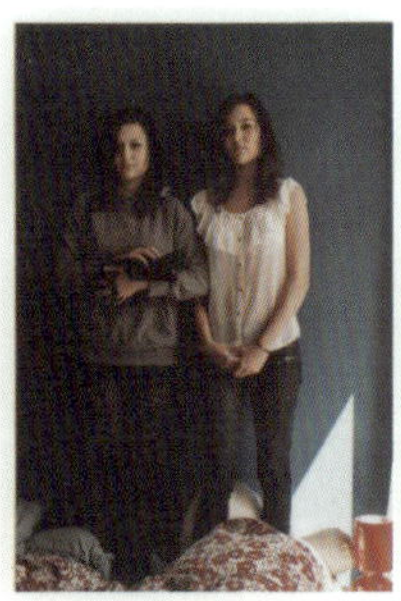

Plate 720
Luca and Madou Ghosh
(P. of a P.) II

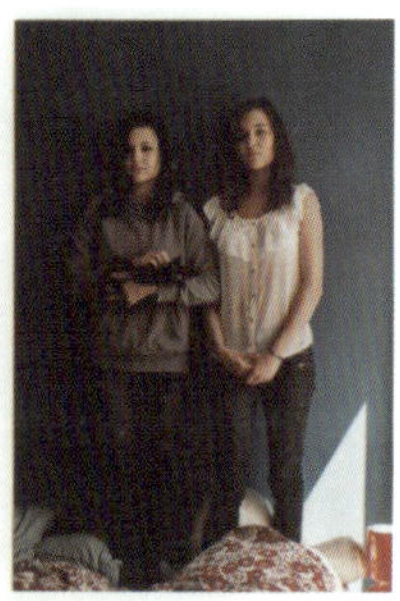

Plate 721
Luca and Madou Ghosh
(P. of a P.) II

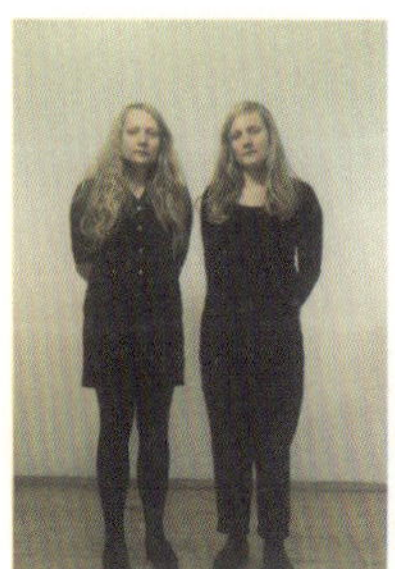

Plate 722
Franziska and Anne Leiste
(P. of a P.) II

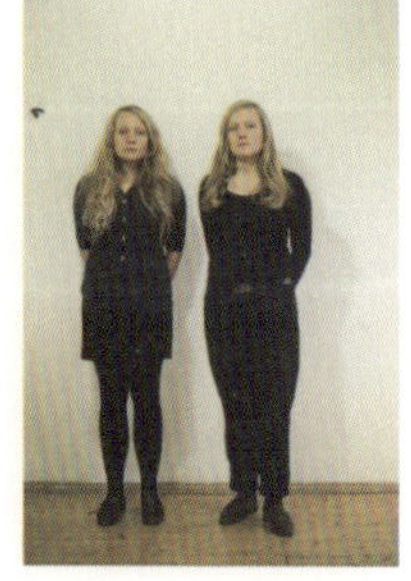

Plate 723
Franziska and Anne Leiste
(P. of a P.) II

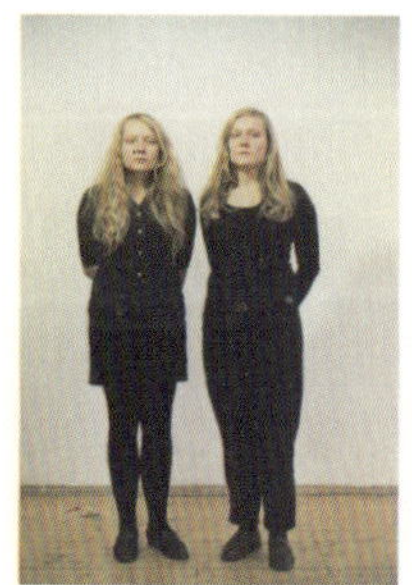

Plate 724
Franziska and Anne Leiste
(P. of a P.) II

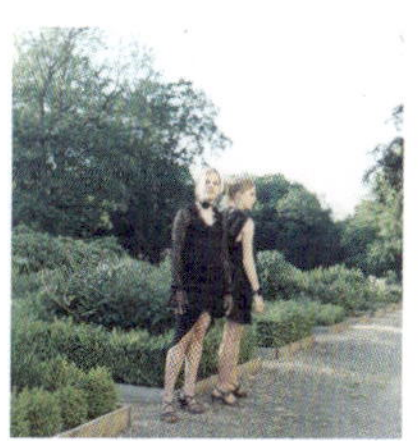

Plate 725
Gothic Wedding (P. of a P.) II

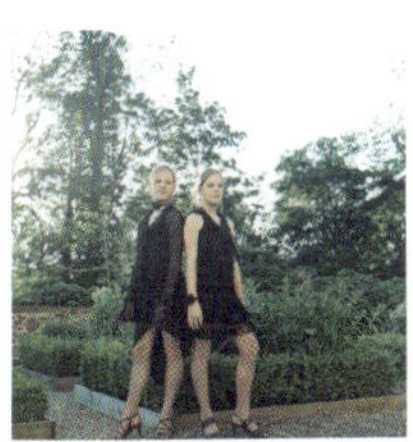

Plate 726
Gothic Wedding (P. of a P.) II

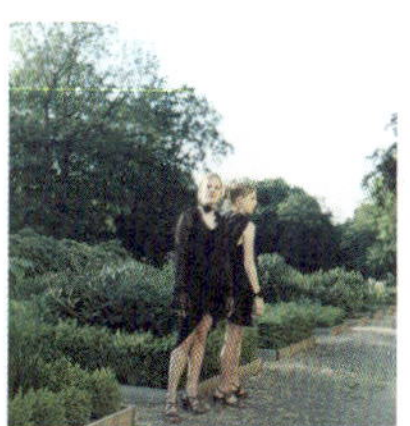

Plate 727
Gothic Wedding (P. of a P.) II

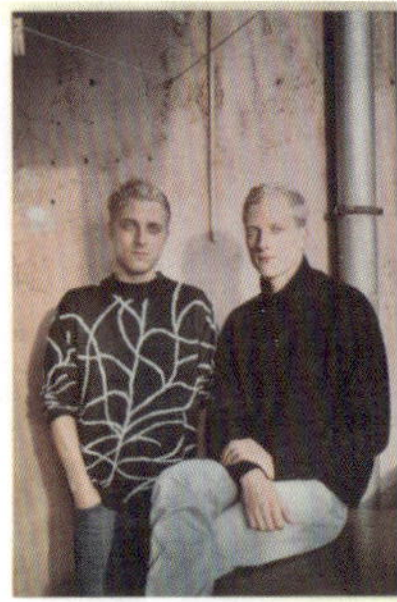

Plate 728
Valentin and Lorenz Just
(P. of a P.) II

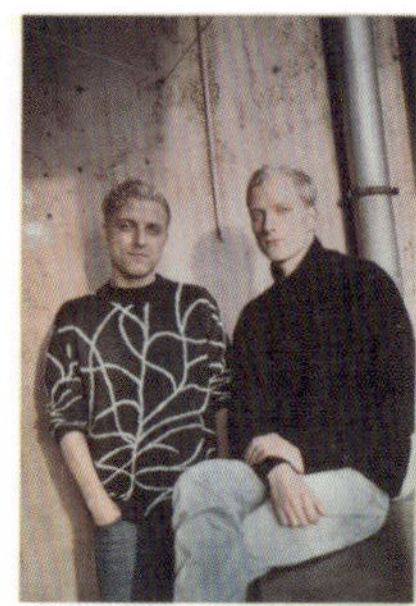

Plate 729
Valentin and Lorenz Just
(P. of a P.) II

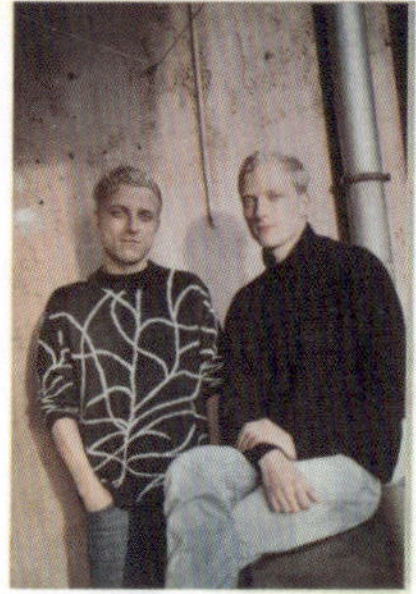

Plate 730
Valentin and Lorenz Just
(P. of a P.) II

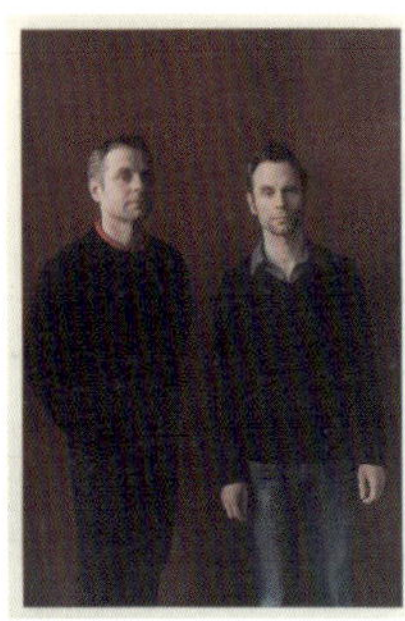

Plate 731
Michael and Matthias Ludwig
(P. of a P.) II

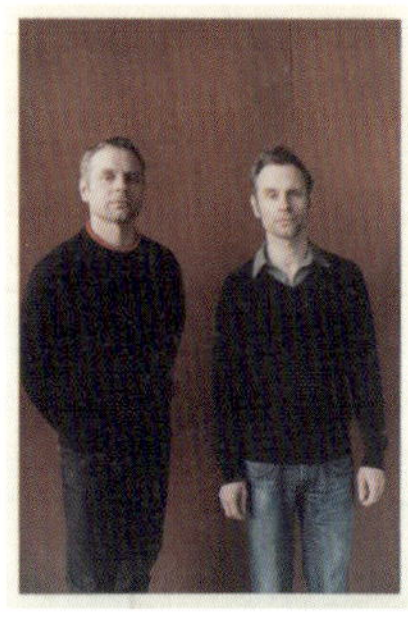

Plate 732
Michael and Matthias Ludwig
(P. of a P.) II

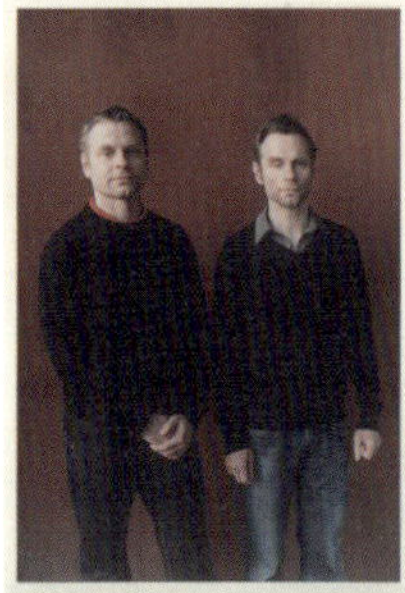

Plate 733
Michael and Matthias Ludwig
(P. of a P.) II

TEXT OF A TALK

BY

LORENZ JUST

TRANSLATED BY LORENZ JUST

C.D. I call for reproduction, more expressly than ever, more than when this was still a factory. No waiting for the lonely hen, to present to us the cracking egg of inspiration: Synthesize instead. Synthesize with minimal differences to the original, so that it remains one original after the other, always another, and in between take your time to catch your breath.

F.G. Below a conceptual superstructure we find those images that elude discussion.

A man perishes in sight of the helpless camera, buried by an avalanche of blankets and cushions. He does not get up, but is arranged in a way suitable for a coffin, until finally all is covered by blackness.

F.G. Furthermore there are objects that elude the image and drift from presence to absence; results of the repeated struggle to bring something to mind, in order to show it; the hope to place an exhibit, or anything, onto a pedestal. But only unfulfilled intention will be visible—over and over again the black veil falls. The objects flee the picture or otherwise have vanished by the end of the series.

A man with a shiny emblem on his blazer, holding out his hand to the two French mastiffs, tied to a staircase railing somewhere at a public space: By the time the dogs notice the camera, the man has disappeared, the steps are deserted.

C.D. The archive is stored inside a cabinet in several banana crates. Material of the past decades, photos that travel through time, to become topical many years later, when the pictures urge to come back to light, to return to the production process. Bit by bit they are integrated into the work cycle, laid out onto the trays of copy machines and scanners. If they still cannot reveal a thing, they are sent back to the crates, at worst they are trashed the next time the archive is cleared out and stock is taken. What remains are palm trees, many flowers, sky, lots of men, women, children.

Landscapes stuck in twilight. Sleeping faces grazed by shadows. Bouquets that remain allusions in the mist and darkness, or those shriveled up, standing in their last vase: a white dustbin or a blue barrel.

F.G. Pictures that preserve transience. Attempts to take brief moments out of time and set an end to decay. And yet every image bears its own traces and hence proves that time has passed. (Inga Kerber's pictures of Native Americans were taken from behind, as if out of hiding.) Eventually the preservation of a moment only reveals a memory far away from reality, a mark on the brain, a picture of faulty visibility. No gaze can be cast a second time. The only thing that has been demonstrated is the defectiveness of technological reproduction.

C.D. The flower five-piece *Cliché of Flowers* is an illustration of imperfect reproduction (the unsuccessful quest for the original black). It is a series of varying shades of black, incapable of returning to its point of origin. It shows the experience which caused the reconsideration of defectiveness that made it the governing principle of serial originality.

F.G. There is a certain cruelty to the series, because the reiterated reproduction of a single subject will finally question that there ever was anything to begin with. Neither the second, third or fourth gaze will make it possible to regain what has been seen. On the contrary: every repetition increases the distance to the first gaze and questions it existentially. A solution is to understand every picture as a moment in itself: a unique, fixed moment, whose place in time originates solely from the viewer's eye. An image that can neither be depicted nor can it be described merely as a depiction itself: the copy moves ahead in time and becomes independent; its point of origin recedes behind a damaged screen and is overwritten.

The Repetitive Singularity

F.G. The motives for choosing the actual subject remain unexplained. Because the picture is being selected from the archive for the reproduction. It is activated out of memory, so to say. Hence the story behind a picture's original creation is subtracted in the process of reproduction. No holiday photos, no pictures from someone's youth taken with their very first camera, no snapshots, and no souvenirs are presented. And yet beneath the conceptual approach in Kerber's work one notices biographical coincidence. The pictures of the man stretched out half asleep are images of a man who needs a lot of sleep, whose girlfriend however sleeps little. Because of a particular situation in someone's life, within the framework of the duration of a relationship the reclining man becomes an established subject of Kerber's work. One's own experience, as the only definite thing to be experienced, becomes abstracted. The bouquets, as a familiar subject, seem to stand outside of history too. And yet they do not:

> I.K. "I picked the green ones myself
> in my garden lot in Clara Park, where all things
> belong to all people, are property of the people,
> found the yellow ones dead on a flea market,
> bought the lilies,
> got the orchids for Valentine's Day
> [...] and left them like that
> without water,
> the yellow and pink bouquet was a birthday
> present from Mo."

F.G. The single case is embedded in established motives: torso,
flower bouquet, landscape, portrait. And yet something remains
that eludes categorization. Just as technological reproduction
always leaves room for mistakes. The general aspects of singularity are revealed in repetition. The conceptual approach
to biographical material merges the particular with the general. The contradiction is made visible as a whole, as a tension
between the two poles of repeatable banality and the singularity of a moment or an instant.

SERIAL SINGULARITY

F.G. It is impossible to discern only a single image in the series.
They all refer to their neighbors. They are pictures of the
same subject, the same moment, and yet they are different
pictures. In the series they immediately enter into a relationship. The dark tint of one picture can be recognized in refer-
ence to the lighter tint of another one and vice versa. As if
one were standing face to face with siblings wondering at the
same time about their great similarity and dissimilarity. As if
a twin could only be conceived in relation to or through his
other twin. As if both were only variations of a third person
occupying the space between them like a phantom. The gaze
must always pass from one to the other; it finds no rest in the
face of only one twin while the other is standing next to him.
The pair, and likewise the series, can only be perceived in
movement; it can never be specified. And yet the movement
does not remain on the side of the viewer alone. The series of
images that differ in minute details is in itself experienced as
motion, as a tiny excerpt from a film sequence; a sequence
that is severed from its prehistory and remains open ended.

Uniqueness in times of mass-reproduction. Human kind still refuses to recognize itself as a part of it. Everyone is merely one more. What remained singular is drowned in the ocean of storage capacity. Eroded to sand it is washed ashore. Forlorn in front of their computers, in common with the world's population. The dream of a language of one's own within the language of all; the dream of a life of one's own within a world of perpetual others. Impatient self-fulfillment. As if time were coming to an end. Since the past does not set free a future. Clearance of all possibilities. And yet a new day is always waiting. Just another final Call. All fades away, imperceptibly slow—futility at the back of the head of all hope. Following the see-through illusion. Another new ending: this age is a path searching for its final point.

I can make it stop, anytime.

Uniqueness in the age of plenty. The vast lands of humanity. Everyone is one more. Diving for singularity in the ocean of storage capacity. Sand on your skin while sun-bathing. All are united in front of the screen. Your own language embedded in the language of all and a life of your own in an ever different world. In the form of self-fulfillment. Time finds its end at the beginning. And the past surrenders to the present. Everything is sold-out at last. Tomorrow becomes today. Infinite outset. At last something new—hope at the back of the head of all futility. Seeing through the see-through illusion. Meeting the target non-stop. This age remains undefined for as long as we haven't been.

TEXT ZUM GESPRÄCH

VON
LORENZ JUST

C.D. Es soll ausdrücklicher reproduziert werden, als es hier in der
Fabrik je der Fall war! Keine Eier legen, wenn es Puff macht,
sondern synthetisieren, mit minimalem Unterschied zum Original, sodass es immer Original bleibt – von einem Stopp zum
nächsten Stopp und Atempausen zwischendurch.

F.G. Unter einem konzeptuellen Überbau bleiben die Bilder, die
sich der Diskussion entziehen.

*Der Mann, der unter der hilflosen Kamera stirbt, zwischen Decken und Kissen,
wie verschütt gegangen. Der nicht aufsteht, sondern in sarggerechte Ordnung
gebracht wird. Bis das Schwarz beginnt ihn endgültig zu überdecken.*

F.G. Des weiteren bleiben die Objekte, die sich dem Bild entziehen und von Anwesenheit zu Abwesenheit driften; Resultate
der wiederholten Anstrengung etwas zu vergegenwärtigen,
um es zu zeigen; der Hoffnung, auf das Podest auch ein Aus-
stellungsstück, irgendetwas setzen zu können. Doch nur die
unerfüllte Absicht wird sichtbar – immer wieder fällt der
schwarze Schleier. Die Gegenstände fliehen das Bild oder sind
am Ende der Reihe restlos verschwunden.

*Der Mann mit dem strahlenden Emblem über der linken Brust, der die Hand
aushält nach den beiden Möpsen, irgendwo an einem öffentlichen Ort, ange-
leint am Treppengeländer: Als die Hunde die Kamera entdecken, ist der
Mann verschwunden, die Stufen sind leer.*

C.D. Das Archiv lagert im Schrank in mehreren Bananen-Kisten.
Material aus Jahrzehnten. Fotos, die die Zeiten durchwan-
dern, um nach Jahren aktuell zu sein; wenn die Bilder
zurück wollen ans Licht, zurück in die Produktion. Stück
für Stück werden sie eingespeist in den Arbeitskreislauf, auf
die Platten der Kopiergeräte und Scanner. Falls sie immer

noch nichts zeigen können, müssen sie zurück in die Kisten,
schlimmstenfalls, wenn ausgemistet wird und Inventur gehalten, endgültig auf den Müll. Es bleiben Palmen, viele Blumen,
Himmel, viele Männer, Frauen, Kinder.

*Landschaften, die in der Dämmerung festhängen. Schlafen mit Schatten im
Gesicht. Blumensträuße, die in Nebel und Dunkelheit nur eine Ahnung bleiben oder längst vertrocknet sind; die in ihrer letzten Vase stehen: im weißen
Mülleimer oder an der blauen Tonne.*

F.G. Bilder, die Vergänglichkeit konservieren. Der Versuch, kurze
Augenblicke aus der Zeit zu lösen und dem Ableben ein Ende
zu setzen. Doch Abbilder tragen ihre eigenen Spuren und haben
den Eintritt in die Vergangenheit sofort herbeigeführt. (Inga
Kerbers Fotos von Indianern sind hinterrücks, wie aus einem
Versteck, geschossen.) Das Festhalten eines Augenblicks zeigt
am Ende nur eine realitätsferne Erinnerung, einen Abdruck im
Gehirn, ein Bild mangelhafter Sichtbarkeit. Kein Blick kann ein
zweites Mal geworfen werden. Deutlich vor Augen geführt, bleibt
einzig die Fehlerhaftigkeit der technischen Reproduktion.

C.D. Der Blumen-5er *Cliché of Flowers* ist die Illustration einer imperfekten Reproduktion, (die vergebliche Suche nach dem anfänglichen Schwarz). Eine Reihe unterschiedlicher Schwarztöne,
die nicht zum Ausgangspunkt zurückführt. Sie zeigt die Erfahrung, die dazu geführt hat, die Fehlerhaftigkeit umzuwerten,
zum leitenden Prinzip reihenweiser Originalität.

F.G. Die Serie wird grausam, weil durch die Wiederholung vom
Motiv nichts mehr bleibt, außer der Frage, ob überhaupt je etwas
gewesen ist. Weder der zweite, dritte noch der vierte Blick wird
es möglich machen, sich des Gesehenen erneut zu bemächtigen. Das Gegenteil ist der Fall: Jede Wiederholung vergrößert
die Entfernung zum ersten Blick und stellt ihn existenziell
in Frage. Ausweg wird es, das Bild selbst zum Augenblick zu

erklären, zu einem einzigartigen, starren Moment, dessen
Zeitlichkeit allein dem Blick des Betrachters entspringt. Ein
Bild, das kein Abbild sein oder haben kann: Denn die Kopie
schreitet in der Zeit voran und wird eigenständig; ihr Ausgangspunkt verblasst unter einer beschädigten Mattscheibe
und wird neu bespielt.

F.G. Der Weg zum eigentlichen Motiv bleibt ungeklärt. Weil das
Bild für die Reproduktion dem Archiv entnommen wird.
Sozusagen aus der Erinnerung heraus aktualisiert wird. Die
ursprüngliche Entstehungsgeschichte des Bildes wird durch
das Verfahren der Reproduktion subtrahiert. Es werden keine
Urlaubsfotos, keine Fotos aus der Jugend, mit der allerersten
Kamera geschossen, keine Schnappschüsse, keine Souvenirs
gezeigt. Doch trotzdem unterliegt dem Konzeptuellen in Inga
Kerbers Arbeiten biographisch Zufälliges. Die Bilder des im
Halbschlaf liegenden Mannes sind Bilder des Mannes, der
viel Schlaf braucht, dessen Freundin aber wenig schläft. Aus
einer konkreten Lebenssituation heraus, im Rahmen der
Dauer einer Beziehung wird der liegende Mann als Motiv
erschlossen. Das eigene Erleben, als das einzig erfahrbare Kon-
krete, wird abstrahiert. Auch die Blumensträuße scheinen als
bekanntes Motiv geschichtslos zu sein. Doch sind sie es nicht:

I.K. „Ich habe die grünen selbst gepflückt
in meinem Garten im Clara-Park, alles gehört allen,
Volkseigentum
die gelben tot auf dem Flohmarkt gefunden,
die Lilien gekauft,
die Orchideen zum Valentinstag bekommen
[...] und dann so gelassen, ohne Wasser,
der gelb rosa Strauß von Mo zum Geburtstag.“

(186)

F.G. Der Einzelfall wird ins bewährte Motiv gebettet: Torso, Blumenstrauß, Landschaft, Portrait. Doch es bleibt etwas bestehen, das sich der Zuordnung entzieht. So wie auch die technische Produktion stets dem Zufall noch Raum lässt. Die allgemeine Qualität des Einzelfalls wird durch die Wiederholung zum Vorschein gebracht. Das konzeptuelle Arbeiten mit biographischem Material lässt das Besondere und das Allgemeine beidseitig ineinander übergehen. Der Widerspruch wird als Ganzes sichtbar gemacht. Als Spannung zwischen den beiden Polen des wiederholbaren Allgemeinen und dem Einzelfall als Moment oder Augenblick.

REIHENWEISER EINZELFALL

F.G. Es ist nicht möglich ein einziges Bild in der Reihe auszumachen. Jedes verweist auf seine Nachbarn. Es sind Bilder desselben Motivs, desselben Augenblicks, aber es sind verschiedene Bilder. In der Reihe gehen sie sofort ein Verhältnis ein. Ein dunkler Farbstich des einen Bildes wird durch den helleren des anderen Bilds erkannt oder andersherum. Als stünde man vor Geschwistern und wäre zur gleichen Zeit über ihre große Ähnlichkeit und ihre große Unterschiedlichkeit verblüfft. Als wäre ein Zwilling nur mit oder sogar durch seinen Zwilling zu denken. Als wären sie beide nur Varianten einer dritten Person, die als Phantom zwischen ihnen schwebt. Der Blick muss immer von einem zum anderen wechseln, er findet keine Ruhe im Gesicht des einen Zwillings, wenn der andere daneben steht. Das Paar, aber auch die Bildreihe, ist nur in Bewegung erfassbar, doch nie dingfest zu machen. Aber die Bewegung bleibt nicht auf Seiten des Betrachters allein. Die Reihe der Bilder, die sich durch minimale Verschiebungen unterscheiden, wird selbst als Bewegung erlebt, als winziger Ausschnitt einer Filmsequenz; einer Sequenz, die losgelöst ist von ihrer Vorgeschichte und mit offenem Ende.

Einzigartigkeit im Zeitalter der Vervielfältigung. Noch weigert sich der Mensch, sich als Teil der Massenware zu erkennen. Jeder ist nur einer mehr. Im Ozean der Speicherkapazität ertrinkt das Unikat. Zu Sand gemahlen findet es zurück an den Strand. Einsam vor dem Rechner, gemeinsam mit der Weltbevölkerung. Der Traum von einer eigenen Sprache in der Sprache aller; der Traum eines eigenen Lebens in der Welt der ewig Anderen. Die Ungeduld zur Selbstverwirklichung. Als fände die Zeit ihr Ende. Und die Vergangenheit gibt keine Zukunft frei. Ausverkauf aller Möglichkeiten. Und trotzdem wartet unentwegt ein nächster Tag. Alles klingt aus, unendlich langsam. Ein neues Letztes. Die Vergeblichkeit im Hinterkopf aller Hoffnung. Weiterführung der längst durchschauten Illusion. Am Ende ohne Anfang. Diese Zeit ist eine Strecke, die ihren Endpunkt sucht.
Ich kann es jederzeit beenden.
Einzigartigkeit im massenhaften Zeitalter. Unüberschaubares Menschenland. Jeder ist einer mehr. Im Ozean der Speicherkapazität auf Tauchgang nach der Einzigart. Sand auf der Haut im Sonnenbad. Am Rechner sind sie alle da. Die eigene Sprache eingebettet in der Sprache aller. Ein eigenes Leben in der ewig anderen Welt. In Gestalt der Selbstverwirklichung. Die Zeit findet ihr Ende am Anfang. Die Vergangenheit ergibt sich der Gegenwart. Und alles ist endlich ausverkauft. Morgen wird heute. Unendlicher Anklang. Zuletzt ein Neues. Hoffnung im Hinterkopf aller Vergeblichkeit. Die durchschaute Illusion durchschaut. Ohne Ende am Ziel. Diese Zeit bleibt unbestimmte Zeit, solange wir nicht gewesen sind.

TEXTE SUR LE DIALOGUE

PAR

LORENZ JUST

Traduit par CAROLINE HUGUENOT

C.D. Il faut absolument s'attacher à une forme de reproduction
bien plus explicite que celle de l'usine ! Ne pas s'efforcer à
pondre une œuvre au moindre «pouf !», mais synthétiser, afin
de minimiser la différence avec l'original, pour que cela reste
un original – d'un stop à l'autre, avec une pause entre-temps
pour respirer.

F.G. Sous une superstructure conceptuelle, restent les images, qui
échappent à la discussion.

*L'homme, qui meurt sous l'oeil impuissant de l'appareil photo, au milieu des
couvertures et des coussins, comme enseveli. Qui ne se lève pas, mais qu'on a
placé comme dans un cercueil. Jusqu'à ce que le noir commence à le recou-
vrir complètement.*

F.G. Il reste en outre les objets, qui se dérobent à l'image et déri-
vent de présence en absence ; résultats de l'effort répété en vue
d'accomplir quelque chose et de le montrer ; l'espoir de pouvoir aussi placer sur l'estrade une pièce d'exposition, n'im-
porte quoi. Mais seul le souhait insatisfait est visible – le voile
noir retombe constamment. Les objets s'échappent hors de
l'image ou ont totalement disparu à la fin de la série.

*L'homme avec l'emblème rayonnant au-dessus du sein gauche, qui tend la
main en direction des deux bouledogues français, dans un quelconque lieu
public, attaché à la barrière de l'escalier : lorsque les chiens découvrent l'appareil photo, l'homme a disparu, les marches sont vides.*

C.D. Les archives sont entreposées dans l'armoire, dans des cartons de bananes. Du matériel vieux de plusieurs décennies,
des photos qui parcourent le temps, pour demeurer actuelles
après des années ; lorsque les images veulent revenir à la lumière, retourner à la production. Pièce après pièce elles vont

être intégrées au cycle de travail, passer sur les photoco-
pieuses et les scanners. Et dans le cas où elles ne peuvent toujours rien révéler, elles doivent retourner dans les cartons,
au pire finir à la poubelle, au moment du tri et de l'inventaire.
Restent des palmiers, beaucoup de fleurs, le ciel, de nombreux
hommes, femmes, enfants.

*Des paysages, qui restent accrochés au crépuscule. Dormir avec des ombres sur
le visage. Des bouquets de fleurs, qui dans la brume et l'obscurité deviennent
flous, ne sont plus qu'une vague idée ou sont depuis longtemps desséchés ;
qui reposent dans leur dernier vase : dans la corbeille blanche ou appuyés
contre la poubelle bleue.*

F.G.   Des images qui conservent l'éphémère. La tentative de ravir
de courts instants au temps et de mettre un terme à la mort.
Mais les représentations conservent leurs propres traces et
ont accès au passé sitôt qu'il est réalisé. (Les photos d'Indiens
d'Inga Kerber sont prises par derrière, comme en cachette).
Le regard soutenu ne montre finalement qu'un souvenir éloi-
gné de la réalité, une empreinte dans le cerveau, une image
d'une visibilité insuffisante. Aucun regard ne peut être jeté
une seconde fois. Il est évident qu'il ne reste pourtant que la
défectuosité de la reproduction technique.

C.D.   Le set de cinq fleurs *Cliché of Flowers* est l'illustration d'une
reproduction imparfaite (la vaine recherche du noir originel).
Une série de tons noirs différents, qui ne ramène pas au point
de départ. Elle montre l'expérience qui a conduit à mettre en
valeur la défectuosité, selon le principe conducteur d'une ori-
ginalité en séries successives.

F.G.   La série devient cruelle, car à travers la répétition du motif,
il ne reste plus rien, hormis la question de savoir s'il y a réel-
lement eu quelque chose. Ni le deuxième, ni le troisième
ni même le quatrième regard n'aura le pouvoir de saisir à

nouveau ce qui a été vu. C'est même le contraire qui se produit : chaque répétition renforce la distance avec le premier
regard et le met en question du point de vue existentiel. La
seule issue consistera à appréhender l'image-même comme
l'instant, comme un moment unique, figé, dont la temporalité prend sa source dans le regard du spectateur. Une image
qui ne peut ni être une représentation ni en avoir une : car
la copie fait son propre chemin dans le temps pour devenir autonome ; son point de départ s'estompe sous une vitre
mate endommagée et se voit renouvelé.

Un Cas Particulier À Répétition

F.G. Le cheminement vers le motif réel demeure inexpliqué. Car
l'image destinée à la reproduction sera retirée des archives.
Pour ainsi dire, réactualisée à partir du souvenir. L'histoire
qui est à l'origine de la création de l'image sera supprimée
par le processus de reproduction. Aucune photo de vacances,
aucune photo de jeunesse, prise avec le tout premier appareil,
aucun instantané, aucun souvenir ne pourra être montré. Le
hasard biographique demeure néanmoins au fondement de
tout concept dans les travaux d'Inga Kerber. Les images de
l'homme allongé à demi endormi sont celles de l'homme qui
a besoin de beaucoup de sommeil, mais dont la compagne
dort peu. C'est à travers une situation concrète de la vie quotidienne, dans le cadre de la durée d'une relation, qu'on retrouve l'homme allongé en tant que motif. L'expérience personnelle, en tant qu'unique fait concret, devient abstraite.
Même le motif bien connu des bouquets de fleurs semble
désormais sans histoire. Et pourtant il n'en est pas dépourvu :

    I.K. « J'ai moi-même cueilli les vertes
          dans mon jardin au parc Clara, tout appartient
          à tout le monde, propriété du peuple,

> les jaunes, je les ai trouvées, mortes, au marché
>   aux puces,
> les lilas, je les ai achetés,
> les orchidées, reçues pour la Saint-Valentin
> […] et les ai laissées ainsi,
> sans eau,
> le bouquet jaune-rose, reçu de Mo pour
>   mon anniversaire. »

F.G. Le cas particulier est ainsi appréhendé à travers un motif qui a fait ses preuves : un torse, un bouquet de fleurs, un paysage, un portrait. Mais il reste néanmoins quelque chose qui échappe à tout classement. De même que la production technique laisse toujours de la place au hasard. L'aspect générique du cas particulier se manifeste à travers la répétition. Dans le travail conceptuel de la matière biographique, le particulier et le général se fondent l'un dans l'autre. L'opposition apparaît comme un tout. Comme une tension entre les deux pôles formés par la réitération du général, et le moment ou l'instantané du cas particulier.

Un Cas Particulier En Séries Successives

F.G. Il est impossible de prendre en compte isolément une image de la série. Chacune renvoie à ses voisines. Ce sont des images du même motif, du même instant, mais toutes sont différentes. Dans la série, elles entrent tout de suite en relation les unes avec les autres. Un voile de couleur sombre est révélé par un autre plus clair sur une autre image, et vice versa. Comme si on se trouvait face à des frères et sœurs, en étant tout à la fois décontenancés par leur grande ressemblance et leur grande différence. Comme si on ne pouvait concevoir un jumeau qu'avec l'autre, voire exclusivement à travers lui. Comme si tous deux n'étaient que des variantes d'une troisième personne, tel un fantôme errant entre eux. Le regard doit toujours alterner de l'un à l'autre, ne trouvant de répit dans le visage de l'un des jumeaux tant que l'autre se trouve à côté. Le couple, mais aussi la série d'images, bien que pouvant n'être compris qu'en mouvement, ne peuvent jamais être apprivoisés. Mais le mouvement ne se produit pas uniquement chez le spectateur. La série d'images, qui se distinguent les unes des autres par d'infimes détails, est elle-même perçue comme mouvement, comme un minuscule extrait d'une séquence de film; une séquence dépouillée de son histoire et à fin ouverte.

Caractère unique à l'ère de la multiplication. L'homme se refuse encore à se reconnaître comme un article de marchandise de masse. Chacun n'est qu'un individu supplémentaire. La pièce unique se noie dans l'océan de la capacité de stockage. Broyée en grains de sable, elle se retrouve sur la plage. Seule devant l'ordinateur, en contact commun la population mondiale. Le rêve d'une langue particulière dans la langue de tous ; le rêve de sa propre vie dans le monde de l'Autre éternel. Épanouissement personnel impatient. Comme si le temps touchait à sa fin. Car le passé ne donne lieu à aucun futur. Et pourtant un lendemain attend constamment. Tout semble infiniment lent. Une fin qui est nouveauté. La vanité en germe dans chaque espoir. Prolongement de l'illusion depuis longtemps percée à jour. Finalement, sans commencement – ce temps est une distance qui cherche son point d'arrivée. Je peux y mettre un terme à tout moment.

Caractère unique à l'ère de la masse. Nul regard d'ensemble qui pût embrasser la terre des hommes. Chacun n'est qu'un individu supplémentaire. Dans l'océan de la capacité de stockage en plongée vers l'Unique. Du sable sur la peau dans un bain de soleil. Tous sont derrière l'ordinateur. La même langue intégrée dans la langue de tous ; sa propre vie dans le monde éternellement autre. Le temps trouve son terme au commencement. Et le passé se résigne au présent. Echo sans fin. En dernier lieu, la nouveauté. L'espoir en germe dans toute vanité. L'illusion percée à jour perce à jour. Sans fin, une fois à destination – ce temps reste indéterminé, aussi longtemps que nous n'avons pas été.

REFRAMING OF AUTHORSHIP

ON INGA KERBER'S PHOTOGRAPHIC WORK

BY

NANNE BUURMAN

TRANSLATED BY GUNNAR WENDEL

I N THE 1950s the *Cahiers du Cinéma* gave voice to an appeal that urged directors to become involved in all stages of film production, so as to develop a signature style. The aim was to liberate directors from the dominant illusionist tradition and to abandon the corresponding impetus for technical perfection in favor of a unique vision [1]. Given the idiosyncratic aesthetics of Inga Kerber's pictures, her photographic work may be conceived as auteur photography, in analogy to the *Politique des Auteurs* of the Nouvelle Vague directors. Even though her photographs, due to the method of their production, have a certain painterly feel, Kerber neither mimicks painting nor engages in a fantasy of authorship akin to the modernist notion of art as the ingenuous expression of a singular individual. Instead, she makes apparent the subjectivity inherent to photography.

However in this case the insistence on subjectivity should neither be mistaken as an affirmation of the idea of seemingly omnipotent authors nor be confused with a desire for absolute control. Similar to Jean-Luc Godard, who clearly marked the fabricated nature of film with his use of dramatic staging of the *mise en scène*, the introduction of a subjective position serves the disillusion and by consequence the relativization of authorial power. I will discuss how Kerber's work reframes the interrelations between authorship, aleatory and automatic elements, as well as the relations between social conventions of seeing and concrete acts of looking. The media-conscious exposure of the ways in which processes of reproduction and reception are interlinked in the creation of images thus calls into question the still widely accepted paradigm of photographic objectivity in favor of revealing the performativity of photographic images.

FRAME I. REPRODUCTION AS PRODUCTION. Inga Kerber's pictures break with several established conventions of photography. Contrary to common practice with its concern to meticulously ensure that negatives, scans and prints are free of dust and smears, Kerber accepts and cultivates these coincidental, unintended traces of manual labor which are usually considered as flaws that disturb the perfect illusion of glossy aesthetics. Likewise, blurs, exposure errors and color shifts are not rejected, but instead treated as constituent parts of the photographic image. Kerber embraces accidents and usually unwanted effects of photographic technology (e.g. color faults, scan lines, printer errors) and gives room for what is generally repressed in photography in the name of neutrality and sterility. The materiality of photographs, for instance, is often neglected in the general emphasis on the indexicality of photographs or in celebrations of their hyperrealistic objectivity. In circumstances where photographs—due to their potential to present images that transcend cultural norms and the limitations of the human capability of seeing—are understood as immediate traces of an outer reality captured by the lens, photography is often rhetorically simplified to almost immaterial, pure referentiality [2]. By reinforcing

---

[1] See Francois Truffaut: A Certain Tendency of the French Cinema [1954], in: *Movies and Methods*, vol. 1, ed. Bill Nichols, Berkeley 1972, pp. 224–37.

[2] This notion ignores the technical coding and physical limitations of photographic devices as well as the corporeality and spatiality of photographic prints. See, for instance, László Moholy-Nagy: *Malerei. Fotografie. Film*, Bauhausbücher, Band 8, Munich 1925; or in a completely different context in Rosalind Krauss: Notes on the Index: Seventies Art in America, in: *October*, 4, 1977, pp. 58–67.

aleatory and automatic effects, Kerber contests the myths of the camera as an omniscient, passive and impartial machinic witness and the idea of the photo as faultless evidence, thus also bestowing the images with a plasticity of their own.

Although the appropriation of accidents and technical traces creates painterly effects –besides the relief-like texture these include, for instance, the color scheme or the distribution of light and dark–Kerber's work is not an attempt to ennoble her photography by means of a painterly aesthetics as was the case with the pictorialists. Instead, her focus is on emphasizing otherwise commonly ignored yet very specific photographic qualities. This is why the materiality of the image carrier–matte rather than standard glossy paper–is intentionally left bare. Furthermore, Kerber does not cut off the reproduction edges and attaches the prints to the wall like posters instead of framing them. She generally abstains from elevating display features such as diasec or picture frames in order to ensure an unobstructed visibility of the subtle differences in the iterations of her photographic reproductions. Here, technical reproduction does not imply the loss of a picture's aura, but instead its augmentation on the basis of the uniqueness of individual reproductions, each of which is inscribed with the culminated traces of the processes of production and reproduction as in a palimpsest. The singularity of individual pictures rather than the identity of mass reproduced images becomes apparent and with it the often neglected productivity and creativity of photographic reproduction. Much more than the outside appearance of the world, the aesthetic dimension of recording it becomes the subject of Kerber's work, without turning the images into untouchable cult objects [3]).

FRAME II. PROJECTION AS RECEPTION. As posters the pictures gain a profane air that counteracts an overly reverential approach towards them. No pane of glass keeps a distance between image and spectator. The matte quality of Kerber's pictures absorbs the gaze instead of reflecting it as a smooth glossy surface would. Blurs, shades and dark areas tempt viewers to draw closer to the images, in hope of identifying more details inside these simultaneously blurred and differentiated areas. Canvas-size formats support the immersion of the spectator into the action within the frame. It is practically impossible to gain a full view of all the pictures simultaneously: once the observer is at a distance that allows an overview of the whole sequence, details begin to disappear. The viewer has no choice but to constantly switch between zoom and long shot [4]). Yet it is not only the eye of the observer that turns into a camera. Given the size of Kerber's pictures, the entire body is forced to engage in a constant to and fro between closeness and distance.

The sequences gain a temporal quality through the spatial synchronization of movements that are in fact diachronous: the optical, bodily and mental movement of the

---

[3]) Concerning the relationship between reproducibility and loss of the aura as well as fetish value and exhibition value of artworks see Walter Benjamin: Das Kunstwerk im Zeitalter seiner technischen Reproduzierbarkeit [1936] and Kleine Geschichte der Photographie [1931] in: idem: *Das Kunstwerk im Zeitalter seiner technischen Reproduzierbarkeit. Drei Studien zur Kunstsoziologie*, Frankfurt am Main 1996, pp. 7–44 and pp. 45–64.

[4]) In a similar way, Roland Barthes argued that the filmic does not lie in the temporality of the film itself, but in the mode of a "simultaneously immediate and vertical reading" (p. 66), which he exemplifies by film stills. See idem: The Third Meaning [*Cahiers du Cinéma*, 1970], in: idem: *Image Music Text*, ed. and transl. by Stephen Heath, London 1977, pp. 52–68.

recipients. This, however, is not a passive repetition of the photographic gaze, but rather an act of performative actualization. The empty spaces inside and between the pictures encourage viewers to supplement the simultaneously blurry and pithy clichés with their own recollections and ideas. Whereas high-definition photographs render a moment in a totality and clarity that could never be perceived by a human being in the blink of an eye, Kerber's photographs come closer to the human way of seeing, including all its limitations and blind spots. It becomes apparent to what huge degree perception depends on supplementation and interpretation of optical information. In this sense, Kerber's pictures also function as projection *screens*[5]) that provoke spectators to reflect on their own projective gaze.

FRAME III. THE OBJECT AS SUBJECT. The encounter of the spectators' and the artist's perspectives on screen causes tensions. Points of view accumulate, compete and oscillate between distance and identification. The intimacy and lure evoked by the materiality of the pictures resurfaces in the photographs' subject matter. A rather intrusive gaze is cast on a man posing in mostly intimate settings, such as in bed or in the bathroom. If spectators adopt the position of this predetermined gaze they inadvertently become voyeurs. In films, voyeuristic perspectives are frequently alleviated by allowing spectators to see the scene through the eyes of another actor in a reverse angle shot[6]). In Kerber's pictures no such counter shot defines the point of view as that of a fellow-actor, hence the spectator is put into the role of the missing other. The standard cut between shot and counter shot is relocated into the gap between the person in the picture and the person looking at the picture. By means of this suture, the spectator is turned into an actor who participates in this photographic 'film.'

Identification with the gaze of the photographer will have to remain ambivalent, because the perspective of the images differs significantly from the dominant western visual regime. According to the norm, both the gaze of the camera and that of the spectator are generally conceived as male. Therefore, in films, women often appear as objects of male desire, a position of female scopophilia is rarely acknowledged[7]). This might explain why Kerber's pictures, which celebrate the female joy of seeing, sometimes trouble viewers or are even occasionally read as 'gay'[8]). In the context of a visual tradition known for depicting women as reclining nudes and passive objects of desire while by contrast

[5]) *Screen Theory* takes up a key notion of *Apparatus Theory*–i.e. how subjects are constituted by spectatorial dispositifs–and extends it with the examination of gender relations in seeing and being seen. See also Laura Mulvey: Visual Pleasure and Narrative Cinema, in: *Screen,* 16 (3), 1975, pp. 6–18; and Kaja Silverman: *Male Subjectivity at the Margins,* New York/London 1992.

[6]) For the function of shot and counter shot in constructing viewers subject positions, see Ute Fenske: *Mannsbilder. Eine geschlechterhistorische Betrachtung von Hollywoodfilmen 1946–1960,* Bielefeld 2008, p. 55.

[7]) For the relationship between scopophilia and gender, see also Laura Mulvey (1975), op. cit., p. 12. For the masculinity of the observer position, see also John Berger: *Ways of Seeing,* London 1972, p. 64.

[8]) For the trouble caused by the "reversal of the gaze" by the "unanticipated agency" of the object that "returns the glance" and thus "contests…the authority of the masculine position", see Judith Butler: *Gender Trouble,* Routledge 1999 [1990], p. xxvii. Seen in this light, reading the pictures as 'gay'–which is reported to have happened repeatedly–reestablishes the dominant order of visibility by imagining a man in the position of the spectator.

presenting men in active movement and vertical positions with flexed muscles, the pose of a reclining, naked man has generally been reserved for hermaphrodites, slaves, the dead or the wounded. It was hence considered 'unmanly' or 'weak.'[9] Identification with the photographer's perspective is therefore not only hampered by intimacy and a possibly divergent sexual or gender identity, but also by the lack of cultural legitimacy of looking at men in this way.

FRAME IV. STYLIZATION AS ANIMATION. References to killing or immobilization are recurrent topoi in discussions of photography. The act of taking pictures has been accused of exposing the subjects of images to violence, either by castrating or killing them or by turning them into stone, immobilising them or strapping them into a corset[10]. On first glance, the treatment of the subjects in Kerber's pictures, with their references to the crucifixion (e.g. pietà poses) and still lifes (e.g. vanitas symbols), seems to affirm this claim. One could even speak of a double petrifiction: flowers and men are styled into clichéd subjects through the composition and captured in freeze frame, their movement arrested as in a film still. While the repetition of photographic shots (bang bang bang/click click click) in a series seems to reinforce the impression of the capital crime of definition, it does in fact also point to an emancipatory potential: the works do not depict total paralysis, but limited freedom of movement, and thus change[11].

With regard to Kerber's works, it is therefore possible to speak of a kind of cinematographic continuous present, not dissimilar from the early writings of Gertrude Stein where this effect was achieved by means of varying repetition, e.g. in the combination of the words 'loving repeating being.'[12] Paradoxically, the repeated stylization of the pose in Kerber's pictures evokes a movement that simultaneously stabilizes and questions this pose[13]. Repetition with slight alterations, created either through different shots of the same subject or through different prints of the same shot, is thus less a consolidation of clichés, but an indication of their potential to actualize sedimented ideas in reproduction. As a series, these pictures also transcend the notion of retrospective referential temporality often associated with photography. Photographs are commonly believed to preserve reality at the past moment of exposure, a view that tends to disregard the ongoing reality of the images themselves, which is directed towards futurity[14].

[9] See also Rozika Parker: Images of Men, in: idem, *Framing Feminism. Art and the Women's Movement 1970–1985*, ed. Griselda Pollock, London/New York 1987, pp. 220–23.

[10] For the topos of death in photography see, for example, Susan Sontag: *On Photography*, London 1977; Roland Barthes: Camera Lucida. Reflections on Photography, New York, 1981, pp. 14–15, pp. 89–91; and Craig Owens: Posing, in: idem: *Beyond Recognition. Representation, Power and Culture*, Los Angeles 1992, pp. 201–17.

[11] Roland Barthes (1981) contrasts the 'lack of a future', the 'stasis', the 'melancholy' in the conservative attitude of photography, which eventually turns photographers into "agents of death", with the advantages of film, whose continuous temporality is similar to that of life itself, op. cit. pp. 89–91.

[12] See Gertrude Stein: *The Making of Americans* [1924], cited in: *A Stein Reader*, ed. Ula E. Dydo, Illinois 1993. p. 62.

[13] According to Diedrich Diederichsen the purpose of a director is to create poses and destroy them at once, so as to create "movement and narration" and to make visible the "genealogy of the pose". See also idem: Queere Pose und erhabene Ungerechtigkeit: Politik und Moral bei Fassbinder und Warhol [2005], in: http://filmkritik.antville.org/stories/1229508 (retrieved 20.12.2010).

CONCLUSION. In Kerber's photographic works the time of exposure is extended for as long as the pictures physically exist. Besides the reproduction processes performed by the artist, the marks of exhibiting and handling, caused by other actors (bent corners, finger prints, scratches, tears, holes) are continually inscribed into the pictures. Because the papers are not protected from light, their exposure time–strictly speaking–only ends with their destruction. Instead of being conserved in status quo inside a glass coffin, the pictures continue to breathe through the open pores of their paper's surfaces. Besides their serial occurrence, it is in fact the specific materiality of these images that invites viewers to think of Kerber's pictures not merely as representations of past realities, but also as presentations that continue into an ongoing present. The pictures are no end points of a past captured and preserved, they are points of departure which open up future possibilities in a performative way.

As screens they mediate between the contexts of production and reception. Yet it is impossible to draw a clear line between these scenes of action, as the work begins with Kerber browsing her archive of images and selecting shots to be cultivated. To some extent, she is the first recipient, whose processes of selecting, experiencing and projecting are taken up by other spectators at the interface between identification and distance, between individuality and sociality. Instead of taking an objective picture of the world or depicting reality in a neutral way, photography is revealed as the interplay of semioticity and materiality, of the intentional and the accidental, of the machinic and the corporeal. Authorship appears less as an authoritarian gesture that simply reverses the relations of production and reception, activity and passivity, but rather as a perpetually changing composition that constantly reconfigures relationally interwoven constellations of photographic agency. This oscillation between production and reproduction, projection and reception, subject and object, animation and stylization opens up a space of possibilities, where authorship and mediality are set into motion and re-framed in manifold ways.

[14] Thierry de Duve for instance associates long time exposure, as an accumulation of time, with "past tense" and the snapshot, as an instant in time, with "present tense." Cf. Thierry de Duve: Time Exposure and Snapshot: The Photographic Paradox [1978], in: *The Cinematic*, ed. David Campany, London 2007, pp. 52–61.

This essay was written in 2010 on the occasion of a planned exhibition project concerned with the relationship of photography and film. It focuses mainly on a selection of images from the categories "Flowers" and "Men."

REKADRIERUNGEN VON AUTORSCHAFT

ZU INGA KERBERS FOTOGRAFISCHEN ARBEITEN

VON
NANNE BUURMAN

I N DEN 1950er Jahren wurde im Kontext der *Cahiers du Cinéma* die Forderung laut, Regisseure sollten sich an allen Schritten der Filmproduktion beteiligen, um einen persönlichen Stil zu entwickeln. Ziel war es, die Regie aus der dominierenden illusionistischen Tradition zu befreien und den Anspruch nach technischer Perfektion zugunsten einer erkennbaren Handschrift hinter sich zu lassen [1]. Angesichts der idiosynkratischen Ästhetik von Inga Kerbers Bildern lässt sich ihre fotografische Arbeit analog zu dieser *Politique des Auteurs* der Nouvelle Vague-Regisseure als Autorenfotografie verstehen. Auch wenn Kerbers Fotografien aufgrund der ihnen zugrunde liegenden Produktionstechnik teilweise malerisch anmuten, wird weder Malerei nachgeahmt noch Autorschaft in Anlehnung an modernistische Künstlervorstellungen als geniale Expression eines singulären Individuums fantasiert. Stattdessen tritt eine dem Fotografischen inhärente Subjektivität in Erscheinung.

Das Betonen von Subjektivität sollte in diesem Zusammenhang jedoch nicht als Affirmation des Glaubens an vermeintlich übermächtige Autorfiguren gelesen oder mit dem Anspruch nach absoluter Werkherrschaft verwechselt werden. Ostentative Subjektivierung wirkt hier – ähnlich wie bei Jean-Luc Godard, der durch das Inszenieren der *Mise en Scène* die Konstruiertheit des Films herausstrich – auch desillusionierend und trägt damit zur Relativierung auktorialer Souveränität bei. In Kerbers Arbeiten wird insofern einerseits das Wechselspiel von Autorschaft, Aleatorik und Automatik sowie andererseits das Verhältnis zwischen gesellschaftlichen Sehkonventionen und konkreten Betrachtungshandlungen rekadriert. Dabei stellt die medienreflexive Exponierung von in der Bildgenese relational ineinandergreifenden Prozessen der Reproduktion und Rezeption das immer noch weit verbreitete Paradigma fotografischer Objektivität zugunsten einer Verhandlung der Performativität fotografischer Bilder in Frage.

FRAME I. REPRODUKTION ALS PRODUKTION. Inga Kerbers Bilder brechen mit einigen gängigen Konventionen der fotografischen Praxis. Während üblicherweise akribisch auf staub- und schlierenfreie Negative, Scans und Drucke geachtet wird – da diese unbeabsichtigten Indizien manueller Produktionsprozesse als Fehler gelten, welche die perfekte Illusion der Hochglanzästhetik stören – akzeptiert und kultiviert Kerber diese koinzidenten Spuren. Auch Unschärfen, Unter/Überbelichtungen und Farbverschiebungen werden nicht verleugnet, sondern als konstitutiver Teil des fotografischen Bildes behandelt. Zufälliges wird ebenso affirmiert wie normalerweise eher unerwünschte maschinelle Effekte der Fototechnik (z.B. Farbstiche, Scanstreifen, Druckkopffehler). Auf diese Weise gibt Kerber dem Raum, was im Namen von Neutalität und Sterilität sonst häufig verdrängt wird. So wird insbesondere die Materialität von Fotografien bei der Betonung ihrer Indexikalität oder in der Feier ihrer hyperrealistischen Objektivität gerne übersehen. Wo Fotos aufgrund ihres Potenzials, Abbildungen unabhängig von kulturellen Kodierungen und Einschränkungen des menschlichen Sehapparats zu bieten, als unvermittelte Abdrücke

---

[1] Siehe Francois Truffaut: „Eine gewisse Tendenz im französischen Film" [1954], in: Ders.: *Die Lust am Sehen*, Frankfurt am Main 1999, S. 295–313.

der vom Objektiv eingefangenen Wirklichkeit rezipiert werden, verflacht Fotografie nicht selten rhetorisch zu einer fast immateriellen reinen Referenzialität[2]. Diesem Mythos der Allwissenheit, Passivität und Unbestechlichkeit des fotografischen Objektivs im Sinne von Maschinen als Augenzeugen oder von Fotos als Beweismitteln setzt Kerber gezielt Effekte der Aleatorik und Automatik entgegen, die den Bildern zudem eine besondere Plastizität verleihen.

Und obwohl durch die Aneignung von Zufällen und technischen Einschreibungen malerische Wirkungen – neben der fast reliefhaften Textur zum Beispiel auch in der Farbigkeit oder Hell-Dunkel-Verteilung – entstehen, ist Kerbers Arbeit kein Versuch, in pictorialistischer Tradition Fotografien über malerische Ästhetik künstlerisch zu adeln. Im Zentrum steht stattdessen das Herausstellen einer sonst oft unbeachteten spezifisch fotografischen Qualität, weshalb auch die Materialität der Bildträger – meist matte Papiere im Gegensatz zum typischen glänzenden Fotopapier – bewusst nackt gezeigt wird. Darüber hinaus lässt Kerber zum Beispiel Reproduktionsränder auf dem Papier stehen und bringt diese ungerahmt wie Poster an die Wand. Auf aufwertende Präsentationstechniken wie Diasec oder Rahmungen wird in der Regel verzichtet, so dass die Differenziertheiten in den Wiederholungen fotografischer Reproduktionen unverstellt sichtbar werden. Die technische Reproduziertheit geht in diesem Fall nicht mit dem Verlust der Aura des Bildes einher – eher potenziert sich diese aufgrund der Einzigartigkeit der einzelnen Reproduktionen, in denen jeweils Spuren der Produktions- und Rezeptionsprozesse kumuliert als Palimpsest präsent sind. Anstelle einer scheinbar identischen Gleichförmigkeit massenhafter Reproduktionen gerät die Singularität der einzelnen Bilder und damit die Produktivität und Kreativität der fotografischen Reproduktion in den Vordergrund. Über die Optik der Realität hinaus wird so vor allem die Ästhetizität des Zugriffs auf die Welt zum Gegenstand von Kerbers Arbeiten, ohne dass die Bilder dabei zu unberührbaren Kultgegenständen würden[3].

FRAME II. PROJEKTION ALS REZEPTION. Die profane Posterhaftigkeit wirkt einer ehrfürchtigen Rezeptionshaltung entgegen. Keine Glasscheibe hält Distanz zwischen Bild und Betrachter\ [4]. Die Mattigkeit der Bilder absorbiert den Blick, anstatt diesen an hochglänzend-glatter Oberfläche abperlen zu lassen. Unschärfen, Schatten, Dunkelheiten verführen dazu, näher an die Bilder heranzutreten, um innerhalb dieser zugleich schemenhaften und differenzierten Bildstellen vielleicht doch noch etwas zu erkennen. Diese Immersion der

[2] Dabei bleiben die technischen Kodierungen und physische Einschränkungen fotografischer Apparaturen ebenso unterbelichtet wie die von den Produktionsbedingungen abhängige Körperlichkeit und Räumlichkeit fotografischer Drucke. So z.B. bei László Moholy-Nagy: *Malerei. Fotografie. Film*, Bauhausbücher, Band 8, München 1925 oder in einem ganz anderen Zusammenhang bei Rosalind Krauss: „Notes on the Index: Seventies Art in America", in: *October*, 4, 1977, S. 58–67.

[3] Zum Verhältnis von Reproduzierbarkeit und Auraverlust, Kultwert und Ausstellungswert von Kunstwerken siehe Walter Benjamin: „Das Kunstwerk im Zeitalter seiner technischen Reproduzierbarkeit" [1936] und „Kleine Geschichte der Photographie" [1931] in: Ders.: *Das Kunstwerk im Zeitalter seiner technischen Reproduzierbarkeit. Drei Studien zur Kunstsoziologie*, Frankfurt am Main 1996, S. 7–44 und S. 45–64.

[4] In diesem Text wird das generische Maskulinum durch einen Backslash ergänzt. Die modifizierte Form soll eine Öffnung auf andere Gender hin anzeigen und zudem problematisieren, wie die sonst übliche Schreibweise dazu beiträgt, bei Generalisierungen stillschweigend männliche Positionen als Norm zu setzen.

Rezipienten\ in das Bildgeschehen wird durch leinwandgroße Formate noch unterstützt. Einen erschöpfenden Überblick über die Bilder zu bekommen, ist kaum möglich, denn aus einer Entfernung, in der man eine gesamte Sequenz im Blick hat, sind Details kaum noch zu erkennen. Die Betrachtung muss sich also zwangsläufig in einem Wechselspiel von Zoom und Totale vollziehen [5]. Aber nicht nur das Auge des\ Betrachters\ wird so zur Kamera. Angesichts der Größe von Kerbers Bildern muss der ganze Körper dieses Hin und Her zwischen Nähe und Distanz vollziehen um den Blick zu tragen.

Die räumliche Synchronisierung eigentlich diachroner Bewegungsläufe innerhalb der Sequenzen wird durch eine optische, physische und mentale Bewegung der Rezipienten\ wieder verzeitlicht. Dabei handelt es sich jedoch nicht um einen passiven Nachvollzug des fotografischen Blicks, sondern um dessen performative Vergegenwärtigung. Die Leerstellen innerhalb und zwischen den Bildern rufen dazu auf, die zugleich unscharfen wie prägnanten Klischees mit eigenen Erinnerungen und Vorstellungen anzureichern. Während gestochen scharfe Fotografien Geschehnisse eines Moments in einer Vollständigkeit und Klarheit festhalten, wie sie ein Mensch in einem Augen-Blick nie sehen könnte, kommen Kerbers Fotos dem menschlichen Sehen mit all seinen Begrenztheiten und blinden Flecken näher. So wird einsichtig, wie stark die Wahrnehmung immer auf Ergänzung und auf Interpretation optischer Informationen angewiesen ist. In diesem Sinne fungieren Kerbers Bilder auch als Projektionsflächen oder *Screens* [6], die Betrachter\ dazu herausfordern, ihren eigenen projektiven Blick zu reflektieren.

FRAME III. OBJEKT ALS SUBJEKT. Das Zusammentreffen der Perspektiven der Rezipienten\ mit der Perspektive der Künstlerin auf diesem Bildschirm provoziert Spannungen. Blicke kumulieren, konkurrieren und oszillieren zwischen Distanzierung und Identifikation. Die Intimität und Sogwirkung, die von der Materialität der Bilder ausgeht, lässt sich auch im Sujet ausmachen. Es wird zum Beispiel ein recht distanzloser Blick auf einen Mann geworfen, der in meist intimen Situationen – wie im Bett oder im Bad – unterschiedliche Posen einnimmt. Identifiziert man sich mit diesem vorgegebenen Blick, wird man unwillkürlich zum Voyeur\. Im Film werden voyeuristische Sehweisen teilweise abgemildert, indem Zuschauern\ durch einen entlastenden Gegenschuss erlaubt wird, die Szene durch die Augen eines\ anderen\ Schauspielers\ zu sehen [7]. Ein solcher, den\ Blickenden\ zeigenden Gegenschuss fehlt jedoch innerhalb von Kerbers Bildern, sodass Betrachter\ dazu gezwungen werden, die Rolle des fehlenden Gegenübers einzunehmen. Der Schnitt, der sonst innerhalb des Filmes zwischen Schuss und Gegenschuss-Einstellung gemacht

---

[5] Ähnlich hat auch Roland Barthes das Filmische nicht in der Zeitlichkeit des Filmes selbst, sondern im Modus einer „zugleich augenblicklichen und vertikalen Lektüre" (S. 66) verortet, die er anhand von Filmstandbildern exemplifiziert. Siehe Ders.: „Der Dritte Sinn" [*Cahier du Cinéma*, 1970], in: Ders.: *Der entgegenkommende und der stumpfe Sinn. Kritische Essays III*, Frankfurt am Main 1990, S. 47–66.

[6] Die *Screen Theory* greift die zentrale Fragestellung der *Apparatustheorie* auf – nämlich wie Subjekte durch Dispositive des Zeigens konstituiert werden – und ergänzt diesen Ansatz durch die Untersuchung gegenderter Blickverhältnisse. Siehe Laura Mulvey: „Visual Pleasure and Narrative Cinema", in: *Screen*, 16 (3), 1975, S. 6–18, und Kaja Silverman: *Male Subjectivity at the Margins*, New York/London 1992.

[7] Zur Funktion von Schuss-Gegenschuss für die Konstruktion der Subjektpositionen von Zuschauern\ siehe Ute Fenske: *Mannsbilder. Eine geschlechterhistorische Betrachtung von Hollywoodfilmen 1946–1960*, Bielefeld 2008, S. 55.

wird, verlagert sich hier als Suture in den Raum zwischen Bildsubjekt und betrachtendes Subjekt, wodurch letzteres als Akteur\ in den ‚Film' involviert wird.

Eine Identifizierung mit dem Blick der Fotografin ist ambivalent, weil die Perspektive der Bilder zum Teil stark vom dominanten westlichen Blickregime abweicht. In dieser Ordnung der Sichtbarkeit ist sowohl der Blick der Kamera als auch der des Betrachters\ in der Regel männlich konnotiert. Im Kino erscheinen Frauen oft als Objekte männlichen Begehrens, eine Position weiblicher Scopophilie ist selten vorgesehen[8]). Dies erklärt vielleicht, warum Kerbers Bilder, die weibliche Schaulust zelebrieren, teilweise Unbehagen hervorrufen oder gar als ‚schwul' rezipiert werden[9]). Angesichts einer Bildtradition, in der Frauen häufig als liegende Akte oder passive Objekte des Begehrens dargestellt werden und Männer überwiegend vertikal, in Bewegung oder muskulärer Anspannung zu sehen sind, ist die Pose des liegenden, unbekleideten Mannes vornehmlich Hermaphroditen, Sklaven, Toten, oder Verletzten vorbehalten und damit als ‚unmännlich' und ‚schwach' konnotiert[10]). Sich mit der Perspektive der Fotografin zu identifizieren, wird also nicht nur durch Intimität, durch eine möglicherweise abweichenden Geschlechteridentität oder Sexualität, sondern auch aufgrund der mangelnden kulturellen Legitimation einer solchen Sichtweise auf den Mann erschwert.

FRAME IV. STILISIERUNG ALS ANIMATION. In der Rede über Fotografie wird immer wieder auf dem Topos der Tötung oder der Stillstellung verwiesen. Fotografieren wird als Gewalt, Kastration, Tötung, Versteinerung, Immobilisierung und Korsettierung der Bildsubjekte diskutiert[11]). Die Behandlung der Bildsujets in Kerbers Bildern scheinen dies auf den ersten Blick durch Kreuzigung (z.B. in Pietà-Pose) sowie Still-Leben (z.B. Vanitas-Symbolik) zu bestätigen. Es lässt sich sogar von einer doppelten Still-Stellung sprechen: Blumen und Männer werden durch Komposition zu klischeehaften Sujets stilisiert und im Freeze-Frame eingefangen, ihre Bewegung wird wie im Filmstill angehalten. Während die Wiederholung des fotografischen Schusses (Peng-Peng-Peng / Klick-Klick-Klick) in der Sequenz einer Bildreihe zunächst wie eine Emphase dieses Tötungsdeliktes der Festschreibung erscheint, verweist sie auch auf ein emanzipatorisches Potenzial: Es wird keine Bewegungslosigkeit, sondern eingeschränkte Bewegungsfreiheit und damit Veränderbarkeit ins Bild gesetzt[12]). So lässt sich in Hinblick auf Kerbers Sequenzen von einer

[8]) Zum Verhältnis von Scopophilie und Gender siehe Laura Mulvey (1975), S. 12, wie Anm. 6. Zur Maskulinität der Betrachter\position siehe auch John Berger: *Ways of Seeing*, London 1972, Kapitel 3, S. 64.

[9]) Zum „Unbehagen" angesichts der Umkehrung des gegenderten Blickverhältnisses in der „unerwarteten Aktivität" des Objekts, welches den Blick erwidert und damit die „Autorität der männlichen Position anficht", siehe Judith Butler: *Das Unbehagen der Geschlechter*, Frankfurt am Main 1991, S. 7f. Die Bilder – wie teilweise geschehen – als ‚schwul' zu rezipieren, stellt die herrschende Ordnung der Sichtbarkeit zumindest insofern wieder her, als ein Mann als Träger des Blicks imaginiert wird.

[10]) Zu Männerbildern siehe auch Rozika Parker: „Images of Men", in: Dies./Griselda Pollock (Hg.): *Framing Feminism. Art and the Women's Movement 1970–1985*, London/New York 1987, S. 220–223.

[11]) Zum Topos des Todes in der Fotografie siehe z.B. Susan Sontag: *Über die Fotografie*, Frankfurt am Main 1980, S. 72, Roland Barthes: Die helle Kammer, Frankfurt am Main 1985, S. 23f, S. 100–103 und Craig Owens: „Posing", in: Ders.: *Beyond Recognition. Representation, Power and Culture*, Los Angeles 1992, S. 201–217.

[12]) Roland Barthes (1985), wie Anm. 11, kontrastiert die ‚Zukunftslosigkeit', den ‚Stillstand', die ‚Melancholie' der Bewahrungshaltung von Fotografie, welche Fotografen zu „Agenten des Todes" mache, mit den Vorteilen des Films, welcher eine ähnlich fortlaufende Zeitlichkeit wie das Leben habe. (S. 100–102)

Art cinematografischem *continuous present* sprechen, wie es Gertrude Stein in ihren frühen Schriften durch variierende Wiederholung, z.B. der Wortkombination „loving repeating being" evozierte[13]. In der wiederholten Stilisierung der Pose entsteht also paradoxerweise eine Bewegung, die diese Pose zugleich stabilisiert und in Frage stellt[14]. Die Wiederholung mit leichten Differenzen, welche entweder in unterschiedlichen Aufnahmen desselben Sujets oder in unterschiedlichen Drucken derselben Aufnahme bestehen, ist also weniger Festschreibung von Klischees, sondern ein Hinweis auf deren Potenzialität und auf die Möglichkeit, in der Iteration sedimentierte Vorstellungen zu aktualisieren. In ihrer Serialität gehen diese Bilder auch über die – häufig im Zusammenhang mit Fotografie angeführte – rückwärtsgerichtete referenzielle Zeitlichkeit der Konservierung von im Moment der Belichtung vorgefundener Realität hinaus, welche das Fortleben des Bildes in Richtung Zukunft unthematisiert lässt[15].

SCHLUSS. In Kerbers fotografischer Arbeit verlängert sich die Zeit der Aufnahme um die physische Lebensdauer der Bilder, denn neben den von der Künstlerin vollzogenen Reproduktionsprozessen schreiben sich auch die Spuren des Ausgestellt-Werdens und der Handhabung durch andere Akteure (abgeknickte Ecken, Fingerabdrücke, Kratzer, Risse, Löcher) in die Bilder ein. Da die Papiere nicht gegen Lichteinfall geschützt sind, endet genau genommen auch die Belichtungszeit erst mit der Zerstörung der Fotografien. Statt im Schneewittchensarg als Status quo konserviert zu werden, atmen die Bilder durch die offenen Poren der Papieroberfläche weiter. Neben der Serialität lädt also gerade die spezifische Materialität der Bilder dazu ein, Kerbers Arbeiten nicht nur als Repräsentationen vergangener Wirklichkeiten zu verstehen, sondern insbesondere auch als Präsentationen, die kontinuierlich eine fortdauernde Gegenwart herstellen. Die Bilder sind keine Endpunkte einer eingefangenen Vergangenheit, sie sind Ausgangspunkte, welche zukünftige Möglichkeiten performativ freisetzen.

Als Bildschirme vermitteln sie zwischen Produktions- und Rezeptionkontext, wobei diese Schauplätze jedoch fließend ineinander übergehen, denn die Arbeit beginnt mit Kerbers Sichtung von gesammeltem Bildmaterial und der Auswahl von zu kultivierenden Aufnahmen. Sie ist gewissermaßen die erste Rezipientin, deren Selektions-, Erfahrungs- und Projektionsprozesse durch andere Betrachter\ im Spannungsfeld zwischen Identifizierung und Distanzierung, Individualität und Sozialität fortgesetzt werden. Statt objektiv die Welt abzulichten oder neutral Realität zu beschreiben, zeigt sich das fotografische Handeln

---

[13] Siehe Gertrude Stein: *The Making of Americans* [1924], Ausschnitt in: Ula E. Dydo (Hg.): *A Stein Reader*, Illinois 1993, S. 62.

[14] Laut Diedrich Diederichsen ist es die Aufgabe des Regisseurs, Posen herzustellen und sogleich wieder zu zerstören, um „Bewegung und Narration" entstehen zu lassen und die „Genealogie der Pose" sichtbar zu machen. (o.S.) Siehe Ders.: „Queere Pose und erhabene Ungerechtigkeit: Politik und Moral bei Fassbinder und Warhol" [2005], in: http://filmkritik.antville.org/stories/1229508 (Zugriff 20.12.2010).

[15] Thierry de Duve assoziiert zum Beispiel die Langzeitbelichtung als Kumulation von Zeit mit „past tense" und den Schnappschuss als Ausschnitt aus der Zeit mit „present tense" (S. 55). Siehe Thierry de Duve: „Time Exposure and Snapshot: The Photographic Paradox" [1978], in: David Campany (Hg.): *The Cinematic*, London 2007, S. 52–61.

Dieser Text entstand 2010 anlässlich eines geplanten Ausstellungsprojektes zum Verhältnis von Fotografie und Film. Er bezieht sich hauptsächlich auf eine dafür vorgesehene Auswahl von Bildern aus den Kategorien ‚Blumen' und ‚Männer'.

also als Zusammenspiel von Semiotizität und Materialität, Intendiertem und Zufälligem, Maschinellem und Körperlichem. Autorschaft erscheint dabei weniger als autoritäre Geste, die Verhältnisse zwischen Produktion und Rezeption, Aktivität und Passivität einfach umkehrt, sondern als immer wieder neu rahmende Komposition, welche relational ineinander verwobene Konstellationen in den Blick bringt. Dieses Oszillieren zwischen Produktion und Reproduktion, Projektion und Rezeption, Subjekt und Objekt, Animation und Stilisierung eröffnet einen Möglichkeitsraum, in dem fotografische Autorschaft und Medialität durch vielfältige Rekadrierungen in Bewegung geraten.

RECADRAGE DU STATUT D'AUTEUR

SUR LES TRAVAUX PHOTOGRAPHIQUES D'INGA KERBER

PAR

NANNE BUURMAN

TRADUIT PAR CAROLINE HUGUENOT

D ANS LES *Cahiers du cinéma* des années cinquante, on recommande de faire participer les réalisateurs à toutes les étapes de la production d'un film, afin de favoriser le développement d'un style personnel. Le but était de libérer le réalisateur, jusqu'alors dominé par la tradition illusionniste, et d'abandonner ainsi l'exigence de perfection qui en découlait, au profit d'une écriture personnelle[1]. Compte tenu de l'esthétique idiosyncrasique de ses images, les travaux d'Inga Kerber peuvent être compris comme de la photographie d'auteur, dans une optique analogue à celle qu'adoptent les réalisateurs de la Nouvelle Vague dans leur *Politique des Auteurs*. Même si les photographies de Kerber revêtent parfois un caractère pictural en raison de leur technique de production, il ne s'agit ni d'imitation de peinture, ni de l'invention d'un statut d'auteur émanant de représentations modernistes d'artistes et qui serait à considérer comme l'expression du génie d'un individu singulier. Au contraire, c'est la subjectivité inhérente à toute photographie qui se manifeste.

Dans ce contexte, il ne faut pas comprendre l'accent sur la subjectivité comme une reconnaissance de figures d'auteur présumées supérieures, ni le confondre avec une exigence de contrôle absolu. La subjectivité ostentatoire joue le même rôle que chez Jean-Luc Godard – qui souligne, à travers la *mise en scène*, l'aspect artificiel du film – celui d'une sorte de désillusion, et par là-même d'une relativité de la souveraineté auctoriale. Dans les travaux de Kerber, le jeu d'alternance entre, d'une part, le statut d'auteur, l'aléatoire et l'automatique, et d'autre part, la relation entre l'aspect conventionnel de prises de vues sociales et le concret des situations d'observation, se voient recadrés, comme je vais l'exposer plus loin. Compte tenu de l'interdépendance des processus de reproduction et de réception dans la genèse des images, cette réflexion sur la médialité remet en question le paradigme toujours très répandu de l'objectivité de la photographie, et ce en faveur de la mise en valeur de la performativité des images photographiques.

CADRE I. LA REPRODUCTION COMME PRODUCTION. Les images d'Inga Kerber rompent avec certaines conventions de la pratique photographique. Tandis que d'ordinaire, on veille méticuleusement à ce que les négatifs, scans et impressions soient propres et nets, sans poussière ni traces – dans la mesure où ces ‹indices› involontaires d'un processus de production manuel sont considérés comme des erreurs venant perturber l'illusion parfaite de l'esthétique sur papier brillant – Kerber accepte en revanche ces traces aléatoires, et même, en quelque sorte, les cultive. Les flous, les sous- ou surexpositions ainsi que les variations chromatiques ne sont même pas corrigés, mais traités comme parties intégrantes de l'image photographique. Les traces survenues par hasard, notamment les effets indésirables de la technique de reproduction (comme par ex. des traits de couleur, des traces de scan, des erreurs de tête d'impression), sont d'ailleurs accentuées. À ce qui est d'habitude refoulé au nom de la neutralité et de la stérilité, Kerber accorde une place. C'est pourquoi la matérialité des photographies en particulier est souvent négligée, l'accent étant mis sur leur indexicalité ou sur leur objectivité hyperréaliste. Si les photos, en

---

[1] Voir François Truffaut, «Une certaine tendance du cinéma français» (1954), dans *id.*, *Le Plaisir des yeux*, Cahiers du Cinéma, Paris 1987, dans *id.*, *Die Lust am Sehen*, Frankfurt am Main (1999) 295-313.

raison de leur potentiel, peuvent apparaître comme des illustrations indépendantes de codes culturels ainsi que des limites des capacités visuelles humaines, et de ce fait être comprises comme des reproductions immédiates de la réalité saisie par l'objectif, c'est que la photographie met à plat, souvent de façon rhétorique, une référentialité propre, presque immatérielle[2]. A travers les effets du hasard et de l'automatisme, qui confèrent aux images leur propre plasticité, Kerber va à l'encontre de ce mythe de l'omniscience, de la passivité et de l'infaillibilité de l'objectif photographique, qui amène à considérer les machines comme des témoins oculaires ou les photos comme des preuves.

Et bien que l'appropriation du hasard et d'empreintes techniques produise un effet pictural – de par une texture presque plastique, ou aussi par ex. à travers la répartition chromatique ou le noir et blanc – le travail de Kerber ne constitue aucunement une tentative d'élever la photographie au noble rang d'art par le recours à l'esthétique de la tradition pictorialiste. Au lieu de cela, c'est la mise en évidence d'une qualité photographique trop souvent négligée qui est au cœur de son travail, voilà pourquoi même la matérialité des supports – le plus souvent du papier mat, par opposition au papier photo brillant classique – est volontairement conservée telle quelle. En outre, Kerber laisse visibles les bords des reproductions, en les affichant simplement sur le mur, telles des posters. En général, elle renonce à des techniques de présentation valorisantes, comme avec du Diasec ou des cadres, de sorte que les légères différences dans les séries répétitives des reproductions photographiques sont rendues visibles sans aucune modification. Le mode de reproduction technique ne conduit toutefois pas dans ce cas à la perte de l'aura de l'image, mais à un renforcement de sa puissance d'action, sur la base du caractère unique de chaque reproduction, qui présente à chaque fois les traces des processus de production et de réception, cumulées telles dans un palimpseste. Loin de l'identité des reproductions de masse, c'est la singularité de chaque image qui apparaît, et au premier plan, la productivité et la créativité des processus de reproduction photographique. Bien plus que l'optique du monde, c'est avant tout l'esthétisme de l'accès au monde tangible qui intéresse Kerber dans ses travaux, sans que les images se transforment pour autant en objets de culte intouchables[3].

CADRE II. LA PROJECTION COMME RÉCEPTION. L'affichage ‹profane› sous forme de poster n'invite pas à un accueil respecteux : aucune vitre pour tenir le spectateur\[4] à distance. L'aspect mat des images absorbe le regard au lieu de le laisser glisser sur une surface lisse et brillante. Des flous, des ombres, des zones obscures amènent à se rapprocher des images,

[2] A ce sujet, les normes techniques ainsi que les limites physiques des appareils photographiques sont tout autant sous-estimées que la corporalité et l'espace des reproductions photographiques dépendant des contraintes de production. Voir p. ex. László"Moholy-Nagy : *Malerei. Fotografie. Film*, Bauhaus Bücher 8, 1925, ou encore Rosalind Krauss : «Notes on the Index: Seventies Art in America», *October*, 4, 1977, 58–67.

[3] Sur la relation entre reproductivité et perte d'aura, valeur de culte et valeur d'exposition des œuvres d'art, voir Walter Benjamin, «Das Kunstwerk im Zeitalter seiner technischen Reproduzierbarkeit» (1936) ainsi que «Kleine Geschichte der Photographie» (1931), dans *id.*, *Das Kunstwerk im Zeitalter seiner technischen Reproduzierbarkeit. Drei Studien zur Kunstsoziologie*, Frankfurt am Main (1996) 7–44 et 45–64.

[4] Dans ce texte, le masculin générique est complété par une barre oblique inversée, ce qui permet la prise en compte de tous. Cette convention vise à attirer l'attention sur la généralisation, très souvent tacite, de la norme androcentrique, favorisée entre autres par l'emploi d'un mode de qualification traditionnel traditionnel.

pour tenter d'y distinguer des formes à la fois schématiques et différenciées. Cette immersion du spectateur\ dans le vécu de l'image est renforcée par des formats grand écran. Il est à peine possible d'avoir une vue d'ensemble des images, car, à partir d'une certaine distance permettant d'embrasser toute une séquence du regard, les détails ne sont plus reconnaissables. L'observation doit donc inévitablement reposer sur un jeu d'alternance entre zoom et vision totale[5]. Mais l'œil du spectateur\ n'est pas le seul à se transformer en caméra. Compte tenu de la taille des images de Kerber, le corps tout entier doit accomplir ce va-et-vient entre proximité et distance, afin de soutenir le regard.

La synchronisation spatiale de mouvements diachroniques enchaînés à l'intérieur de séquences se temporalise à nouveau à travers le mouvement optique, physique et mental du spectateur\. Dans ce cas, il ne s'agit toutefois pas d'une compréhension passive du regard photographique, mais de sa réalisation performative. Les espaces vides à l'intérieur et entre les images appellent à enrichir les clichés à la fois flous et prégnants à l'aide de ses propres souvenirs et représentations. Tandis que des photos très nettes retiennent les événements d'un moment dans son intégralité et sa clarté, tels qu'un homme ne pourrait jamais les percevoir en un seul instant, on peut considérer que les photos de Kerber sont plus proches de la vision humaine, avec toutes ses limites et ses zones d'ombres. Cela démontre à quel point la perception est toujours tributaire de compléments ainsi que de l'interprétation d'informations optiques. En ce sens, les images de Kerber fonction-comme des surfaces de projection ou *screens*[6]), qui incitent le spectateur\ à projeter son propre regard réflexif.

CADRE III. L'OBJET COMME SUJET. La rencontre sur cet écran de la perspective du spectateur\ avec celle de l'artiste génère des tensions. Les regards se cumulent, entrent en concurrence et oscillent entre prise de distance et identification. L'intimité et l'attraction qui se dégagent de la matérialité des images sont aussi perceptibles dans le sujet. Un regard sans aucune distance est par exemple porté sur un homme qui, dans des situations le plus souvent intimes, comme par exemple au lit ou dans son bain, est présenté dans différentes poses. Pour peu que les spectateurs\ s'identifient avec ce regard tout tracé, ils se transforment involontairement en voyeurs. Dans un film, les prises de vue voyeuristes sont partiellement atténuées, dans la mesure où il est permis au spectateur\, grâce à un contrechamp, de voir la scène à travers les yeux d'un autre acteur\[7]. Un tel contrechamp pour le spectateur\ fait cependant défaut dans les images de Kerber, de telle sorte qu'il se voit contraint d'assumer le rôle de la personne qui lui fait face. Le montage, qui intervient d'ordinaire entre champ et réglage du contrechamp, est ici comme une suture dans

[5] De la même manière, Roland Barthes concevait le film non pas dans sa temporalité, mais dans une «lecture à la fois instantanée et verticale» (66), illustrée à l'aide des arrêts sur images. Voir id., «Le troisième sens», *Cahiers du cinéma* No.222, 1970, dans *id., Der entgegenkommende und der stumpfe Sinn. Kritische Essays III*, Frankfurt am Main (1990) 47-66. (Cette citation est une traduction rétroactive du texte initial allemand).

[6] La Screen-Theory reprend la problématique centrale de *l'Apparatustheorie*, à savoir comment des sujets sont constitués à travers les dispositifs de mise en valeur et de diffusion de l'image et complète cette approche par une étude de genre sur les relations de regards, voir Laura Mulvey, «Visual Pleasure and Narrative Cinema», in *Screen*, 16 (3), 1975, 6–18, et Kaja Silverman, *Male Subjectivity at the Margins*, New York/London (1992).

[7] Sur le rôle de champ-contrechamp dans la détermination du positionnement des sujets, voir Ute Fenske, *Mannsbilder. Eine geschlechterhistorische Betrachtung von Hollywoodfilmen 1946–1960*, Bielefeld (2008) 55.

l'espace entre le sujet de l'image et le sujet-spectateur\, par lequel ce dernier est impliqué en tant qu'acteur\ dans le ‹film photographique›.

Une identification avec le regard de la photographe est ambivalente, car la perspective des images diverge parfois nettement du régime de regard occidental. Sous ce régime de visibilité, le regard de la caméra aussi bien que celui du spectateur\ sont en général connotés de façon masculine. Au cinéma, les femmes apparaissent souvent comme des objets du désir masculin, un angle scopophile féminin n'est que rarement prévu[8]). Cela explique peut-être pourquoi les images de Kerber célèbrent le voyeurisme féminin, parfois suggéré sans gêne ou pouvant même être perçu comme ‹gay›[9]). Dans la lignée d'une tradition iconographique où les femmes sont fréquemment représentées nues, comme des objets du désir masculin, allongées et passives, et les hommes pour la plupart verticalement, en mouvement ou parcourus de tensions musculaires, la pose de l'homme allongé, dévêtu, étant essentiellement réservée aux hermaphrodites, aux esclaves, aux morts ou aux blessés, et se voit ainsi connotée comme ‹efféminée› et ‹faible›[10]). S'identifier avec la perspective de la photographe est ainsi rendu plus difficile non seulement en raison de l'intimité, d'une identité sexuelle ou d'une sexualité peut-être différente, mais aussi à cause du manque de légitimité culturelle d'un telle perspective phallocratique.

Cadre IV. La Représentation Stylisée comme Animation. Dans le discours sur la photographie, il est souvent fait référence au *topos* du meurtre ou de la position immobile. La photographie est considérée comme un acte de violence, de castration, de meurtre, de pétrification, comme l'immobilisation et le corsetage du sujet représenté[11]). Dans les images de Kerber, le traitement des sujets, à travers l'idée de crucifixion (voir par ex. la pose de *Pietà*) ou le concept de nature morte (par ex. la symbolique de la *Vanitas*), semble au premier abord confirmer cet aspect. On peut même parler d'une position doublement immobile : par leur composition, les images de fleurs et d'hommes sont stylisées en sujets stéréotypés, puis capturées en arrêt sur image, leur mouvement étant stoppé comme dans un plan fixe. Tandis que la répétition de la prise photographique (clic-clic-clic/pam-pam-pam) dans la séquence d'une série d'images apparaît au premier abord comme une emphase de ce délit de meurtre par fixation dans le temps, elle renvoie également à un potentiel émancipatoire : aucune immobilité n'est fixée dans l'image, mais plutôt une liberté de mouvement restreinte, et donc une certaine capacité de modification[12]).

---

[8]) Sur le rapport entre scopophilie et genre, voir Laura Mulvey (1975), *supra* n. 8. (12). Sur la masculinité de la perspective du spectateur\, voir aussi John Berger, *Ways of Seeing*, Londres (1972) chap. 3 (64).

[9]) Sur les troubles par rapport à l'inversion des relations de regard sexuées, dans le cadre de l'activité inattendue de l'objet, qui répond au regard et conteste ainsi l'autorité de la position masculine, voir Judith Butler, *Das Unbehagen der Geschlechter*, Frankfurt am Main (1991) 7/8. La perception ‹gay› des images rétablit au moins sur ce point l'ordre dominant de la visibilité, dans la mesure où on imagine un homme comme porteur du regard.

[10]) Sur les images d'hommes, voir aussi Rozika Parker, «Images of Men», dans ead., Griselda Pollock (éd.) : *Framing Feminism. Art and the Women's Movement 1970–1985*, Londres/New York (1987) 220–223.

[11]) Sur le topos de la mort en photographie, voir p. ex. Susan Sontag, *Über die Fotografie*, Frankfurt am Main (1980) 72 ; Roland Barthes, La chambre claire, Frankfurt am Main (1985) 23–24, 100–103 et Craig Owens, «Posing», dans *id., Beyond Recognition. Representation, Power and Culture*, Los Angeles (1992) 201–217.

[12]) Roland Barthes (1985), voir *supra* n°12, oppose le ‹manque d'avenir›, l'‹immobilité›, la ‹mélancolie› de l'aspect conservateur de la photographie, qui transforment les photographes en «agents de la mort», aux avantages du film, qui adopte une temporalité comparable à celle de la vie (100–102).

Dans cette optique, les séquences de Kerber peuvent être comprises comme une sorte de *présent continu* cinématographique, tel qu'il est évoqué par Gertrude Stein dans ses premiers écrits à travers la répétition diversifiée d'infimes modifications, p. ex. la combinaison des mots ‹loving repeating being›[13]. Paradoxalement, un mouvement se crée grâce à la stylisation répétée de la pose, qui en même temps la stabilise et la remet en question[14]. La répétition avec d'infimes modifications, qui consistent soit en prises différentes d'un même sujet, soit en impressions différentes de la même photo, apparaît ainsi moins comme la fixation d'un cliché que comme un indice de sa capacité à actualiser des représentations sédimentées au moyen de l'itération. Par leur sérialité, ces images vont aussi au-delà de l'idée de temporalité rétrospective qui, dans le discours sur la référentialité photographique, est fréquemment associée à la conservation de la réalité au moment de l'exposition, et par conséquent ne prend pas en considération la persistance de l'image dans le futur[15].

CONCLUSION. Dans le travail photographique de Kerber, le temps des prises se prolonge aussi longtemps que les images existent physiquement, car à côté des processus de reproduction mis en œuvre par l'artiste, les traces de l'exposition et du maniement par d'autres agents (angles pliés, empreintes de doigts, griffures, déchirures, trous) s'inscrivent également dans les images. Comme le papier n'est pas protégé contre les effets de la lumière, le temps de pose ne s'achève à proprement parler qu'avec la destruction de la photographie. Au lieu d'être conservées dans un cercueil de verre, les images continuent à respirer à travers les pores ouverts de la surface en papier. A côté de leur sérialité, la matérialité spécifique des images de Kerber invite donc justement à les comprendre non seulement comme des représentations de réalités passées, mais également en particulier comme des présentations qui instaurent continuellement un présent persistant. Les images ne constituent pas le point final d'un passé capturé, elles sont le point de départ qui donne lieu à de futures possibilités performatives.

En tant qu'écrans, elles servent d'intermédiaires entre contexte de production et de réception, qui se recoupent du reste couramment, car le travail commence par le tri de la collection du matériel iconographique et la sélection des photos à traiter effectués par Kerber. Elle est d'une certaine façon la première destinataire des processus de sélection et d'expérimentation, qui seront poursuivis par d'autres spectateurs\ à travers des dynamiques d'identification et de distanciation, d'individualité et de collectivité. Au lieu de

---

[13] Voir Gertrude Stein, *The Making of Americans* (1924), extrait de Ula E. Dydo (éd.), *A Stein Reader,* Illinois (1993) 62.

[14] Selon Diedrich Diederichsen, c'est au réalisateur qu'incombe la tâche de créer et de défaire immédiatement les poses, pour que se crée du «mouvement et de la narration» et rendre ainsi visible la «généalogie des poses» voir *id.,* «Queere Pose und erhabene Ungerechtigkeit: Politik und Moral bei Fassbinder und Warhol» (2005), dans http://filmkritik.antville.org/stories/1229508 (dernier accès le 20.12.2010).

[15] Thierry de Duve associe par ex. une longue durée d'exposition comme cumulation de temps à un «past tense», et la prise de vue instantanée comme extrait du temps avec un «present tense» (55), voir *id.,* «Time Exposure and Snapshot: The Photographic Paradox» (1978), dans David Campany (éd.), *The Cinematic,* London (2007) 52–61.

Ce texte a été rédigé en 2010 dans le cadre d'un projet d'exposition sur la relation entre photographie et cinéma. Il se fonde principalement sur une sélection d'images appartenant aux catégories ‹fleurs› et ‹hommes›.

reproduire le monde de manière objective ou de décrire la réalité de façon neutre, l'action photographique se présente comme un jeu collectif entre la sémioticité et la matérialité, l'intentionnel et l'aléatoire, le machinique et la corporalité. Le statut d'auteur apparaît ainsi moins comme une manifestation d'autorité inversant simplement les relations entre production et réception, activité et passivité, mais plutôt comme une composition constamment réencadrante, qui met en lumière des constellations entrelacées. Cette oscillation entre production et reproduction, projection et réception, sujet et objet, animation et stylisation, ouvre un champ de possibilités dans lequel le statut d'auteur et la médialité photographique se mettent en marche et se recadrent de diverses manières.

TABLE OF CONTENTS

Thank You

The authors and contributors would like to thank: Andrea Baier, Helke Beyersdorf, Steven Black, Joscha Bruckert, Merret Buurman, Sebastian Burger, Anne Büttner, Damien Florébert Cuypers, Liviu Dalateanu, Brooke Arnao Dixit, Markus Dreßen, Isabelle Dutoit, Julia Fischer, Matthias Friederich, Madou Ghosh, Molina Ghosh, Luca Ghosh, Lætitia Gorsy, Anaïs Goupy, Roman Graneist, Anni Gratenau, Ella Gratenau, Harald Gratenau, Harald Gratenau Jr., Susanne Gratenau-Linke, Stefan Guggisberg, Beate Gütschow, Noémie Hauduroy, Sophie Herr, Amrai Hofmann, Mette Hofmann, Sylvie Hofmann, Thomas Hofmann, Caroline Huguenot, Stefan Hurtig, Justus Jager, Luka Savelii Jager, Thomas Janitzky, Friederike Jokisch, Valentin Just, Andy Kania, Anne Kerber, Berthold Kerber, Markus Kerber, Sebastian Kerber, Thea Kerber, Tilman Kerber, Yvette Kießling, Maximilian Kirmse, Martin Kobe, Annett Krause, Lasse Laskowski, Corinne von Lebusa, Edgar Leciejewski, Anne Leiste, Franziska Leiste, Michael Link, Gesine Linke, Harald Linke, Jan Linke, Jonas Linke, Hanjo Lu, Matthias Ludwig, Michael Ludwig, Nicolas Malclès-Sanuy, Oliver Mark, Carsten Martin, Inga Martin, Skadi Martin, Susanne Martin, Malte Masemann, Minoo Pelle Meinen, Christa Müller, Sebastian Nebe, Sascha Neitzel, David O'Kane, Jakob Ottilinger, Baptiste Perrin, Jochen Plogsties, Anja Predeick, Nans Quetel, Pascal Renger, Dominik Renner, Johannes Rochhausen, Andrea Sartorius, Anna Sartorius, Titus Schade, Philipp Scharf, Katharina Schilling, Kristina Schuldt, Tristan Schulze, Robert Seidel, Juli Sinios, Minou Sinios, Stella Sinios, Matthias Sommerer, Wolfgang Stahr, Johannes Tiepelmann, Ira Tolstaya, Julia Uebermuth, Gunnar Wendel, Jan Wenzel, Karin Werner, Konstantin Wiegandt, Holiday Zahl, Toni Jin Zeidler, Uta Zeidler

Catalogue Raisonné (Clichés)
by Inga Kerber

All images by Inga Kerber. *Concept* Inga Kerber, Daniel Rother. *Texts by* Nanne Buurman, Lorenz Just. *Translations by* Lorenz Just, Caroline Hugenot, Gunnar Wendel. *Text Editors* Jan Wenzel, Eva Wilson, Cyril Bernard. *Prepress by* Joscha Bruckert. *Graphic Design by* Daniel Rother, Berlin. *Printer* Elbe Druckerei, Wittenberg. *Binding* Stein+ Lehmann, Berlin.

The plates are numbered according to a system designed especially for the Catalogue Raisonné (Clichés).

ISBN: 978-3-940064-76-9

Published by Spector Books, Hartkortstraße 10, D–04107 Leipzig, T: 49. 341. 264 510 12, F: 49. 341. 212 24 11, www.spectorbooks.com

Distribution Germany/Austria GVA Gemeinsame Verlagsauslieferung Göttingen, GmbH & Co. KG, www.gva-verlage.de. *Switzerland* AVA Verlagsauslieferung AG, www.ava.ch. *UK/France/Japan* Anagram Books Ltd, www.anagrambooks.com. *North America* RAM Publications + Distribution Inc., www.rampub.com

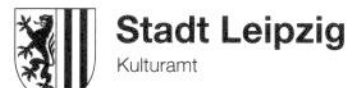

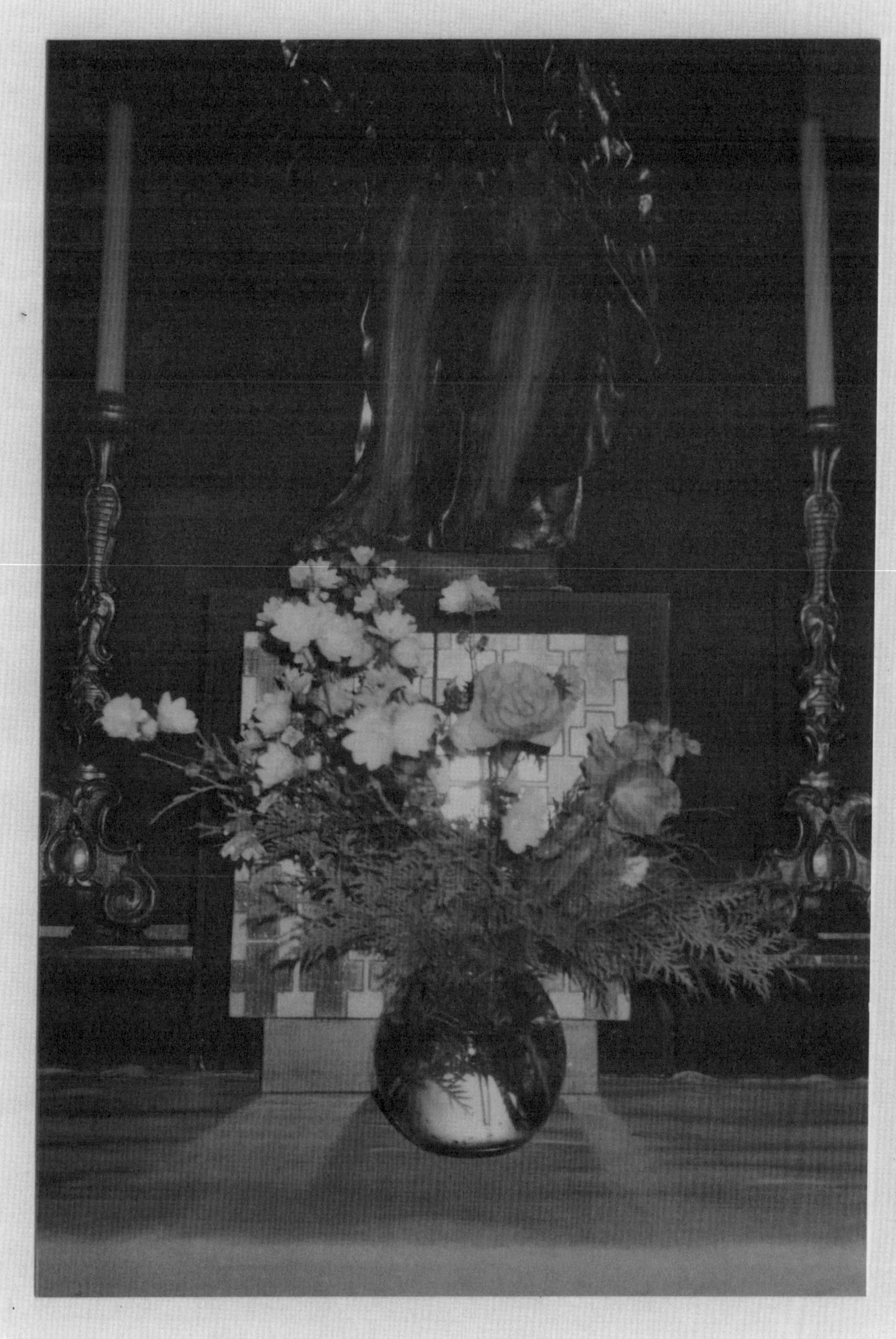